# New Directions in Human Associative Learning

# New Directions in Human Associative Learning

**A. J. Wills**
*University of Exeter*

2005

LAWRENCE ERLBAUM ASSOCIATES, PUBLISHERS
Mahwah, New Jersey                                    London

Lawrence Erlbaum Associates, Inc., Publishers
10 Industrial Avenue
Mahwah, New Jersey 07430

Cover design by Kathryn Houghtaling Lacey

**Library of Congress Cataloging-in-Publication Data**

New directions in human associative learning / edited by A.J.
Wills.
    p.  cm.
Includes bibliographical references and index.
ISBN 0-8058-5081-3 (c. : alk. paper)
    1. Paired-association learning—Textbooks.   I. Wills, A. J.
(Andy J.)

BF319.5.P34N48 2004
153.1'526—dc22                                  2004046980
                                                     CIP

Books published by Lawrence Erlbaum Associates are printed
on acid-free paper, and their bindings are chosen for strength
and durability.

Printed in the United States of America
10  9  8  7  6  5  4  3  2  1

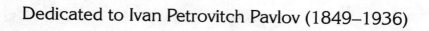

Dedicated to Ivan Petrovitch Pavlov (1849–1936)

# Contents

**PREFACE**         xiii

**ACKNOWLEDGMENTS**         xv

**LIST OF CONTRIBUTORS**         xvii

**1. ASSOCIATION AND COGNITION**         1

*A. J. Wills*

WHAT IS ASSOCIATIVE LEARNING?    1

*Associative Learning and Humans*    2

*"Associative" (Connectionist) Theories of Human Behavior*    3

*"I Tell My Students Pavlov Was a Genius and They Just Gape at Me"*    4

OUTLINE OF THIS BOOK    5

OUTLINE OF THIS SECTION    6

REFERENCES    7

**2. MENTAL MODELS OF CAUSATION: A COMPARATIVE VIEW**         11

*A. G. Baker, Robin Murphy, Rick Mehta, and Irina Baetu*

A ROAD MAP    13

TWO VIEWS OF CAUSAL REPRESENTATION    13

*Data Processing With Probabilistic Causes (Contingency Theory)*    15

*Associative Approaches and the Rescorla–Wagner Model*    21

SINGLE-CAUSE TESTS CONTRASTING CONTINGENCY
($\Delta P_{tc}$), POWER ($P_{tc}$), AND ASSOCIATIVE STRENGTH
($V_{tc}$)   24

*Do These Experiments Evaluate Causal Power?*   26

CAUSE COMPETITION AND CAUSAL ORDER
WITH TWO CAUSES   28

*Experiment 1*   28

*Experiment 2*   34

*Experiments 3 and 4*   34

*Experiment 5*   35

CONCLUSIONS   37

REFERENCES   38

**3. ON THE ROLE OF CONTROLLED COGNITIVE**   **41**
**PROCESSES IN HUMAN ASSOCIATIVE LEARNING**

*Jan De Houwer, Stefaan Vandorpe, and Tom Beckers*

EMPIRICAL EVIDENCE   42

*Associative Learning is Typically Accompanied
by Awareness of the Learned Associations*   43

*Associative Learning is Effortful*   44

*Associative Learning Can Depend on Verbal Instructions
About Contingencies*   45

*Associative Learning Can Depend on Abstract
Rules*   46

*Associative Learning Can Depend on Deductive
Reasoning*   46

THEORETICAL IMPLICATIONS   50

*Only Automatic Associative Processes Determine Human
Associative Learning*   50

*Only Controlled Processes Determine Human Associative
Learning*   51

*Associative Learning is Determined by Both Controlled
and Automatic Processes*   54

*Some Pointers for Future Theoretical Developments*   57

*Why Have Associative Models Fared so Well?*   59

CONCLUSION   60

REFERENCES   60

**4. ASSESSING (IN)SENSITIVITY TO CAUSAL     65
   ASYMMETRY: A MATTER OF DEGREE**

*Jason M. Tangen, Lorraine G. Allan, and Hedyeh Sadeghi*

BLOCKING EFFECTS AND ASSOCIATIONS   65

BLOCKING EFFECTS IN HUMAN LEARNING   67

CAUSAL–MODEL THEORY   68

CAUSAL–MODEL THEORY AND CONDITIONAL ΔP   70

ALLEGED CAUSAL–MODEL INFLUENCES   73

GENERAL METHOD   73

   *Participants and Design   73*

   *Procedure and Materials   75*

EXPERIMENT 1: CLARITY OF THE CAUSAL MODEL—
   REMINDERS   76

   *Method   76*

   *Results   77*

   *Discussion   80*

EXPERIMENT 2: CLARITY OF THE CAUSAL MODEL—
   COVER STORY   80

   *Method   81*

   *Results   81*

   *Discussion   83*

EXPERIMENT 3: INTEGRATION   84

   *Method   84*

   *Results   85*

   *Discussion   87*

GENERAL DISCUSSION   88

REFERENCES   89

APPENDIX—CAUSAL–MODEL PROMPTS   92

   *2C–1E   92*

   *2E–1C   92*

**5. CONNECTIONIST MODELS OF HUMAN     95
   ASSOCIATIVE LEARNING**

*A. J. Wills*

ASSOCIATIVE LEARNING → LEARNING
   OF ASSOCIATIONS   95

ASSOCIATIVE LEARNING → CONNECTIONISM   96

OUTLINE OF THIS SECTION   98

REFERENCES   99

**6. INTEGRATING ASSOCIATIVE MODELS           101
OF SUPERVISED AND UNSUPERVISED
CATEGORIZATION**

*Jan Zwickel and A. J. Wills*

HEBBIAN LEARNING AND AN INTRODUCTION
    TO CONNECTIONISM   102

COMPETITIVE LEARNING   103

THE RESCORLA–WAGNER MODEL (OR DELTA
    RULE)   105

INTEGRATING SUPERVISED AND UNSUPERVISED
    LEARNING   108

AN INTEGRATED MODEL   108

BLOCKING   110

EXPERIMENT   111

    *Method*   112

    *Results and Discussion*   114

MODELING   116

OTHER MODELS   117

    *Stimulus Representation*   117

    *Attentional Processes*   118

    *Plasticity–Stability Dilemma*   118

    *Decision Processes*   119

    *Level of Analysis*   120

SUMMARY   120

REFERENCES   121

**7. THE ROLE OF ASSOCIATIVE HISTORY IN HUMAN   125
CAUSAL LEARNING**

*M. E. Le Pelley and I. P. L. McLaren*

THE RESCORLA–WAGNER MODEL   126

EXPERIMENT 1: ASSOCIATIVE CHANGE FOR EXCITORS
    AND INHIBITORS TRAINED IN COMPOUND   127

APECS AND ADAPTIVE GENERALIZATION   130

EXPERIMENT 2: ASSOCIATIVE CHANGE
    IN RETROSPECTIVE REVALUATION   136

*The Modified Rescorla–Wagner Model  137*

*APECS and Retrospective Revaluation  141*

EXPERIMENT 3: LEARNED ASSOCIABILITY IN HUMAN
CAUSAL LEARNING  147

REFERENCES  152

**8. ELEMENTAL REPRESENTATION**                          **155**
**AND ASSOCIABILITY: AN INTEGRATED MODEL**

*Mark Suret and I. P. L. McLaren*

EMPIRICAL BACKGROUND  157

EMPIRICAL EVIDENCE FOR ASSOCIABILITY
PROCESSES  159

EXPERIMENT 1  161

*Stimulus Construction  161*

*Design  161*

*Procedure  163*

*Results  164*

*Discussion  167*

MODELING ASSOCIABILITY IN REAL TIME  171

AN ELEMENTAL ANALYSIS OF REVERSAL
AND TRANSFER ALONG A CONTINUUM  172

A NEW MODEL: FROM TRIAL-BASED TO A REAL-TIME
FRAMEWORK  173

SIMULATIONS OF EXPERIMENT 1  178

*Simulation Design  178*

*Simulation Procedure  178*

SIMULATION RESULTS  179

DISCUSSION  181

CONCLUSIONS  184

REFERENCES  186

**9. APPLICATIONS AND EXTENSIONS**                       **189**

*A. J. Wills*

REFERENCES  191

**10. SIGNAL–OUTCOME CONTINGENCY, CONTIGUITY,**          **193**
**AND THE DEPRESSIVE REALISM EFFECT**

*Robin A. Murphy, Frédéric Vallée-Tourangeau,*
*Rachel Msetfi, and Andy G. Baker*

ASSOCIATIVE THEORY AND CONTINGENCY   194

SIGNAL–OUTCOME PAIRINGS VERSUS
   CONTINGENCY   195

MEASURING SIGNAL–OUTCOME CONTINGENCY   197

ASSESSING CONTINGENCY LEARNING   199

BASE RATE DEPARTURES FROM CONTINGENCY   203

THE INSTRUMENTAL LEARNING DENSITY EFFECTS   205

TEST OF THE CONTIGUITY HYPOTHESIS OF DENSITY
   EFFECTS   206

TESTING THE ROLE OF THE CELL D
   IN DEPRESSIVE REALISM   211

SUMMARY AND CONCLUSIONS   216

REFERENCES   217

**11. LEARNING TO LIKE (OR DISLIKE):**       **221**
**ASSOCIATIVE LEARNING OF PREFERENCES**
   *Andy P. Field*

A BRIEF(ISH) HISTORY OF EVALUATIVE
   CONDITIONING   222

   *A Typical Experiment Using Visual Stimuli*   223

   *A Typical Experiment Using Taste Stimuli*   224

   *Preferences for Visual Stimuli: Basic Findings*   225

   *Preferences for Tastes: Basic Findings*   228

   *Preferences for Odors: Basic Findings*   229

   *Preferences Conditioned Cross–Modally*   229

   *Interim Summary*   231

ENTER THE HARBINGER OF DOOM   231

   *The Squid of Despair*   231

THE HAMSTER OF HOPE   234

   *Interim Summary*   239

IS EVALUATIVE CONDITIONING A QUALITATIVELY
   DISTINCT FORM OF ASSOCIATIVE LEARNING?   239

   *Learning Without Contingency Awareness*   239

   *Resistance to Extinction*   242

   *Contingency*   243

*Feature Modulation    244*
*Other Characteristics    244*
SUMMARY    245
REFERENCES    246

**AUTHOR INDEX**                                                    **253**

**SUBJECT INDEX**                                                   **259**

# Preface

April 2003 marked the centenary of Pavlov's first public presentation on the conditioned reflex, work that subsequently made him one of the best-known figures in psychology. Pavlov's contribution to the study of animal cognition is well known, but two international symposia held last spring at Exeter and Cardiff universities underlined his influence on the study of *human* cognition. *New Directions in Human Associative Learning* collects together previously unpublished work presented at these symposia in to an integrated volume. It seeks to introduce the reader to some of the cutting-edge theories and findings in the study of the cognitive processes that underlie associative learning processes in humans.

This book is designed to be accessible to undergraduates, providing a clear illustration of how the principles of animal cognition studied in introductory and intermediate-level courses apply to the contemporary study of human cognition. It would be ideal as supplementary reading for an intermediate-level animal or human cognition course, and as a core text for a senior-level seminar option in human learning processes. A high school level of familiarity with mathematics is assumed.

# Acknowledgments

The research presented in chapter 4 was supported by a Natural Sciences and Engineering Research Council of Canada research grant to Lorraine Allan and by a Natural Sciences and Engineering Research Council of Canada Graduate Scholarship to Jason Tangen, and is part of a PhD dissertation by Jason Tangen to McMaster University.

The authors of chapter 6 would like to thank Katrin Scharpf for helpful comments on the first draft of the chapter and Professor Joachim Funke and Dr. Klaus Rogge for helpful discussions.

The research presented in chapters 7 and 8 was supported by a grant from the Economic and Social Research Council to I. P. L. McLaren.

The research reported in chapter 10 was supported in part by grants from the Biotechnology and Biological Sciences Research Council and the Economic and Social Research Council. The authors of chapter 10 thank Doree Levine and Jasmine Hastings for recruiting and testing of human participants for some of the experiments reported therein.

Finally, thanks to the Experimental Psychology Society for hosting the symposium (Exeter, 2003), from which many of the chapters of this book emerged, and to John Pearce and Rob Honey for their excellent associative learning symposium (Gregynog, 2003).

# Contributors

**Lorraine G. Allan**
Department of Psychology, McMaster University
Hamilton, ON, L8S 4K1, Canada

**Andy G. Baker**
Department of Psychology, McGill University
1205 Dr. Penfield Avenue
Montreal, Quebec, H3A 1B1, Canada

**Irena Baetu**
Department of Psychology, McGill University
1205 Dr. Penfield Avenue
Montreal, Quebec, H3A 1B1, Canada

**Tom Beckers**
Department of Psychology, University of Leuven
Tiensestraat 102, B-3000
Leuven, Belgium

**Jan De Houwer**
Department of Psychology, Ghent University
Henri Dunantlaan 2, B-9000
Ghent, Belgium

**Andy P. Field**
Department of Psychology, University of Sussex
Falmer, Brighton, England

**M. E. Le Pelley**
School of Psychology, Cardiff University
Cardiff, UK

**I. P. L. McLaren**
Department of Experimental Psychology, University of Cambridge
Cambridge, England

**Rick Mehta**
Psychology Department, Acadia University
18 University Avenue
Wolfville, Nova Scotia, B4P 2R6, Canada

**Rachel Msetfi**
Psychology Department, University of Hertfordshire
College Lane
Hatfield, Hertfordshire, England AL10 9AB

**Robin A. Murphy**
University College London, Department of Psychology
26 Bedford Way
London, England WC1H 0AP

**Hedyeh Sadeghi**
Department of Psychology, McMaster University
Hamilton, ON, L8S 4K1, Canada

**Mark Suret**
Department of Experimental Psychology
Downing Street
Cambridge, England CB2 3EB

**Jason M. Tangen**
Department of Psychology, McMaster University
Hamilton, ON, L8S 4K1, Canada

**Frédéric Vallée-Tourangeau**
Department of Psychology, Kingston University
Penrhyn Road Centre, Kingston upon Thames
Surrey, England KT1 2EE

**Stefaan Vandorpe**
Department of Psychology, Ghent University
Henri Dunantlaan 2, B-9000
Ghent, Belgium

**Andy J. Wills**
School of Psychology, University of Exeter
Perry Road
Exeter, England

**Jan Zwickel**
Department of Psychology, Heidelberg University
Hauptstraße 47-51, 69117
Heidelberg, Germany

# Chapter 1

# Association and Cognition

A. J. Wills

In April 1903, Pavlov presented his early work on the conditioned reflex to the International Congress of Medicine, Madrid (Pavlov, 1903/1928a). Two of the, no doubt numerous, events that celebrated the centenary of this event were the Spring meeting of the Experimental Psychology Society at Exeter (for which I was the local organizer) and the annual Associative Learning Symposium organized by Professors Rob Honey and John Pearce of Cardiff University.

As the date of the Experimental Psychology Society (EPS) conference approached, my thoughts turned increasingly to the nature of the man and the work we were about to celebrate, and how both were considered today. I repeatedly recalled a conversation with a colleague about a year earlier that started with him saying, "Associative learning ... isn't that something they did in the 1950s when they thought pigeons could be trained to guide missiles?"

It's probably best that this particular opinion remains anonymous but, in less extreme forms, it probably reflects the attitude of a considerable minority of today's professional psychologists. Breaking down the opinion into its constituents, it seems to center on the ideas that the study of associative learning is (a) entirely concerned with nonhuman animals, and is (b) part of an episode in the history of psychology that ended with the "cognitive revolution" of the 1960s and 1970s. Both components of this opinion are fundamentally incorrect, as I indicate later in this chapter. However, first there is a need to define terms.

## WHAT IS ASSOCIATIVE LEARNING?

In some senses, there is a tension in talking about Pavlov and "associative learning" in the same breath. The term *associative* was in use throughout Pavlov's career, but it was not a term that he favored. For example, in his Madrid lecture he deliberately eschews the term associative, stating that "habits and associations ... are also reflexes, but condi-

1

tioned reflexes" (Pavlov, 1903/1928a). This perhaps explains, in part, the reaction of another one of my to-remain-anonymous colleagues. I asked her whether she thought Pavlov would have approved of a human associative learning symposium being held in his honor, particularly given that much of his work was with nonhuman animals. Her reply was, "Human testing no problem, I'd guess. It's the arty-farty cognitive empire-building 'conditioning is just one corner of the empire of associative learning' that he might balk at."

This concern can, I think, be partially addressed by a proper definition of terms. In the context of the title and content of this book, "associative learning" is intended to be a description of a class of problem facing the organism. It is not a statement about the nature of the internal processes by which the organism solves that problem. It is also not a statement about the suitability or otherwise of particular theoretical constructs to explain the organism's behavioral reactions. For example, in 1932 Pavlov concluded a discussion of teaching a dog to raise its paw in response to a verbal command in the following way: "Why this is merely simple association, as psychologists usually assume, and by no means not an act of intelligence, of ingenuity-even if of elementary things-remains unclear to me" (p. 124).

In this statement, Pavlov is presumably using the term *simple association* to refer to certain specific process theories discussed earlier in that paper. Hence, the term *association* is being used to describe a specific theory of which he is critical. However, there seems little doubt that the appropriate behavior of the dog in this situation is contingent upon it detecting a reliable associative relationship between a particular type of sound emitted by the trainer and the action that is rewarded. In this manner, the situation Pavlov describes necessarily involves associative learning, but may or may not involve the formation of the "simple associations" assumed by a particular process theory. The confusion inherent in using such similar terms for such different concepts perhaps leads to the conclusion that a more distinct terminology should be used. The preferred nomenclature of this volume is to use "associative learning" to describe a class of problem facing the organism, and to use (somewhat) more theoretically specific terms to describe and differentiate process accounts (e.g., connectionist models, controlled processes).

## Associative Learning and Humans

Let's return to the misconception that the study of associative learning is wholly concerned with nonhuman animals. There can be absolutely no doubt that Pavlov considered his work to be of great importance to the understanding of the human condition. Perhaps the most striking manifestation of this view was the 2 months in the summer of 1918 that Pavlov spent studying psychiatric patients. This work resulted in a tentative theory of catalepsy derived by analogy to experiments he had previously performed with dogs (Pavlov, 1919/1928c). A large part of his last 7 years of research were also dedicated to the application of his findings to psychiatry. Another example of Pavlov's direct interest in human behavior is his article on the "reflex of purpose" (Pavlov, 1916/1928d). In this he suggests that activities such as stamp collecting are natural results of this reflex (Pavlov was a keen stamp collector, by the way). Pavlov also suggests that suicide can result from the chronic inhibition of the reflex of purpose. Against a context of such liberal extrapolations, it would seem unlikely that Pavlov could have had a principled objection to the study of associative learning in humans.

More generally, a minimal knowledge of the history of psychology draws one to the inevitable conclusion that the study of associative learning has always been deep at the heart of human experimental psychology. From early examples such as the "Little Albert" experiments of Watson and Rayner (1920), through studies of the modification of the galvanic skin response (Cook & Harris, 1937), the learning of preferences (Razran, 1938), simulated medical diagnosis (Smedslund, 1963), stereotype formation (Hamilton & Gifford, 1976), right up to recent work on causal reasoning (Cheng, 1997) and the complexities of retrospective revaluation (e.g., Dickinson & Burke, 1996), psychology has seldom strayed far from the consideration of this basic form of activity.

## "Associative" (Connectionist) Theories of Human Behavior

If one accepts that associative learning is, and is likely to remain, a topic of core interest in psychology, this does not necessarily mean that "associative" theories (recall our earlier distinction) are of any current use in the explanation of human behavior. One of the most overstated and misunderstood aspects of the history of psychology is the idea that there was a kind of "cognitive revolution" in the 1960s and 1970s. In the "dark ages" that preceded this revolution, behaviorists ruled with an iron first, disallowing any explanation of behavior that hinted at the presence of an internal state. After the revolution, psychologists were once again free to invoke any mental states and processes they liked and everyone was much happier and more productive. It sometimes seems to be assumed that associative theories vaporized at around that time. Recent histories of psychology sometimes add a final chapter. In this part of the story, everyone reads McClelland and Rumelhart's *Parallel Distributed Processing* (Rumelhart, McClelland, & the PDP Research Group, 1986) and has another conversion experience because here is an approach that permits internal states but that is constrained by certain types of neurophysiological data.

This caricatured history is wrong in every important respect. For example, it combines the experimental methodology of behaviorism (reliance on observable behavior) with its philosophy (inappropriateness of mental states as a subject for study). A cursory glance at any modern textbook of cognitive psychology will demonstrate that the methodology of behaviorism survived the cognitive revolution. Similarly, when Pavlov explains that his approach focuses the whole of attention "upon the correlation between external phenomena and the reaction of the organism" (Pavlov, 1903/1928a, p. 50), it is the methodology rather than the philosophy that he is endorsing. This distinction is supported by the clear line he draws between his approach and that of investigators such as Watson: "The practical American mind ... found that it is more important to be acquainted with the exact outward behavior of man than with guesses about his internal states ... I and my co-workers hold another position" (Pavlov, 1903/1928a, p. 40).

What was Pavlov's position on internal states? One clear illustration can be found in the article "Natural Science and the Brain" (Pavlov, 1909/1928b). In this, he proposed that the conditioned reflex developed through the action of two types of brain process. The first of these was a "temporary union, i.e., the establishment of a new connection in the conducting paths" (p. 122). This idea is foreshadows the concept of the "associative link" or "connection weight" employed in many contemporary connectionist (or "associative") models. The second type of brain process was the action of "analyzers." The concept of analyzers corresponds closely to the "nodes" of a contemporary connectionist system.

It's worth just underlining the implications of this article. In 1909, Pavlov (1909/1928b) proposed a theory of associative learning that is recognizably a form of connectionist theory—the sort of approach that a caricatured history of psychology attributes to postcognitive research almost 80 years later. One standard response to this objection is that although associative theories were popular for a time, the work of Minsky and Papert (1969) led to psychologists abandoning associative theory until Rumelhart, Hinton, and Williams (1986) invented back-propagation. One minor problem with this account is that back-propagation was discovered at least 12 years earlier (Werbos, 1974). A more major problem is the simple fact that associative theories were *not* abandoned. One can trace a steady development of associative theory from Thorndike (1898) and Pavlov, through (to name but a few) Spence (1936), Hull (1943), Konorski (1948), Hebb (1949), Rescorla and Wagner (1972), Mackintosh (1975), Grossberg (1976), Pearce and Hall (1980), Wagner (1981), and Pearce (1987). Much of this theoretical work predates *Parallel Distributed Processing* and even some much later work (e.g., Kruschke, 1992, 2001).

### "I Tell My Students Pavlov Was a Genius and They Just Gape at Me"

This is another quote from a colleague. I think it reflects a lack of understanding (on the students' part) of the nature and extent of Pavlov's contribution to cognitive psychology. Pavlov was one of the pioneers of the objective, scientific study of associative learning. He was also a pioneer of a theoretical approach to explaining behavior that eventually became known as connectionism. This combination alone makes him a critical figure in the development of cognitive psychology as we know it today. Additionally, people tend to forget the breadth of phenomena within classical conditioning that are attributable to him. Pavlov's body of work goes far beyond the basic demonstration of the development of a conditioned response. Pavlov also demonstrated extinction, and showed through reminder treatments that extinction was not simply unlearning. He provided experimental demonstrations of generalization decrement, context-specificity, and the importance of contiguity. All of this appears in his first public presentation in 1903. By 1912 he had developed the contemporary concept of conditioned inhibition (although his tests for the presence of conditioned inhibition are now generally acknowledged as inadequate).

What makes this all the more remarkable is the fact that Pavlov was over 50 before he started work on the conditioned reflex. In fact, it was not until he was 21 that he decided against becoming a priest, and started to train as a physician. He became a physician at 30, a professor of pharmacology at 41, and a professor of physiology at 46. He won the Nobel prize at 55 for his work on the digestive glands. His most famous book, *The Conditioned Reflexes* (Pavlov, 1927), was published when he was 78.

There is not the space in this volume to provide a detailed biography (Gantt, 1928, provides an excellent introduction). Nevertheless, some aspects of Pavlov's personality are worth mentioning briefly. In one respect, Pavlov was a stereotypical academic. He is reported to have had extraordinarily poor dress sense and that on the rare occasions he bought his own clothes "his choice of colors ... made his friends laugh and his family angry" (Gantt, 1928, p. 14). In other respects, he is much harder to pigeonhole. Pavlov was a keen gymnast in his youth, a keen gardener throughout his life, and a proponent of the importance of physical exercise. He had a very high level of manual dexterity, being a highly accomplished surgeon, and he also had an exceptionally good memory. He was widely regarded as a clear, energetic, and popular lecturer. This comes across in his collected lectures (Gantt, 1928) despite the barriers of the intervening century and the translation from Russian into English. Within the context of his times, Pavlov was also distinguished by his regard for animal welfare, pioneering postoperative care for experimental animals and developing alternatives to vivisection. In 1924, he resigned his professorship in protest at student expulsions. He didn't smoke or drink, but did swear copiously. He worked 7 days a week, but took at least 2 months off each summer.

## OUTLINE OF THIS BOOK

This book emerged from the work presented at the "New Directions in Human Associative Learning" symposium (Experimental Psychology Society meeting, Exeter, England, April 10–11, 2003) and some of the human work presented at the "Associative Learning Symposium" (Gregynog, Wales, April 15–17, 2003). Chapters 3, 6, 7, 10, and 11 were from the Experimental Psychology meeting, whereas chapters 2, 4, and 8 emerged from the Associative Learning Symposium.

This book has been divided into three sections. In the first section (chaps. 1–4) the reader is introduced to some recent data and controversies in the study of associative learning. In the second section (chaps. 5–8) the focus shifts to recent developments in the formal theories of how associative learning occurs. All three chapters are written from the perspective of connectionist modeling and are contributed by a group of authors who have a broadly similar outlook and background. The final section (chaps. 9–11) turns to some of the more applied work on human associative learning; specifically, its application to depression and to the development of preferences (e.g., product preferences). The first chapter of each section provides a short introduction to the material covered.

## OUTLINE OF THIS SECTION

This first section of the book begins with a chapter by Andy Baker, Robin Murphy, and Rick Mehta, in which they introduce two well-known theories of human associative learning. First up is Patricia Cheng's PowerPC theory, which is one example of the class of *statistical* (or *normative*) accounts. Next up is Bob Rescorla and Alan Wagner's eponymous theory. Rescorla–Wagner theory is one example of the class of *associative* (or *connectionist*) accounts. Baker, Murphy, and Mehta then go on to review some of the previous attempts to determine whether PowerPC or Rescorla–Wagner is the better theory of human causality judgments. Five of these studies (from Rick Mehta's doctoral thesis) are presented in detail, and are concerned with the role of causal order (i.e., whether causes are observed prior to effects, or effects prior to causes). Neither PowerPC nor Rescorla–Wagner adequately accounts for the causal-order effects presented. Additionally, the authors lead us to the conclusion that the comparison of a specific statistical account with a specific connectionist account tells us little about the relative merits of the class of theory from which each come. Indeed, their final conclusion is that statistical and connectionist accounts exist at different levels of explanation and hence should not be considered as being directly in competition. Statistical accounts help us understand what might need to be computed in order for us to behave adaptively. Associative accounts provide potential mechanisms for these computations.

In contrast, Jan De Houwer, Stefaan Vandorpe, and Tom Beckers argue (chap. 3) that associative accounts as a class fail to provide a mechanism for certain known and important phenomena in human associative learning. They attribute this failure to the fact that associative theories are typically accounts of automatic (i.e., unintentional or unconscious) processes. Human behavior presumably also results from nonautomatic processes, in other words processes that are intentional, conscious, or effortful. Jan and colleagues review the evidence that human associative learning (a) requires awareness of the learned associations, (b) is effortful in the sense that it disrupts demanding secondary tasks, and (c) can result from both direct experience and verbal instruction. They also point out that human associative learning can show generalizations to novel situations of a type difficult to explain without recourse to abstract rules.

Finally, they review evidence that suggests deductive reasoning can play an important role in determining causal judgments. Perhaps the most striking of these demonstrations is the presence of higher order retrospective revaluation effects in human associative learning. This phenomenon (which is described more fully in the chapter itself) is naturally explained by the recursive application of a deductive rule but is particularly problematic for many associative accounts. De Houwer and colleagues conclude that an understanding of controlled processes is crucial to our understanding of human associative learning. As they readily admit, this conclusion introduces an additional challenge to theorists. Theories of human associative learning that include controlled processes are currently highly descriptive and hence poorly specified. This is in stark contrast to associative theories of automatic processes, which have reached a high level of formal specification (see chaps. 5, 6, 7, and 8). Jan and colleagues' chapter was almost certainly the most controversial in the process of internal peer review this book went through, and seems likely to stimulate debate for some time to come.

In chapter 4, Jason Tangen, Lorraine Allan, and Hedyeh Sadeghi combine some of the themes of chapters 2 and 3. They start with a brief review of certain basic effects in human associative learning, and of the Rescorla–Wagner theory. Then, similarly to Andy Baker's chapter, they discuss the challenges causal-order effects present to both normative and associative accounts of human associative learning. Jason Tangen's suggested resolution of this problem is that normative accounts and associative accounts represent different strategies that can be applied by the human participant. From this starting point, Jason reports a series of experiments designed to investigate the conditions under which an associative or a normative strategy is most likely to be applied.

## REFERENCES

Cheng, P. W. (1997). From covariation to causation: A causal power theory. *Psychological Review, 104,* 367–405.

Cook, S. W., & Harris, R. E. (1937). The verbal conditioning of the galvanic skin reflex. *Journal of Experimental Psychology, 21,* 202–210.

Dickinson, A., & Burke, J. (1996). Within-compound associations mediate the retrospective revaluation of causality judgements. *The Quarterly Journal of Experimental Psychology, 49B,* 60–80.

Gantt, W. H. (1928). Ivan P. Pavlov: A biographical sketch. In W. H. Gantt (Ed.), *Lectures on conditioned reflexes* (pp. 11–34). London: Lawrence & Wishart.

Grossberg, S. (1976). Adaptive pattern classification and universal recoding: Part I. Parallel development and coding of neural feature detectors. *Biological Cybernetics, 23*, 121–134.

Hamilton, D. L., & Gifford, R. K. (1976). Illusory correlation in interpersonal perception: A cognitive basis of stereotypic judgments. *Journal of Experimental Social Psychology, 12*, 392–407.

Hebb, D. O. (1949). *The organization of behavior.* New York: Wiley.

Hull, C. L. (1943). *Principles of behavior.* New York: Appelton–Century–Crofts.

Konorski, J. (1948). *Conditioned reflexes and neuron organization.* Cambridge, England: Cambridge University Press.

Kruschke, J. K. (1992). ALCOVE: An exemplar-based connectionist model of category learning. *Psychological Review, 99*, 22–44.

Kruschke, J. K. (2001). Toward a unified model of attention in associative learning. *Journal of Mathematical Psychology, 45*, 812–863.

Mackintosh, N. J. (1975). A theory of attention: Variations in the associability of stimuli with reinforcement. *Psychological Review, 82*, 276–298.

Minsky, M. L., & Papert, S. A. (1969). *Perceptrons: An introduction to computational geometry.* Cambridge, MA: MIT Press.

Pavlov, I. P. (1928a). Experimental psychology and psycho-pathology in animals. In W. H. Gantt (Ed.), *Lectures on conditioned reflexes* (Vol. 1, pp. 47–60). London: Lawrence & Wishart. (Original work published 1903).

Pavlov, I. P. (1928b). Natural science and the brain. In W. H. Gantt (Ed.), *Lectures on conditioned reflexes* (Vol. 1, pp. 120–130). London: Lawrence & Wishart. (Original work published 1916).

Pavlov, I. P. (1928c). How psychiatry may help us to understand the physiology of the cerebral hemispheres. In W. H. Gantt (Ed.), *Lectures on conditioned reflexes* (Vol. 1, pp. 287–293). London: Lawrence & Wishart. (Original work published 1919).

Pavlov, I. P. (1928d). The reflex of purpose. In W. H. Gantt (Ed.), *Lectures on conditioned reflexes* (Vol. 1, pp. 275–281). London: Lawrence & Wishart. (Original work published 1916).

Pavlov, I. P. (1927). *Conditioned reflexes.* New York: Dover.

Pavlov, I. P. (1932). The reply of a physiologist to psychologists. *Psychological Review, 39*(2), 91–127.

Pearce, J. M. (1987). A model of stimulus generalization for Pavlovian conditioning. *Psychological Review, 94*, 61–73.

Pearce, J. M., & Hall, G. (1980). A model for Pavlovian learning: Variations in the effectiveness of conditioned but not of unconditioned stimuli. *Psychological Review, 87*, 532–552.

Razran, G. (1938). Conditioning away social bias by the luncheon technique. *Psychological Bulletin, 35*, 693.

Rescorla, R. A., & Wagner, A. R. (1972). A theory of Pavlovian conditioning: Variations in the effectiveness of reinforcement and nonreinforcement. In A. H. Black & W. F. Prokasy (Eds.), *Classical conditioning II: Current research* (pp. 64–99). New York: Appleton–Century–Crofts.

Rumelhart, D. E., Hinton, G. E., & Williams, R. J. (1986). Learning internal representations by error propagation. In D. E. Rumelhart & J. L. McClelland (Eds.), *Parallel distributed processing: Explorations in the microstructure of cognition* (Vol. 1, pp. 318–364). Cambridge, MA: MIT Press.

Rumelhart, D. E., McClelland, J. L., & the PDP Research Group. (1986). *Parallel distributed processing.* Cambridge, MA: MIT Press.

Smedslund, J. (1963). The concept of correlation in adults. *Scandinavian Journal of Psychology*, *4*(3), 165–173.

Spence, K. W. (1936). The nature of discrimination learning in animals. *Psychological Review*, *43*, 427–449.

Thorndike, E. L. (1898). Animal intelligence: An experimental study of the associative processes in animals. *Psychological Review, 8.*

Wagner, A. R. (1981). SOP: A model of automatic memory processing in animal behavior. In N. E. Spear & R. R. Miller (Eds.), *Information processing in animals: Memory mechanisms* (pp. 5–47). Hillsdale, NJ: Lawrence Erlbaum Associates.

Watson, J. B., & Rayner, R. (1920). Conditioned emotional reactions. *Journal of Experimental Psychology*, *3*, 1–14.

Werbos, P. J. (1974). *Beyond regression: New tools for prediction and analysis in the behavioral sciences.* Unpublished doctoral dissertation, Harvard University, Cambridge, MA.

# Chapter 2

# Mental Models of Causation: A Comparative View

A. G. Baker, Robin Murphy, Rick Mehta, and Irina Baetu

It is customary to introduce a chapter like this with a global statement about how adaptive it is for organisms to have an appreciation of the causal structure of the world, or the more modest claim that it is useful to have an appreciation of contingencies between events in the world. In some sense we do not disagree with this as we have each written several of these statements ourselves. They are written to attract interest in a, perhaps, rather arcane and technical area of research. However, each element of this statement requires careful consideration. The claim that it is a useful or an adaptive skill seems commonsense, but it, like many similar arguments, has little empirical justification. Few experiments demonstrate the skill is adaptive. Even if we grant there is something adaptive about understanding the causal structure of the world, what do we mean by understanding? Probably the ability to predict a future event or the consequences of action is the adaptive function, but a number of possible cognitive structures can make predictions about possible future events. In a classical conditioning experiment a metronome might be paired with food. With training, a dog will come to salivate when the metronome is activated. Contrast this with a chemist who might stop a student from trying to drop a bar of sodium into a beaker because she expects a rather violent reaction. An alien observing each scenario might infer that the dog and the chemist both have some understanding of the causal structure or at least the contingencies in their world. Important to note, the predictive or anticipatory behavior of both actors implies that they have internalized some sort of information that will allow them to predict the future.

If a naive human, rather than the alien observer, were asked what sort of mechanism was involved in these behaviors, he would be unlikely to assume that they were the same. Undergraduates in psychology might suggest that some associative mechanism involving reinforcement, or some such process, has stamped in a behavioral tendency and this more or less reflexively allows the dog to "predict" future food. With the chemist, they might argue that through experience or perhaps just the process of education she has developed some sort of rich representation of the causal structure of the situation. After all, we have never seen sodium dropped into water yet we can visualize what will happen. Moreover, most of us would agree that the chemist need not ever have had any experience or specific training with this particular scenario in order to save the student from his folly. Some understanding of chemistry and of the possible effects of a vigorous reaction is all that is necessary. This ability to represent causal structure and use this causal knowledge in novel situations is a keystone to our conceptualization of human causal reasoning. Indeed, it is this ability to transfer knowledge that is a critical distinction between causal power and statistical theories of causal reasoning, but more on that later.

Before we go on though, we must examine this notion of transfer of learning to a novel situation. First one needs to consider just what constitutes a novel situation. Again some cases are clear but many are less so. It has been known for a long time that animals and people will respond to stimuli similar to those that they have previously experienced. It is easy to demonstrate that animals will respond to stimuli that are similar to those they have been trained on. This process is called generalization. The response is generally stronger the more similar are the stimuli. Furthermore it could be argued that even a test trial with the same stimulus is a generalization test. Animals are sensitive to time and place and even metabolic changes, and these are probably incorporated into their representation of a stimulus. Moreover, the neural response to two presentations of exactly the same tone will not be identical. Thus every conditioning trial could be argued as novel and thus a demonstration of transfer.

Most observers would probably believe that the transfer in the case of the chemist is somehow fundamentally different than that in a generalization test, and we probably would not argue about that. However, the chemist has had experience with similar chemical reactions. She has probably had safety training. She probably has read about or seen scenarios in which responsible adults behave to protect younger people. She may have seen other lab accidents. Moreover, it is likely that at least part of this behavior, even if only the motivation to protect younger people, is genetically determined. Thus, it could be argued that is not a pure case of transfer of abstract causal knowledge to a novel situation. Rather, each subcomponent is simply generalized, perhaps in a rather reflexive manner, from past experience. An argument that might be used to counter this position is that, although this particular case may be similar to others, it would still be possible to transfer this knowledge to a completely novel case. This begs the argument about what a completely novel case might be. If it were completely novel then what handle would there be to transfer to it? What of your present knowledge would be relevant and what would not? Moreover, if these apparently rare cases of pure transfer are so rare how could they be adaptive? Leaving this issue aside leaves us with the question as to what empirical criteria might be used to discriminate between the two types of transfer. If they are, indeed, two types.

## A ROAD MAP

Up to this point we have informally outlined two views of how people and other organisms might deal with causal information. They might form a complex rule-based representation or respond in a rather simple or almost reflexive way. The first view roughly maps onto what researchers might call causal power or generative models of cause. Sometimes they are, more simply, called mental models of cause. The second maps onto what are called associative models of information processing and these, not surprisingly, arise from research in conditioning. In the remainder of this chapter we try to do three things. We, somewhat more formally, describe the theories behind these two positions. We then describe two general empirical attempts to compare and contrast them. In the first we investigate experiments studying single causes. We conclude that in spite of a great deal of research that tells us much about how people deal with causes, what is lacking is good data to discriminate the two views. We argue that this is the case because the research has not been driven by a clear understanding of the crucial feature that distinguishes these views—transfer to a novel situation. Finally, we outline experiments using multiple causes and varying causal order (whether information about the effect precedes or follows the cause). Again we conclude that the results of these experiments are not conclusive.

## TWO VIEWS OF CAUSAL REPRESENTATION

Two main perspectives on causal reasoning at least partly reflect two philosophical traditions. The British Empiricists argued that all information about cause must come in through the senses (e.g., Hume 1737/1960). These impressions are then associated with one another using temporal, or spatial, contiguity, similarity, and other empirical cues to causality. Knowledge about cause arises from these associations. The modern cognitive jargon is that this is a bottom-up process in that the cognition is constructed from and driven by experience in the world. The alternative view, normally associated with Kant (1781/1929), is that people judge cause using some preconceived notion of generative transmission or causal power. This process may be innate or learned. Thus, an experience, or data from the senses, is interpreted in light of these generative processes that impose constraints on how the data is interpreted. In fact, it has even been argued that these causal models that include reference to causal order, cause before effect, and some mechanism of causal transmission can transcend empirical cues to causality such as spatial and temporal contiguity.

An experiment by Shultz (1982) demonstrates this principle. He showed that temporal contiguity alone did not drive children's judgments of cause. Children observed a candle with an electric blower on either side of it. A screen was placed to protect the candle when the first blower was turned on. A few seconds later the second blower was turned on and at the same time the screen was moved in front of it, thus preventing it from extinguishing the candle. But this now allowed the first blower to blow the candle out. Even though switching on the second blower was contiguous with the candle going out, the children had little trouble identifying the first blower as the cause. This result was replicated with young African bush children, thus weakening the possible claim that it was a consequence of the children's familiarity with the blowers. In a second experiment Shultz showed that the process for identifying candidate causes with their effects was quite constrained. Children showed that they identified specific causes with only certain types of effects. They were able to identify a lamp rather than a blower as the cause of a spot of light. They identified the blower, rather than a tuning fork, as the culprit when a candle was extinguished. Finally, they asserted that the tuning fork, rather than the light, was responsible for causing a box to resonate. This demonstration showed that no one cause was intrinsically more salient than the others but, rather, that specific causes were identified with effects that were appropriate to the physical reality of the world. Furthermore, when asked to describe the scenarios, the children used language that referred to mechanisms of generative transmission and not to factors such as temporal contiguity and so forth. These results were interpreted to show that subjects' interpretations of the data were influenced, and even dominated, in a top-down manner by some sort of internal models of cause.

No rational psychologist would argue that people cannot describe causal mechanisms. So that cannot be the crucial controversial issue in this debate. Moreover, the children are likely to have had considerable experience with some of the physical systems used in these experiments and with any others must have had at least some minimal instruction. So it is possible that they were simply applying, or generalizing, already learned causal knowledge, in spite of the fact that Shultz used quite young children and rather elegantly tried to control for this. Furthermore, schoolchildren are encouraged to give rational reasons for things and causal models are rational. Who is to say how much of our discourse with young children includes and thus encourages description using causal models? One thing seems certain, however, and that is at a very early age children are very good at identifying causal mechanisms. This does not necessarily enlighten us about the mechanism but does imply that this is an adaptive ability.

Although the argument is intuitively attractive, these data do not easily distinguish whether this reflects a top-down cognitive mechanism that involves a representation of the causal structure or an emergent property of some simpler more reflexive process. A classic animal-learning experiment will illustrate this point. Animals develop food aversions if they have experienced pairings of the flavor of that food with illness and they do so very rapidly, even with a single pairing. They will also develop a conditioned emotional response (anxiety) if an audiovisual cue is paired with electric shock. Garcia and Koelling (1966) reported an experiment with rats in which they paired a compound of an audiovisual cue and a flavor with either electric shock or illness. They found that the animals associated the flavor with illness and the audiovisual cue with shock. This experiment and its outcome are very similar to Shultz's experiments described previously. In spite of equivalent temporal contiguity, the animals only associate certain predictors with certain outcomes. As such, the results are consistent with the idea that the rats had an internal model of cause in which they portrayed novel foods as possible causes of gastric distress and audiovisual cues as related to possible causal mechanisms for external threats. Many people would argue that the underlying mechanisms for the results with rats and children differ, but the point here is that the surface data are the same. That is to say, the children and rats make very similar "reports." If the mechanisms differ, perhaps because the children "reflect" on the data and the rats do something more reflexive, then this implies that very disparate mechanisms can generate very similar behaviors. These behaviors are consistent with mental models of cause. It is a tenet of the associative position that very complex processes arise from very simple mechanisms. Thus, in some situations a simple system can act like it has complex models of causal power integrated into it. These might not transfer to all possible situations but if they do to most common situations, and if occasional errors are not too costly, then they are adaptive. Interestingly, it is the situations in which they don't transfer that are most useful in identifying the mechanisms.

## Data Processing With Probabilistic Causes (Contingency Theory)

Given that even judgments of cause using generative transmission must partly be informed by experience, it is necessary to consider the mechanism that processes this information. And again, there are two main camps loosely associated with the associationist and the generative traditions in philosophy. We first discuss what we call normative but what are also called statistical models of causal reasoning with particular emphasis on Cheng's work (e.g., Cheng, 1997; Cheng & Novick, 1990, 1992; Cheng, Park, Yarlas, & Holyoak, 1996). Because this approach involves suggesting that reasoners use a measure of correlation or contingency to inform their judgment, we must first understand the normative statistic that describes a binary contingency between two outcomes.

It has long been known that to understand the relationship between a cause and an effect, one must consider what happens in the presence of a cause but also what happens in its absence. Every morning the rooster crows and every morning the sun rises. Does the rooster cause the sun to rise? Without knowing what happens on mornings when the rooster is absent we cannot tell. Cook the rooster for supper and the problem is solved; the sun still rises. This example represents a deterministic situation in which there was a direct one-to-one mapping of cause onto effect. More difficult are probabilistic situations in which the events do not always co-occur but nevertheless a relationship may exist between them. Bad health behaviors like smoking are causal factors in many heath problems but they are not perfect causes. Not all people who smoke get lung cancer. Some people who do not smoke get lung cancer. What smoking does, is increase the probability that someone will get lung cancer. The unbiased statistic that describes the one-way contingency of a cause, like smoking, and an effect, like cancer, is $\Delta p$ and was popularized by Allan (1980). The contingency table shown in Fig. 2.1 outlines the four possible conjunctions of a binary cause and effect.

Cell A represents cases where the cause and effect occur together. Cell B represents cases where the cause occurs and the effect does not. Cell C represents cases in which the effect occurs and the cause does not. Finally, in Cell D neither the cause nor effect occurs. This final cell can sometimes lead to problems because it involves the absence of two events; so unless the trial opportunity is clearly marked it poses the logical issue of determining how many times something did not happen. Estimates of Cell D can also be inflated because subjects may use their experience from outside the specific experimental or trial context because this experience usually involves the absence of the two events (see Murphy et al., chap. 10, this volume, for a discussion of this). From the point of view of evidence for a contingency, all cells should have equal

|  | Effect present | Effect absent |
|---|---|---|
| **Cause present** | A | B |
| **Cause absent** | C | D |

FIG. 2.1. A contingency table depicting the events in a one-way contingency between cause and effect.

weight. Cells A and D provide evidence for a positive contingency or a facilitatory causal relationship, because when the cause is there so should the effect (Cell A) and when the cause is not there then the effect should not be (Cell D). High frequencies in Cells B and C provide evidence against a positive contingency because neither the effect nor the cause should occur without the other. Put another way, if there is a positive relationship between cause and effect, then the probability of the effect given that the cause has recently occurred ($P(O|C)$) should be greater than the probability of the effect given that the cause has not recently occurred ($P(O|\sim C)$). In our notation, we use O for outcome event rather than the more common E for effect in order to distinguish between the concrete event that occurs and the causal mechanism implied by the word *effect*. This is not an issue with excitatory causes. For example, the effect and the outcome in the smoking example is cancer. However, with a preventive or inhibitory cause the effect is the absence of the outcome event. The effect of a treatment for cancer is no cancer. Thus the formula for the unbiased statistic for a one-way contingency is the difference between these two probabilities:

$$\Delta p = P(O|C) - P(O|\sim C) \quad \text{range} = -1 \text{ to } +1 \tag{2.1}$$

In terms of cell frequencies:

$$\Delta p = A/(A + B) - C/(C + D) \tag{2.2}$$

Thus, if a human's judgments of the contingency between a cause and an effect are to be normative, they should fairly accurately reflect $\Delta p$. And they often do. For instance, Wasserman, Elek, Chatlosh, and Baker (1993) exposed subjects to 25 contingencies ranging from $-1$ to $1$ with varying cause-and-effect densities and found that the correlation between $\Delta p$ and the ratings was over .9.

Statistical models of causal perception (i.e., Cheng & Novick, 1990) have claimed that people actually compute $\Delta p$ and that that is their representation of the mechanism of causal induction. It is certainly clear that $\Delta p$ does describe the effectiveness of the cause in the situation in which they are trained, but does it represent a good model of the mechanism of cause? Some thought will suggest that it is not.

Cheng's (1997) PowerPC theory deals with this issue. As we mentioned earlier, the notion of generative transmission implies that some generative force exists within the cause. With certain constraints, this power is independent of the causal context, whereas $\Delta p$ is a description of what happens in a specific causal context. That is to say, the power of a cause will transfer from one situation to another. PowerPC makes straightforward assumptions about a causal situation in which there is one binary target cause and in which all causes are independent of one another. First, it is assumed that all outcomes have a cause, so those that occur in the absence of the target cause (e.g., smoking for cancer) must be caused by known or unknown alternative causes (e.g., environmental factors or genetic predisposition) that have identifiable power. It is possible that more than one cause on a given trial has generative power but, because the outcome is binary and can occur only once, it is impossible to determine in a single case if one or more causes had generative power. This situation can be differentiated from a situation in which the outcome is continuous. For example, bad eating habits and lack of exercise contribute to weight gain. An individual person who eats poorly and rarely exercises will be expected to be heavier than someone who only eats poorly. With binary causes and outcomes, the presence of two potential causal agents will change only the distribution and number of outcomes.

If the target cause is not present and there are no alternative causes, the outcome would not occur. When the target cause is not present but the alternative causes are present the net power of these alternatives ($p_{alt}$) is just the conditional probability of an outcome given the absence of the target [i.e., $p_{alt} = P(\text{Outcome}|\text{no Cause}) = P(O|\sim C)$]. This is the outcome base rate. In fact, the power of the target cause ($p_{tc}$) is also defined the same way. The power of a cause can be conceptualized as the proportion of trials on which the outcome would occur in its presence when it is the only effective cause present. This pure situation only occurs when the base rate is zero (i.e., the conditional probability of an effect given the absence of the target cause is zero [i.e., $P(O|\sim C) = 0$]). It is illustrated in the top row of Table 2.1. In this first example, $P(O|C) = .5$ and $P(O|\sim C) = 0$ so $\Delta p = .5$. Because the base rate [i.e., $P(O|\sim C)$] is zero, by definition there must be no effective alternative causes, so the power, $p_{tc}$, of the target is $P(O|C) = .5$. That is, in the presence of the target the likelihood of an outcome increases from 0 to .5.

When the base rate is not zero, the situation is more complicated, because the target cause is no longer the only effective cause and is al-

TABLE 2.1

Three Moderate ($\Delta p = .5$) Positive and Negative ($\Delta p = -.5$) Contingencies With Different Base Rates and Hence Differing Causal Power

| $\Delta p$ | Density | $P(O|C)$ | $P(O|\sim C)$ | $P_{alt}$ | $P_{tc}$ |
|---|---|---|---|---|---|
| .5 | .25 | .5 | 0 | 0 | .5 |
| .5 | .5 | .75 | .25 | .25 | .67 |
| .5 | .75 | 1 | .5 | .5 | 1 |
| −.5 | .25 | 0 | .5 | .5 | −1 |
| −.5 | .5 | .25 | .75 | .75 | −.67 |
| −.5 | .75 | .5 | 1 | 1 | −.5 |

ways presented in the presence of possible unobserved alternative causes. Therefore, at least some of the outcomes that occur on cause-present trials must be caused by the alternatives. We can calculate the power of the alternatives from the base rate calculated on the cause-not-present trials because we assume that in the absence of all alternatives no outcome would occur. Consider the third row in Table 2.1. Here the base rate $P(O|\sim C)$ is .5 so the power of the alternatives is .5. Thus, we know that on the trials when the target cause is present an outcome would occur at least 50% of the time, even if the target cause is completely ineffective, because the unobserved alternatives with their causal power ($p_{alt}$ = .5) will be present. Moreover, because the alternatives and the target cause are assumed to have independent causal power, one cannot determine the power of the target on that proportion of the trials because, regardless of the effectiveness of the target cause, those outcomes would already have been caused by the alternatives. Thus the only trials that could be used to determine the power or effectiveness of the target are those 50% of the trials on which the alternatives would not have caused an outcome. In the third row of the table, the probability of an outcome given the target cause ($P(O|C)$) is 1. This requires that on every instance in which the alternatives did not cause an effect the target must have. It follows from this that its power must be one. This is true because it must cause an outcome on all trials on which the alternatives were not effective or were not present. On these trials the base rate must be zero and outcomes caused by the target cause occur on each of them. Even though the power of the target is different, the contingency $\Delta p$ is the same as in the earlier example [$\Delta p = P(O|C) - P(O|\sim C) = .5$]. Thus, in the two cases we have discussed we have equivalent $\Delta p$s and differing power.

From the discussion it is now very easy to derive Cheng's (1997) formula for the causal power of positive or facilitatory causes. Power may be determined on those trials in which the target cause is present but the alternative causes are not effective. This portion of trials is (1 – the base rate) or ($1 - p_{alt}$) or [$1 - P(O|\sim C)$]. The power of the target is the proportion of these trials on which an outcome occurs. The amount the cause raises the probability of the effect over baseline is simply $\Delta p$. However, $\Delta p$ underestimates the number of trials on which the target would have been effective because, on some of the target's presentations, both it and the alternatives would have had generative power. Thus, $\Delta p$ actually represents the trials on which only the target is effective (i.e., the outcomes on the noneffective alternative trials). We know those trials are ($1 - p_{alt}$) so the power of the target is just the ratio of $\Delta p$ and this value. Thus, the formula for the power of a positive or excitatory cause may be written:

$$p_{tce} = \Delta p/(1 - p_{alt}) = \Delta p/(1 - P(O|\sim C)) \qquad (2.3)$$

The moderate base rate contingency in the second row of Table 2.1 will illustrate this calculation. $P(O|\sim C) = .25$ thus the power of the alternatives $p_{alt} = .25$ and $\Delta p = P(O|C) - P(O|\sim C) = .75 - .25 = .5$. Hence $P_{tce} = \Delta p/(1 - p_{alt}) = .5/(1 - .25) = .67$.

It is sometimes difficult to follow probabilistic arguments such as the preceding one, so it might be helpful to consider an analogy with the more familiar case of coin tosses. The case of two independent causes, one representing the target (t) and the other the alternatives (a), can be understood by considering independent coin tosses. Any time a head (H) occurs the coin toss is considered to have generated an outcome. The alternative-cause coin is tossed on every trial and the target coin is tossed on some proportion of the trials. On trials in which only the alternative coin is tossed, it will come up heads and generate an effect 50% of the time. Therefore its power $(p_a)$ is .5. This is also the base rate of the outcome. When both coins are tossed, there are the usual conjunctions of events $(H_aH_t, H_aT_t, T_aH_t,$ and $T_aT_t)$. Any time at least one head occurs the conditions for an outcome are met. Thus, outcomes will occur on 75% of the trials in which both coins are tossed. We can now see that $\Delta p_t$ for the target is .25 because $p(O|t) = .75$ and $p(O|\sim t) = .5$. The power of the target can be easily calculated. We must simply ignore the trials on which the alternative would have caused an outcome $(H_aH_t, H_aT_t)$ and consider those trials on which only the target coin could have caused the outcome $(T_aH_t, T_aT_t)$. On 50% of those trials, the target turns up heads and an outcome is caused. Thus, the power of the target coin will be calculated to be $p_t = .5$. In the case of this unbiased coin we already know its power is .5 because, by definition, it comes up heads 50% of the time. Cheng's formula $p_t = \Delta p/(1 - p_a) = .25/(1 - .5) = .5$ can also calculate the power. Thus, one can see from this example how two independent causes of power .5 can generate a $\Delta p$ of .25.

Three parallel examples of preventive or inhibitory causes are shown in the bottom three rows of Table 2.1. A preventive cause causes an outcome that would otherwise occur, not to occur. Thus, in order for a preventive cause to be effective, there must be some alternative causes with some power or there would be no outcomes to prevent. It will be recalled that the ideal situation for computing positive power was when no outcomes were otherwise expected—when $P(O|\sim C) = 0$. For an inhibitory cause, the ideal situation to compute its power would be when the probability of an outcome in its absence was 1. An alternative way to look at it is to consider the effect of a preventive cause to be no-outcome. Thus, the ideal situation would occur when the probability of no-outcome given the alternatives was zero $P(\sim O|\sim C) = 0$. If one follows the aforementioned derivation for excitatory causes, the formula for an inhibitory target cause may be written:

$$P_{tci} = -\Delta p/(1 - P(\sim O|\sim C)) \qquad (2.4)$$

But $P(O|{\sim}C) = (1 - P({\sim}O|{\sim}C))$ so we are left with Cheng's:

$$P_{tci} = -\Delta p / P(O|{\sim}C) \tag{2.5}$$

We prefer to leave off the negative sign so that inhibitory power is a negative entity. The bottom three rows of Table 2.1 show the power for three different negative causes with a constant $\Delta p = -.5$ and varying power of the target cause.

Again, the important point is that, because power is defined for each cause independent of all alternatives, power can be seen as a property of the cause, and not the context in which it is presented. Thus power can be used to make reasoned theoretically based predictions about what would happen if a cause is transferred to another context. For example, the cause from the third row of Table 2.1 has a power $p_{tc} = 1$. Thus, if it is present in a situation in which the base rate is zero (i.e., $p_{alt} = 0$) one would expect it to cause an outcome on every trial. Thus $P(O|C)$ would always be 1 and in this case $\Delta p$ would be 1. Alternatively people might just transfer $\Delta p$ from one situation to the other and thus predict that $P(O|C)$ would be .5 because that is the probability generated by $\Delta p = .5$ if $p_{alt} = 0$.

## Associative Approaches and the Rescorla–Wagner Model

The most commonly tested associative model has been the Rescorla–Wagner (Rescorla & Wagner, 1972) model but several others have been considered as well (e.g., Baker, Murphy, & Vallée-Tourangeau, 1996; Miller & Matzel, 1988; Pearce 1987, 1994; Pearce & Hall, 1980; van Hamme & Wasserman, 1994). According to these models, causal information is processed through the formation of associative links between representations of the cues and the outcomes. Throughout this discussion we assume that the input cues are representations of the cause and the outcomes are representations of the effects. Although the exact mechanisms differ, generally the output of associative links increases when a cause and effect occur together and weakens when the effect occurs without the cause. Most associative interpretations have several things in common:

1. The links are considered to be unidirectional. If a cause–effect link exists, activating the representation of the cause will increase the likelihood the link will be activated but activating the effect will not.
2. The representations are organized in, at least, two levels, according to their temporal order, with the causes on the input level and outcomes on the output level.
3. There is no bias in the network in the sense that an association may form equally well between any input node and output node.
4. If a cause and an outcome occur close together in time the net association is strengthened. If the cause occurs by itself the net associ-

ation is weakened. We refer to net associations because some theories posit the weakening and strengthening of a single link (e.g., Rescorla & Wagner, 1972) and others posit separate generative and preventive links (e.g., Pearce & Hall, 1980).

A simple version of such a net is shown in Fig. 2.2. It can be seen that the input nodes are causes and the output nodes are effects. This example has nodes for two target causes and a third node for the alternative causes. The alternative causes are often referred to as the context in these associative models. And, analogous to the notion of power for the alternative causes, if there is a nonzero base rate of outcomes in the absence of the causes, associations between the context and the outcome are formed. The model we have described is not biologically realistic because biological systems do have predispositions to form some associations rather than others, as in flavor aversion learning, and here all links have an equal probability of being strengthened. However, because it is unbiased, it is ideal for demonstrating the flexibility and power of this approach.

A further feature of associative models, as they have been applied to contingency learning, is that many posit competition between cues when more than one cue or cause are paired with the outcome. An example of an experiment in which cue competition occurred is the rela-

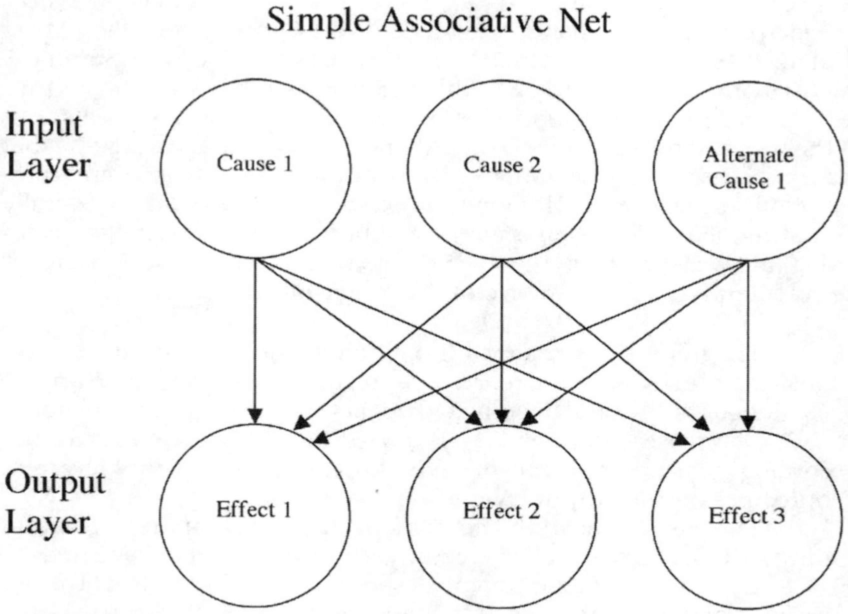

## Simple Associative Net

FIG. 2.2 A simple version of a two-layer associative net.

tive validity experiment (Wagner, Logan, Haberlandt, & Price, 1968). In this experiment rats were exposed to trials of two compounds, each consisting of a unique tone (*A* or *B*) and a common light (*X*), the target stimulus. One group received a true discrimination treatment in which one of the compounds (*AX*) was always paired with shock and the other (*BX*) never was. Therefore, the presence of *A* or *B* perfectly predicted the outcome. In the pseudodiscrimination group each of *AX* and *BX* was paired with shock 50% of the time and therefore neither *A* nor *B* was informative about the presence of the outcome. Because the compounds occurred an equal number of times, *X* was paired with shock an equal number, and an equal proportion (50%) of times in each group. When *X* was later tested alone it generated a much stronger conditioned response in the pseudodiscrimination than in the true discrimination. It was as if the cues competed for a fixed pool of associative strength and in the true discrimination *A* won that competition because it was a stronger predictor than *X*. The most popular cue competition model is that of Rescorla and Wagner (1972).

This model assumes that, if one or more causes are paired with an outcome, changes in each individual bond between these causes and the outcome will be inversely proportional to the associative strength of all other causes present on that trial. Thus, if one cause already has a very strong association with the outcome, it will limit the ability of other causes to acquire associative strength. This is the mechanism for cue competition. The following formula describes the changes of associative strength ($\Delta V_i$) of each individual cause $i$ on a single trial:

$$\Delta V_i = \alpha_i \beta_O (\lambda_O - \Sigma V_{all}) \qquad (2.6)$$

$V_i$ represents the associative strength of each individual cue or cause $i$. $\alpha$ represents the learning rate parameter for $i$ and roughly corresponds to its salience (or associability, see chaps. 6 and 7). $\beta_O$ represents the learning rate parameter for the unconditioned stimulus (US). The common assumption, and a necessary one to account for the relative validity effect, is that this parameter is higher on outcome trials than on those for which the outcome is not present ($\beta_O > \beta_{\sim O}$) (see Murphy, Baker, & Fouquet, 2001). This reasonable assumption formalizes the claim that the presence of the outcome is more salient than its absence. $\lambda_O$ represents the total or asymptotic associative strength that will be supported by the outcome once learning is complete and is proportional to the outcome strength. If the outcome does not occur on a trial, $\lambda_{\sim O} = 0$. The final term $\Sigma V_{all}$ represents the total associative strength of all causes present on that trial.

When there is a single cause, only two nodes are required to describe the learning, one for the context and one for the cause. When the cause is present, it and the context compete for any increases or decreases in associative strength elicited by the presence or absence of the outcome. When the cause is not present, the context benefits from the presence and absence of the outcome. When outcomes occur only in the presence of the cause, the context quickly loses the competition for associative strength. However, in nondeterministic situations when outcomes occur in the presence and the absence of the target cause, the cause and context compete for associative strength. Higher proportions of outcomes during the cause (high $P(O|C)$) favor the cause and high proportions in its absence (high $P(O|{\sim}C)$) favor the context. This should be reminiscent of the formula for calculating $\Delta p$. Interestingly, Chapman and Robbins (1990) have shown that once enough trials have been given and asymptote has been achieved the associative strength of the target ($V_{tc}$) is equal to $\Delta p_{tc}$ if it is assumed that $\lambda_O = 1$ and that ($\beta_O = \beta_{\sim O}$). We mentioned earlier that it is normally assumed that ($\beta_O > \beta_{\sim O}$). Wasserman et al. (1993) demonstrated that with this assumption the asymptotic values for $V_{tc}$ showed a modest bias with higher values at low densities but these values were still very highly correlated with $\Delta p_{tc}$.

## SINGLE-CAUSE TESTS CONTRASTING CONTINGENCY ($\Delta p_{tc}$), POWER ($p_{tc}$), AND ASSOCIATIVE STRENGTH ($V_{tc}$).

It would seem very easy to determine if observers use contingency, power, or associative strength to evaluate contingencies. Table 2.1 showed that power not contingency varies with outcome base rate. Two common strategies to contrast the measures involve holding contingency constant and varying power, or holding power constant and varying contingency, and observing whether judgments follow one measure or the other. Table 2.1 illustrates the former strategy in which contingency is held constant at either $\Delta p_{tc} = \pm.5$ and power varying from $\pm.5$ to $\pm 1$. The original experiment by Wasserman et al. (1993) used just this strategy and, among other contingencies, included those in Table 2.1.

The experiment used an instrumental paradigm in which participants pushed a button to attempt to control the illumination of the light. The sessions were divided into 1–second time bins. If one or more responses were made in a bin it was called a response and if none were made it was called a nonresponse. Following each bin, the light could be illuminated with varying probabilities depending on whether it was a response or nonresponse bin. Thus, the two conditional probabilities for the calculation of $\Delta p$ were defined. In the overall experiment subjects were exposed to conditional probabilities of an outcome given the response and given no response that varied from 0 to 1 in steps of .25. This generated 25 contingencies varying in outcome density and varying from $\Delta p = -1$ to $\Delta p = 1$. We have already mentioned that in both experiments humans' judgments were very highly correlated with $\Delta p$ ($r^2 > .9$). This implies that they did not match power well because we know it varies with base rate.

Figure 2.3 shows the results from Wasserman et al. (1993) for the six contingencies from Table 2.1. It is clear from this figure that subjects' judgments do largely track the two contingencies. All judgments of Δp = .5 are greater than those of the Δp = –.5 contingency. However, there is also a fanlike density bias in which subjects' estimates of low base rate contingencies diverge more from zero. As well as the estimates, power and asymptotic associative strengths from the Rescorla–Wagner model are plotted on the graph. It is clear that estimates are closely related to associative strengths. Although the estimates of the negative contingency are proportional, but of a different magnitude, to preventive or inhibitory power, the estimates of the positive contingency diverge greatly from power. Quite clearly, the results of this experiment are consistent with the Rescorla–Wagner (1972) associative model and not consistent with Cheng's (1997) PowerPC.

Since the publication of Cheng's formulae for power, several researchers have contrasted power with contingency or associative strength as explanations of human causal judgments and the results have been mixed (see Allan, 2003). For example, Buehner and Cheng (1997) repeated Wasserman et al.'s (1993) design but used a passive classical conditioning design and found that estimates were moderately consistent

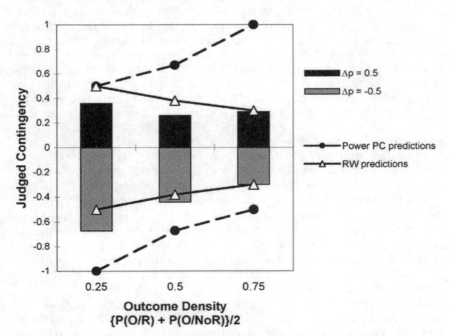

FIG. 2.3. Selected results from Wasserman et al. (1993). Also plotted are predictions from the PowerPC model and the Rescorla–Wagner model.

with power. Vallée-Tourangeau and colleagues reported results that were not consistent with power but also were not strongly supportive of the associative model (Vallée-Tourangeau, Murphy, & Drew, 1997; Vallée-Tourangeau, Murphy, Drew, & Baker, 1998). Lober and Shanks (2000) reported a similar series of experiments in which they found evidence that was inconsistent with power. The results have been mixed and, often arcane, arguments have been mounted to defend both sides. It is our impression that the weight of the data is on the side of the contingency or the Rescorla–Wagner model. However, we now believe that these tests do not represent an appropriate evaluation of causal power theories.

## Do These Experiments Evaluate Causal Power?

Causal-power theory states that people's behavior in causal situations is guided by some internal representation of causal models, including generative transmission. For it to be adaptive, it does not require the person to be able to report power when asked; rather it requires the person to generate behavior in the world that is consistent with the generative structure of the environment. People may or may not be aware of the mechanism or process. Even if they are aware of the mechanism, they likely do not have clear verbal distinctions between power ($p_{tc}$), contingency ($\Delta p$), or even certain conditional probabilities. This is not to say we cannot teach people the distinction; it is just that the "ordinary" person may not have it at the tip of her or his tongue. When we ask them for a judgment of the causal mechanism, they may mix up these questions or not understand exactly what is meant. We may ask them to report the relationship of cause $X$ with effect $Y$. They might think we mean power, or contingency, or they might even think we mean the conditional probability of $Y$ given $X$ [i.e., $P(O|C)$]. Even though a panel of eminent scientists has decided that the wording of a question clearly allows a distinction between two factors, say power and contingency, this does not mean it will distinguish between the subjects', possibly subconscious, calculation of these entities. An accurate appreciation of each of these entities has adaptive consequences. Replying with $P(O|C)$ answers the question of what will happen when the cause is there. Answering with $\Delta p$ allows decisions to be made about which of two states is better and helps with choice tasks or in deciding to initiate a response. Answering with power potentially allows the participant to predict what will happen in other contexts as well as the present one. From the perspective of generating adaptive behavior nearly any of these answers is correct in some situations.

Another issue is the level of analysis. $\Delta p$ is a normative statistic that simply describes the one-way contingency between the cause and the effect. It is a normative description of the world. If it is adaptive to be sensitive to this contingency, then a person's behavior should map onto this contingency. Thus, as a preliminary goal, it is worthwhile to ask if a person's behavior maps onto or computes $\Delta p$. (The terms *computation* and *algorithm*, which we use shortly, come from Marr's, 1982, analysis of explanation in vision.) If a person's behavior "computes" $\Delta p$, it is possible that the internal psychological mechanism involves a process in which conditional probabilities are somehow calculated and compared and that this is the internal mechanism, rule, or algorithm that generates the behavior that corresponds to $\Delta p$. However, we have also seen that associative strength (V) can generate outputs that correlate with $\Delta p$, so it is possible that an associative mechanism is able to generate the adaptive behavior that is required. In effect, at the computational level, contingency theory appears to be correct; people largely behave as if they are computing $\Delta p$. However the mechanism by which $\Delta p$ is calculated may bear no resemblance to how a statistician would calculate $\Delta p$. One point that is important is that even if the algorithm is different a correct normative description or theory is always valuable because it outlines the appropriate adaptive ideal to which the actual psychological algorithm must aspire.

Now consider power. Cheng's $p$ is also a normative statistic. It is a normative description of what will happen when two independent events, like the tossing of two coins, co-occur. It is possible that people extract this sort of information in a causal-induction task along with whatever is necessary for generative transmission. If they have this ability, then the interesting thing is what happens when they apply this information. Assume a moderate power for the target cause $p_{tc}$ = .5 and a base rate of .5 (i.e., $p_{alt}$ = .5). If the person applies power, they will be able to calculate $\Delta p_{tc}$ by solving the power formula for it (i.e., $\Delta p_{tc} = p_{tc}(1 - p_{alt})$ = .5 (1 – .5) = .25). They can then calculate P(O|C) by adding $p_{alt}$ and $\Delta p_{tc}$. Thus, if a person has a representation of power (remember power also implies the generative mechanism) this will generate each of the preceding answers. Moreover, if the cause is transferred to another context with a different base rate it will also generate answers to each of the three questions. This is just the critical and possibly adaptive feature of a representation of power over a simple representation of the relationships between the events in the learning context.

The next issue is what negative data on Cheng's (1997) PowerPC model means for mental models of cause or generative transmission. The answer to this is "very little." $p_{tc}$ as defined here is only one of many possible mental models of cause and Cheng has never denied this. This is an independent-cause model. However, even if it is disconfirmed in any individual case, it could mean that any one of many other possible causal models was being applied in this particular experiment. The models could be additive rather than multiplicative. They might involve interactions between the target and the alternative causes. People might impose their own natural causal models on the data as was done in Shultz's (1982) experiments. And any of these options is consistent with mental models of cause or generative transmission. Therefore, experiments targeting Cheng's specific theory of power cannot rule out this general approach or even particularly weaken it. Similarly, we argue in the section that follows on causal order that experiments targeted at specific associative models do very little to weaken the general associative strategy.

We have pointed out that the basic data from ours and other research cannot really rule out theories of generative transmission. If people report $\Delta p_{tc}$ rather than $p_{tc}$, then it is quite possible that this was an emergent property of the representation of $p_{tc}$. Alternatively, it could result from $V_{tc}$ from the Rescorla–Wagner model. It could also be that the participants had an additive model of cause in which they represented a generative process whereby some calculation of $\Delta p_{tc}$ was internalized. Clearly the only way to being to investigate possible mechanisms of generative transmission is to stop asking people for reports of what they believe the causal relation to be and begin asking them for predictions about what would happen in other causal contexts. The main beauty of generative theories is the natural way in which mental models of cause transfer from one situation to another. If we wish to understand cause we should design studies that investigate its main adaptive function; namely transfer. There are very few such studies. Most certainly if we wish to understand how people represent causal power it is important that such experiments be done.

Up to this point, we have discussed causal power of a single target cause. This topic was relatively easy because there existed a formal model of power that could be tested and evaluated. In the subsequent section we are moving on to less formal aspects of mental models of cause. These aspects have more semantic content and are much less clearly specified. In the real world causes generally precede effects. However, sometimes people perceive the effects before the cause and they can induce cause from these events. For example, a person might have various symptoms and a physician would diagnose a bacterial infection. Causes usually match their effects. People often have preexisting causal models and these causal models often are involved in causal induction. Much of the work on possible rich representations of causal structure has been done in the context of cue competition experiments. So we discuss these first.

## CAUSE COMPETITION AND CAUSAL ORDER WITH TWO CAUSES

### Experiment 1

It will be recalled that in selective association experiments such as those of Wagner et al. (1968) judgments of a moderate cue are influenced by the presence of a second stronger cue. Mehta (2000) carried out a series of experiments designed to contrast predictions of the causal-model theories with the associative perspective by manipulating causal order and the number of causes and effects. Discussion of his first experiment illustrates the paradigm and outlines the two classes of explanation. This experiment was a replication of an experiment reported by Baker, Mercier, Vallée-Tourangeau, Frank and Pan (1993) but used a different cover story that was appropriate for manipulating causal order and the number of causes. In this procedure subjects were exposed to two causes ($A_C$ & $B_C$) and one effect ($X_E$). In this experiment, and each of the others, A was the target event. In these experiments the contingency of A was held constant at $\Delta p_A = .5$ with $P(O|C_A) = .75$ and $P(O|\sim C_A) = .25$. In each experiment, $B_C$ the competing cause was either uncorrelated with the outcome [$\Delta p_B = 0$ with $P(O|C_B) = .5$ and $P(O|\sim C_B) = .5$] or perfectly correlated with it [$\Delta p_B = 1$ with $P(O|C_B) = 1$ and $P(O|\sim C_B) = 0$]. The two treatments used the notation $\Delta p_A/\Delta p_B$ and were labeled .5/1 and .5/0. If cue competition was found, it would be expected that judgments of $A_C$ would be much lower when it was contrasted with a strong $B_C$ (.5/1).

The scenario for this experiment was straightforward but was crucial for the design of the subsequent experiments. $A_C$ and $B_C$ were two fictitious chemicals and $X_E$ was a fictitious strain of bacteria. The cover story stated that scientists were interested in whether the two chemicals affected the survival of the strain of bacteria. The scientists would add either both chemicals, one of the chemicals, or no chemicals to a culture and then it was determined whether the culture had survived (the effect or outcome). They were further told that the chemicals could help, hinder, or have no effect on the survival of the bacteria. Thus, it was possible to program both facilitatory or preventive causal relationships. Moreover, it was possible to change the cover story so that the chemicals were no longer causes but were effects and the bacteria were the cause. This modified scenario would thus have one cause and two effects rather than two causes and one effect. In this second scenario, the scientists were interested in whether the bacteria influenced the presence of the two chemicals. Again it was described so that the bacteria could be either a preventive or facilitatory cause.

All experiments consisted of 48 trials per treatment and participants made causal ratings of A and B after 32 and 48 trials. The rating scale ranged from −100 for a perfect preventive cause to 100 for a perfect facilitative cause. All subjects received both treatments in counterbalanced orders. Each treatment was couched as a separate game. The frequency of each of the event conjunctions is shown in Table 2.2.

On each trial the participants were shown which of the causes was present, as text on the computer screen, and then were asked to guess whether the outcome would occur on that trial. Once they had guessed they were shown whether or not the outcome had occurred. We only report the ratings after 48 trials as the ratings after 32 trials were very similar. We also do not report the ratings for $B_C$ because they were very similar in all the experiments and tracked $\Delta p_B$. Finally, each of the first four experiments had two more contingencies presented in counterbal-

TABLE 2.2

Frequency of Events for the Two Contingencies in Experiments 1 – 5

| | Experimental Treatment | |
| Event Conjunction | 0.5/0 | 0.5/1 |
|---|---|---|
| AB → X | 9 | 18 |
| A~B → X | 9 | 0 |
| ~AB → X | 3 | 6 |
| ~A~B → X | 3 | 0 |
| AB → ~X | 3 | 0 |
| A~B → ~X | 3 | 6 |
| ~AB → ~X | 9 | 0 |
| ~A~B → ~X | 9 | 18 |
| Total trials | 48 | 48 |
| $\Delta p_A$ | .5 | .5 |
| $\Delta p_B$ | 0 | 1 |
| $\Delta p_{A|\sim B}$ | .5 | 0 |
| $\Delta p_{A|B}$ | .5 | 0 |

anced order with the others. In each of these contingencies $A_C$ was uncorrelated with the outcome $\Delta p_A = 0$ and the contingency for $B_C$ was again 0 or 1. These treatments were also included in Baker et al. (1993) and they were included in Mehta's (2000) experiments to make the experiments comparable. Just as we had in the original experiments, these treatments also generated a cue competition effect comparable to that of the ones we report here. Although we report no statistics here, we carried out standard analyses of variance on all data and standard a posteriori tests on the data. All assertions about differences between means we make here are reliable at the $\alpha = .05$ level.

The estimates of $A_C$ are shown in the left panel of Figure 2.4. When $A_C$ was paired with a weak second cause ($\Delta p_B = 0$) in treatment .5/0 it was given a moderately positive causal rating. However, when it was paired with a strong cause in the competition treatment (.5/1) the estimates were quite low.

***Causal Competition and Causal Models.*** Certainly experiments showing cue competition are consistent with the Rescorla–Wagner model. It was also argued that because people are making inaccurate judgments of $A_C$'s absolute contingency they are also inconsistent with contingency theory (e.g., Dickinson, Shanks, & Evenden, 1984).

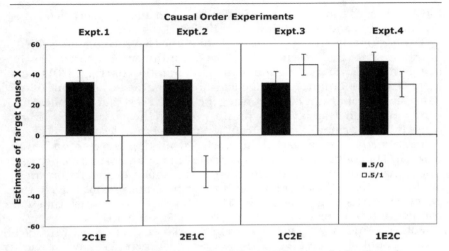

FIG. 2.4. Estimates of the strength of the target cause $A_C$ for Experiments 1–4. The error bars represent standard errors of the means.

But it turns out that this is not true (e.g., see Baker et al., 1996; Spellman, 1996). When there are two possible causes of an outcome that are at least partly independent of one another the unconditional contingency is not the appropriate measure of their contribution to the effect. The true measure is their contingency conditional upon one another. To understand this, consider two causes, say a diet high in fat ($A_C$) and smoking ($B_C$). Both are possible causes of heart troubles ($X_E$). If we had a sample of people of whom some smoked, some had fatty diets, some had both risk factors, and some had neither factor and we wished to study the effects of fatty foods on heart disease, one strategy would be to hold the other factor, smoking, constant and then study the effect of high-fat diets at each level of smoking. For example, we might look at all the people who did not smoke and then calculate the proportion of nonsmokers who had a fatty diet and who contracted heart disease [$P(X_E|A_C{\sim}B_C)$]. This could be compared with the proportion of nonsmokers with no fatty diet who had heart disease [$P(X_E|{\sim}A_C{\sim}B_C)$]. If these two values are subtracted, we have the contingency for $A_C$ conditional on the absence of $B_C$ [$\Delta p_{A|{\sim}B} = P(X_E|A_C{\sim}B_C) - P(X_E|{\sim}A_C{\sim}B_C)$]. A similar contingency could be calculated given the presence of smoking [$\Delta p_{A|B} = P(X_E|A_CB_C) - P(X_E|{\sim}A_CB_C)$]. For the same reasons it is easier to calculate power when the base rate of outcomes is zero, it is argued that the contingency of $A_C$ is more informative in the absence of other facilitatory causes (i.e., $\Delta p_{A|{\sim}B}$). For preventive causes it is just the opposite $\Delta p_{A|B}$ is more useful. From an information-processing point of view, if these conditionalized contingencies are very low this means that the target cue does not add any extra predictive information beyond that supplied by the blocking cue.

The bottom two rows of Table 2.2 show the two contingencies for $A_C$ in the presence and absence of $B_C$. These contingencies are zero in the competition (5./1) treatment and are still .5 in the control (.5/0) treatment. These conditional contingencies are normative so again one of the valuable contributions of the contingency analysis is that it implies that cue competition, that is the discounting of $A_C$ in the presence of a strong cause $B_C$, is a normative effect. Traditional associative descriptions of cue competition have emphasized that such discounting represents a failure to learn. The contingency analysis implies that it is a normative process. Cue competition is one of the cornerstones of modern associationism so at the very least the associationists must be grateful that the contingency theorists (e.g., Spellman, 1996) have demonstrated that cue competition is a normative information-processing strategy.

Both contingency theory and the Rescorla–Wagner model provide a good account of the result of Mehta's first experiment. We have provided considerable evidence in similar preparations that we believe weakens both accounts of information processing (e.g., Baker et al., 1993), however the critical point here is not the information-processing mechanism but the causal-model mechanism as applied to this paradigm.

Waldmann and Holyoak (1992) have pointed out an interesting asymmetry between the predictions of causal-model theory and associative models such as the Rescorla–Wagner model when causal order and the number of causes and effects are manipulated. They point out that associative models are founded on contiguity and temporal order. Figure 2.5 shows two fragments of an associative net involving three events. In the left panel we have two input events and one output event. Because there are two bonds connected to a single output, the

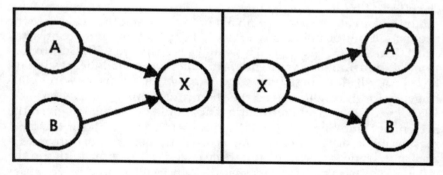

FIG. 2.5. Two fragments of an associative network showing connections with one input variable and two output variables and with two input variables and one output variable.

Rescorla–Wagner model will predict cue competition through its linear operator $(\lambda_O - \Sigma V_{all})$. However, when there is one input and two outputs there are two independent bonds so in this case there are two separate linear operators, each of the form $(\lambda_O - V_{TC})$, so no competition should occur because two bonds do not have to share the asymptotic strength $\lambda_O$ of either outcome. This is an oversimplification because both bonds share the context and other common cues, but that can be ignored for this analysis. Thus, the Rescorla–Wagner model would predict cue competition whenever there are two inputs and one output. Although learning rate parameters will differ, there should be no principled difference whether these events are causes or effects.

Causal-power theory takes a different perspective. This theory implies that people have a causal model of the events and the semantic content of these models imposes constraints on the situations in which they might show cue competition. Although the normal structure of a causal relationship is that causes precede effects, and this order should be easiest to learn, they also acknowledge that sometimes information about the effects is presented before knowledge of the cause. For example, people often find out about symptoms before they find out about causes. People can use this information to make diagnoses of new cases where they know the symptoms. This is called diagnostic reasoning. They can also make predictions if later they are told the cause is present.

Cue competition occurs when people impose conditionalized contingencies on the data as we have described previously. If we have a situation in which there are two causes, it is appropriate to impose such conditionalized contingencies. So we would expect cue competition whenever there are two causes and one effect regardless of the order. One the other hand it is argued that effects do not compete for causes so it does not matter what the causal order is. This contrasts with the associative models' prediction that, regardless of whether there are two causes followed by one effect or two effects followed by one cause, cue competition will occur. Competition will not occur when there is one cause or one effect followed by two effects or two causes.

A number of researchers have tested these predictions; the results have been somewhat mixed and the tone has often but not always been very adversarial (e.g., compare Melz, Cheng, Holyoak, & Waldmann, 1993; Shanks & Lopez, 1996; Waldmann, 2000; Waldmann & Holyoak, 1997; with Tangen & Allan, 2004). We do not review these studies in any depth, but before we go on it is worthwhile pointing out that the major assumption that effects should not compete is by no means exclusive. There are many examples where effects are not independent of one another. For example, a person who eats large meals may, as a consequence, get fat, however the large meals might also support a high level of activity. Presumably there is an inverse relationship between the two processes and cue competition would be appropriate. Similarly, anxiety causes freezing, aggression, and flight in rats. It is difficult to imagine that these are independent. Thus one of the major tenets of this research is on rather shaky ground. It would not be an issue if the content of people's models of the effects were independently assessed to make sure that the assumption of effect–cause independence is met but this is rarely done. There are other pitfalls and empirical difficulties.

## Experiment 2

Waldmann and Holyoak (1992) carried out a series of experiments in which they had two causes and one effect or two effects and one cause. From the previous arguments it seems clear that they would expect to get cue competition with two causes but not with two effects. The results of their series of experiments were equivocal. Experiments 1 and 3 confirmed their expectations but in Experiment 2 they found that they got strong cue competition in both situations. They argued that this anomalous result was caused by already-formed causal models involving alternative causes that were not mentioned in the experiment. This caused the participants to discount the weaker cause because they believed hypothetical alternatives were the actual cause of the effect. The problem with this analysis is that they did not independently assess these alternatives in Experiment 2 so the demonstration is entirely circular. This criticism of Waldmann and Holyoak's experiment ignores other treatments in the experiments that generated results consistent with mental models of cause and that were also very difficult for the associative position. Nonetheless, the issue about the ad hoc postulation of unmeasured causal models to deal with awkward data is a serious one and not uncommon. Also their experiments did not fully explore the number of causes and effects and causal order. We now discuss Mehta's other experiments that were designed to do this.

It will be recalled that in Mehta's first experiment the two chemicals were defined as causes ($A_C$ and $B_C$) and the fate of the bacteria as a single effect $X_E$. In Experiment 2 the two chemicals were now defined as effects ($A_E$ and $B_E$) and the bacteria was the single cause. As in Experiment 1, the chemicals were presented first followed by the cause ($A_E B_E \rightarrow X_C$). This is a diagnostic situation but because there are two effects and one cause, causal-model theory predicts that there should not be cue competition. Because there are two inputs and one output as in the left panel of Figure 2.5, the associative model would predict cue competition. The second panel of Figure 2.4 shows estimates of $A_E$ in both the control (.5/0) and the blocking contingency (5./1). There is a strong cue competition effect and again the estimates for treatment .5/1 are very much below zero.

## Experiments 3 and 4

Experiments 3 and 4 involved a similar contrast between predictive and diagnostic preparations except that in both of these experiments the events are presented as one input and two outputs. Experiment 3 involved the one-cause/two-effects scenario ($X_C \rightarrow A_E B_E$) and Experiment 4 used the one-effect/two-cause scenario ($X_E \rightarrow A_C B_C$). According to the aforementioned simplified associative model we would not expect cue competition in either experiment. Causal-model theory would expect cue competition in Experiment 4 in which there are two causes and one effect but not in Experiment 3.

The results for Experiments 3 and 4 are shown in the two right panels of Figure 2.4. Although there is some hint of cue competition in Experiment 4, it is of a much lesser magnitude than that in either Experiment 1 or 2 and is not statistically reliable. With the exception of a study by Tangen and Allan (2004) that borrowed Mehta's design and scenario, this is the most complete investigation of causal order and input–output order. It also uses identical cues for both causes and effects so it is unlikely that there would be any biases. The results of these experiments clearly support the simple associative model.

There is, however, a methodological problem with many of the experiments including these. That is that subjects were asked on each trial to predict the outcome. This is done to encourage them to pay attention. On two-event $\rightarrow$ one-event pairings this required predicting a single event, and in the cue competition (.5/1) group the perfect stimulus could do that perfectly well. This might encourage the participants to simply reduce their attention to the target cue. Such a process would encourage cue competition. On the one-event $\rightarrow$ two-event procedure the subjects needed to predict the occurrence of both events. This should maintain their attention to both the competing event and the target. Thus they might learn about both events and cue competition might be reduced.

## Experiment 5

In order to investigate this possibility, Mehta (2000) repeated the treatments of Experiments 1–4 in a single experiment but did not ask the participants to make any predictions on any of the trials. We were encouraged to do this by a series of experiments reported by Tangen and Allan (2004; see also Tangen, Allan, & Sedeghi, chap. 4, this volume), which did not use trial-by-trial predictions and under some circumstances found single-cause/two-effect cue competition. Because there were two different scenarios, the subjects were divided into two groups. One group was the predictive group and received only cause $\rightarrow$ effect orderings. The second group received only diagnostic treatments (i.e., effect $\rightarrow$ cause). Each group received the two orders of presentation (i.e., one event followed by two events and vice versa). Within each order, subjects were presented with the cue competition (.5/1) and the control (.5/0) treatment contingencies. Thus contingency and event order were within-subjects factors and causal order was a between-subjects factor.

The results of this experiment are shown in Figure 2.6. It is quite clear from this figure that there was a cue competition following each treat-

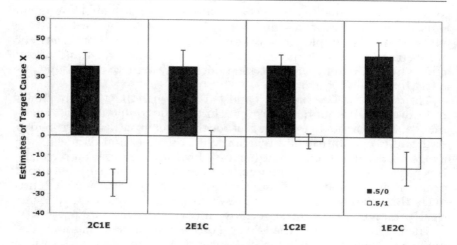

FIG. 2.6. Results of Experiment 5. In this experiment subjects were not required to make predictions on each trial.

ment. This is clearly inconsistent with power theory because there is cue competition both when there are two causes and when there is one. But it is also inconsistent with the simple associative model that we have been considering. Cue competition was found with either one or two antecedent events.

As we mentioned, causal-model theory can explain unexpected cue competition such as that found in the one-cause/two-effect treatments by suggesting that a participant might have some strong alternative causal model that causes them to discount the weaker cue. However, in this experiment and several others, Mehta gave the participants questionnaires that assessed whether they believed there were any important uncontrolled factors in the fictitious experiments. In general they reported no such alternative causes. Thus, he found no evidence of any consistent competing models that might cause the cue competition effect. It is always possible that there are subconscious models involved but these data considerably weaken this argument.

It should be pointed out, however, that there is more than one associative model and they do not all have the same architecture or properties. In associative models with direct cue competition such as Rescorla–Wagner the target stimulus fails to develop associative strength, so information about its pairings with the outcome is lost. Many associative models do not posit cue competition during training; rather all links are learned separately. It is at the point of the decision that the relative strengths of the links are evaluated and cue competition occurs. Miller and Matzel (1988) have called this a comparator process. Because the actual causal representations reach full strength and cue competition comes at the decision or output stage, these associative mechanisms maintain enough information to support either cue competition or an accurate representation of the unconditional contingencies.

The simple associative net has also assumed that links were unidirectional but this is not biologically necessary. It is possible the links are bidirectional. This could occur either because the links themselves are bidirectional or because separate links, or several neuron loops, in both directions are formed. In any case it is possible to conceptualize an associative net with only unidirectional links that allows effect–cause cue competition.

Given the causal order Event 1 to Event 2 (E1 → E2) it is easy to see how a link E1–E2 would form. We would write the net with E1 in the input layer and E2 in the output layer. But how would an E2–E1 link form given the standard net described earlier? It is easy to overlook, given their privileged semantic roles in causal model theory as causes and effects, but both E1 and E2 are sensory events, and, thus, when either is presented some initial sensory representation might be activated. Therefore, either could easily act as the input for an association. Likewise it is possible that each could exist in the output layer as the second element in an association and would in a reinforcement-like way strengthen a link through back propagation. Thus, it is possible that at some place in the net E2 is an input and E1 is an output. This would allow E2–E1 associations to form. However, because E2 generally follows rather than precedes E1, the problem is to provide temporal precedence and contiguity to drive the system. The simplest mechanism to do this is to posit a slow decay function for the representation of E1 and E2. With this decay function, the representation of E1 would still be active when E2 is present so backward associations would be able to form. Interestingly, if we minimize the E1–E2 delay this would facilitate this process, and that is exactly what we did in Experiment 5. In this experiment we eliminated the predictions on each trial; this reduced the delay between stimulus presentations and we found cue competition everywhere.

Thus a modified, and admittedly ad hoc, associative model can account for our results. What is clear is that our data and much of the data from others are not well accounted for by Waldmann and Holyoak's (1992) description of mental models of cause. By the same token the simple associative net illustrated in Figure 2.5 also requires considerable modification in order to account for the data.

## CONCLUSIONS

There has been a great deal of often conflicting and adversarial work on the notion of causal power. In the first section we outlined how power theories were derived and discussed some attempts to test them by asking for ratings of power. We concluded that most of these tests were inadequate because the same intervening variable, namely power ($P_{tc}$), could generate a number of possible correct answers to questions. We concluded that the ideal situation in which to study the internal representations of power would be the transfer situation. Causal power serves an adaptive function if it allows the observer to accurately predict future events and the consequences of present behaviors. Moreover, although the majority of data we discussed does not strongly support Cheng's (1997) PowerPC model, this in no way can be seen as undermining the strength of causal power. It only weakens one of many possible mechanisms of power.

In the second section of this chapter we evaluated the role of the semantic content of mental models of power on cue competition. Generally our results were not consistent with models of power. They were also not consistent with the Rescorla–Wagner model. Rather they were more consistent with a general associative model that allows bidirectional associative links.

These results have not been particularly supportive of causal-model theory. However, causal-power theories represent a normative description of the environment. They lead to what we believe to be adaptive behavior. It is our firm belief that at the computational level organisms must compute at least some of the many aspects of models of cause. It may be that these adaptive behaviors are an emergent property of mechanisms that do not look much like our conceptualization of models of cause. Associative models provide one such candidate. This is as it should be. The goal of science is to provide simpler explanations of complex behaviors and cognitions.

## REFERENCES

Allan, L. G. (1980). A note on measurement of contingency between two binary variables in judgment tasks. *Bulletin of the Psychonomic Society, 15*, 147–149.

Allan, L. G. (2003). Assessing PowerPC. *Learning and Behavior, 31*, 192–204.

Baker, A. G., Mercier, P., Vallée-Tourangeau, F., Frank, R., & Pan, M. (1993). Selective associations and causality judgments: Presence of a strong causal factor may reduce judgments of a weaker one. *Journal of Experimental Psychology: Learning, Memory, and Cognition, 19*, 414–432.

Baker, A. G., Murphy, R. A., & Vallée-Tourangeau, F. (1996). Associative and normative models of causal induction: Reacting to versus understanding cause. In D. R. Shanks, K. J. Holyoak, & D. L. Medin (Eds.), *The psychology of learning and motivation.* Causal Learning (Vol. 34, pp. 1–45). San Diego: Academic Press.

Buehner, M. J., & Cheng, P. W. (1997). Causal induction: The PowerPC theory versus the Rescorla–Wagner theory. In M. G. Shafot & P. Langley (Eds.), *The proceedings of the Nineteenth Annual Conference of the Cognitive Science Society* (pp 55–60). Mahwah, NJ: Lawrence Erlbaum Associates.

Chapman, G., & Robbins, S. J. (1990). Cue interaction in human contingency judgments. *Memory and Cognition, 18*, 537–545.

Cheng, P. W. (1997). From covariation to causation: A causal power theory. *Psychological Review, 104*, 367–405.

Cheng, P. W., & Novick, L. R. (1990). A probabilistic contrast model of causal induction. *Journal of Personality and Social Psychology, 58*, 545–567.

Cheng, P. W., & Novick, L. R. (1992). Covariation in natural causal induction. *Psychological Review, 99*, 365–382.

Cheng, P. W., Park, J., Yarlas, A. S., & Holyoak, K. J. (1996). A causal-power theory of focal sets. In D. R. Shanks, K. J. Holyoak, & D. L. Medin (Eds.), *The psychology of learning and motivation: Causal learning* (Vol. 34, pp. 313–355). San Diego: Academic Press.

Dickinson, A., Shanks, D. R., & Evenden, J. L. (1984). Judgment of act-outcome contingency: The role of selective attribution. *Quarterly Journal of Experimental Psychology, 36A*, 29–50.

Garcia, J. & Koelling, R. A. (1966). Relation of cue to consequence in avoidance learning. *Psychonomic Science, 4*, 123–124.

Hume, D. (1960). *A Treatise on Human Nature.* Oxford, England: Clarendon Press. (Original work published 1737)

Kant, I. (1929). *Critique of pure reason.* London: Macmillan. (Original work published 1781)

Lober, K., & Shanks, D. R. (2000). Is causal induction based on causal power? A critique of Cheng (1997). *Psychological Review, 107*, 195–212.

Marr, D. (1982). *Vision: A computational investigation into the human representation and processing of visual information.* San Francisco: Freeman.

Mehta, R. (2000). *Contrasting associative and statistical theories of contingency judgments.* Unpublished doctoral dissertation, McGill University, Montreal, Quebec, Canada.

Melz, E. R., Cheng, P. W., Holyoak, K. J., & Waldmann, M. R. (1993). Cue competition in human categorization: Contingency or the Rescorla–Wagner learning rule. Comment on Shanks (1991). *Journal of Experimental Psychology: Learning, Memory, and Cognition, 19*, 1398–1410.

Miller, R. R., & Matzel, L. D. (1988). The comparator hypothesis: A response rule for the expression of associations. In G. H. Bower (Ed.), *The psychology of learning and motivation* (Vol. 22, pp. 51–92). San Diego: Academic Press.

Murphy, R. A., Baker, A. G., & Fouquet, N. (2001). Relative validity of contextual and discrete cues. *Journal of Experimental Psychology: Animal Behavior Processes, 27*, 137–152.

Pearce, J. M. (1987). A model for stimulus generalization in Pavlovian conditioning. *Psychological Review, 94*, 61–73.

Pearce, J. M. (1994). Similarity and discrimination: A selective review and a connectionist model. *Psychological Review, 101*, 587–607.

Pearce, J. M., & Hall, G. (1980). A model for Pavlovian learning: Variations in the effectiveness of conditioned but not unconditioned stimuli. *Psychological Review, 87*, 532–552.

Rescorla, R. A., & Wagner, A. R. (1972). A theory of Pavlovian conditioning: Variations in the effectiveness of reinforcement and nonreinforcement. In A. H. Black & W. F. Prokasy (Eds.), *Classical conditioning II: Current research and theory* (pp. 64–99). New York: Appleton–Century–Crofts.

Shanks, D. R., & Lopez, F. J. (1996). Causal order does not affect cue selection in human associative learning. *Memory & Cognition, 24*, 511–522.

Shultz, T. R. (1982). Rules of causal attribution. *Monograph of the Society for Research into Child Development, 47* (1, Serial No. 194).

Spellman, B. A. (1996). Acting as intuitive scientists: Contingency judgments are made while controlling for alternative potential causes. *Psychological Science, 7*, 337–342.

Tangen, J. M., & Allan, L. G. (2004). Cue interaction and judgments of causality: Contributions of causal and associative processes. *Memory & Cognition, 32*, 107–124.

Vallée-Tourangeau, F., Murphy, R. A., & Drew, S. (1997). Causal judgments that violate the predictions of the power PC theory of causal induction. In M. G.

Shafto & P. Langley (Eds.), *Proceedings of the Nineteenth Annual Conference of the Cognitive Science Society* (pp. 775–780). Mahwah, NJ: Lawrence Erlbaum Associates.

Vallée-Tourangeau, F., Murphy, R. A., Drew, S., & Baker, A. G. (1998). Judging the importance of constant and variable candidate causes: A test of the power PC theory. *Quarterly Journal of Experimental Psychology, 51A,* 65–84.

van Hamme, L. J., & Wasserman, E. A. (1994). Cue competition in causality judgments: The role of nonpresentations of compound stimulus elements. *Learning and Motivation, 25,* 127–151.

Wagner, A. R., Logan, F. A., Haberlandt, K., & Price, T. (1968). Stimulus selection in animal discrimination learning. *Journal of Experimental Psychology, 76,* 171–180.

Waldmann, M. R. (2000). Competition among causes but not effects in predictive and diagnostic learning. *Journal of Experimental Psychology: Learning Memory and Cognition, 26,* 53–76.

Waldmann, M. R., & Holyoak, K. J. (1992). Predictive and diagnostic learning within causal models: Asymmetries in cue competition. *Journal of Experimental Psychology: General, 121,* 222–236.

Waldmann, M. R., & Holyoak, K. J. (1997). Determining whether causal order affects cue selection in human contingency learning: Comments on Shanks and Lopez (1996). *Memory & Cognition, 25,* 125–134.

Wasserman, E. A., Elek, S. M., Chatlosh, D. L., & Baker, A. G. (1993). Rating causal relations: The role of probability in judgments of response-outcome contingency. *Journal of Experimental Psychology: Learning, Memory, and Cognition, 19,* 174–188.

# Chapter 3

# On the Role of Controlled Cognitive Processes in Human Associative Learning

Jan De Houwer, Stefaan Vandorpe, Tom Beckers

Several researchers have suggested that there are two ways in which humans can learn that two events are associated (e.g., McLaren, Green, & Mackintosh, 1994; Pavlov, 1927; Razran, 1971). On the one hand, learning can proceed as the result of associative processes that capture regularities in the environment by forming associations between representations. These processes are typically characterized as automatic (in the sense of unintentional, unconscious, or efficient) and stimulus–driven (i.e., determined mainly by the experienced events). On the other hand, people can learn associations by engaging in rule-based processing.[1] Such processing is controlled (in the sense of intentional, conscious, or effortful) and driven not only by experience but also by language and formal reasoning (e.g., Sloman, 1996). Brewer (1974), for instance, explicitly put forward the idea that humans learn associations by generating and evaluating hypothetical rules about associations in a conscious and controlled manner. As we see later on, this idea is supported by a substantial amount of evidence.

Nevertheless, the probabilistic and associative models that dominate modern research on human associative learning say little about the role of controlled processes. According to probabilistic models (sometimes also referred to as statistical models), behavioral effects of associative learning can be predicted on the basis of the actual conditional probabilities with which events occur (e.g., Allan, 1980; Cheng, 1997; Cheng & Novick, 1990). The well-known $\Delta P$ model, for instance, postulates that judgments

---

[1]Note that when we talk about the learning of associations, we thus do not mean the formation of associations between representations. Rather, we use the term *associative learning* to refer to the fact that individuals somehow register that the occurrence of events is related in a certain way.

about the contingency between event A and event O will reflect the difference between the probability that O is present when A is present [P(O/A)] and the probability that O is present when A is absent [P(O/~A)]. Most probabilistic models are, however, normative and do not incorporate assumptions about the processes that are involved. They are therefore also silent about the role of controlled processes in human associative learning.

The second class of dominant models are the associative models. They are basically hypotheses about the nature of the automatic associative processes by which regularities in the environment can be learned. The fact that modern associative models focus on automatic processes is sometimes made explicit (e.g., McLaren et al., 1994; Wagner, 1981) but can also be inferred from the fact that controlled processes or conscious beliefs are regarded as factors that should be eliminated when studying associative learning (e.g., Dickinson, 2001; Razran, 1971) or from the fact that the models say little or nothing about the impact of controlled processes on learning. It thus comes as no surprise that many associative learning psychologists "continue to think of associative learning as a basic process that is quite divorced from higher order cognitive processes" (Lovibond & Shanks, 2002, p. 23).

The aim of this chapter is to make explicit the fact that controlled processes are important in human associative learning and to discuss the possible theoretical implications of this fact. We are certainly not the first to emphasize the role of controlled processes in human associative learning. Brewer (1974) and Dawson and Schell (1985, 1987), for example, communicated the same message in their excellent chapters several decades ago. Nevertheless, there are various reasons why we believe that the present chapter serves a purpose. First, the lack of attention for controlled processes in modern research on human associative learning shows that the message of people like Brewer and Dawson needs to be reiterated. Second, we also discuss recent findings that support and extend their views. Third, we look at theoretical implications that were not considered in detail before.

In the first part of this chapter, we discuss the available evidence for the role of controlled processes in human associative learning. Because most of this evidence has been reviewed elsewhere (e.g., Brewer, 1974; Davey, 1987; Dawson & Schell, 1985, 1987; De Houwer, Beckers, & Vandorpe, in press; Lovibond & Shanks, 2002), this section is fairly short. The second part consists of an in-depth discussion of the theoretical implications of these findings. Here we address issues such as the implications for associative models, the plausibility of dual-process models, the apparent irrationality of behavior, and the implications of our conclusions for animal research.

## EMPIRICAL EVIDENCE

Let us assume that people learn associations by generating and testing hypotheses in a conscious and controlled manner and that associatively induced changes in behavior are a reflection of the conscious hypothesis that the person holds. This assumption leads to several predictions (also see Brewer, 1974; Dawson & Schell, 1985). First, because people are conscious about the hypotheses they entertain, evidence for the learning of a particular association should be accompanied by awareness of that association. Second, because generating and testing hypotheses are effortful processes, associative learning should interfere with other effortful processes and should depend on the availability of sufficient cognitive resources. Third, because conscious hypotheses can be derived not only from experience but also from verbal instructions, abstract rules, and deductive reasoning, one can predict that associative learning can be influenced by these factors. We now discuss the evidence regarding these predictions.

## Associative Learning Is Typically Accompanied by Awareness of the Learned Associations

A huge number of studies have looked at the role of awareness in associative learning (for reviews, see Brewer, 1974; Dawson & Schell, 1985; Lovibond & Shanks, 2002; Shanks & St. John, 1994). Although there still is strong disagreement about whether associative learning can be unconscious in some situations, most of the data can be interpreted as consistent with the hypothesis that evidence for learning is found only when participants have conscious knowledge of the learned information.

The evidence for this conclusion is particularly strong in the case of Pavlovian conditioning of human autonomic responses. In a typical study, an innocuous stimulus (e.g., a light; conditioned stimulus or CS) is paired in a certain manner with an affectively and biologically relevant stimulus that evokes a clear unconditioned response (e.g., an electric shock; unconditioned stimulus or US). It is then examined whether pairing the CS with the US results in a change in the autonomic responses (e.g., galvanic skin responses or GSRs) that are evoked by the CS. Such conditioned responses (CRs) provide evidence that the association between the CS and US has been learned. Importantly, in most studies (for reviews, see Dawson & Schell, 1985; Lovibond & Shanks, 2002) it is found that only participants who are aware of the CS–US contingency show CRs. Moreover, the CRs tend to occur only after the participants become aware of the CS–US contingency. Such results have led to the conclusion that awareness of the CS–US contingency is a necessary condition for Pavlovian conditioning to occur (e.g., Dawson & Schell, 1985).

Other results suggest that the close link between learning and awareness is due to the fact that conscious hypotheses determine how the participant will respond. For instance, interindividual differences in human autonomic conditioning are closely related to interindividual differences in the extent to which the US is expected at a particular moment in time (e.g., Epstein & Roupenian, 1970). Moreover, when participants have incorrect beliefs about the association between events or between a behavior and an event, their conditioned behavior is most often in line with the incorrect beliefs rather than the objective contingencies (e.g., Parton & DeNike, 1966).

## Associative Learning Is Effortful

Controlled cognitive processes can be characterized as effortful. One can conceptualize this by assuming that such processes take up a certain amount of cognitive resources. Because the pool of available cognitive resources is limited, a particular controlled process will interfere with the simultaneous operation of another controlled process. Therefore, if controlled processes are involved in associative learning, learning that one event is associated with another event should interfere with performance on a secondary task that also depends on the operation of controlled processes. Dawson, Schell, Beers, and Kelly (1982) tested this prediction by asking participants to respond to tones while being presented with CSs during a Pavlovian conditioning phase. Results showed that participants responded more slowly to tones that were presented on trials with a CS+ (i.e., a CS that was associated with the US) than to tones presented on trials with a CS− (i.e., a CS that was not associated with the US). Moreover, this difference was particularly pronounced shortly after the onset of the CS+ (early effect) and shortly before the US was delivered (late effect). Dawson et al. attributed the early effect to the (effortful) retrieval and evaluation of evidence regarding the US-signaling properties of the CS+ and the late effect to anticipation and preparation for the US. These and other aspects of the data of Dawson et al. suggest that shortly after the onset of the CS+, people generate a conscious expectation that the US will occur in the near future. Forming or entertaining such a conscious belief draws attention away from the secondary task.[2]

If learning a simple association between two stimuli depends on effortful controlled processes, one would a fortiori expect that more complex learning phenomena also depend on such processes. Recent results regarding blocking in human contingency learning confirm this prediction. Studies on human contingency learning are procedurally similar to studies on Pavlovian conditioning. Participants see situations

---

[2]One could argue that (effortful) learning should take place on both the CS+ and the CS− trials. Whereas on the CS+ trials, participants learn that the CS+ is followed by the US, on the CS− trials, they learn that the CS− is not followed by the US. It is therefore unlikely that the observed difference between CS+ and CS− trials was due to the fact that participants retrieved and evaluated evidence only on the CS+ trials. A more likely explanation is that participants realized that the CS+ (but not CS−) was a signal for an upcoming aversive event. Note, however, that this also implies that conscious beliefs are important in associative learning.

in which certain cues and outcomes are present or absent and are afterward asked to judge the contingency between the cues and outcomes. The cues are thus equivalent to CSs, the outcomes to USs, and the contingency judgments to CRs. Human contingency learning and Pavlovian conditioning studies are not only procedurally similar, they also, by and large, generate similar results (see De Houwer & Beckers, 2002b, for a review). For instance, blocking can be found in both types of studies. In studies on blocking, an outcome stimulus O appears when stimulus A is presented on its own (A+) and when stimulus A is presented together with a target stimulus T (AT+). Results typically show that less evidence is found for the learning of the T–O contingency when A+ trials are also presented than when only AT+ trials are presented. De Houwer and Beckers (2003) recently found that blocking in human contingency learning was less pronounced when participants performed a demanding secondary task during the learning and test phase than when they performed an easy secondary task. This result is in line with the hypothesis that blocking depends on effortful controlled processes and thus illustrates that such processes play an important role in human associative learning.

## Associative Learning Can Depend on Verbal Instructions About Contingencies

Many studies showed that merely telling participants that there will be an association between stimuli is sufficient to produce evidence for learning. For instance, if one informs a participant that a tone will always be followed by a shock, the tone will afterward evoke a conditioned GSR even though the tone and shock have never actually been presented together (e.g., Cook & Harris, 1937). Likewise, if one first presents tone-shock trials and then informs the participants that the tone will no longer be followed by the shock, the conditioned GSR will be dramatically reduced (e.g., Colgan, 1970). The latter result demonstrates not only that verbal instructions can lead to the same effects as the actual experience of a contingency, but also suggests that conscious beliefs that are derived from actual experience can interact with conscious beliefs that are derived from verbal instructions.

Recent studies showed that these conclusions also hold for more complex learning phenomena. Lovibond (2003) found that presenting A– trials (CS A is presented without the US) after AT+ trials resulted in an increase in the conditioned GSR toward T. We discuss a likely explanation for this finding later on. For now it is important to note that the exact same result was found when the AT+ and A– were described verbally rather than actually presented (Experiment 2) or when the AT+ trials were actually presented but the subsequent A– trials were replaced by the verbal message that A was a safe cue that would not be followed by the US (Experiment 3).

## Associative Learning Can Depend on Abstract Rules

An important advantage of controlled processing is that it allows one to reason about unprecedented situations (e.g., James, 1890). One way to achieve this is by inferring abstract rules from specific experienced events and to use those rules to make conscious hypotheses about what would happen in new situations. In a recent paper, Shanks and Darby (1998) summarized several studies that confirm that people do use rules to arrive at conscious hypotheses about associations and that they behave according to those rules. Shanks and Darby also reported a striking demonstration of the use of rules in associative learning. They presented A+, B+, AB–, C–, D–, CD+ trials together with I+, J+, M–, and N– trials. During a test phase, participants judged that the outcome was more likely to occur after the (previously unseen) compound MN than after the (also previously unseen) IJ compound. Judgments thus reflected the rule that the likelihood of the outcome after a compound of two stimuli (i.e., AB–, CD+) is the reverse of the likelihood of the outcome after the elements of the compound (i.e., A+, B+, C–, D–). This important ability of people to infer and use abstract rules fits perfectly with the idea that controlled, rule-based processes have an important impact on human associative learning.

## Associative Learning Can Depend on Deductive Reasoning

Evidence for the role of deductive reasoning in human associative learning comes mainly from studies on cue competition. Because these studies are fairly new, we devote somewhat more space to them. Cue competition refers to the fact that associatively induced changes in behavior (e.g., CRs or contingency judgments) toward a particular target stimulus T depend not only on the objective contingency between stimulus T and the outcome (or US) but also on the contingency between the outcome and an alternative stimulus A. Blocking is one example of cue competition: Associatively induced changes in behavior toward T are less pronounced when AT+ trials are presented in combination with A+ trials than when only AT+ trials are presented. Associative models attribute blocking to the operation of automatic, stimulus-driven processes. Recently, Mitchell and Lovibond (2002) and De Houwer and Beckers (2003) have proposed that blocking could, however, also be due to controlled reasoning processes (see Waldmann, 2000, for a related proposal). They argued that people intentionally apply the following deductive rule: *"If Cues A and T together cause the outcome to occur with the same intensity and probability as A alone, this implies that Cue T is not a cause of the outcome."* Therefore, if participants see A+ and AT+ trials, they can infer that T is not associated with the outcome and thus show no behavioral evidence of having learned the T–O association.

Importantly, however, the deductive rule is valid only under certain conditions. Therefore, if blocking is produced by the controlled application of the rule, it should depend on whether the conditions for applying the rule are fulfilled. Several experiments have confirmed this prediction (see De Houwer et al., in press, for a more detailed overview of the evidence for a deductive reasoning account of blocking). First, the deductive rule applies only when Cues A and T are regarded as causes of the outcome O. Effects of causes are most often additive. Therefore, a comparison of the intensity or probability of the outcome on A+ and AT+ trials can provide information about the causal impact of Cue T. The additivity assumption (and thus the deductive rule) does not apply for noncausal stimuli such as stimuli that are believed to be mere predictors or effects of the outcome. For instance, the fact that the ringing of a bell at a railway crossing (A) predicts the arrival of a train (O) to the same extent than the ringing of a bell and the flickering of lights together (AT) does not imply that the flickering of lights (T) on its own is not a valid signal for the arrival of the train. Therefore, if blocking depends on a controlled application of the deductive rule, blocking should be influenced by whether participants are led to believe that the cues are causal or noncausal.

This prediction has been verified in a number of experiments (e.g., De Houwer, Beckers, & Glautier, 2002; Waldmann, 2000). For instance, in the study of De Houwer et al., participants saw several squares, some of which lit up when a drawing of an army tank moved across the computer screen. The tank exploded after certain squares lit up but not when other squares lit up. Half of the participants were told that the squares represented weapons and that a weapon fired at the tank when the square representing that weapon lit up. This should encourage participants to believe that the cues (squares lighting up) were potential causes of the outcome (explosion of the tank), in which case the deductive rule is valid. The other participants were told that the squares represented indicators that could be used to predict the explosion of the tank. In this scenario, the cues were thus noncausal and the rule could not be applied. Results showed that blocking was much stronger and significant only when the cues were said to be weapons. This supports the hypothesis that blocking is due to the fact that participants infer that T is not a cause of the outcome because the intensity and probability of the outcome is the same when A and T are presented together (i.e., Weapons A and T fire together) than when only A is presented.

The deductive rule that can produce blocking is also invalid if outcomes always occur to a maximal extent. If A on its own always causes the outcome to a maximal extent and A and T together cause the outcome to occur to the same extent, ceiling effects prevent one from making a definite conclusion about the causal status of T. For instance, if T is a cause of the outcome, one would not be able to observe its effect because A already has a maximal effect. Therefore, if blocking is due the fact that people engage in controlled reasoning, it should depend on whether the outcome occurs to a maximal or submaximal extent on the A+ and AT+ trials. De Houwer et al. (2002) tested this prediction using the tank paradigm that we described previously. All participants saw that the impact of weapon A corresponded to a value of 10 and that the combined impact of weapons A and T together also corresponded to a value of 10. In one condition, participants were told that the maximal impact that could be measured corresponded to a value of 10. Because weapon A on its own already caused the outcome to the maximal extent, it was not possible to make a definite conclusion about the association between T and the outcome. Hence, blocking should not occur. In the second condition, the maximal impact that could be measured corresponded to a value of 20. Because both A on its own and A and T together caused the outcome to a submaximal extent, participants could infer that T did not have an effect on the outcome and blocking should thus occur. The results confirmed these predictions: Blocking was much stronger and significant only when outcomes occurred to a submaximal extent.

A third condition that needs to be fulfilled in order to apply the blocking rule is that information should be available about both the AT+ trials and the A+ trials. If, for instance, participants have reason to believe that T was present on the A+ trials, they cannot arrive at a valid conclusion regarding the causal status of T. De Houwer (2002) conducted a blocking study in which participants could not determine whether cue T was present or absent during the A+ trials that preceded the AT+ trials. At the end of the experiment, participants were asked whether they believed cue T was present during the A+ trials. Only those participants who did believe that T was present on the A+ trials showed a blocking effect. In a second experiment, participants received verbal information about the presence of T during A+ trials. Despite the fact that they received this information only after all A+ and AT+ trials were presented, participants who were told that T was absent on the A+ trials showed a strong blocking effect whereas no blocking was found in a group of participants who were told that T was present during the A+ trials.

When there is no information about A+ trials, participants can also apply the blocking rule recursively to arrive at a hypothesis about what would happen when A is presented on its own. In another series of experiments that were conducted at our lab (De Houwer & Beckers, 2002a, 2002c), participants were exposed to AB+, AT+, and B– or B+ trials. At first sight, participants cannot use the deductive rule to arrive at a conclusion about T because no A+ trials are presented. When, however, participants see AB+ and B– trials, they can deduce that A is a cause of the outcome because the outcome occurs on the AB+ trials despite the fact that B on its own does not cause the outcome. Given this hypothesis, they can infer that T is not a cause of the outcome because the observed effect of A and T together is the same as the hypothesized effect of A alone. If B+ trials are presented rather than B– trials, participants can conclude that A is not a cause of the outcome (because B alone has the same effect as A and B together) and thus that T is a cause of the outcome (because the outcome is more likely when A and T together are presented than when A is presented on its own).

One could argue that deductive reasoning plays a role only in situations in which participants are asked to make explicit judgments about the contingency between events (as is the case in human contingency learning studies that were conducted at our lab) whereas automatic processes operate in more traditional conditioning studies with non-verbal indices of learning (as is the case in human autonomic conditioning). The studies of Mitchell and Lovibond (2002) and Lovibond (2003), however, suggests otherwise. Mitchell and Lovibond used colored squares as CSs, electric shocks as USs, and measured associatively induced changes in GSR to the CSs. One color (Color A) was followed by a shock both when it was presented on its own (A+) and when it was presented in compound with a second colored square (Color T; AT+). During a training phase that preceded the learning phase, participants saw two other colors that were also always followed by the shock when presented on their own (X+, Y+) and when presented in compound (XY+). However, for half of the participants, the shock on the XY+ trials was twice as intense as on the X+ and Y+ trials whereas for the other participants, the intensity of the shock on the XY+ trials was the same as on the X+ and Y+ trials. Increasing the intensity of the shock on the XY trials should encourage participants to believe that the effects of the various CSs are additive. Therefore, if they subsequently learn that A and T together have the same effect as A alone, they can infer that T is not associated with the shock. Hence, this group should show a clear blocking effect. When participants learn during the training phase that the shock is as intense after XY than after X or Y on their own, they are likely to believe that the effects of the various CSs are not additive. This should discourage them from concluding that T is not associated with the outcome and hence from showing blocking. Mitchell and Lovibond found blocking only when the intensity of the shock on XY+ trials was higher than on X+ and Y+ trials. This clearly supports the thesis that deductive reasoning does play an important role in human autonomic conditioning. Also note that Lovibond, Been, Mitchell, Bouton, and Frohart (2003) have recently found similar effects of pretraining on blocking in human contingency learning.

The results of Lovibond (2003) that we discussed earlier also support the idea that cue competition in human autonomic conditioning depends on deductive reasoning. He showed that presenting A– trials after AT+ trials increased conditioned autonomic responding to T regardless of whether the trials were actually presented or only described verbally. Lovibond argued that this result was due to the fact that the A– trials allowed people to infer that T was responsible for the US on the AT+ trials. The fact that the manner in which the information was conveyed did not matter strongly suggests that the result was indeed based on deductive reasoning rather than on automatic, stimulus-driven associative processes.

## THEORETICAL IMPLICATIONS

What do all these findings tell us about the processes that are involved in human associative learning? First of all, they seem to clearly indicate that a single process view according to which only automatic associative processes determine learning is incorrect. But before we accept this conclusion, we consider some arguments that might be raised against this interpretation of the data. Second, one could regard the data as evidence for a single-process view according to which only controlled, rule-based processes are important in human associative learning. We also discuss the pros and cons of this idea. Third, one might conclude that both automatic and controlled processes are involved in human associative learning. Although such a dual-process view is appealing, we point out that certain considerations need to be taken into account.

### Only Automatic Associative Processes Determine Human Associative Learning

Until now we have implicitly assumed that if only automatic associative processes are important for learning, then conscious, controlled processes should play no role whatsoever in associative learning. One could, however, argue that this assumption is flawed. Since the late 1960s in particular, associative psychologists have acknowledged that conscious cognitive factors such as conscious expectancies are involved in associative learning. For instance, CRs in human (and animal) autonomic conditioning are often regarded as resulting from the fact that the participant has learned to expect the US after the presentation of the CS. Such US expectancies can be modeled as the level of activation of the US representation. Associative processes underlie the activation of the US representations (and thus US expectancy) because activation can spread from the CS representation to the US representations as the result of the association that links both representations. These CS–US associations are formed according to the principles that are put forward in the associative models. One could even argue that a conscious expectancy (i.e., a certain level of activation of the US representation) needs to be present in order to observe CRs. What is crucial, however, is that conscious expectancies are regarded as being the *product* of automatic associative processes. As such, no causal role is assigned to controlled *processes* such as the generation and testing of hypotheses.

Even this cognitive interpretation of associative models is, however, not compatible with the results that we discussed. First, we have seen that associative learning is typically accompanied by awareness of the associations that are presented, that is, awareness of the fact that two stimuli co-occur in a certain manner (e.g., that the CS always precedes the US). As Lovibond and Shanks (2002) pointed out, a cognitive associative view can explain why CRs are typically accompanied by a conscious expectancy that the US will occur (expectancy awareness) because conscious expectancies can be the product of automatic associative processes (i.e., automatic activation of the US representation). But the cognitive associative view cannot explain why learning typically depends on awareness of the fact that there is a contingency between the presence of the CS and the presence of the US (contingency awareness). Associative psychologists could try to explain the role of contingency awareness by assuming that activation spreads from the CS to the US representation only when participants are aware of the CS–US relation (i.e., when there is contingency awareness), but this would imply that conscious knowledge is not merely a product of automatic associative learning but has a profound impact on the operation of associative processes. Hence, one could no longer argue that associative learning depends only on automatic associative processes. The close link between contingency awareness and associative learning does, however, make perfect sense if one assumes that people learn by generating and testing hypotheses about associations in a conscious and controlled manner. According to this view, one needs to form a conscious hypothesis about the CS–US association before learning can be observed. Therefore, contingency awareness is crucial.

Second, the cognitive associative view can also not explain how factors such as instructions, rules, and deductive reasoning can have an impact on associative learning. It does not solve this issue because the cognitive view still does not acknowledge the role of controlled *processes*. This is also clear from the fact that the current "cognitive" associative models assume that learning is almost exclusively stimulus-driven. These models thus focus on the results of direct experience and have no way to accommodate other sources of conscious expectancies or hypotheses about contingencies. It is also difficult to see how the operation of controlled processes such as reasoning could ever be modeled solely in terms of automatic associative processes (e.g., Fodor & Pylyshyn, 1988).

## Only Controlled Processes Determine Human Associative Learning

If automatic associative processes are not the beginning and end of associative learning, maybe controlled processes are? At the very least, the idea that controlled processes are important is clearly supported by the evidence that we reviewed earlier. But some might argue that it is unlikely that only controlled processes determine associative learning. For one thing, it seems unlikely that people constantly calculate and compare probabilities when learning associations on the basis of direct experience. In principle, such an approach would be feasible (e.g., Cheng & Holyoak, 1995; Wasserman, 1990). For instance, in order to determine whether there is an association between a cue A and an outcome O, people might compare the probability that O is present when A is also present [P(O/A)] with the probability that O is present when A is absent [P(O/~A)]. This hypothesis corresponds to the $\Delta P$ model with this difference: that it does not stipulate what people should do (i.e., is not merely a normative hypothesis) but what people actually do (i.e., it specifies the nature of the actual processes). In fact, it can be regarded as a form of deductive reasoning that depends on the following rule: "Events A and B are associated if the probability of B is higher when A is present than when A is absent."

There is good evidence that associative learning about simple associations often corresponds to what could be expected on the basis of the $\Delta P$ model (see Shanks, 1995, and Baker, Murphy, Vallée-Tourangeau, & Mehta, 2001, for reviews). However, is there also evidence that humans actually calculate and compare probabilities when learning about associations? In one of the few recent papers that addressed this issue, Shanks came to the conclusion that it is unlikely that humans learn associations in this manner. On the one hand, he acknowledged that the data of Wasserman, Elek, Chatlosh, and Baker (1993) do support the hypothesis. Wasserman et al. found that judgments about the contingency between events (in this case, an action A and an outcome O) closely corresponded to subjective estimates of the probabilities P(O/A) and P(O/~A). In fact, in those cases where contingency judgments deviated from the objective contingency, they still corresponded to the difference between the estimates of P(O/A) and P(O/~A).

On the other hand, Shanks (1995) also discussed some findings that in his opinion argue against the hypothesis that people calculate and compare probabilities when learning about associations. First, research shows that people can arrive at judgments about contingencies even when they cannot calculate the relevant probabilities. For instance, when AB+ and AC– trials are presented, one cannot calculate appropriate probabilistic contrasts for Cue B because B always occurs together with cue A and neither B nor A are ever presented on their own (e.g., Cheng & Holyoak, 1995; Cheng & Novick, 1990). Nevertheless, people will often be confident that B is strongly related to the outcome. However, Shanks failed to acknowledge the role of deductive reasoning. For instance, from the fact that A and C together do not lead to the outcome (AC–), one can conclude that neither A nor C is associated with the outcome, provided that one makes certain assumptions about the nature of Cue C (e.g., that it is not a preventative cause) and the interaction between cues (e.g., that effects of multiple cues are additive). Once it has been concluded that A is not a cause of the outcome, one can deduce that B is a cause of the outcome because the outcome does occur on the AB+ trials. Therefore, in this example, learning might not be based entirely on direct experience but also on deductive reasoning. In fact, our analysis leads to the prediction that people will not regard B as a cause of the outcome if there are reasons to doubt the assumptions that underlie the deductive reasoning (e.g., by telling the participants that the effects of the multiple causes interact).

Shanks (1995) pointed to trial-order effects as a second argument against the hypothesis that people calculate and compare associations when learning about associations. Many studies have shown that contingency judgments are often influenced more by recent trials than by trials that are presented at the beginning of the learning phase (e.g., Lopez, Shanks, Almaraz, & Fernandez, 1998). Such recency effects should not occur when contingency judgments are based on probabilities because conditional probabilities are not affected by trial order. But more recent studies, however, suggest that trial-order effects depend on beliefs that participants have about what information is relevant in a given test context (Matute, Vegas, & De Marez, 2002). For instance, if participants are required to give a contingency judgment after every trial, they are inclined to think that their judgments should reflect the most recent information that they received. If, however, they are asked to give only one rating at the end of all trials, this encourages them to think that all the presented information should be taken into account when making the judgment. In line with this prediction, recency effects are much stronger when judgments need to be made on each trial than when only one judgment at the end of the learning phase is required (e.g., Collins & Shanks, 2002; see Matute et al. for an in-depth discussion of this issue). Research on trial-order effects is thus compatible with the idea that people arrive at contingency judgments by calculating and comparing probabilities. Trial-order effects seem to be due to factors that determine which information participants will use in order to calculate the relevant probabilities. In conclusion, unlike Shanks, we believe that the available evidence does not contradict the idea that people can learn about associations by calculating and comparing probabilities.

But this conclusion does not imply that *only* controlled processes are important for associative learning. Perhaps one of the reasons why it is so difficult to accept this idea is that it seems to entail that learning should always be rational and effortful. If associative learning reflects the actual probabilities in the environment, rule learning, or deductive reasoning, we should be able to behave in a perfectly appropriate and rational manner. On the one hand, associative learning often does correspond to what is normatively appropriate (see Baker et al., 2001; Shanks, 1995). But sometimes people do get it wrong and behave irrationally, that is, in ways that do not correspond to the objective contingencies. Does this not imply that there is more to learning than just controlled processes?

There are two arguments against this conclusion. First, the fact that learning depends on controlled processes does not mean that the controlled processes are always applied in an appropriate manner. For instance, there are various reasons why people's estimates of probabilities can be incorrect (e.g., baseline effects, confirmation bias, e.g., Tversky & Kahneman, 1974). If they are incorrect, this can result in irrational behavior. Second, once a conscious hypothesis about an association has been inferred or deduced, it can be stored in memory and subsequently activated automatically (e.g., Öhman & Soares, 1993). This could lead to situations where a once entertained hypothesis can exert an automatic impact on behavior even when that hypothesis has subsequently been rejected on the basis of more recent evidence. Therefore, one would expect a certain degree of irrationality in behavior even when associative learning depends only on controlled cognitive processes.

Although it is reasonable to believe that only controlled processes are responsible for associative learning, it is difficult to conclude with certainty that automatic associative processes play no role in associative learning whatsoever. Not only are there logical problems with reaching such conclusion (how can one prove beyond any doubt that something never has any effect at all?), there are also certain findings that strongly suggest that at least some forms of associative learning can be unconscious and thus based on automatic processes (see De Houwer, Thomas, & Baeyens, 2001, and Lovibond & Shanks, 2002, for a discussion of some likely candidates). We therefore do not exclude the possibility that associative learning depends to a certain extent on automatic processes, but believe that the available evidence supports the conclusion that most often, controlled processes are crucial.

### Associative Learning Is Determined by Both Controlled and Automatic Processes

As we noted at the start of this chapter, the idea that associative learning is based on both automatic and controlled processes has been popular for a long time. Most often, however, the emphasis in these dual-process models is on the automatic processes. As was noted by Dawson and Schell (1985), the standard view has always been that learning psychologists should try to unravel the exact nature of the automatic associative processes. When doing so, they should try to control for cognitive variables and processes because these can contaminate the results. Hence, controlled processes are most often viewed as little more than "nuisance variables."

The evidence that we reviewed shows, however, that controlled processes are much more than nuisance variables. They are an integral and important factor in human associative learning. Learning psychologists can no longer simply ignore controlled processes such as hypothesis testing and deductive reasoning. If they want to understand human associative learning, they should take these processes into account.

It is likely that some associative psychologists will nevertheless try to model the effects of controlled processes by using associative principles only. There are two potential problems with this approach. First, as noted earlier, one can argue that it is difficult (if not impossible) to model the operation of controlled processes on the basis of associative processes (Fodor & Pylyshyn, 1988). Even if one believes that it should be possible in principle, one should acknowledge that constructing associative models of controlled processes such as reasoning is a formidable task that associative researchers have not even begun to tackle. Second, there is a clear risk of making the associative models too complex and no longer representative of the associative processes that do play a role in associative learning. Let us, take the example of blocking (i.e., less conditioned responding to a target cue T when AT+ trials are presented in combination with A+ trials). Most associative models explain this effect by assuming that the automatic formation of associations depends on the extent to which the presence of the outcome is already predicted: The association between T and the outcome O does not increase in strength on the AT+ trials because A already has a strong association with the outcome due to the A+ trials that preceded the AT+ trials (e.g., Rescorla & Wagner, 1972; Wagner, 1981). But what if blocking is due solely to the operation of controlled processes such as deductive reasoning or the strategic allocation of attention? Such an idea is perhaps not implausible in light of the existing evidence on blocking and the fact that controlled processes seem to be crucial even for the acquisition of simple associations between stimuli (see De Houwer et al., in press, for an in-depth discussion). If one accepts this idea, it would imply that associative models do not need to incorporate the assumption that changes in associative strength depend on the existing associative strength of other cues. It would thus favor associative models that are much less complex than modern associative theories (and, in fact, more similar to the contiguity-driven models that were commonplace in the 1950s and 1960s, e.g., Hebb, 1949). Even if one believes that our conclusion about blocking is unlikely to be correct, one should accept that there is a risk of making associative models too complex if one sets the aim of explaining all findings on associative learning with these models, even the findings that could be due to controlled processes.

This brings us back to the idea of controlled processes as nuisance factors. Although researchers should, in our opinion, accept the fact that controlled processes contribute to associative learning, some might want to limit themselves to study of the nature of the automatic associative processes that are also involved in associative learning (assuming that such processes are involved). In order to do so, one should be able to eliminate or independently assess the contribution of controlled processes. This endeavor, however, is not a straightforward one. Existing research on automatic processes shows that there are many problems in establishing that controlled processes are not involved in a certain effect. For example, most of the evidence on learning without awareness can be criticized on the basis of the manner in which the absence of contingency awareness was established (e.g., Lovibond & Shanks, 2002; Shanks & St. John, 1994). Likewise, implicit-memory researchers have struggled to find ways to avoid that indices of implicit memory are contaminated by controlled retrieval processes (e.g., Jacoby, 1991; Richardson-Klavehn, Lee, Jourban, & Bjork, 1994).

From this perspective, it is ironic to see that associative-learning psychologists have always implicitly assumed that performance in simple, transparent learning experiments could inform them about the nature of automatic associative processes. Except for studies on learning and awareness, they rarely took precautions to avoid a contribution of controlled processes, nor did they check whether controlled processes were involved. In more recent research, certain precautions have sometimes been taken. For example, some researchers have started to use many different stimuli in their experiments in the hope that participants would no longer be able to deal with this overload of information by using controlled processes (e.g., Larkin, Aitken, & Dickinson, 1998; LePelley & McLaren, 2001; see Dickinson, 2001, p. 23). Unfortunately, they never reported clear evidence that corroborated the claim that participants did not use controlled processes. Obtaining such evidence would also not be simple. Merely asking participants to justify their contingency ratings at the end of the experiment, for instance, would be a very insensitive way to check whether participants used controlled processes. If one found that participants could not justify their ratings, this could simply indicate that they have forgotten the inferences and deductions that formed the basis for their ratings.

One also faces a second problem when trying to study automatic associative processes by excluding controlled processes. As is evidenced by research on learning and awareness, most often one does not find evidence for learning when there is no evidence for contingency awareness (and thus controlled processes). This is probably the reason why until now little or no research has been done on the processes that underlie learning without awareness. Interestingly, there are some indications that the processes that are involved in learning without awareness are much more simple than is assumed by modern associative theories (e.g., De Houwer et al., 2001; Hendrickx & De Houwer, 1997; Stevenson, Prescott, & Boakes, 1998). This is in line with the idea that the automatic associative processes that are involved in human associative learning in general could be much more simple than has been assumed until now (see De Houwer et al., 2001, p. 865, for an outline of a model in which learning is based merely on contiguity but performance can be based either on an automatic activation of stored associations or on a controlled retrieval and comparison of stored associations).

One could argue that another way to exclude any impact of controlled processes is by studying associative learning in nonhuman animals. Assuming that animals are not capable of controlled, conscious thought, this research should provide a unique insight in the automatic associative processes that play a role in associative learning. There are, however, a few considerations that one should take into account. First, there is no guarantee that the learning processes that operate in animals are the same as those that operate in humans. Dawson and Schell (1987, p. 50) cite Hebb in this context: "Because a simple task could, theoretically, be handled by a simple mechanism does not mean in fact that the brain handles it that way. In an uncomplicated nervous system, yes: but in the complex brain of a higher animal other mechanisms may insist on getting into the act and turn the simple task into a complex one." Second, it is possible that at least some nonhuman animals are capable of certain forms of controlled processing. Research on animal cognition has indeed generated some interesting results that are in line with this hypothesis (e.g., Clayton, Yu, & Dickinson, 2003). Therefore, one cannot simply assume that associative learning in animals is due solely to automatic associative processes. As Brewer (1974) pointed out, it might well be interesting to entertain the hypothesis that nonhuman animals also use controlled processes when learning about associations. Of course, it will be difficult (if not impossible) to establish the role of consciousness in animal learning. But controlled processes are characterized also by other features, for instance the fact that they are effortful. It might therefore be interesting to use variants of secondary probe tasks (see Dawson et al., 1982) or implement demanding secondary tasks (see De Houwer & Beckers, 2003) in order to examine the extent to which associative learning in nonhuman animals can be characterized as effortful. Likewise, one could examine whether other findings that provide strong support for the role of controlled processing in humans (e.g., the impact of ceiling effects on blocking) can be replicated in studies with other animals. In other words, research on human associative learning could provide an interesting source of inspiration for research on associative learning in nonhuman animals.

## Some Pointers for Future Theoretical Developments

As we pointed out in the introduction, none of the dominant models of human associative learning incorporate clear assumptions about the role of controlled cognitive processes. Those researchers that do acknowledge the fact that controlled processes are important, provide only descriptive accounts of how these processes influence learning (e.g., De Houwer & Beckers, 2003; Lovibond, 2003; Waldmann, 2000). There thus is a clear need for detailed models of associative learning that explain why controlled processes are so important for learning and how they operate.

Dawson and Schell (1985) argued that the information processing model of Shiffrin and Schneider (1977) as applied by Öhman (1979) could provide an interesting starting point for modeling the role of controlled processes in associative learning. This model clarifies the differences between automatic and controlled processes and incorporates the assumption that controlled processing is necessary for learning. That is, new associations will be stored in memory only if the relationship between the associated stimuli is detected by a central, capacity-limited system. Because central processing is available to consciousness, it follows that awareness of the associations is a prerequisite for associative learning. Although this model has the virtue of showing how associative learning can be regarded as an instance of information processing in general, it remains largely descriptive and provides little details about the way in which controlled processes operate in the context of associative learning.

In order to find clues about the operation of controlled processes, one could turn to the literature on human reasoning and problem solving. The aim of most research on reasoning has been to uncover the way in which humans arrive at conclusions about relations in the environment on the basis of certain rules and premises. Associative learning is also about detecting relations in the environment. In fact, it is likely that most people who participate in a learning experiment regard the task as an intellectual problem (e.g., "try to figure out which stimuli go together") that they need to solve in a rational manner (see Brewer, 1974, and Maltzman, 1977, for similar suggestions). Moreover, much of the research that we have reviewed suggests that participants indeed solve the problem (i.e., learn about associations) by applying rules in a controlled manner. For instance, in order to decide whether an event A and an event O are related, one can estimate the likelihood that O occurs when A occurs, the likelihood that O occurs when A is absent, and use these estimates as premises for the rule "if O is more likely to occur when A is present than when A is absent, then the presence of A is associated with the presence of O." What the literature on reasoning can offer us is ways to formalize and model such controlled reasoning processes. This would allow us to developed more detailed and complete models of associative learning. Research on reasoning has also provided insights on when and why human reasoning is normatively incorrect. It would be interesting to see whether the same reasoning errors can influence associative learning.

In order to reason deductively, one of course needs premises. These premises can be provided through instructions or result from previous reasoning processes, but can also be induced on the basis of experience. A crucial question is how this induction on the basis of experience is achieved. Previously we have argued that learning simple associations is achieved by a rule-based comparison of estimated probabilities [i.e., $P(O/A)$ and $P(O/\sim A)$]. In order to arrive at these estimates, one needs to access memories of past situations in which the events were present or absent. This access can be either controlled or automatic. Controlled retrieval of memory traces would imply that one intentionally and consciously tries to recollect relevant past events. Once recalled, one can combine the relevant information in a controlled manner and arrive at an estimate of the probabilities. Although such an approach is feasible, it is likely that humans will often use shortcuts. For instance, Dougherty, Gettys, and Ogden (1999) provide an elegant proposal on how people can estimate probabilities in a relatively effortless manner. Such a spontaneous use of memory could often form the basis of the premises for deductive reasoning about events. Therefore, existing memory research can provide helpful information about factors that influence associative learning.

We believe that a model that integrates principles from human reasoning and human memory could go a long way in providing a full account of human associative learning. However, many issues remain problematic. For instance, where do deductive rules come from? Are they based on experience (and thus perhaps associative processes), enculturation, or maybe even genetic makeup? One way to tackle this issue is to do research on infants and children in order to establish how deductive rules develop (e.g., Gopnik, Sobel, Schulz, & Glymour, 2001). Such research could also lead to interesting new insights in human associative learning. For instance, if the deductive rules that are used in associative learning develop during childhood, one would expect that the functional characteristics of learning also change as a function of the changes in the underlying rules. Developing a model that is based on principles from human reasoning and memory will be a formidable task. But we are convinced that taking up this challenge will lead to fascinating new insights. Moreover, we believe that it is a better approach than to keep deluding ourselves that automatic associative processes are the beginning and end of human associative learning.

## Why Have Associative Models Fared So Well?

In hindsight, it seems obvious that people can learn about associations by using controlled processes such as reasoning and hypothesis testing. Why, then, are associative models still dominant in modern research? One reason is that the associationistic view has a long tradition in psychology (and philosophy). It is thus difficult for many people to leave behind the associationistic view that has guided their thinking and research for many years. Another important reason is that associative models do quite well in accounting for the available empirical data. The well-known Rescorla–Wagner model (Rescorla & Wagner, 1972), for instance, is compatible with a huge number of findings while being relatively simple. If our argument is correct that associative models do not provide an accurate account of the processes that underlie associative learning, how is it possible that they are able to account for so much of the data? We agree with Lovibond (2003) that "the success of these models is due to them capturing, at least in part, the operating characteristics of the inferential learning system" (p. 105). What this means is that associative models (as well as probabilistic models for that matter) can be seen as (mathematical) formalisations of certain deductive reasoning processes. A system that operates on the basis of associative models does not reason, but acts very much as if it is reasoning. The associative models will thus often predict the same result as a model that is based on the assumption that humans actually generate and test hypothesis or reason in a controlled, conscious manner. The two types of models can be differentiated, however, by manipulating variables that influence the likelihood that people will reason in a certain manner, but that should have no impact on the operation of the associative model. We have seen that such variables (e.g., instructions, secondary tasks, ceiling effects, nature of the cues and outcomes) do indeed have a huge effect. Given these results, it is justified to entertain the belief that participants are using controlled processes such as reasoning and to look for new ways to model and understand these processes.

## CONCLUSION

Having come to the end of writing this chapter, we are left with an ambiguous feeling. On the one hand, we feel a bit embarrassed because our message seems so simple and obvious: People think and reason when they learn about associations. We often experience the same feeling when explaining our work on learning to colleagues, friends, and (especially) family. But at the same time there is the conviction that our aim to communicate this message is just and important. Unlike what many learning psychologists still implicitly or explicitly believe, controlled processes are crucial in associative learning. The processes are not just nuisance factors but an integral part of learning. If our aim is to understand human associative learning, we thus need to take these factors into account in our experiments and theories.

## REFERENCES

Allan, L. G. (1980). A note on the measurement of contingency between two binary variables in judgment tasks. *Bulletin of the Psychonomic Society, 15,* 147–149.

Baker, A. G., Murphy, R. A., Vallée-Tourangeau, F., & Mehta, R. (2001). Contingency learning and causal reasoning. In R. R. Mowrer & S. B. Klein (Eds.), *Handbook of contemporary learning theories* (pp. 255–306). Mahwah, NJ: Lawrence Erlbaum Associates.

Brewer, W. F. (1974). There is no convincing evidence of conditioning in adult humans. In W. B. Weimer & D. S. Palermo (Eds.), *Cognition and the symbolic processes* (pp. 1–42). Hillsdale, NJ: Lawrence Erlbaum Associates.

Cheng, P. W. (1997). From covariation to causation: A causal power theory. *Psychological Review, 104,* 367–405.

Cheng, P. W., & Holyoak, K. J. (1995). Complex adaptive systems as intuitive statisticians: Causality, contingency, and prediction. In J.-A. Meyer & H. Roitblat (Eds.), *Comparative approaches to cognition* (pp. 271–302). Cambridge, MA: MIT Press.

Cheng, P. W., & Novick, L. R. (1990). A probabilistic contrast model of causal induction. *Journal of Personality and Social Psychology, 58,* 545–567.

Clayton, N. S., Yu, K. S., & Dickinson, A. (2003). Interacting cache memories: Evidence for flexible memory use by Western scrub-jays *(Aphelocoma californica). Journal of Experimental Psychology: Animal Behavior Processes, 29,* 14–22.

Colgan, D. M. (1970). Effect of instructions on the skin conductance response. *Journal of Experimental Psychology, 86,* 108–112.

Collins, D. J., & Shanks, D. R. (2002). Momentary and integrative response strategies in causal judgment. *Memory & Cognition, 30,* 1138–1147.

Cook, S. W., & Harris, R. E. (1937). The verbal conditioning of the galvanic skin reflex. *Journal of Experimental Psychology, 21,* 202–210.

Davey, G. L. (1987). An integration of human and animal models of Pavlovian conditioning: Associations, cognitions, and attributions. In G. L. Davey (Ed.), *Cognitive processes and Pavlovian conditioning in humans* (pp. 83–114). Chichester, England: Wiley.

Dawson, M. E., & Schell, A. M. (1985). Information processing and human autonomic classical conditioning. In P. K. Ackles, J. R. Jennings, & M. G. H. Coles (Eds.), *Advances in Psychophysiology* (pp. 89–165). Greenwich, CT: JAI Press.

Dawson, M. E., & Schell, A. M. (1987). Human autonomic and skeletal classical conditioning: The role of conscious cognitive factors. In G. L. Davey (Ed.), *Cognitive processes and Pavlovian conditioning in humans* (pp. 27–55). Chichester, England: Wiley.

Dawson, M. E., Schell, A. M., Beers, J. R., & Kelly, A. (1982). Allocation of cognitive processing capacity during human autonomic classical conditioning. *Journal of Experimental Psychology: General, 111,* 273–295.

De Houwer, J. (2002). Forward blocking depends on retrospective inferences about the presence of the blocked cue during the elemental phase. *Memory & Cognition, 30,* 24–33.

De Houwer, J., & Beckers, T. (2002a). Higher-order retrospective revaluation in human causal learning. *Quarterly Journal of Experimental Psychology, 55B,* 137–151.

De Houwer, J., & Beckers, T. (2002b). A review of recent developments in research and theory on human contingency learning. *Quarterly Journal of Experimental Psychology, 55B,* 289–310.

De Houwer, J., & Beckers, T. (2002c). Second-order backward blocking and unovershadowing in human causal learning. *Experimental Psychology, 49,* 27–33.

De Houwer, J., & Beckers, T. (2003). Secondary task difficulty modulates forward blocking in human contingency learning. *Quarterly Journal of Experimental Psychology, 56B,* 345–357.

De Houwer, J., Beckers, T., & Glautier, S. (2002). Outcome and cue properties modulate blocking. *Quarterly Journal of Experimental Psychology, 55A,* 965–985.

De Houwer, J., Beckers, T., & Vandorpe, S. (in press). Evidence for the role of higher-order reasoning processes in cue competition and other learning phenomena. *Learning and Behavior.*

De Houwer, J., Thomas, S., & Baeyens, F. (2001). Associative learning of likes and dislikes: A review of 25 years of research on human evaluative conditioning. *Psychological Bulletin, 127,* 853–869.

Dickinson, A. (2001). The 28th Bartlett memorial lecture: Causal learning: An associative analysis. *Quarterly Journal of Experimental Psychology, 54B,* 3–25.

Dougherty, M. R., Gettys, C. F., & Ogden, E. E. (1999). MINERVA-DM: A memory processes model for judgments of likelihood. *Psychological Review, 106,* 180–209.

Epstein, S., & Roupenian, A. (1970). Heart rate and skin conductance during experimentally induced anxiety: The effect of uncertainty about receiving noxious stimuli. *Journal of Personality and Social Psychology, 16,* 20–28.

Fodor, J. A., & Pylyshyn, Z. W. (1988). Connectionism and cognitive architecture: A critical analysis. *Cognition, 28,* 3–71.

Gopnik, A., Sobel, D. M., Schulz, L. E., & Glymour, C. (2001). Causal learning mechanisms in very young children: Two-, three-, and four-year-olds infer causal relations from patterns of variation and covariation. *Developmental Psychology, 37,* 620–629.

Hebb, D. (1949). *The organization of behaviour.* New York: Wiley.

Hendrickx, H., & De Houwer, J. (1997). Implicit covariation detection. *Psychologica Belgica, 37,* 29–50.

Jacoby, L. L. (1991). A process dissociation framework: Separating automatic from intentional uses of memory. *Journal of Memory and Language, 30,* 513–541.

James, W. (1890). *The principles of psychology.* New York: Holt.

Larkin, M. J. W., Aitken, M. R. F., & Dickinson, A. (1998). Retrospective revaluation of causal judgements under positive and negative contingencies. *Journal of Experimental Psychology: Learning, Memory, & Cognition, 24,* 1331–1352.

Le Pelley, M. E., & McLaren, I. P. L. (2001). Retrospective revaluation in humans: Learning or memory? *Quarterly Journal of Experimental Psychology, 54B,* 311–352.

Logan, G. D. (1988). Toward an instance theory of automatization. *Psychological Review, 95,* 492–527.

Lopez, F. J., Shanks, D. R., Almaraz, J., & Fernandez, P. (1998). Effects of trial order on contingency judgements: A comparison of associative and probabilistic contrast accounts. *Journal of Experimental Psychology: Learning, Memory, and Cognition, 24,* 672–694.

Lovibond, P. F. (2003). Causal belies and conditioned responses: Retrospective revaluation induced by experience and by instruction. *Journal of Experimental Psychology: Learning, Memory, and Cognition, 29,* 97–106.

Lovibond, P. F., Been S.-L., Mitchell, C. J., Bouton, M. E., & Frohart, R. (2003). Forward and backward blocking of causal judgment is enhanced by additivity of effect magnitude. *Memory and Cognition, 31,* 133–142.

Lovibond, P. F., & Shanks, D. R. (2002). The role of awareness in Pavlovian conditioning: Empirical evidence and theoretical implications. *Journal of Experimental Psychology: Animal Behavior Processes, 28,* 3–26.

Maltzman, I. (1977). Orienting in classical conditioning and generalization of the galvanic skin response: An overview. *Journal of Experimental Psychology: General, 105,* 111–119.

Matute, H., Vegas, S., & De Marez, P.-J. (2002). Flexible use of recent information in causal and predictive judgment. *Journal of Experimental Psychology: Learning, Memory, & Cognition, 28,* 714–725.

McLaren, I. P. L., Green, R. E. A., & Mackintosh, N. J. (1994). Animal learning and the implicit/explicit distinction. In N. C. Ellis (Ed.), *Implicit and explicit learning of languages* (pp. 313–332). London: Academic Press.

Mitchell, C. J., & Lovibond, P. F. (2002). Backward and forward blocking in human electrodermal conditioning: Blocking requires an assumption of outcome additivity. *Quarterly Journal of Experimental Psychology, 55B,* 311–330.

Öhman, A. (1979). The orienting response, attention, and learning: An information-processing perspective. In H. D. Kimmel, E. H. van Olst, & J. F. Orlebeke (Eds.), *The orienting reflex in humans* (pp. 5–26). Hillsdale, NJ: Lawrence Erlbaum Associates.

Öhman, A., & Soares, J. J. F. (1993). On the automatic nature of phobic fear: Conditioned electrodermal responses to masked fear-relevant stimuli. *Journal of Abnormal Psychology, 102,* 121–132.

Parton, D. A., & DeNike, L. D. (1966). Performance hypotheses of children and response to social reinforcement. *Journal of Personality and Social Psychology, 4,* 444–447.

Pavlov, I. P. (1927). *Conditioned reflexes*. London: Oxford University Press.

Razran, G. (1971). *Mind in evolution*. Boston: Houghton Mifflin.

Rescorla, R. A., & Wagner, A. R. (1972). A theory of Pavlovian conditioning: Variations in the effectiveness of reinforcement and nonreinforcement. In A. H. Black & W. F. Prokasy (Eds.), *Classical conditioning II: Current research and theory* (pp. 64–99). New York: Appleton–Century–Crofts.

Richardson-Klavehn, A., Lee, M. G., Jourban, R., & Bjork, R. A. (1994). Intention and awareness in perceptual identification priming. *Memory and Cognition, 22*, 293–312.

Shanks, D. R. (1995). Is human learning rational? *Quarterly Journal of Experimental Psychology, 48A*, 257–279.

Shanks, D. R., & Darby, R. J. (1998). Feature- and rule-based generalization in human associative learning. *Journal of Experimental Psychology: Animal Behavior Processes, 24*, 405–415.

Shanks, D. R., & St. John, M. F. (1994). Characteristics of dissociable human learning systems. *Behavioural and Brain Sciences, 17*, 367–447.

Shiffrin, R. M., & Schneider, W. (1977). Controlled and automatic human information processing II: Perceptual learning, automatic attending, and a general theory. *Psychological Review, 84*, 127–190.

Sloman, S. A. (1996). The empirical case for two systems of reasoning. *Psychological Bulletin, 119*, 3–22.

Stevenson, R. J., Prescott, J., & Boakes, R. A. (1998). Changes in odor sweetness resulting from implicit learning of a simultaneous odor-sweetness association: An example of learned synesthesia. *Learning and Motivation, 29*, 113–132.

Tversky, A., & Kahneman, D. (1974). Judgment under uncertainty: Heuristics and biases. *Science, 184*, 1124–1131.

Wagner, A. R. (1981). SOP. A model of automatic memory processing in animal behavior. In N. E. Spear & R. R. Miller (Eds.), *Information processing in animals: Memory mechanisms* (pp. 5–47). Hillsdale, NJ: Lawrence Erlbaum Associates.

Waldmann, M. R. (2000). Competition among causes but not effects in predictive and diagnostic learning. *Journal of Experimental Psychology: Learning, Memory, & Cognition, 26*, 53–76.

Wasserman, E. A. (1990). Detecting response-outcome relations: Toward an understanding of the causal texture of the environment. In G. H. Bower (Ed.), *The psychology of learning and motivation* (Vol 26, pp. 27–82). New York: Academic Press.

Wasserman, E. A., Elek, S. M., Chatlosh, D. L., & Baker, A. G. (1993). Rating causal relations: The role of probability in judgments of response-outcome contingency. *Journal of Experimental Psychology: Learning, Memory, & Cognition, 19*, 174–188.

# Chapter 4

# Assessing (In)sensitivity to Causal Asymmetry: A Matter of Degree

Jason M. Tangen, Lorraine G. Allan, Hedyeh Sadeghi

## BLOCKING EFFECTS AND ASSOCIATIONS

Contiguity or the pairing of events has long been recognized by learning theorists as insufficient to explain basic associative processes. In 1968, Leon Kamin described the blocking phenomenon as a demonstration of this insufficiency. Using a two-phase design, as shown in Table 4.1, Kamin conditioned a group of animals to associate a single cue with an outcome (i.e., A → O). In Phase 2, a second cue was paired alongside the first (i.e., AB → O). A second group of animals were exposed to only the latter phase. Despite the extensive pairing of Cue B and the outcome, Group 1 learned very little about B compared to Group 2 (and other relevant control groups). The initial training with A blocked conditioning to the superimposed cue and resulted in an attenuated response to B at test.

At the same time, Wagner, Logan, Haberlandt, and Price (1968) demonstrated a related phenomenon they labeled relative validity to demonstrate the same insufficiency of contiguity. Table 4.2 illustrates the design used by Wagner and his colleagues. They exposed animals to two compounds containing a common A cue that was paired with either Cue

**TABLE 4.1**

**Experimental Design by Kamin (1968)**

|         | Phase 1 | Phase 2 | Test     |
|---------|---------|---------|----------|
| Group 1 | A → O   | AB → O  | B (low)  |
| Group 2 |         | AB → O  | B (high) |

TABLE 4.2
Experimental Design by Wagner et al. (1968)

|  | Learning Phase | Test |
|---|---|---|
| Group 1 | AB → O (100%) | A (low) |
|  | AC → O (0%) |  |
| Group 2 | AB → O (50%) | A (high) |
|  | AC → O (50%) |  |

B or C. The animals were assigned to one of two groups: In Group 1, the AB compound was always paired with the outcome (100%) whereas the AC compound was never paired with the outcome (0%). In Group 2, each compound was paired with the outcome on 50% of the trials. During the test phase, the animals responded less to Cue A in Group 1 than in Group 2, even though A was paired with the outcome on 50% of the trials in both groups. These results demonstrate that the animals were not sensitive to the absolute validity of each cue, but rather were sensitive to the validity of each cue relative to one another.

The blocking and relative validity effects initiated the development of associative learning models such as that proposed by Rescorla and Wagner (1972). Following Kamin's suggestion that the "surprisingness" of an outcome determines the extent that events become associated to it (Kamin, 1969a, 1969b), Rescorla and Wagner developed a model of Pavlovian conditioning based on the difference between the expected status of an outcome and its actual status (see Allan, 1993; Miller, Barnet, & Grahame, 1995, for review). The more unexpected or surprising an outcome, the more conditioning will occur. According to the model, the strength of association between a cue and outcome changes as a function of the equation

$$\Delta V = \alpha\beta(\lambda - \Sigma V), \tag{4.1}$$

where $\Delta V$ represents the change in associative strength of the cue. $\alpha$ is the learning rate parameter that is unique to each cue and represents its salience; it is positive when the cue is present, and zero when it is absent. $\beta$ is the learning rate parameter associated with the outcome. $\lambda$ is the upper limit of associative strength that the outcome will support. Finally, $\Sigma V$ is the sum of associative strengths for all of the cues present on a given trial. Because the outcome can support only a limited amount of associative strength, each cue that is presented must compete to be associated with the outcome.

In Group 1 of Kamin's blocking experiment, the associative strength between Cue A and the outcome quickly approaches asymptote ($\lambda$) in the first phase. In the second phase, when the redundant B cue is presented with A, because A has already acquired most of the associative strength available, the sum of associative strength for A and B ($\Sigma V$) is already near $\lambda$. Therefore, the level of surprise ($\lambda - \Sigma V$) is nearly zero and very little associative strength would accrue to B. At test, Rescorla and Wagner's (1972) model predicts very little responding to Cue B.

In the relative validity experiment by Wagner et al. (1968), the individual cues compete to be associated with the outcome just as they did in the blocking paradigm. In Group 1, Cues B and C perfectly predict the presence and absence of the outcome respectively, the sum of the associative strength ($\Sigma V$) will quickly approach asymptote, and little will be learned about Cue A. In Group 2, because B and C predict the outcome only 50% of the time, they require more trials to reach asymptote. As a result, A can accrue more associative strength. Therefore, the animals will respond more at test to A in Group 2 compared to Group 1. Because B quickly approaches $\lambda$ in Group 1, thereby reducing the associative strength available to A, some would say that Cue B "blocks" conditioning to A (e.g., Baker, Mercier, Vallée-Tourangeau, Frank, & Pan, 1993; Baker, Murphy, & Vallée-Tourangeau, 1996; Mehta, 2000; Vallée-Tourangeau, Baker, & Mercier, 1994). Note, however, that in order for the Rescorla–Wagner model to account for this relative validity effect, one must assume that $\beta_O$ (outcome present) is greater than $\beta_{\sim O}$ (outcome absent), as indicated by Baker et al. (chap. 2, this volume). In addition to blocking and relative validity, the Rescorla–Wagner model been successful in predicting several counterintuitive phenomena (see Siegel & Allan, 1996, for review).

## BLOCKING EFFECTS IN HUMAN LEARNING

Wasserman (1990) extended the relative validity paradigm to human participants by asking them to judge the efficacy of certain foods in causing an allergic reaction. As in the original relative validity experiment, a common A cue (e.g., shrimp) was paired with either Cue B (e.g., strawberries) or C (e.g., peanuts). The "differential correlation" of the AB and AC compounds with the allergic reaction (O) was varied across five conditions maintaining the original 100%–0% and 50%–50% manipulation, as well as three intermediate conditions, i.e., 87.5%–12.5%, 75%–25%, and 62.5%–37.5%. Participants' ratings of the redundant A cue increased as a function of the differential correlation between the AB and AC compounds. That is, judgments of A were lowest in the 100%–0% condition and highest in the 50%–50% condition, and gradually increased among the three intermediate conditions.

Blocking was first demonstrated in humans by Shanks and his colleagues (Dickinson & Shanks, 1985; Dickinson, Shanks, & Evenden 1984; Shanks, 1985) using a computer game. The experiment followed the two-phase blocking paradigm described earlier. During the first phase of the experiment, participants watched a series of trials where a tank successfully or unsuccessfully traversed a minefield (A → O). In the second phase, they were instructed to shoot down the tank. The participants were unable to determine whether the tank was destroyed by a mine or their own gunfire (AB → O). During the test phase, they were asked to rate both the influence of their shooting and the effectiveness of the mines in destroying the tank. Those who were exposed to the initial phase of the experiment rated the their own gunfire as being less effective compared to those not exposed to Phase 1. Learning that the minefield was effective in the destruction of the tank seemed to have blocked learning about the influence of their own gunfire in the latter phase of the experiment.

Subsequently, Chapman and Robbins (1990) investigated blocking by presenting participants with information about a fictitious stock market and individual stocks. Over a series of trials, participants were told whether the price of individual stocks increased or not, followed by information about the rise or fall of the entire stock market. The objective was to indicate how predictive each stock was in the fluctuation of the stock market. In the first phase of the experiment, a rise in Stock P (predictive) always resulted in a rise in the market, whereas a rise in Stock N (nonpredictive) resulted in no change in the market. In the second phase, two novel stocks were presented alongside Stocks P and N: Stock B (blocking) was paired with P resulting in a rise in the market; and the pairing of Stock C (control) and N also resulted in a rise in the stock market. During the test phase, participants provided higher predictiveness ratings for C than for B, even though the two stocks were equally predictive. As in the previous blocking demonstrations, learning about the predictive cue in the first phase blocks learning about the cue it is paired with in the subsequent phase. P blocked the equally predictive association between B and the stock market.

## CAUSAL-MODEL THEORY

As humans became the subject of cue-interaction paradigms, Waldmann and Holyoak (1992) noted the shortcoming of associative models to encode the asymmetry of causal relationships. Causes influence effects, but effects do not influence causes. According to Waldmann (Waldmann, 2000, 2001; Waldmann & Holyoak, 1990, 1992, 1997), associative models neglect the causal status among events by simply encoding the antecedent events as cues and subsequent events as outcomes. For example, in Figure 4.1, the generic events A1, A2, and A3 can be interpreted as either causes or effects. Waldmann argues that humans will rate the influence of each cue differently depending on their causal interpretation and how the cues are interconnected. Specifically, if A1 and A2 are interpreted as two causes that jointly influence a common effect (A3), then according to a common-effect model

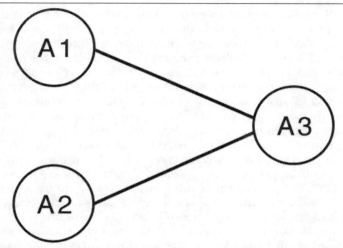

FIG. 4.1.  Generic casual structure among three interconnected events. A1, A2, and A3 each represent a cause or an effect.

(2C–1E), one should consider each cause conditional upon the other re-sulting in an interaction between A1 and A2. On the other hand, if the causal arrows are reversed, and A3 is interpreted as a common cause of two effects (A1 and A2), then according to a common-cause model (2E–1C), the two effects should be considered independently while as-sessing the causal strength of A3. Both effects are the product of the common cause. Therefore, when one is asked to rate the effectiveness of the cause, because A1 and A2 are effects, they have no causal influ-ence on A3. One should, therefore, estimate the unconditional influ-ence on each effect resulting in no cue interaction. Waldmann maintains that associationist learning theories predict cue interaction between cues regardless of their causal status, whereas causal-model theory predicts cue interaction only between causes.

The data reported by Waldmann and Holyoak (1992) prompted a re-sponse among several associative-learning theorists, who questioned the results and disputed the necessity of causal models in explaining the presence and absence of cue interaction. The contentious result was the absence of cue interaction when two effects preceded a single cause (2E–1C). Because identical cues were used in both the 2C–1E and 2E–1C scenarios, associative models predict an attenuated response in both conditions. In support of associative models, Shanks and López (1996), Matute, Arcediano, and Miller (1996), and Price and Yates (1995) using different cue-interaction paradigms with various materials, reported a cue-interaction effect regardless of whether two causes preceded a sin-gle effect or whether two effects preceded a single cause. Van Hamme, Kao, and Wasserman (1993), however, obtained results that were consistent with causal-model theory in which causes interact and effects do not. The authors, however, did not consider their results to be inconsistent with associative theories (see Waldmann, 2000, for review). Waldmann (2000) responded to the criticisms made by the associative theorists by replicating no cue interaction in the 2E–1C scenario using a novel design to address the criticisms raised against the experiments in Waldmann and Holyoak's (1992) article. He also demonstrated the same sensitivity to causal asymmetry using a one-phase overshadowing design (Waldmann, 2001), Simpson's paradox (Waldmann & Hagmayer, 2001), and he generalized causal-model theory to human categorization (Waldmann & Hagmayer, 1999; Waldmann, Holyoak, & Fratianne, 1995). In response, Cobos, López, Caño, Almaraz, and Shanks (2002) improved upon the methodology used by Shanks and López (1996) and presented a series of experiments in an attempt to address each of the criticisms proposed by Waldmann (2000, 2001). The results from their analyses reaffirm their previous findings (Shanks & López, 1996) of cue interaction in the 2E–1C scenario in which multiple effects indicate the presence of a common cause. Cobos et al. (2002) argue that causal asymmetry does not influence the acquisition and use of inferential knowledge.

Recently, however, Tangen and Allan (2004) provided evidence for both high-level (causal reasoning) processes and low-level (associative) processes. They argued that both factors influence causal assessment depending on what is being asked about the events, and participants' experience with those events. In particular, in two experiments, they demonstrated how expectations of the structure of causal relationships influence overall causal ratings. In two other experiments, they showed that participants are insensitive to causal structure in their trial-by-trial prediction responses in contrast to their overall ratings, and that this sensitivity to causal direction in their overall ratings becomes less evident as trials progress. Tangen and Allan concluded that people engage in both causal reasoning and associative learning (see also chap. 3, this volume, for discussion of controlled processes).

Several potential factors have been suggested to explain the presence or absence of a causal model effect. The present chapter examines the influence of three such factors in the one-phase simultaneous blocking design used by Tangen and Allan (2004). The following experiments were not designed to set associative and causal-model theories in opposition (see Tangen & Allan, 2004, for contrast), but rather to examine three circumstances under which a causal-model effect occurs or not, and to further examine the role of conditionalization in causal-model theory.

## CAUSAL-MODEL THEORY AND CONDITIONAL $\Delta P$

The one-phase simultaneous blocking design initially proposed by Baker et al. (1993) makes use of all possible event combinations for two cues (A and B) and a common outcome (O): Both cues may be present (AB), one may be present and the other absent (A~B or ~AB), or both may be absent (~A~B) as illustrated in Figure 4.2. For each cue combination, the outcome either occurs (O) or not (~O). In such a task, after being presented with a cue combination, participants are typically asked to predict whether the outcome will occur or not (Yes, No), which is also represented in Figure 4.2. By calculating the frequency with which each event combination occurred, Cues A and B can be expressed in terms of their unconditional or conditional ΔP values respectively:

$$\Delta P_A = P(O|A) - P(O|\sim A) = \frac{a+c}{a+b+c+d} - \frac{e+g}{e+f+g+h} \qquad (4.2)$$

$$\Delta P_B = P(O|B) - P(O|\sim B) = \frac{a+e}{a+b+e+b} - \frac{c+g}{c+d+g+h} \qquad (4.3)$$

$$\Delta P_{A|B} = P(O|AB) - P(O|\sim AB) = \frac{a}{a+b} - \frac{e}{e+f} \qquad (4.4)$$

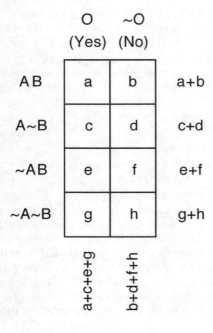

FIG. 4.2.  4 × 2 contingency matrix illustrating the eight possible cue-outcome combinations for two cues. Each cell represents the frequency of each event type.

$$\Delta P_{A|\sim B} = P(O|A \sim B) - P(O|\sim A \sim B) = \frac{c}{c+d} - \frac{g}{g+h} \tag{4.5}$$

$$\Delta P_{B|A} = P(O|BA) - P(O|\sim BA) = \frac{a}{a+b} - \frac{c}{c+d} \tag{4.6}$$

$$\Delta P_{B|\sim A} = P(O|B \sim A) - P(O|\sim B \sim A) = \frac{e}{e+f} - \frac{g}{g+h} \tag{4.7}$$

in which the two unconditional $\Delta P$ values (Equations 4.2 and 4.3) correspond to the difference between the proportion of times the outcome occurs given the cue and the proportion of times the outcome occurs not given the cue. The conditional $\Delta P$ values in Equations 4.4–4.7 allow one to assess the influence of each cue in both the presence and absence of the other cue.

Cue interaction by means of conditionalization occurs if participants' ratings better correspond with conditional, rather than unconditional, $\Delta P$. When two cues described as causes precede a single outcome described as an effect (2C–1E), a causal-model account predicts that participants should conditionalize by rating the influence of each cause relative to the other. Associative models also predict that the cues should interact but by means of cue competition as opposed to conditionalization. Alternatively, if the two cues are described as effects whereas the outcome is described as a cause (2E–1C), a causal-model account predicts that participants should rate each effect independently coinciding with unconditional $\Delta P$ described previously. Because associative accounts disregard the causal description of the events, they would again predict that the cues would interact by means of cue competition.

Each of the experiments described in Tangen and Allan (2004) were designed to set apart the two accounts of cue interaction. In each case, two cues were paired with a single outcome where Cue A was always moderately contingent ($\Delta P_A = 0.5$), and was paired with Cue B, which ranged from being non-contingent ($\Delta P_B = 0$) to perfectly contingent ($\Delta P_B = 1$). If participants' ratings or predictions of A changed as the contingency of B increased, then they were judging A relative to B. In contrast, if their judgment of A did not change as B increased, then they were judging A independently of B. Throughout each of the four experiments, Tangen and Allan found that on early trials there was a significant causal model effect in participants' ratings where the causal scenario (2C–1E and 2E–1C) significantly interacted with Cue B contingency. In Experiment 4, they showed that the causal-model effect dissipated as the trials progressed. Furthermore, they revealed a dissociation between ratings and prediction responses where participants' ratings were sensitive to the causal scenario (at least on early trials), whereas their prediction responses were insensitive to the causal scenario instead reflecting what seems to be the current level of associative strength.

## ALLEGED CAUSAL-MODEL INFLUENCES

The debate between associative and causal–model theorists prompted a number of experiments examining the influence of causal asymmetry on judgments of contingency, and has resulted in a number of positive and negative results (Cobos et al., 2002; Price & Yates, 1995; Shanks & López, 1996; Tangen & Allan, 2004; Van Hamme et al., 1993; Waldmann, 2001; Waldmann & Holyoak, 1992). Several potential factors have been suggested to explain the presence or absence of a causal-model effect. We examine the influence of three such factors using the one-phase blocking design described earlier. Recall that in Tangen and Allan (2004, Experiment 4), participants became less sensitive to the causal direction of the events as trials progressed. The purpose of the present series of experiments is to examine the specific circumstances under which we can alter participants' sensitivity to the direction of the causal relationship. In order to determine whether each of the alleged causal-model influences was effective in bringing about a causal-model effect, we compare each experiment in turn with the results obtained in Experiment 4 of Tangen and Allan. Therefore, using those data as a template, we compare them with the data obtained from each experiment in sequence by including both in an analysis of variance (ANOVA), and we report any significant differences between them that are consistent or inconsistent with a causal-model account. Specifically, we indicate whether the main effect of experiment interacted with the causal scenario and any other relevant factors.

## GENERAL METHOD

### Participants and Design

A total of 100 undergraduate students at McMaster University volunteered for course credit (40 participants in Experiments 1 and 3, and 20 participants in Experiment 2). All of the experiments used the same one-phase blocking design described in Tangen and Allan (2004, Experiment 4). Sixty-four trials were presented to each participant. On each trial, one of four possible cue combinations was presented (AB, A~B, A~B, ~A~B) at which point participants were asked to predict whether the outcome on that particular trial would occur or not (Yes, No). The actual outcome of the trial (O, ~O) followed along with corrective feedback on their decision (Correct, Incorrect). Eight trial types were therefore possible and are presented in Table 4.3. The number of times that each trial type was presented was determined by pairing moderately

**TABLE 4.3**
**Frequency of Events In Experiment 1–3.**

| Trial Type | 0.5/0 | 0.5/0.25 | 0.5/0.75 | 0.5/1 |
|---|---|---|---|---|
| ABO | 12 | 16 | 22 | 24 |
| A~BO | 12 | 8 | 2 | 0 |
| ~ABO | 4 | 4 | 6 | 8 |
| ~A~BO | 4 | 4 | 2 | 0 |
| AB~O | 4 | 4 | 2 | 0 |
| A~B~O | 4 | 4 | 6 | 8 |
| ~AB~O | 12 | 8 | 2 | 0 |
| ~A~B~O | 12 | 16 | 22 | 24 |
| | | | | |
| # of Trials | 64 | 64 | 64 | 64 |
| $\Delta PA$ | 0.5 | 0.5 | 0.5 | 0.5 |
| $\Delta PA|B$ | 0.5 | 0.47 | 0.17 | 0 |
| $\Delta PA|{\sim}B$ | 0.5 | 0.47 | 0.17 | 0 |
| $\Delta PB$ | 0 | 0.25 | 0.75 | 1 |
| $\Delta PB|A$ | 0 | 0.13 | 0.67 | 1 |
| $\Delta PB|{\sim}A$ | 0 | 0.13 | 0.67 | 1 |

*Note.* Unconditional $\Delta P$ values were calculated using Equations 4.2 and 4.3. Conditional $\Delta P$ values were calculated using Equations 4.4–4.7.

contingent Cue A ($\Delta P_A = 0.5$) with Cue B, which varied in contingency ($\Delta P_B$: 0, 0.25, 0.75, 1). The particular event frequencies were selected so that the conditional $\Delta P_A$ values would gradually diverge from the unconditional $\Delta P_A$ values as $\Delta P_B$ increased.

Cue interaction was measured by the pattern of data obtained from ratings of Cue A: If ratings of A changed as a function of $\Delta P_B$, then the cues interacted; if ratings of A did not vary, then the cues did not interact. According to causal-model theory, by means of conditional $\Delta P$, participants in the 2C–1E scenario should rate A conditional on B thereby tracking the pattern of conditional $\Delta P_A$ values across the four contingency pairs (0.5, 0.47, 0.17, 0). Participants in the 2E–1C scenario should rate A independently of B thereby tracking the pattern of unconditional $\Delta P_A$ values across the four contingency pairs (0.5, 0.5, 0.5, 0.5).

Throughout each set of 64 trials, participants were asked to rate Cues A and B after 16, 32, 48, and 64 trials. On each trial, they were asked to predict the outcome. The cue combinations and their corresponding predictions (Yes, No) were mapped onto the $4 \times 2$ matrix presented in Figure 4.2 and used as an indirect measure of participants' conditional $\Delta P$ estimates (see also López, Shanks, Almaraz, & Fernandez, 1998; Tangen & Allan, 2003).

## Procedure and Materials

In Experiments 1 and 3, participants received instructions on a computer screen where they were informed about four strains of bacteria that have been discovered in the mammalian digestive system (see Experiment 2 methods section for a different cover story). In the 2C–1E scenario, they were told that scientists were testing whether a pair of chemicals affected the strain's survival, whereas, in the 2E–1C scenario, the scientists were testing whether the bacteria affected the production of a pair of chemicals.

Up to four participants at a time performed the experiment on Power Macintosh computers. Each experiment was programmed in MetaCard 2.5. In the instructions, the four contingency pairs were identified as separate "experiments" to test the influence of the chemicals on the bacteria, or vice versa. Within each causal scenario, the 64 trials were presented in random order according to the frequencies presented in Table 4.3. A computer-rendered movie of a colored three-dimensional chemical spinning along its axis indicated the addition or production of a chemical, and actual footage of moving bacteria was displayed when the bacteria survived or were added. Faded, unmoving grayscale images of the same chemicals and bacteria were displayed to indicate their absence on a given trial. The names of the chemicals and bacteria were displayed only when the events occurred. Each of the movies and images were randomly assigned fictitious names from a set of eight chemicals and four bacteria, and were randomly assigned to appear on the left- or right-hand side of the screen for each of the 64 trials.

Participants were presented with one of four cue combinations consisting of the presence or absence of two chemicals and were then asked to indicate whether they thought the bacterial strain survived/was added or not by clicking one of two buttons on the computer screen. Once they made their selection, they were presented with the outcome along with Correct or Incorrect as feedback. After viewing and predicting the outcome for 16 trials, participants in the 2C–1E causal scenario were asked to rate how strongly each chemical (Cues A and B) affected the bacteria, and those in the 2E–1C scenario were asked to rate how strongly the bacteria affected the production of each chemical (Cues A and B). Ratings were made on a scale ranging from –100 to 100 by moving a horizontal scrollbar with a mouse ranging from –100 at the leftmost position to 100 at the rightmost position, anchored at 0 at the center. The trials resumed and participants were asked to repeat the rating process after 32, 48, and 64 trials.

## EXPERIMENT 1: CLARITY OF THE CAUSAL MODEL—REMINDERS

Waldmann and Holyoak (1997) presented a list of methodological requirements for investigating causal directionality, the first of which is to "ensure that participants consistently interpret the learning situation in terms of directed cause–effect relations" (p. 127). In criticizing the methodology used by Shanks and López (1996), Waldmann and Holyoak insisted on the necessity of making the causal relationship in the instructions and materials unmistakable. They argued that if there is any ambiguity in participants' interpretation of the event relations, then one cannot accurately measure the influence of their causal interpretation on learning. Though Shanks and López used a cover story in which various symptoms (effects) were diagnostic of a disease (cause), Waldmann and Holyoak argued that the directionality of the causal relationship could be misinterpreted.

Tangen and Allan (2004) used materials that could also be interpreted as causally ambiguous. Participants were told that scientists have recently discovered several strains of bacteria that exist in the mammalian digestive system. In the 2C–1E scenario, they were told that the scientists were testing whether certain pairs of chemicals (causes) affect the survival of the bacteria (effects). In the 2E–1C scenario, they were told that the scientists were testing whether a certain pairs of chemicals (effects) were produced as a result of the addition of the bacteria (cause). Tangen and Allan selected materials particularly for the potential to reverse causal direction, in which the chemicals could be described as causes just as easily as effects. In their final experiment, Tangen and Allan demonstrated that the influence of the causal model decreased as the number of trials increased. It is possible that over time, the causal relationship between the events became less clear where participants misinterpreted the cues as causes and the outcome as an effect in the 2E–1C scenario. In their methodological requirements, Waldmann and Holyoak (1997) made a point of noting that participants must consistently interpret the learning situation in terms of directed cause–effect relations. Experiment 1 was designed to serve this purpose by consistently reminding participants about the direction of the causal relationship at hand.

### Method

Participants in Experiment 1 were asked to provide contingency ratings for Cues A and B after 16, 32, 48, and 64 trials. After every eight trials, they were exposed to the 16 causal model prompts given in the Appendix to consistently and explicitly remind them about the direction and nature of the causal relationship. Half of the participants were assigned to the 2C–1E scenario and half were assigned to the 2E–1C scenario, and the four contingency pairs were presented to each participant in random order. Those in the 2C–1E condition were given 2C–1E prompts whereas those in the 2E–1C condition were given 2E–1C prompts. Each participant was therefore presented with each of the 16 prompts two times, in random order, after Trials 8, 16, 24, 32, 40, 48, 56, and 64 for each of the four contingency pairs shown in Table 4.3.

## Results

*Ratings.* The data from Tangen and Allan (2004, Experiment 4) were used as a template to compare the results from the present experiment and the two subsequent experiments. In Tangen and Allan (2004, Experiment 4), at 32 trials, the pattern of results was similar to that of the previous three experiments. In the 2C–1E scenario, ratings of A tracked the pattern of conditional $\Delta P$ values presented in Table 4.3, whereas in the 2E–1C scenario the ratings tracked the pattern of unconditional $\Delta P$ values. After 48 and 64 trials, however, a different pattern of results emerged. Ratings of A declined as $\Delta P_B$ increased, regardless of the causal scenario. The effect of the causal model seemed to have dissipated over trials, and cue interaction occurred for both scenarios. This was confirmed by the statistical analyses reported by Tangen and Allan. A 2 (scenario: 2C–1E, 2E–1C) × 4 ($\Delta P_B$: 0, 0.25, 0.75, 1) × 3 (trial: 32, 48, 64) mixed ANOVA on the ratings of A revealed a significant two-way interaction of scenario with $\Delta P_B$, $F(3, 114) = 3.33$, $p < .05$, and a significant three-way interaction of scenario with $\Delta P_B$ and trial, $F(6, 228) = 3.13$, $p < .01$. The two-way interaction of scenario with $\Delta P_B$ indicates that cue interaction was greater for 2C–1E than for 2E–1C, and the three-way interaction of scenario with $\Delta P_B$ and trial indicates that this difference between the two scenarios decreased over trials.

Figure 4.3 illustrates the mean ratings of Cue A after 64 trials, and Table 4.4 provides the mean ratings of Cue A after 32, 48, and 64 trials. The ratings and estimated $\Delta P$ values after 16 trials are not reported as participants' prediction responses of the randomly presented events occasionally resulted in 4 × 2 matrices with row frequencies of zero. The data are presented for each of the four contingency pairs. The pattern of data for ratings of Cue A is virtually identical to the results obtained in Tangen and Allan (2004, Experiment 4), which are reproduced in Figure 4.4 for trial 64. Trial 64 ratings of Cue A decrease as $\Delta P_B$ increases closely tracking the pattern of conditional $\Delta P$ values presented in Table 4.1 regardless of whether the two cues were described as causes (2C–1E) or effects (2E–1C).

Using the results from Tangen and Allan (2004) as a template, a 2 (experiment: Exp. 4, Exp 1.) × 2 (scenario: 2C–1E, 2E–1C) × 4 ($\Delta P_B$: 0, 0.25, 0.75, 1) × 3 (trial: 32, 48, 64) mixed ANOVA was conducted on the ratings of Cue A. Participants' sensitivity to causal direction did not differ between the two experiments as indicated by the experiment × scenario

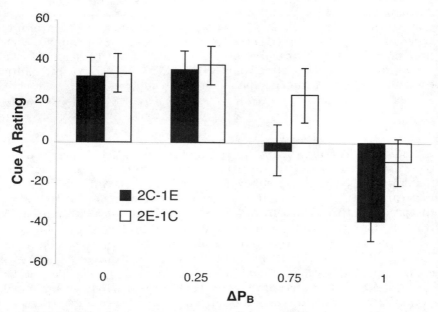

FIG. 4.3. Mean ratings of Cue A in Experiment 1 after 64 trials. The ratings are shown as a function of $\Delta P_B$ (0, 0.25, 0.75, 1) separately for each of the two conditions. Error bars represent standard errors of the means.

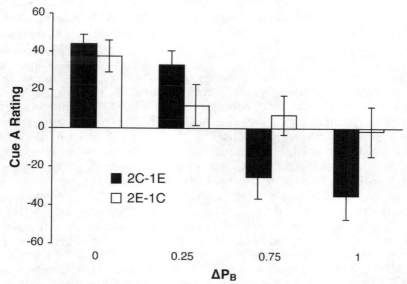

FIG. 4.4. Mean ratings of Cue A after 64 trials reproduced from Experiment 4 of Tangen and Allan (2004). The ratings are shown as a function of $\Delta P_B$ (0, 0.25, 0.75, 1) separately for each of the two conditions. Error bars represent standard errors of the means.

## TABLE 4.4

**Experiment 1 Mean Ratings and Estimated ΔP Values of Cue A Conditional on the Presence of Cue B (est$\Delta P_{A|B}$) and the Absence of Cue B (est$\Delta P_{A|\sim B}$) After 32, 48, and 64 Trials**

| | | 2C–1E | | | | | | | |
|---|---|---|---|---|---|---|---|---|---|
| | | 0.5/0 | | 0.5/0.25 | | 0.5/0.75 | | 0.5/1 | |
| 32 | Rating | 39.7 | (8.6) | 29.5 | (11.5) | −16 | (12.6) | −39.7 | (9.7) |
| | est$\Delta P_{A|B}$ | 0.39 | (0.08) | 0.3 | (0.09) | 0.19 | (0.07) | 0.09 | (0.06) |
| | est$\Delta P_{A|\sim B}$ | 0.46 | (0.08) | 0.38 | (0.09) | 0.37 | (0.05) | 0.16 | (0.04) |
| 48 | Rating | 25.3 | (9.8) | 26.6 | (9.8) | 0.2 | (12) | −45.7 | (10.4) |
| | est$\Delta P_{A|B}$ | 0.38 | (0.07) | 0.36 | (0.08) | 0.16 | (0.05) | 0.07 | (0.03) |
| | est$\Delta P_{A|\sim B}$ | 0.5 | (0.07) | 0.44 | (0.07) | 0.29 | (0.05) | 0.09 | (0.03) |
| 64 | Rating | 32.5 | (9) | 35.6 | (9.4) | −3.7 | (12.4) | −38.5 | (9.6) |
| | est$\Delta P_{A|B}$ | 0.39 | (0.07) | 0.42 | (0.07) | 0.13 | (0.04) | 0.06 | (0.02) |
| | est$\Delta P_{A|\sim B}$ | 0.51 | (0.07) | 0.48 | (0.06) | 0.27 | (0.05) | 0.08 | (0.02) |
| | | 2E–1C | | | | | | | |
| | | 0.5/0 | | 0.5/0.25 | | 0.5/0.75 | | 0.5/1 | |
| 32 | Rating | 35.4 | (11.1) | 45.6 | (10.1) | 11.4 | (10.8) | 0.1 | (13.9) |
| | est$\Delta P_{A|B}$ | 0.39 | (0.08) | 0.59 | (0.05) | 0.3 | (0.07) | 0.15 | (0.06) |
| | est$\Delta P_{A|\sim B}$ | 0.61 | (0.05) | 0.61 | (0.08) | 0.44 | (0.08) | 0.23 | (0.07) |
| 48 | Rating | 27.4 | (11.9) | 50.8 | (5.8) | 28.1 | (10.3) | −1.6 | (14.1) |
| | est$\Delta P_{A|B}$ | 0.46 | (0.07) | 0.54 | (0.05) | 0.32 | (0.06) | 0.09 | (0.04) |
| | est$\Delta P_{A|\sim B}$ | 0.62 | (0.06) | 0.6 | (0.08) | 0.38 | (0.07) | 0.16 | (0.06) |
| 64 | Rating | 33.9 | (9.5) | 38 | (9.5) | 23.2 | (13.3) | −9.4 | (11.6) |
| | est$\Delta P_{A|B}$ | 0.48 | (0.07) | 0.54 | (0.06) | 0.27 | (0.05) | 0.07 | (0.03) |
| | est$\Delta P_{A|\sim B}$ | 0.64 | (0.05) | 0.59 | (0.07) | 0.37 | (0.06) | 0.11 | (0.04) |

*Note.* Standard errors of the means are given in parentheses.

× $\Delta P_B$ interaction, which was not significant, $F(3, 228) = .62, p > .05$, and the experiment × scenario × $\Delta P_B$ × trial interaction, which also was not significant, $F(6, 456) = 1.34, p > .05$.

***Predictions.*** Table 4.4 also provides the mean estimated ΔP values conditional on the presence and absence of Cue B after 32, 48, and 64 trials. In Tangen and Allan (2004, Experiment 4), the mean estimated conditional ΔP values for A calculated after 32, 48, and 64 trials closely tracked the conditional $\Delta P$ values presented in Table 4.3 for both causal scenarios. A 2 (scenario: 2C–1E, 2E–1C) × 4 ($\Delta P_B$: 0, 0.25, 0.75, 1) × 3 (trial: 32, 48, 64) × 2 (Cue B status: present, absent) mixed ANOVA on the estimated values for A revealed a significant main effect of $\Delta P_B$, $F(3, 114) = 33.71$, $p < .001$, and contributed to a significant interaction with trial, $F(6, 228) = 9.39$, $p < .001$. However, the scenario did not interact with either $\Delta P_B$ or trial, $p > .05$, indicating that the estimated values for A decreased as $\Delta P_B$ increased for both scenarios.

Again, using these data as a template, a 2 (experiment: Exp. 4, Exp. 1) × 2 (scenario: 2C–1E, 2E–1C) × 4 ($\Delta P_B$: 0, 0.25, 0.75, 1) × 3 (trial: 32, 48, 64) × 2 (Cue B status: present, absent) mixed ANOVA was conducted on the estimated conditional $\Delta P$ values for Cue A. Participants' sensitivity to causal direction did not differ between the two experiments as indicated by the experiment × scenario × $\Delta P_B$ interaction, which was not significant, $F(3, 228) = .15$, $p > .05$. The only effect (that interacted with experiment) to reach significance in the prediction data was a four-way interaction between experiment, scenario, $\Delta P_B$, and trial, $F(6, 456) = 2.97$, $p < .01$. This significant interaction arises from a descending pattern of estimated $\Delta P$ values across trials when $\Delta P_B = 0.25$ for the 2C–1E scenario, whereas estimated $\Delta P$ tended to increase across trials when $\Delta P_B = 0.25$ for the 2E–1C scenario. This interaction is anomalous: it was not found by Tangen and Allan (2004) nor replicated in any of the present experiments.

## Discussion

Experiment 1 tested the methodological requirement proposed by Waldmann and Holyoak (1997) for clarity of the causal model by explicitly reminding participants about the direction and nature of the causal relationship for two causal scenarios. The results indicate that the frequent presentation of causal prompts did not influence sensitivity to causal directionality. Reminding participants about the direction and nature of the causal relationship after every eight trials was actually our second attempt to produce a causal-model effect. The first attempt presented the same causal model prompts after every 16 trials. The results from the two experiments were virtually identical. Neither participants' ratings nor predictions differed between the data obtained from the present experiment and Tangen and Allan (2004, Experiment 4).

### EXPERIMENT 2: CLARITY OF THE CAUSAL MODEL—COVER STORY

As indicated above, Tangen and Allan (2004) selected their materials to provide causal exchangeability whereby two cues can be described as either causes or effects followed by an outcome that can be described as an effect or a cause. In particular, the participants had no prior expectations about the causal nature of the chemicals and bacteria in the cover story. It seems just as plausible for the chemicals to influence the survival of the bacteria as the bacteria to influence the production of the chemicals. It may be this exchangeable property of the stimuli that is responsible for the similar treatment of the events. After all, prototypical causal events in the world cannot plausibly be exchanged with their effects. For example, it is unlikely that one would mistakenly interpret smoke as a cause of fire or pain as a cause in stubbing one's toe. Waldmann and Holyoak (1997) insist that the causal nature of the events be absolutely transparent in order to ensure an appropriate test of causal-model theory. Experiment 2 adopted materials in which the cover story described causes that could not conceivably be exchanged with effects or vice versa.

In each of the experiments described by Tangen and Allan (2004), and in the aforementioned Experiment 1, participants demonstrated a strong cue-interaction effect in the 2C–1E scenario. The particular result of interest here, then, is the extent to which participants will assess one effect in light of the other in the 2E–1C scenario using a cover story describing two effects that could not plausibly influence the root cause. Therefore, only the 2E–1C scenario could be tested and the 2C–1E scenario in Experiment 4 of Tangen and Allan was used as a control.

## Method

The design and procedure for Experiment 2 was identical to that of Experiment 1 without the 2C–1E scenario or the causal-model prompts. Rather than assessing the extent to which a bacterial strain produced a pair of chemicals as in Experiment 1, participants were asked to assess the extent to which a particular food caused a patient to experience a pair of symptoms. Thus, each trial presented a pair of movies denoting whether a patient suffered from a migraine headache and/or stomach pains. Participants were then asked to indicate whether they thought the patient ate the particular food or not, and were then provided with corrective feedback along with a static image of the food indicating whether it was indeed consumed or not. Therefore, the four different bacterial strains being tested in Experiment 1 were substituted with different foods (avocado, bananas, carrots, grapes, and strawberries) being tested in Experiment 2. All aspects of the experiment were designed to be identical to the 2E–1C scenario of Experiment 1 with the exception of the materials presented.

## Results

*Ratings.* Figure 4.5 illustrates the mean ratings of Cue A after 64 trials for the 2E–1C scenario and the mean ratings of Cue A after 64 trials for the 2E–1C scenario reproduced from Experiment 4 of Tangen and

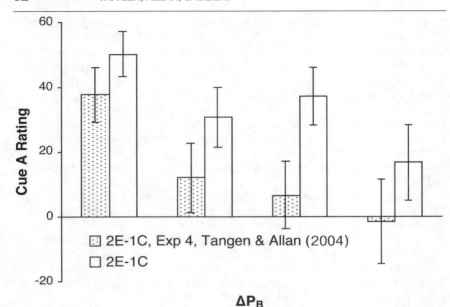

FIG. 4.5. Mean ratings of Cue A in Experiment 2 after 64 trials for the 2E–1C scenario. The dotted bars are reproduced from Tangen and Allan (2004) and represent the mean ratings of Cue A in Experiment 4 after 64 trials for the 2E–1C scenario. The ratings are shown as a function of $DP_B$ (0, 0.25, 0.75, 1) separately for each of the two conditions. Error bars represent standard errors of the means.

Allan (2004). Table 4.5 provides the mean ratings of Cue A after 32, 48, and 64 trials. The data are presented for each of the four contingency pairs. As in Experiment 1, the pattern of data for ratings of Cue A is similar to the results obtained in Tangen and Allan (Experiment 4). Ratings of Cue A generally decrease as $\Delta P_B$ increases tracking the pattern of conditional $\Delta P$ values presented in Table 4.3.

Again, using the data from Tangen and Allan (2004, Experiment 4) as a template, a 2 (experiment: Exp. 4, Exp. 2) × 4($\Delta P_B$: 0, 0.25, 0.75, 1) × 3 (trial: 32, 48, 64) mixed ANOVA was conducted on the ratings of Cue A for the 2E–1C causal scenario. As in the previous experiment, there was no effect of the causal model as indicated by the experiment × $\Delta P_B$ interaction, which was not significant, $F(3, 114) = .75, p > .05$. Although there was a significant main effect of experiment, $F(1, 38) = 4.5, p < .05$, indicating overall higher ratings in Experiment 2, no other effects or interactions reached significance.

*Predictions.*    Table 4.5 also depicts the mean estimated conditional $\Delta P$ values of Cue A conditional on the presence and absence of Cue B for

## TABLE 4.5

**Experiment 2 Mean Ratings and Estimated ΔP Values of Cue A Conditional on the Presence of Cue B (estΔP$_{A|B}$) and the Absence of Cue B (estΔP$_{A|\sim B}$) After 32, 48, and 64 Trials**

| | | 2E–1C | | | | | | | |
|---|---|---|---|---|---|---|---|---|---|
| | | 0.5/0 | | 0.5/0.25 | | 0.5/0.75 | | 0.5/1 | |
| 32 | Rating | 29.8 | (8.6) | 40.6 | (9.4) | 19.1 | (11.1) | 3.6 | (14.1) |
| | estΔP$_{A|B}$ | 0.4 | (0.08) | 0.42 | (0.06) | 0.19 | (0.07) | 0.04 | (0.04) |
| | estΔP$_{A|\sim B}$ | 0.46 | (0.08) | 0.55 | (0.08) | 0.35 | (0.06) | 0.25 | (0.06) |
| 48 | Rating | 35.8 | (10.4) | 47.5 | (8.9) | 23.5 | (12.7) | 16.9 | (12.9) |
| | estΔP$_{A|B}$ | 0.41 | (0.06) | 0.41 | (0.05) | 0.13 | (0.04) | 0.02 | (0.03) |
| | estΔP$_{A|\sim B}$ | 0.48 | (0.06) | 0.55 | (0.07) | 0.4 | (0.06) | 0.23 | (0.05) |
| 64 | Rating | 50.3 | (6.9) | 30.7 | (9.3) | 37.1 | (8.9) | 16.8 | (11.6) |
| | estΔP$_{A|B}$ | 0.42 | (0.05) | 0.39 | (0.04) | 0.13 | (0.04) | 0.04 | (0.03) |

*Note.* Standard errors of the means are given in parentheses.

Experiment 2. The data are presented for each of the four contingency pairs after 32, 48, and 64 trials. The prediction responses are similar to the rating data in that estimated conditional ΔP decreases as ΔP$_B$ increases. Again, using the data from Tangen and Allan (2004, Experiment 4) as a template, a 2 (experiment: Exp. 4, Exp. 2) × 4 (ΔP$_B$: 0, 0.25, 0.75, 1) × 3 (trial: 32, 48, 64) × 2 (Cue B status: present, absent) mixed ANOVA was conducted on the estimated conditional ΔP values for Cue A. As in the rating data, there was no significant effect of the causal model between the two experiments as indicated by the experiment × ΔP$_B$ interaction, which was not significant, $F(3, 114) = .44, p > .05$. No other effects interacted significantly with the experiment main effect.

## Discussion

Experiments 1 and 2 were designed to address the objection made by Waldmann and Holyoak (1997) for the clarity of the causal model when investigating causal judgments. In Experiment 1, we explicitly reminded participants about the nature and direction of the causal relationship by presenting dialogues prompting them with information about the causal status of the events. In Experiment 2, we implicitly emphasized the causal model by using materials that were congruent with participants' prior assumptions about direction the relationship. Neither experiment, however, significantly increased their sensitivity to the causal description of the events. Therefore, the alleged causal model influence of emphasizing the clarity of the causal model (implicitly or explicitly) has proven to be ineffective.

## EXPERIMENT 3: INTEGRATION

In discussing the results from their four experiments, Tangen and Allan (2004) drew an analogy between their findings and the primacy-recency effect obtained by Collins and Shanks (2002). In the primacy-recency effect, Collins and Shanks described the "momentary" strategy where judgments reflect the current associative strength of the cue, and the "integrative" strategy where participants do not constrain their judgments on the current perception of the relationship, but instead integrate information across a number of trials. Tangen and Allan proposed that similar strategies might be operating in assessing causally asymmetric events. Participants' sensitivity to causal structure can vary in degree according to what they are asked about the events and according to their experience with them. They argued that if participants were asked to use the causal model for some particular purpose, then they would likely be more sensitive to the causal structure. Similarly, if participants were asked an integrative rating question that reflected the general relationship of the events, then their assessments would better coincide with the predictions made by causal-model theory.

Experiment 3 was designed to investigate whether participants' ratings would better reflect the causal structure of the events if asked to provide an integrative rating. That is, in contrast to the prediction responses required on every trial, and the four ratings requested every 16 trials, participants were told that a pharmaceutical company was interested in manufacturing the two chemicals (2C–1E) or the bacterial strain (2E–1C) based on their observations. They were asked to assess the effectiveness of each chemical on the survival of the bacteria (2C–1E) or assess the effectiveness of the bacterial strain on the production of each chemical (2E–1C) based on the entire set of 64 trials. The wording of this "integration" question was intended to suggest that they should consider the causal description of the events rather than identifying them as generic cues and outcomes.

### Method

The design of Experiment 3 was similar to Experiment 1, but without the probes. Participants were asked to provide prediction responses on each trial and rate the relationship every 16 trials based on the contingencies presented in Table 4.3. After rating each chemical following Trial 64, participants were presented with the following dialogue:

*2C–1E:* You have just observed a series of 64 experimental trials. DrugCorp—a large pharmaceutical company—is interested in your assessment of each chemical on the survival of the bacteria and they intend to allocate funds to manufacture the chemicals on the basis of your observations. It is important that your estimate best reflects the effectiveness of each chemical across the entire set of 64 trials. Please use the scrollbar below each chemical to make a rating on a scale from −100 to +100.

*2E–1C:* You have just observed a series of 64 experimental trials. DrugCorp—a large pharmaceutical company—is interested in your assessment of the bacteria on the production of each chemical and they intend to allocate funds to manufacture the bacteria on the basis of your observations. It is important that your estimate best reflects the effectiveness of the bacteria across the entire set of 64 trials. Please use the scrollbar below each chemical to make a rating on a scale from −100 to +100.

After providing a rating for each chemical, another series of trials would begin based on one of the four contingency pairs listed in Table 4.3.

### Results

In Experiment 3, there were three dependent measures: ratings, integrative ratings, and predictions.

***Ratings.***    Figure 4.6 illustrates the mean ratings of Cue A after 64 trials and Table 4.6 provides the mean ratings of Cue A after 32, 48, and 64 trials. The data are presented for each of the four contingency pairs.

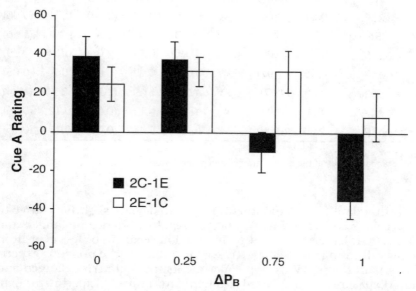

FIG. 4.6. Mean ratings of Cue A in Experiment 3 after 64 trials. The ratings are shown as a function of $\Delta P_B$ (0, 0.25, 0.75, 1) separately for each of the two conditions. Error bars represent standard errors of the means.

## TABLE 4.6
**Experiment 3 Mean Ratings and Estimated ΔP Values of Cue A Conditional on the Presence of Cue B (est$\Delta P_{A|B}$) and the Absence of Cue B (est$\Delta P_{A|\sim B}$) After 32, 48, and 64 Trials**

| | | 2C–1E | | | | | | | |
|---|---|---|---|---|---|---|---|---|---|
| | | *0.5/0* | | *0.5/0.25* | | *0.5/0.75* | | *0.5/1* | |
| 32 | Rating | 31.4 | (8) | 42.1 | (9.8) | 6.2 | (10.7) | −13.3 | (9.3) |
| | est$\Delta P_{A|B}$ | 0.44 | (0.07) | 0.45 | (0.08) | 0.26 | (0.06) | 0.12 | (0.06) |
| | est$\Delta P_{A|\sim B}$ | 0.52 | (0.07) | 0.56 | (0.06) | 0.33 | (0.07) | 0.32 | (0.08) |
| 48 | Rating | 39.9 | (9.1) | 36.9 | (8.7) | −4.6 | (10.6) | −23.6 | (8.9) |
| | est$\Delta P_{A|B}$ | 0.52 | (0.06) | 0.44 | (0.06) | 0.17 | (0.04) | 0.05 | (0.03) |
| | est$\Delta P_{A|\sim B}$ | 0.58 | (0.06) | 0.57 | (0.05) | 0.27 | (0.06) | 0.21 | (0.07) |
| 64 | Rating | 39.1 | (10) | 37.8 | (8.9) | −9.8 | (10.5) | −35.3 | (9.2) |
| | est$\Delta P_{A|B}$ | 0.53 | (0.07) | 0.42 | (0.06) | 0.1 | (0.04) | 0.04 | (0.03) |
| | est$\Delta P_{A|\sim B}$ | 0.59 | (0.06) | 0.56 | (0.05) | 0.27 | (0.06) | 0.13 | (0.04) |
| | | 2E–1C | | | | | | | |
| | | *0.5/0* | | *0.5/0.25* | | *0.5/0.75* | | *0.5/1* | |
| 32 | Rating | 27.2 | (10.2) | 19.7 | (11) | 50.9 | (9.3) | 4 | (13.2) |
| | est$\Delta P_{A|B}$ | 0.29 | (0.07) | 0.36 | (0.07) | 0.16 | (0.04) | 0.18 | (0.07) |
| | est$\Delta P_{A|\sim B}$ | 0.51 | (0.08) | 0.48 | (0.06) | 0.44 | (0.08) | 0.21 | (0.06) |
| 48 | Rating | 29.7 | (7.8) | 24.3 | (10.8) | 34 | (9.7) | −1.4 | (11.6) |
| | est$\Delta P_{A|B}$ | 0.36 | (0.07) | 0.38 | (0.06) | 0.17 | (0.06) | 0.14 | (0.05) |
| | est$\Delta P_{A|\sim B}$ | 0.55 | (0.07) | 0.47 | (0.05) | 0.47 | (0.07) | 0.2 | (0.06) |
| 64 | Rating | 24.9 | (8.7) | 31.6 | (7.5) | 31.9 | (10.6) | 8.5 | (12.4) |
| | est$\Delta P_{A|B}$ | 0.4 | (0.07) | 0.42 | (0.06) | 0.17 | (0.06) | 0.12 | (0.05) |
| | est$\Delta P_{A|\sim B}$ | 0.58 | (0.06) | 0.53 | (0.06) | 0.45 | (0.06) | 0.19 | (0.05) |

*Note.* Standard errors of the means are given in parentheses.

The rating data from Experiment 3 seem to deviate slightly relative to the previous two experiments and the results obtained in Tangen and Allan (2004, Experiment 4). Cue interaction seems to be less evident in the overall ratings for the 2E–1C scenario than in the previous experiment. As in the previous two experiments, the data from Tangen and Allan (Experiment 4) was used as a template, and a 2 (experiment: Exp. 4, Exp. 3) × 2 (scenario: 2C–1E, 2E–1C) × 4 ($\Delta P_B$: 0, 0.25, 0.75, 1) × 3 (trial: 32, 48, 64) mixed ANOVA was conducted. Unlike the previous experiments, there was a significant effect of the causal model as indicated by the significant experiment × scenario × $\Delta P_B$ interaction, $F(3, 228) = 3.04, p < .05$, and the significant four-way interaction between experiment, scenario, $\Delta P_B$, and trial, $F(6, 456) = 2.65, p < .05$.

**Integrative Ratings.**    Table 4.7 presents the mean integrative ratings of Cue A for each of the four contingency pairs after 32, 48, and 64 trials. As in the rating data, there seems to be an effect of the causal model. A 2 (scenario: 2C–1E, 2E–1C) × 4 ($\Delta P_B$: 0, 0.25, 0.75, 1) mixed ANOVA conducted on the integrative judgments of Cue A confirms these observations. The ANOVA revealed significant main effects of scenario, $F(1, 38) = 6.66, p < .05$, and $\Delta P_B$, $F(3, 114) = 20.79, p < .001$, as well as a significant interaction between them, $F(3, 114) = 3.73, p < .05$.

**Predictions.**    Table 4.6 also depicts the estimated $\Delta P$ values conditional on the presence and absence of Cue B. The data are presented for each of the four contingency pairs after 32, 48, and 64 trials. The prediction response data do not seem to differ from those in the previous two experiments. Again, using the data from Tangen and Allan (2004, Experiment 4) as a template, a 2 (experiment: Exp. 4, Exp. 3) × 2 (scenario: 2C–1E, 2E–1C) × 4 ($\Delta P_B$: 0, 0.25, 0.75, 1) × 3 (trial: 32, 48, 64) × 2 (Cue B status: present, absent) mixed ANOVA was conducted on the estimated conditional $\Delta P$ values for Cue A. Unlike the rating data, there was no significant influence of the causal model as indicated by the experiment × scenario × $\Delta P_B$ interaction, which was not significant, $F(3, 228) = 1.5, p > .05$.

## Discussion

Overall, we see that participants are more sensitive to the structure of the causal relationship when asked to provide an integrative judgment than

TABLE 4.7
**Experiment 3 Mean Integrative Ratings of Cue A**

|  | 2C–1E | | | |
| --- | --- | --- | --- | --- |
|  | *0.5/0* | *0.5/0.25* | *0.5/0.75* | *0.5/1* |
| Rating | 41.3 | 33.6 | −4.4 | −27.9 |
|  | (7.9) | (8.8) | (9.3) | (10) |
|  | 2E–1C | | | |
|  | *0.5/0* | *0.5/0.25* | *0.5/0.75* | *0.5/1* |
| Rating | 37.8 | 46.4 | 45.1 | −3.9 |
|  | (7.1) | (8) | (8.9) | (11.6) |

*Note.* Standard errors of the means are given in parentheses.

in the previous two experiments and in Tangen and Allan (2004, Experiment 4). Asking participants to integrate the causal information over trials seems to have increased their sensitivity to the direction of the causal relationship as indicated by the integrative ratings after every 64 trials. Introducing this integrative question seems to have also influenced their subsequent causal ratings as indicated by the significant experiment × scenario × ΔPB interaction described earlier. Therefore, the alleged causal-model influence of an integrative test question was effective. However, the dissociation between ratings and trial-by-trial predictions remains. Participants conditionalize in their prediction responses for both scenarios despite the circumstances. The effect of the integration question on ratings is not large by any means, but it nicely demonstrates how the relative weighting of causal and associative factors vary in a matter of degree depending on what is being asked about the events.

## GENERAL DISCUSSION

Tangen and Allan (2004) have demonstrated that the contribution of causal and associative processes depends on what the participant is being asked about the events, and on their experience with those events. They presented two experiments providing evidence for high-level (causal reasoning) processes, and two experiments providing evidence for low-level (associative) processes. They argued that both factors influence causal assessment. The present series of experiments provides additional evidence for this dual-process argument.

Experiment 1 was designed to investigate whether emphasizing the direction of the causal relationship would influence assessments of that relationship as suggested by Waldmann and Holyoak (1997). Participants were presented with causal model "prompts" every eight trials designed to remind them about the direction of the causal relationship. Even though they were presented with information signaling the direction of the relationship immediately prior to rating that relationship, it did not influence their sensitivity to causal directionality. Experiment 2 elaborated on this investigation by implicitly emphasizing the independence between the two effects in the 2E–1C scenario by using a cover story that was congruent with participants' expectations about the direction of the causal events. Again, however, emphasizing the direction of the causal relationship did not influence their causal assessments. Following a prediction made by Tangen and Allan (2004), Experiment 3 required participants to respond to an integrative test question designed so they would weight the causal description of the events more heavily than their associative nature by regarding the causal description of the events rather than identifying them as generic cues and outcomes. The manipulation was successful, in that the influence of the causal model was evident both in participants' ratings and integrative ratings.

According to causal-model theory, our knowledge of causal asymmetry provides us with the capacity to ignore the order in which events are presented thereby transforming them into causal-model representations that reflect their asymmetry (Waldmann, 2000). However, the extent and circumstances of our disregard for temporal order has not been specified. A conditional $\Delta P$ account of causal-model theory suggests that participants will conditionalize between causes, but not effects. Thus, causal assessments should coincide with conditional $\Delta P$ when two causes produce a common effect (2C–1E), and unconditional $\Delta P$ when two effects result from a common cause (2E–1C). The pattern of results obtained in Experiments 1–3 is not consistent with causal-model theory in the strictest sense. Causal assessments of the moderately contingent Cue A ($\Delta P_A = 0.5$) should be identical in the 2E–1C scenario regardless of the contingency for Cue B. This is not the case. We see that cues interact in both scenarios. However, according to an associative account, the two cues should interact the same amount regardless of their causal description. This is not the case. We see a larger cue-interaction effect for the 2C–1E scenario than for 2E–1C scenario. We also see from Experiment 3 that this sensitivity to causal asymmetry can change depending on what participants are asked about the events.

The results from Experiments 1–3 indicate that causal assessments are influenced by both the causal description and the associative nature of the events. Throughout the three experiments, participants' A ratings seem to be higher in the 2E–1C scenario when it is paired with a stronger Cue B (indicating their sensitivity to the causal structure of the events). This difference is especially pronounced in both the rating and integration data from Experiment 3 when participants are provided with an integrative question. On the other hand, the analyses reveal significant cue-interaction effects for both scenarios in Experiments 1 and 2. As well, participants' prediction response data indicate no sensitivity whatsoever to causal asymmetry (indicating their sensitivity to the associative structure of the events). This mixture of high- and low-level processing is consistent with the results from Tangen and Allan (2004) and Price and Yates (1995), who argue for the joint contribution of associative and causal factors in judgments of contingency.

Furthermore, as predicted by Tangen and Allan (in press), the balance of sensitivity to the associative and causal structure of the events can be shifted depending on what participants are asked about the events as indicated by the results from Experiment 3. Indeed, it seems as though assessing (in)sensitivity to causal asymmetry cannot be explained solely by an associative account or causal-model theory, but may be better explained in terms of their joint contribution.

## REFERENCES

Allan, L. G. (1993). Human contingency judgments: Rule based or associative? *Psychological Bulletin, 114*, 435–448.

Baker, A. G., Mercier, P., Vallée-Tourangeau, F., Frank, R., & Pan, M. (1993). Selective association and causality judgments: Presence of a strong causal factor may reduce judgments of a weaker one. *Journal of Experimental Psychology: Learning, Memory, and Cognition, 19,* 414–432.

Baker, A. G., Murphy, R. A., & Vallée-Tourangeau, F. (1996). Associative and normative models of cause. In D. R. Shanks, K. J. Holyoak, & D. L. Medin (Eds.), *The psychology of learning and motivation* (pp. 1–45). San Diego: Academic Press.

Chapman, G. B., & Robbins, S. J. (1990). Cue interaction in human contingency judgment. *Memory & Cognition, 18,* 537–545.

Cobos, P. L., López, F. J., Caño, A., Almaraz, J., & Shanks, D. R. (2002). Mechanisms of predictive and diagnostic causal induction. *Journal of Experimental Psychology: Animal Behavior Processes, 28,* 331–346.

Collins, D. J., & Shanks, D. R. (2002). Momentary and integrative response strategies in causal judgment. *Memory & Cognition, 30,* 1138–1147.

Dickinson, A., & Shanks, D. R. (1985). Animal learning and human causality judgment. In L. G. Nilson & T. Archer (Eds.), *Perspectives on learning and memory* (pp. 167–191). Hillsdale, NJ: Lawrence Erlbaum Associates.

Dickinson, A., Shanks, D. R., & Evenden, J. (1984). Judgment of act–outcome contingency: The role of selective attribution. *Quarterly Journal of Experimental Psychology, 36A,* 29–50.

Kamin, L. J. (1968). "Attention-like" processes in classical conditioning. In M. R. Jones (Ed.), *Miami symposium on the production of behavior: Aversive stimulation* (pp. 9–33). Miami, FL: University of Miami Press.

Kamin, L. J. (1969a). Predictability, surprise, attention, and conditioning. In B. A. Campbell & R. M. Church (Eds.), *Punishment and aversive behavior* (pp. 279–296). New York: Appleton–Century–Crofts.

Kamin, L. J. (1969b). Selective association and conditioning. In N. J. Mackintosh & W. K. Honig (Eds.), *Fundamental issues in associative learning* (pp. 42–64). Halifax, Nova Scotia, Canada: Dalhousie University Press.

López, F. J., Shanks, D. R., Almaraz, J., & Fernandez, P. (1998). Effects of trial order on contingency judgments: A comparison of associative and probabilistic contrast accounts. *Journal of Experimental Psychology: Learning, Memory, and Cognition, 24,* 672–694.

Matute, H., Arcediano, F., & Miller, R. R. (1996). Test question modulates cue competition between causes and between effects. *Journal of Experimental Psychology: Learning Memory, and Cognition, 22,* 182–196.

Mehta, R. R. (2000). *Contrasting associative and statistical theories of contingency judgments.* Unpublished doctoral dissertation, McGill University, Montreal, Quebec, Canada.

Miller, R. R., Barnet, R. C., & Grahame, N. J. (1995). Assessment of the Rescorla–Wagner model. *Psychological Bulletin, 117,* 363–386.

Price, P. C., & Yates, F. (1995). Associative and rule-based accounts of cue interaction in contingency judgment. *Journal of Experimental Psychology: Learning, Memory, and Cognition, 21,* 1639–1655.

Rescorla, R. A., & Wagner, A. R. (1972). A theory of Pavlovian conditioning: Variations in the effectiveness of reinforcement and non-reinforcement. In A. H. Black & W. F. Prokosy (Eds.), *Classical conditioning II: Current research and theory* (pp. 64–99). New York: Appleton–Century–Crofts.

Shanks, D. R. (1985). Forward and backward blocking in human contingency judgement. *Quarterly Journal of Experimental Psychology. B, Comparative and Physiological Psychology, 37B,* 1–21.

Shanks, D. R., & López, F. J. (1996). Causal order does not affect cue selection in human associative learning. *Memory & Cognition, 24,* 511–522.

Siegel, S., & Allan, L. G. (1996). The widespread influence of the Rescorla–Wagner model. *Psychological Bulletin and Review, 3,* 314–321.

Tangen, J. M., & Allan, L. G. (2003). The relative effect of cue-interaction. *Quarterly Journal of Experimental Psychology. B, Comparative and Physiological Psychology, 56B,* 279–300.

Tangen, J. M., & Allan, L. G. (2004). Cue-interaction and judgments of causality: Contributions of causal and associative processes. *Memory.& Cognition, 32,* 107–124.

Vallée-Tourangeau, F., Baker, A. G., & Mercier, P. (1994). Discounting in causality and covariation judgements. *Quarterly Journal of Experimental Psychology. B, Comparative and Physiological Psychology, 47B,* 151–171.

Van Hamme, L. J., Kao, S. F., & Wasserman, E. A. (1993). Judging interevent relations: From cause to effect and from effect to cause. *Memory & Cognition, 21,* 802–808.

Wagner, A. R., Logan, F. A., Haberlandt, K., & Price, T. (1968). Stimulus selection in animal discrimination learning. *Journal of Experimental Psychology, 76,* 171–180.

Waldmann, M. R. (2000). Competition among causes but not effects in predictive and diagnostic learning. *Journal of Experimental Psychology: Learning, Memory, and Cognition, 26,* 53–76.

Waldmann, M. R. (2001). Predictive versus diagnostic causal learning: Evidence from an overshadowing paradigm. *Psychonomic Bulletin and Review, 8,* 600–608.

Waldmann, M. R., & Hagmayer, Y. (1999). How categories shape causality. In M. Hahn & S. C. Stoness (Eds.), Proceedings of the twenty-first annual conference of the Cognitive Science Society (Vol. 82, pp. 761–766). Mahwah, NJ: Lawrence Erlbaum Associates.

Waldmann, M. R., & Hagmayer, Y. (2001). Estimating causal strength: The role of structural knowledge and processing effort. *Cognition, 82,* 27–58.

Waldmann, M. R., & Holyoak, K. J. (1990). Can causal induction be reduced to associative learning? In *Proceedings of the twelfth annual conference of the Cognitive Science Society* (pp. 190–197). Hillsdale, NJ: Lawrence Erlbaum Associates.

Waldmann, M. R., & Holyoak, K. J. (1992). Predictive and diagnostic learning within causal models: Asymmetries in cue competition. *Journal of Experimental Psychology: General, 121,* 222–236.

Waldmann, M. R., & Holyoak, K. J. (1997). Determining whether causal order affects cue selection in human contingency learning: Comments on Shanks and Lopez (1996). *Memory & Cognition, 25,* 125–134.

Waldmann, M. R., Holyoak, K. J., & Fratianne, A. (1995). Causal models and the acquisition of category structure. *Journal of Experimental Psychology: General, 124,* 181–206.

Wasserman, E. A. (1990). Attribution of causality to common and distinctive elements of compound stimuli. *Psychological Science, 1,* 298–302.

Williams, D. A. (1996). A comparative analysis of negative contingency learning in humans and nonhumans. In D. R. Shanks, K. J. Holyoak, & D. L. Medin (Eds.), *The psychology of learning and motivation* (pp. 89–125). San Diego: Academic Press.

## APPENDIX—CAUSAL MODEL PROMPTS

### 2C–1E

1. You are assessing how well each chemical causes the strain of bacteria to survive.
2. The two chemicals are causes and the bacteria is the effect.
3. Each of the two chemicals may have a positive, negative, or no influence on the survival of the bacteria.
4. Your job is to evaluate the extent to which each chemical aids in or interferes with the survival of the bacterial strain.
5. Consider the causal influence of each chemical on the survival of the bacteria.
6. The goal is to predict whether the bacterial strain will survive given the presence or absence of the chemicals.
7. You are trying to determine the influence of each chemical on the survival of the bacteria.
8. Think about the effect each chemical has on the bacterial strain.
9. Consider the causal strength of each chemical.
10. Try to judge the effectiveness of each chemical by its influence on the bacteria.
11. Keep in mind that each chemical affects the bacterial strain.
12. Decide the degree to which the bacterial strain depends on the addition of each chemical.
13. Try to keep track of what happens to the bacterial strain when one, both, or neither chemical was added.
14. Each chemical may cause the bacteria to survive more often, less often, or may have no influence on the strain's survival.
15. Evaluate the extent to which each chemical caused the strain of bacteria to survive.
16. Try to ascertain the causal influence of each chemical on the bacteria.

### 2E–1C

1. You are assessing how well the bacterial strain causes each of the two chemicals to be produced.
2. The bacteria is the cause and the two chemicals are the effects.
3. The bacteria may have a positive, negative, or no influence on the production of each chemical.
4. Your job is to evaluate the extent to which the bacterial strain aids in or interferes with the production of each chemical.
5. Consider the causal influence of the bacteria on the production of each chemical.
6. The goal is to diagnose whether the bacteria were added to the digestive system given the presence or absence of the chemicals.

7. You are trying to determine the influence of the bacteria on the production of the two chemicals.
8. Think about the effect the bacterial strain has on each chemical.
9. Consider the causal strength of the bacterial strain.
10. Try to judge the effectiveness of the bacteria by its influence on each chemical.
11. Keep in mind that the bacterial strain affects each chemical.
12. Decide the degree to which each chemical depends on the addition of the bacterial strain.
13. Try to keep track of whether one, both, or neither chemical was produced when the bacterial strain was added.
14. The bacteria may cause the production of each chemical more often, less often, or may have no influence on whether the chemical is produced.
15. Evaluate the extent to which the strain of bacteria caused each chemical to be produced.
16. Try to ascertain the causal influence of the bacteria on each chemical.

# Chapter 5

# Connectionist Models
# of Human Associative Learning

A. J. Wills

*Warning:* If you are new to the study of human associative learning and have skipped the first four chapters you're going to find the next four pretty tough. This is because all these chapters, particularly this one, draw on concepts introduced in chapters 1–4.

In chapter 1, I drew a distinction between two quite different concepts that sometimes both attract the term *associative learning*. On some occasions, "associative learning" is used to define a particular type of problem that an organism has to solve. On other occasions, "associative learning" is used as a theoretical statement about the sorts of mental processes by which the organism solves this type of problem.

## ASSOCIATIVE LEARNING → LEARNING OF ASSOCIATIONS

Let's consider "associative learning" as a problem definition first. In this sense of the term, "learning" refers to a relatively permanent change in response potentiality caused by information available from the organism's perceptual receptors. This rather technical definition is a variant of the definition offered by Reber (1985, p. 395).

Breaking this definition of "learning" down into its constituent components, "response potentiality" indicates that learning results in a potential to respond differently. Sometimes the organism actually will act differently. At other times, no immediate behavioral change is observed but evidence that learning has occurred emerges later. The use of "response potentiality" also underlines the important idea that learning is a hypothetical event for which behavior provides evidence.

The phrase "relatively permanent change" is intended to exclude various types of momentary changes in response potentiality. This is a fuzzy boundary, but changes in response potentiality that persist for no more than a few hundred milliseconds are not generally considered as "learning." The phrase "caused by information available from the organism's perceptual receptors" is a statement about the data upon which learning operates. "Perceptual receptors" indicates structures such as the retina, the cochlea, the somatosensory receptors, and so on. One important aspect of this definition is that it is not intended as a statement of process. Hence, no assumption is being made about an upper limit to the amount of processing that results from sensory information, the time course over which that happens, or the extent to which the learning process importantly involves integration with already learned information.

When "associative learning" is used as a definition of a type of problem facing an organism, the intent behind this phrase is perhaps better expressed as "the learning of one or more associations." The intent behind the term *association* is statistical; it is the extent to which changes in one environmental variable are related to changes in another. The provision of an appropriate statistical measure of association is not a trivial problem. For example, one is likely to use a different measure depending on whether a predictive or correlational relation is being considered. A predictive relation has a particular direction. For example, if you know a car has a dead battery you can predict pretty reliably that the car will not start. However, if a car will not start, you should be much less confident about predicting the presence of a dead battery. Delta P (chaps. 2 & 4) is one example of a measure of a predictive associative relationship. In contrast, a correlational relationship as measured by, for example, Pearson's *r* is bidirectional. Even within these two classes (predictive and correlational) the choice of statistic is not straightforward. Recall, for example, from chapter 2 that the delta P and PowerPC equations provide two different potential measures of the strength of a predictive relationship.

## ASSOCIATIVE LEARNING → CONNECTIONISM

Now let's turn to the usage of "associative learning" in the sense of a class of theory about the processes involved in the "learning of associations." Here we can haul ourselves out of the linguistic treacle by using the term *connectionism*. As I said in chapter 1, there is an unfortunate tendency when discussing the history of psychology to assume that connectionism started in 1986 with the publication of the PDP manuals (Rumelhart, McClelland, & The PDP Research Group, 1986). These manuals undoubtedly had an enormous impact; they encouraged the mainstream of human cognitive psychology to reconsider the usefulness of connectionism as a theoretical system. However, connectionism is much more than 20 years old. The word *connectionism* can be traced back at least as far as Thorndike (1898), whereas the development of associationism can be traced from Aristotle, through the British Empiricists (e.g., Hume, 1739/1978), to Ebbinghaus (1885/1913) and Pavlov (1909/1928) and, from there, throughout the 20th century.

Connectionism is a theoretical approach that assumes learning results from the formation of connections between representations. These representations (often called "nodes") have a variable level of activation. The activation of a node is passed through all of its outward connections to other nodes, hence determining the activity level of those nodes. The connections between nodes have a variable "strength" or "weight." The stronger the connection, the more efficient it is at transmitting activation. The strength of connections is changed by a learning algorithm. Many different learning algorithms have been proposed, the simplest of which is probably the Hebbian algorithm (Hebb, 1949). In Hebbian learning, the connection weight between two representations increases if they are cojointly active.

For many, one of the appeals of a connectionist approach is that it appears to be a simplified model of the action of neurons. This perhaps gives the potential, in the long term, for more unified accounts of the human mind that incorporate both physiological and psychological observations. On the other hand, one of the most commonly used learning algorithms (Rumelhart, Hinton, & Williams, 1986) allows information to travel in both directions down the same connections; something that given our current understanding of neurophysiology seems rather unlikely. So, whereas some theorists do see the integration of physiology and psychology as an important goal, to others the neuron is more like a descriptive metaphor for the operations of a connectionist system. The implication of this must be that connectionist theories have (at least perceived) virtues other than the potential to integrate physiology and psychology.

Probably the other main appeal of connectionist models is the level of specificity that is gained. A theory expressed in connectionist terms seems to leave much less room for ambiguity and interpretation than a theory expressed in more informal terms. One example of an informally expressed theory is Alan Baddeley's visuo-spatial sketchpad (see, e.g., Baddeley, 1986). Yet, a theory can clearly reach a high level of mathematical specificity without being connectionist. For example, Ashby's accounts of categorical decisions (e.g., Ashby, 2000) are expressed specifically and mathematically but are not connectionist. Connectionist accounts can even have certain pragmatic disadvantages compared to some other kinds of mathematical model. For example, deriving predictions from connectionist systems can become quite involved because they are generally nonlinear systems (which makes the mathematics more complex). For similar reasons, it can also be difficult to determine whether a particular behavior of a connectionist system is a general property of the model or whether it is parameter-specific. Such complexity may be necessary to explain human behavior but it is not, in itself, a virtue.

Probably the best way to consider connectionist systems are as theoretical accounts that have a high level of specificity while simultaneously taking into account certain basic principles of neural function. It is this combination that presumably leads to their continued popularity.

## OUTLINE OF THIS SECTION

The following three chapters are examples of how connectionist models can be employed as theories of human associative learning. All three chapters are broadly similar in approach, probably because four of the five authors have worked closely with each other for some years (Mark Suret, Mike Le Pelley, and I were all members of Ian McLaren's research group for a number of years during the period 1994–2003). As a result of these close links, the level of agreement across these chapters is greater than it is across the field of connectionist modeling of human associative learning as a whole.

Chapter 6 starts with an introduction to connectionism and describes the Hebbian learning algorithm alluded to in the previous section. Jan and I then continue with a consideration of how connectionist systems account for the learning that undoubtedly can occur in the absence of feedback. We then consider the Rescorla–Wagner rule (Rescorla & Wagner, 1972) but, in contrast to previous chapters, the concentration is on the general strengths and limitations of the rule as an algorithm for learning from feedback, rather than on its ability to predict specific experimental results. Next, Jan and I make a case for the need to combine feedback and no-feedback learning systems. A simple integrated model is proposed as one example of how this could be done, and is tested against the results of a novel experiment. The chapter closes with a consideration of some of the more obvious limitations of the integrated model proposed.

Chapter 7 reprises the Rescorla–Wagner model, this time drawing attention to its prediction that all cues present on a given trial are subject to the same change in associative strength (assuming the cues are of equal salience). Following a very elegant demonstration by Rescorla (2000) that this is not the case for rats, Mike and Ian demonstrate that it is also not true for humans performing an allergy prediction task. They then introduce their APECS model—a different type of connectionist system—and show that it can predict the results found. Next, they demonstrate the presence, in humans, of a related effect with absent-but-expected, rather than present, cues (retrospective revaluation, see chap. 3). The APECS model is also able to predict these entirely novel results. Finally they present a study (based on work by Lochmann & Wills, 2003) that indicates that the APECS model needs to be modified to explain certain predictive history effects. Predictive history is the idea that cues that have a history of being predictive form associations more quickly than those that have a history of being nonpredictive, even when the outcomes being learned about are novel.

In order to explain the results found, Mike and Ian suggest the adoption of the associability change processes proposed by Nick Mackintosh

(1975). The basic idea is that, in addition to their variable activity, nodes representing stimuli have a variable "associability" that modulates the rate at which associative links from this node change in strength. In the Mackintosh system, if a stimulus is a good predictor its associability increases whereas if it is a poor predictor its associability decreases.

In chapter 8, Mark and Ian continue the theme of associability processes. They start by introducing Lawrence's (1952) "Transfer along a continuum" (TAC) finding with rats. TAC, roughly stated, is a demonstration that training on an easy discrimination (e.g., black vs. white) before transferring to a difficult discrimination (e.g., light gray vs. dark gray) can result in better performance on the "hard" discrimination than an equivalent amount of training on the "hard" discrimination from the outset. The basic result can be explained without recourse to the concept of associability. However, a more sophisticated version of the experiment, again performed with rats (Mackintosh & Little, 1970), seems to require some kind of associability process. Mark and Ian demonstrate that effects analogous to those found by Mackintosh and Little can also be found in humans. They then go on to demonstrate how the McLaren and Mackintosh (2000, 2002) connectionist model can be modified to include the sort of associability process originally proposed by Mackintosh some 25 years earlier. They also demonstrate that this modified model can reproduce in detail the patterns of results found in their human experiments.

## REFERENCES

Ashby, F. G. (2000). A stochastic version of general recognition theory. *Journal of Mathematical Psychology, 44,* 310–329.

Baddeley, A. (1986). *Working memory.* New York: Oxford University Press.

Ebbinghaus, H. (1913). *Über das Gedächtnis* (H. Ruyer & C. E. Bussenius, Trans.). New York: Teachers College, Columbia University. (Original work published 1885)

Hebb, D. O. (1949). *The organization of behavior.* New York: Wiley.

Hume, D. (1978). *A treatise of human nature.* New York: Oxford University Press. (Original work published 1739)

Lawrence, D. H. (1952). The transfer of a discrimination along a continuum. *Journal of Comparative and Physiological Psychology, 45,* 511–516.

Lochmann, T., & Wills, A. J. (2003). Predictive history in an allergy prediction task. In F. Schmalhofer, R. M. Young, & G. Katz (Eds.), *Proceedings of EuroCogSci03: The European Cognitive Science Conference* (pp. 217–222). Mahwah, NJ: Lawrence Erlbaum Associates.

Mackintosh, N. J. (1975). A theory of attention: Variations in the associability of stimuli with reinforcement. *Psychological Review, 82,* 276–298.

Mackintosh, N. J., & Little, L. (1970). An analysis of transfer along a continuum. *Canadian Journal of Psychology, 24,* 362–369.

McLaren, I. P. L., & Mackintosh, N. J. (2000). An elemental model of associative learning: I. Latent inhibition and perceptual learning. *Animal Learning & Behavior, 28*(3), 211–246.

McLaren, I. P. L., & Mackintosh, N. J. (2002). An elemental model of associative learning: II. Generalization and discrimination. *Animal Learning & Behavior*, *30*, 177–200.

Pavlov, I. P. (1928). Natural science and the brain. In W. H. Gantt (Ed.), *Lectures on conditioned reflexes* (Vol. 1, pp. 120–130). London: Lawrence & Wishart. (Original work published 1909)

Reber, A. S. (1985). *Dictionary of psychology*. London: Penguin.

Rescorla, R. A. (2000). Associative changes in excitors and inhibitors differ when they are conditioned in compound. *Journal of Experimental Psychology: Animal Behavior Processes*, *26*, 428–438.

Rescorla, R. A., & Wagner, A. R. (1972). A theory of Pavlovian conditioning: Variations in the effectiveness of reinforcement and nonreinforcement. In A. H. Black & W. F. Prokasy (Eds.), *Classical conditioning II: Current research* (pp. 64–99). New York: Appleton–Century–Crofts.

Rumelhart, D. E., Hinton, G. E., & Williams, R. J. (1986). Learning internal representations by error propagation. In D. E. Rumelhart & J. L. McClelland (Eds.), *Parallel distributed processing: Explorations in the microstructure of cognition* (Vol. 1, pp. 318–362). Cambridge, MA: MIT Press.

Rumelhart, D. E., McClelland, J. L., & The PDP Research Group. (1986). *Parallel distributed processing*. Cambridge, MA: MIT Press.

Thorndike, E. L. (1898). Animal intelligence: An experimental study of the associative processes in animals. *Psychological Review, 8*.

# Chapter 6

# Integrating Associative Models of Supervised and Unsupervised Categorization

Jan Zwickel and A. J. Wills

Categorization—dividing the world into groups of things—is one of the core mechanisms behind many cognitive abilities. Categorization enables people to cope with the otherwise overwhelming complexity of objects and situations by reducing information. It also allows people to generate predictions by generalizing what they already know to novel situations. For example, if you meet, say, a new doctor, you can make certain inferences about how they will act based on what you already know about the category "doctor." As two situations are rarely (if ever) identical such an ability seems essential to everyday life. On the other hand, overgeneralization can be problematic. For example, it might be useful to have a "cat" category that covers both your own pet and other similar animals. It would, however, be potentially disastrous if you generalized what you knew about this category to the first lion you met.

Most of the psychological research into our ability to categorize has employed a *supervised learning* paradigm (e.g., Bruner, Goodnow, & Austin, 1956; Gluck & Bower, 1988; Medin & Schaffer, 1978). Prototypically, supervised learning assumes the presence of a perfect teacher, who observes *every* category choice and provides correct feedback on *every* decision (i.e., which category was the correct one to choose). This technique has undoubtedly revealed important information about the psychological processes of categorization. Nevertheless, it seems unlikely that this level of information is commonly available outside of the laboratory.

*Free classification*, which can also be described as *unsupervised learning*, is a methodology that goes to the opposite extreme. Participants are typically asked to partition stimuli into groups that seem reasonable or "natural" to them (e.g., Ahn & Medin, 1992; Bersted, Brown, & Evans,

1969; Medin, Wattenmaker, & Hampson, 1987; Wills & McLaren, 1998). No feedback on categorization decisions is given.

In this chapter, we describe three basic associative theories of learning as they might be applied to the problem of category learning. First, we describe *Hebbian learning*, which was one of the earliest formal associative theories of learning. Second, we describe *competitive learning*, which can, in some ways, been seen as a development of Hebbian learning, and is a theory of *unsupervised learning*. Next, we describe the *Rescorla–Wagner* theory, which is a theory of *supervised learning*. We then argue that there is a need for a mechanism that can use feedback when it is available (supervised learning) but will continue to learn if feedback is absent (unsupervised learning). We propose a possible mechanism that involves adding certain aspects of the Rescorla–Wagner theory to competitive learning. Our proposed system makes a clear prediction about people's behavior in a free-classification task, and we describe how we have begun to test that prediction. The chapter ends with a consideration of other theoretical approaches to the problem of category learning, both within the domain of associative learning and more generally.

## HEBBIAN LEARNING AND AN INTRODUCTION TO CONNECTIONISM

Hebb (1949) postulated that "when an axon of cell A is near enough to excite a cell B and repeatedly or persistently takes part in firing it, some growth process or metabolic change takes place in one or both cells such that A's efficiency, as one of the cells firing B, is increased" (p. 62). One way of expressing *Hebbian* learning formally is shown in Equation 6.1:

$$\Delta w_{ij} = G a_i a_j \qquad (6.1)$$

where $a_i$ and $a_j$ are the activities of two different neurons, $i$ and $j$, $\Delta w_{ij}$ is the change in strength of the connection $w_{ij}$ between neuron $i$ and neuron $j$, and $G$ is a parameter that affects the rate of learning. For simplicity, let's assume that $a_i$ and $a_j$ can take only values of 0 and 1. If $a_i$ and $a_j$ are both 1, then the connection strength increases by $G$. However, if either $i$ or $j$ is not active, the equation is zero and the connection strength doesn't change. By this equation, strong connections are developed between neurons that are active at the same time and weak connections between neurons that seldom fire together.

Hebbian learning has the potential to acquire the sort of information we need to learn categories. For example, imagine a situation where neuron $i$ represents a feature of a category, and neuron $j$ represents the category label. If feature $i$ is typical of category $j$ then a strong link will form between the two, and so a novel object that has feature $i$ is likely (other things being equal) to be categorized as a member of group $j$. However, it's worth making clear at this point that we are not assuming there is necessarily a *single* neuron that uniquely represents, say, the category "football player." This may be the case, or it might be that categories are represented as a pattern of activity distributed over many neurons (see Page, 2000, for an excellent review of this issue).

In what follows, the neuron or neurons that represent a stimulus feature are called an *input unit* and the neuron or neurons that represent a category are called an *output unit*. The strength of the connection between an input unit and an output unit represents the strength of the learned association between a stimulus feature and a category. The set of input units, output units, and the connections between them is described as a connectionist, or neural, network.

## COMPETITIVE LEARNING

This section is an introduction to competitive networks as a model of unsupervised category learning. In an unsupervised category-learning situation, stimuli are presented but the category membership of those stimuli is not given. The network must therefore decide which category the stimulus belongs to. One way of doing this is to assume that the output unit made most active by the presentation of the stimulus is the one that represents the category.

In a standard competitive network (and many other kinds of networks), the activity of an output unit is the sum of the activities of the input units multiplied by the connection weights from the inputs units to the output unit. Formally,

$$O_j = \sum_i a_i w_{ij} \qquad (6.2)$$

where $o_j$ is the activity of output unit $j$, $a_i$ is the activation of input unit $i$, and $w_{ij}$ is the connection strength between input unit $i$ and the output unit $j$.

Assuming that connection strengths start with random values, it is likely that the first stimulus presented will make one of the output units more active than any of the others. Under competitive learning, this output unit is considered the "winner" and its activity is set to one. The activity of all other output units is set to zero. A learning rule can then be applied. For example, if one applies Hebbian learning, the connection strengths between the active input units and the winning output units would be increased. All other connection strengths would remain unchanged.

Through the application of a learning rule such as Hebbian learning, the winning output unit comes to more strongly represent the presented stimulus, and hence is more likely to win again if a similar stimulus is presented in the future (similar in the sense of having many features in common). However, if a substantially different stimulus is presented, it is possible that a different output unit will win. In turn, that output unit will begin, through the action of the learning rule, to more strongly represent this substantially different stimulus and those similar to it. The system has therefore begun to develop the ability to categorize, despite the absence of external information about category membership.

One problem with using basic Hebbian learning in this way is that, in practice, one output unit can often end up representing all the stimuli. In an attempt to reduce this problem, Rumelhart and Zipser (1986) introduced further competition between the output units by introducing a limit on the sum of all connection strengths to any given output unit. This means that, after a certain point, the only way a connection strength to a particular output unit can increase is if other connection strengths to that output unit decrease. This encourages output units to specialize on different kinds of feature patterns.

Rumelhart and Zipser restrict the maximum level of connection strengths by assuming the presence of a kind of "decay" process that operates every time the connection strengths are changed. Formally, if unit $j$ loses,

$$\Delta w_{ij} = 0 \qquad (6.3a)$$

and hence connection strengths to losing output units remains unchanged but, if unit $j$ wins then

$$\Delta w_{ij} = G\frac{a_i}{n} - Gw_{ij} \qquad (6.3b)$$

where $G$ is again a learning parameter, $a_i$ is one if input unit $i$ is active but zero otherwise, and $n$ is the number of active input units. Note that the inclusion of $n$ means that the increase in connection strength is greater the fewer the number of active input units. This compensates an output unit that is supported by few input neurons.

Equations 6.3a and 6.3b implement a mechanism similar but not identical to Hebbian learning. If input unit $i$ is active when the winning unit is active, the connection strengths increase. However, the connection strengths also decay a bit because of the last term of Equation 6.3b. Inclusion of the connection strength $w_{ij}$ in that decay process means that strong connections decay more rapidly than weak connections. If input unit $i$ is not active, then there is no increase in connection strength. However, the decay process ($-Gw_{ij}$) still operates. One outcome of the learning rules expressed in Equations 6.3a and 6.3b is that, once the sum of connection strengths to a given output node reaches 1 it stays there—further learning can only redistribute the total weight across different connections.

Competitive networks suffer from a fundamental limitation. If the task is learning to partition patterns into groups on the basis of overall similarity (measured in terms of feature overlap), then competitive learning may succeed. However, if the task requires overall similarity to be ignored and category responses to be made on the basis of a particular subset of features, then competitive learning will necessarily fail. For example, imagine that you have three objects in front of you to put into two groups—a newspaper, a beer bottle, and a plastic bottle. In terms of overall similarity, the two bottles seem likely to form one category and the newspaper another. However, if the task requires you to separate the items into "recyclable" and "nonrecyclable" then (in some districts), the newspaper and the glass bottle go into the recycling bin, but the plastic bottle goes into the landfill bill.

How could a neural network create a different grouping than one that is based on overall similarity? One possible solution is feedback. Feedback provides information from outside, enriches gathered information, and thereby changes the priority of different features through the knowledge of an "expert." This external knowledge is not commonly used in a competitive network; it is the realm of another class of networks that engage in *supervised* learning. In the next section, we consider one such theory.

## THE RESCORLA–WAGNER MODEL (OR DELTA RULE)

The Rescorla–Wagner model (Rescorla & Wagner, 1972) was developed in the domain of animal-learning theory, although similar models can be traced back to Widrow and Hoff's (1960) work on electronic switching circuits. In connectionist modeling, the model is often referred to as the delta rule.

Roughly speaking, the model works in the following way. After a stimulus is presented, the model predicts whether or not an outcome will occur. The environment then provides the model with feedback about whether the predicted outcome did in fact occur. If the model made the correct prediction then it assumes there is no need for further learning. However, if there is a discrepancy between the model's prediction and the feedback, learning takes place by adjusting connection strengths. These are adjusted in a manner that should reduce the error in future. How does the model achieve this? In what follows we describe the model in terms as similar as possible to those used in our description of competitive learning. As a result, the terminology is more similar to that used in connectionist modeling than that originally used by Rescorla and Wagner. The basic concepts, however, remain unchanged.

The model has, as before, a set of input units and a set of output units and associative connections from the former to the latter. As with competitive networks, the activity of an output unit is the sum of the activities of input units multiplied by their corresponding connection strengths. The learning rule works in the following way. If output unit $j$ should (on the basis of feedback) be highly active, but the activation coming from the input units is insufficient, the connection strengths from active input units increase. On the other hand, if output unit $j$ should not be active, but activation is coming from the input units, then the connection strengths between active input units and output unit $j$ is reduced. Formally, the change in connection strength between input unit $i$ and output unit $j$ is

$$\Delta w_{ij} = G\left(\lambda_j - \sum_k a_k w_{kj}\right)a_i \tag{6.4}$$

where $a_i$ represents the activity of input unit $i$, $\lambda_j$ represents the correct activation of the output unit $j$, provided by the feedback from the environment, and $k$ sums over all input units. The term in parentheses denotes the difference between the model's prediction and the feedback. This difference is weighted by the activation of the input unit—only active input units can drive changes in connection strength in this system. Stone (1986) demonstrates that the delta rule essentially carries out the equivalent of multiple linear regression.

The delta rule is at the heart of many models of supervised categorization (e.g., Gluck & Bower, 1988; Kruschke, 1996; McClelland & Rumelhart, 1985). In this section, we outline one simple way in which it can be used, based closely on Gluck and Bower's work.

In the system we consider, features of objects are represented by input units and categories are represented by output units. Input units have an activity of one if the feature they represent is present, and zero otherwise. The output unit representing the correct category is assumed to have a $\lambda$ of one, whereas all other category units have a $\lambda$ of zero.

The system as described has two well-known properties (see, e.g., Minsky & Papert, 1969). First, if there is a configuration of connection strengths that yields all the right answers, the delta rule is guaranteed to find it. Second, there are a number of problems that the delta rule, in this form, is unable to learn. For example, it cannot learn the exclusive-or (XOR) problem. In the XOR problem, there are two input units and one output unit. If just one of those input units is active, then the output unit should be active. However, if both input units are active or inactive, then the output unit should be inactive. For example, when playing a simple card game, you may be able "stick" or "twist," but you have to do one of the two and you can't do both. If "stick" was represented by one input unit and "twist" by another, the delta rule could never learn which of the four possible responses (stick, twist, stick & twist, neither) were allowed. This is because it needs to form a positive connection between "twist" and "allowed," and also between "stick" and "allowed," so stick and twist together would inevitably result in the response "allowed."

The XOR problem can be solved by introducing a different coding scheme; more specifically one can introduce input units that represent the combination of features. These kind of models are commonly referred to as configural cue or unique cue models (Gluck, 1991; Rescorla, 1973). In our card game example, this would mean a third input unit that represents "stick and twist" that is only active when both the "stick" and the "twist" input units are active. This "stick and twist" unit could then form a strong negative connection to the "allowed" output unit. Together with weaker positive connections from "stick" to "allowed" and "twist" to "allowed," the system could solve this XOR problem. This solution effectively involves turning the XOR problem into a different problem that the network can solve.

Another solution to the XOR problem is to introduce a layer of units between the input and output units. These are generally described as "hidden" units and they allow the network to recode the input it receives. For example, it is possible to create a hidden unit that is active only when both input units are active. If this hidden unit has a sufficiently strong *negative* connection to the output unit, then the output unit's activity will be close to zero when both input units are active (the input units will increase the activity of the output unit, but this will be offset by the reduction in activity caused by the hidden unit).

The delta rule needs to be modified before one can apply it to a system with hidden units. This is because the environment provides no direct information about what the "correct" activity of a hidden unit should be, so the error $(\lambda - \Sigma aw)$ for a hidden unit does not have an obvious value. One solution is to calculate the error for output units as normal and then pass that error to the hidden units via the connections between the two. This solution is often described as "back–propagation" and is described in detail by Rumelhart, Hinton and Williams (1986). The history of this back-propagation algorithm can be traced back to Werbos (1974).

The back-propagation system has a number of well-known properties, three of which we consider here because they highlight how the system differs from a simpler delta-rule system with no hidden layer. First, Hornik, Stinchcombe, and White (1989) demonstrated that a delta-rule network with a hidden layer is a universal function approximator. Roughly speaking, this means that if there is a stable relationship between the input patterns and the output patterns, then there is a hidden-layer network with a particular pattern of connection strengths that can reproduce it. This contrasts starkly with the simple delta-rule system, which has clear limitations to the patterns it can reproduce.

A second well-known property of back-propagation is that, although there is always a pattern of connection strengths in some hidden-layer network that will reproduce any given function, back-propagation is not guaranteed to find it. Instead it may, during the course of learning, get stuck in what are described as *local minima*. Roughly speaking, this is where the network finds itself in a position where its current performance is not correct but where any small change in connection strengths makes its performance worse than it already is. This again puts back-propagation into stark contrast with the simple delta-rule system, which will always find the solution if one exists.

Back-propagation is also generally considered to be a neurally implausible system. In other words, given what we currently know about the brain, it seems unlikely that neurons could engage in the sorts of processes back-propagation requires. Again, this is in stark contrast to the simple delta-rule system, which can be constructed from the known properties of neurons (see McLaren, 1989).

## INTEGRATING SUPERVISED AND UNSUPERVISED LEARNING

So far, we have discussed one model of learning in unsupervised situations (competitive learning) and a different model of learning in supervised situations (the Rescorla–Wagner model). In this section, we consider the merits of integrated theories that can learn in both supervised and unsupervised situations.

Why is the integration of supervised and unsupervised learning desirable? This is most easily illustrated by considering the alternative, which is that the learner must determine in advance whether to engage in supervised or unsupervised learning. If the world was neatly and predictably divided into situations where no feedback is ever received and situations where feedback is always received, then this might not be too much of a problem. However, it seems likely that for most situations feedback is received sporadically and not entirely predictably. One would therefore be likely to encounter the joint problems of ignoring available feedback and failing to learn anything when feedback is unexpectedly absent. There are also potential issues of how information gained by the supervised and unsupervised systems would be integrated.

Another reason why the integration of supervised and unsupervised learning might be desirable is that it reduces the number of theories needed to explain learning. Following the reasoning of Occam (a medieval monk), scientists often argue that if you have a choice between two explanations, both of which explain the available data, you should pick the simpler ("Occam's razor"). It's our contention that the integrated theory we discuss next is a simpler explanation than one that posits separate systems for supervised and unsupervised learning.

## AN INTEGRATED MODEL

In the following, we show one way in which a simple associative model of supervised learning (a single-layer delta-rule network) can be integrated with a simple associative model of unsupervised learning (a Rumelhart and Zipser competitive network). Our approach was to start with the delta-rule system and consider how it could be modified to also account for situations where feedback is missing. When feedback is present, the delta rule tries to minimize the difference between the feedback ($\lambda$) and the prediction delivered by the weights ($\Sigma aw$). One way to generalize this principle to situations where feedback is absent is for the network to produce its own feedback signal, which we designate as $\lambda'$. If feedback is present, $\lambda'$ is determined by that feedback. However, when feedback is absent $\lambda'$ is set to one for the most active output unit and zero for all other output units (an idea borrowed from competitive learning). Such a system does not need to know in advance whether feedback is going to occur, and could be implemented by introducing fixed inhibitory links between the output units (see Wills, Reimers, Stewart, Suret, & McLaren, 2000, for an example of this type of decision mechanism).

Allowing the delta-rule system to generate its own feedback in this way provides a potential integrated model of supervised and unsupervised learning. However, from our earlier discussion of competitive learning it seems likely that such a system would suffer from a potentially serious problem. Like a competitive system with Hebbian learning, there is a real danger that in unsupervised situations one output unit could come to represent all presented stimuli. This is because there are only very rarely situations where stimuli from different categories have absolutely nothing in common. If stimuli from different categories have some common features, then the "winner" of the first stimulus has an advantage when the second stimulus is applied, due to its stronger connections to the features the first and second stimuli have in common.

Rumelhart and Zipser (1986) included further sources of competition besides the "winner-take-all" competition in an attempt to reduce this problem, and we modified the delta rule in a similar way. Specifically, we modified the delta rule so that it included a sort of weight decay process and a process that scales weight changes by the number of active input units. Hence, our modified delta rule is

$$\Delta w_{ij} = G\left(\lambda'_j - \sum_k a_k w_{kj}\right)\frac{a_i}{n} - G\left(\lambda'_j - \sum_k a_i w_{kj}\right)w_{ij} \qquad (6.5)$$

where $G$ is a learning rate parameter, $n$ is the number of active input units, $a_i$ is the activity of input unit $i$, $w_{ij}$ is the connection strength from input unit $i$ to winning output unit $j$, and $\lambda'$ is the internally generated feedback signal discussed earlier. $k$ sums over all input units.

All that we've done here is add the error-correcting component of the delta rule ($\lambda' - \Sigma aw$) to Rumelhart and Zipser's learning algorithm (Equation 6.3b). As a result, this integrated model makes predictions about unsupervised learning that differ from those made by Rumelhart and Zipser's competitive learning system. Specifically, our system adds the constraint that connection strengths will change only if the internal feedback signal $\lambda'$ is not fully predicted by the network (i.e., if $\lambda' - \Sigma aw$ does not equal zero). This leads to the prediction that effects such as *blocking* (described in the next section) should be observable in unsupervised learning. In contrast, Rumelhart and Zipser's model predicts that blocking will not be observed in unsupervised learning because their learning rule is a variant of Hebbian learning and hence contains no error-correcting component. In later sections, we report data that indicates blocking does occur in free classification, and discuss simulations that show that our system can predict blocking in free classification but that the Rumelhart and Zipser system cannot. In the next section we provide a very brief outline of the phenomenon of blocking for the benefit of those who are not familiar with it.

## BLOCKING

The term *blocking* was coined by Kamin (1969) to describe a phenomenon he observed in rats. In Kamin's experiment, rats learned in an initial phase that pressing a bar leads to a food pellet. After this contingency was established, the first phase started. In the first phase, a noise was sometimes presented. When the noise was on, the rat received an electric shock. Rats quickly suppressed responding in the presence of the noise, as measured by frequency of pressing the bar. In the second phase, the noise was always accompanied by a light. When the noise and the light were on, the rats got shocked. Again, the rats avoided pressing the bar during presentations of the noise–light compound. In the final phase, the light was presented alone, and Kamin found that the rats did not suppress responding in the presence of the light. In other words, the rats appeared not to have learned the association between light and shock.

Kamin also ran a control group of rats. The control group was identical to the experimental group with one exception–the control group skipped the first phase (noise only). In the final phase, the control group showed strong suppression in response to the light, thereby indicating that they had learned the connection between the light and the shock in the second phase. Table 6.1 summarizes the design of Kamin's experiment.

How might this difference between the control and experimental groups be explained? Kamin's explanation employed the notion of "surprise." The experimental group had learned that the noise predicts shock in the first phase. Therefore, the shock was not surprising in the second phase. According to Kamin, learning only occurs if the outcome is surprising, so the rats didn't learn the connection between the light and the shock. However, the control group skipped the first phase and therefore was surprised in the second phase by the shock. Consequentially in the second phase, the rats learned the connection between the light and the shock as well.

### TABLE 6.1
### Kamin's (1969) Blocking Experiment

| Group | Stage One | Stage Two | Test |
|---|---|---|---|
| Experimental | N → Shock | LN → Shock | L |
| Control | | LN → Shock | L |

*Note.* "L" denotes a light, "N" a noise.

The delta rule predicts that blocking should occur. Consider a simple representation of the problem where one input unit represents "tone," another "light," and an output unit represents "shock." There are connections from the input units to the output units, which start at zero. Assuming sufficient training, Phase 1 leads to the connection strength between the "tone" input unit and the "shock" output unit being close to $\lambda$. Therefore, in Phase 2 when both the "tone" and "light" input units are active and a shock occurs, there is only a very small error ($\lambda - \Sigma aw$) at the "shock" output unit because $\Sigma aw$ is close to $\lambda$. This means that the connection strength between the "light" and "shock" units cannot increase substantially, leading to blocking. However, if the first stage is skipped the initial error when the tone and light are presented together is high, so substantial connections form from both input units to the output unit.

Evidence for blocking can also be found in humans. For example, Dickinson, Shanks, and Evenden (1984) demonstrated a blocking effect in the context of a simple computer game. The game involved tanks driving through an invisible minefield. In the experimental condition, participants first experienced an "observation" phase, where they were asked to observe a number of occasions of a tank driving through the minefield and either blowing up or not. Following this, the participants were given the opportunity to shoot at the tanks. Finally, they were asked to rate the effectiveness of the gun in destroying the tanks. In the control condition, the initial observation phase was omitted. Participants in the experimental condition gave lower ratings of the gun's effectiveness than participants in the control condition did. For the experimental group, the development of a "minefield" $\rightarrow$ "tank explodes" association in the observation phase blocks the development of a "gun fired" $\rightarrow$ "tank explodes" association in the second phase.

The demonstration of blocking in humans is not limited to this kind of "ratings" task. For example, Martin and Levy (1991) demonstrated blocking in human eyelid conditioning.

## EXPERIMENT

The purpose of our experiment was to demonstrate an effect analogous to blocking in the absence of feedback. Previous research demonstrates that category learning can proceed successfully in the absence of feedback (e.g., Homa & Cultice, 1984; Wills & McLaren, 1998). Additionally, the current study follows on from Zwickel and Wills's (2002) demonstration of a blocking-like effect in a situation where some feedback was present, but it was very sparse and not item specific.

The design of the current experiment is shown in Table 6.2; the letters indicate sets of features that make up the abstract stimuli we presented. In Phase 1, examples of Category 1 were created from a base pattern that contained feature sets A and B. Examples of Category 2 were created from a base pattern that contained feature sets C and D.

TABLE 6.2

Experimental Design

| | Phase 1 | Phase 2 | Test |
|---|---|---|---|
| Category 1 | AB | A<u>E</u> | |
| | | | <u>E</u>F |
| Category 2 | CD | GF | |

*Note.* Each letter represents a set of six features. For example, Category 2 in Phase 2 contains feature sets G and F. The redundant feature set E is underlined.

Note that the labels Category 1 and Category 2 are essentially arbitrary in a free-classification task—they could be reversed without changing anything in the design or execution of the experiment. As Table 6.2 illustrates, once the participant had mastered the AB versus CD categorization they were transferred to a second categorization. The testing phase started after the participants had mastered this second categorization. The datum of central importance in this design is the category to which the test stimulus presented in the test phase is allocated. The response to a single stimulus is chosen as the dependent variable because subsequent decisions may be contaminated by learning on previous test trials.

Note that feature set E occurs only in situations where the information it provides is redundant. In Phase 2 the stimuli can be identified as Category 1 on the basis of whether they contain "A" features—an association already learned in Phase 1. Hence, through analogy to selective learning effects in tasks with feedback, one might consider that E develops little control over responding. In contrast, G and F may develop more control over responding as they are the only features in Phase 2 that predict the presence of a Category 2 stimulus. If blocking occurs in free classification, one would therefore expect participants to place stimulus EF into Category 2 (i.e., the same category as they used for stimulus GF). This is because F's association to Category 2 is predicted to be greater than E's association to Category 1, due to E, but not F, being blocked.

## Method

*Participants and Apparatus.* Thirty-two psychology students from the University of Heidelberg participated to fulfill partial course requirements or for a small reward. Participants were tested in groups in a quiet computer room. Stimulus presentation was on color monitors connected to standard PCs running the DMDX software package (Forster & Forster, 2003). Responses were collected via the left and right CTRL keys on standard PC keyboards.

*Stimuli.*   Each stimulus was made up of 12 small pictures (hereafter "elements") taken from a set of 72 that have been used in a number of previous experiments (e.g., Jones, Wills, & McLaren, 1998). See Fig. 6.1 for an example stimulus. For any given stimulus, the 12 elements were randomly arranged in a square of three rows with 4 elements in each row, and were surrounded by a gray rectangle outline 5 cm in height and 4 cm in width. Each of the letters A to G in Table 6.2 represents a set of six elements. The stimuli actually presented to participants were generated by random distortion of the base patterns described in Table 6.2. Each element in a base pattern was given a 10% chance of being replaced by a randomly selected element from the other base pattern. An example may be helpful. To create an AB stimulus in Phase 1, the six A elements and the six B elements were randomly arranged in the four-by-three grid of the stimulus. Each element was then given a 10% chance of being replaced by a randomly selected element from set C or D. This method of stimulus construction produces training examples that are composed predominantly of elements characteristic of a particular category but that also exhibit considerable variability.

In order to control for effects of the differential salience of the elements, participants were divided into pairs. The assignment of picture elements

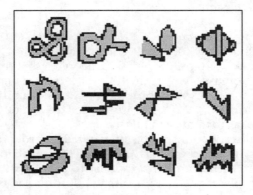

FIG. 6.1.  An example stimulus.

to letters was randomly determined for each pair of participants. One participant in each pair received the stimuli described in Table 6.2 whereas the other received a design where E was transposed with F and A with G. Hence, the putatively redundant elements were E for one member of the participant pair, whereas they were F for the other member.

*Procedure.* The main experiment was preceded by some general written instructions and a brief practice phase to familiarize participants with the procedure. The experiment then proceeded in blocks of 24 trials. On each trial, a stimulus was presented for 800 ms and followed by a mid-gray mask that was presented for 1,200 ms. If a response was not detected within 2,000 ms of stimulus onset, the trial terminated with a message stating that the participant had responded too slowly and asked them to speed up. The participant was then moved on to the next trial.

Each block comprised the sequential presentation of 24 stimuli, 12 from each of the two categories. At the end of each block the percentage of correct responses made by the participant was calculated, but *not* presented to the participant. Clearly, percentage correct has a slightly different interpretation in a free classification task to a task with trial-specific feedback as the relationship between Categories 1 and 2 and the two response keys is arbitrary. Hence, percentage correct was computed by assuming for each block that the key that was pressed most often when stimuli of Category 1 were presented represented the correct answer to Category 1. The other key was assumed to be the correct answer for Category 2. When this "percentage correct" score exceeded 83%, the participant was moved on to the next phase of the experiment. Participants were also moved on to the next phase if they completed six blocks without reaching this criterion.

## Results and Discussion

Participants completed a mean of 5.19 blocks in Phase 1, and a mean of 5.25 blocks in Phase 2. Most people did not achieve high levels of performance in this task, with only 4 of the 32 people tested reaching the 83% criterion in both phases. Given the total lack of feedback and the relatively small amount of exposure to complex and unfamiliar stimuli, this is perhaps unsurprising. We therefore decided to exclude only those participants whose performance in Phase 2 was so poor that their response to the test stimulus EF could not be interpreted. In order to be included, a participant's dominant response to Category 1 stimuli in Phase 2 had to be different from their dominant response to Category 2 stimuli in that phase. For example, if when a Category 1 stimulus was presented the participant was more likely to press the right-hand key, then in order to be included they had to be more likely to press the left-hand key in response to Category 2. In other words, they should not predominantly assign the stimuli of both categories to the same key.

Sixteen of the 32 participants passed this criterion. However, one would not expect participants to demonstrate blocking unless they have learned the Phase 1 categorization to some extent. We therefore divided our remaining participants into "learners" and "nonlearners" by applying the same criterion to performance in Phase 1. Finally, we classified all 16 participants on the basis of whether their response to the EF test stimulus was consistent or inconsistent with blocking. Their response was classified as consistent if they responded to EF using the key they had predominantly used to respond to GF in Phase 2. If they used the other key, they were classified as inconsistent with the blocking hypothesis.

Looking at Table 6.3, one can see that the majority of the learner's classifications of the test stimulus were consistent with the blocking hypothesis. Tested against a null hypothesis of random responding, the evidence for our blocking hypothesis misses significance by the narrowest of margins, $p = 0.05$, one-tailed, on a binomial test. A one-tailed test is appropriate here because the direction of the effect was predicted in advance on the basis of previous evidence in supervised learning (see earlier Blocking section) and in a situation where trial-specific feedback was absent (Zwickel & Wills, 2002).

Further inspection of Table 6.3 indicates that nonlearners do not show behavior consistent with blocking. This is as we would predict, because blocking should occur only if the Phase 1 categorization is learned. A contingency chi-square confirms that the proportion of blocking-consistent responses is significantly affected by performance in Phase 1, $\chi^2(1)=6.11$[1], $p < 0.05$. Taking these two analyses together, our data seem to support the conclusion that a blocking-like effect occurs in unsupervised learning. Additionally, all four participants that passed the 83% criterion in both phases made a blocking-consistent response to the test stimulus, $p = 0.06$, one-tailed, on a binomial test.

One further aspect of these results is that nonlearners appear to show nonrandom responding in the opposite direction to that pre-

TABLE 6.3

Results of the Experiment

|  | Learners | Nonlearners |
|---|---|---|
| Consistent with blocking | 8 | 1 |
| Inconsistent with blocking | 2 | 5 |

[1]No corrections have been applied for the low expected frequencies of some of the cells. It has been found that even small expected frequencies do not increase the chance of type I errors (Overall, 1980). A general discussion of this issue can be found in Howell (2002, pp. 151–152).

dicted by the blocking hypothesis. Although this effect falls short of significance, $p = 0.22$, two-tailed, on a binomial test, it is interesting to speculate what may be behind this pattern. One possibility is that participants who did not learn the category structure in Phase 1 developed something of a mix of the Phase 1 and Phase 2 prototypes. These people might therefore represent the stimuli of Category 1 as derived from a prototype ABE and stimuli of Category 2 as derived from a prototype CDGF. If one accepts Pearce's (1987) assumptions about the relationship between shared elements and similarity, then test stimulus EF is more similar to ABE than to CDGF. This is because Pearce assumes that similarity is affected by the *proportion* of shared elements. EF contains one third of ABE's elements but only one quarter of CDGF's elements, so EF is predicted to be more similar to ABE than to CDGF. As a result, participants would be predicted to place EF into Category 1, which is opposite to the effect predicted by blocking.

## MODELING

The results of our experiment indicate that a blocking-like phenomenon occurs in unsupervised learning. It has been our contention throughout this chapter that such an effect is predicted by our integrated model but not by Rumelhart and Zipser's (1986) competitive-learning model. In this section we show how we've supported this conclusion through computer simulations of both models.

We implemented the Rumelhart and Zipser learning rule (Equations 6.3a and 6.3b) in a network consisting of 60 input units and 2 output units. Each of the elements composing our stimuli was assigned to an input unit and the activation of that unit was set to one if the feature was present and zero otherwise. We ran the simulation 32 times, once for each participant in our experiment. For each simulation, each stimulus presented to a given participant was presented to the input units of the corresponding simulation. Stimuli were presented sequentially, and in the same order as they had been to the corresponding participant. The winning output unit for the presented stimulus was simply defined as the most active output unit. The learning rule was then applied and the next stimulus presented. The network's response to the test stimulus was coded as blocking-consistent or blocking-inconsistent using the same procedure we had used for the participants' responses (see the section Results and Discussion). Simulated participants were also categorized as "learners" or "nonlearners" using the same procedures we had used for the participants. The data from the "learners" in this simulated experiment were then assessed for the significance of the blocking effect, tested against a null hypothesis of random responding.

Equation 6.3b includes the learning rate parameter $G$. We therefore performed 50 simulated experiments across which $G$ varied from 0.001 to 0.491 in steps of 0.01. None of our 50 simulated experiments produced a significant blocking effect, reinforcing our conclusion that the Rumelhart and Zipser system does not predict blocking in this experiment.

Next we replaced the Rumelhart and Zipser learning rule with our modified delta rule (Equation 6.5) and repeated the 50 simulated experiments. This time, out of the 50 runs, 42 runs were significant. The non-significant runs all occurred between the learning rates of 0.001 and 0.081, indicating that this prediction of our model is robust across a wide range of learning rates.

## OTHER MODELS

Throughout this chapter, we've deliberately concentrated on two well-known and comparatively simple associative models of categorization that can be straightforwardly applied to the experimental procedures and stimuli we employed. In so doing, it was not our intention to suggest that the Rumelhart and Zipser or the Rescorla–Wagner models are the only, or even the best, models of unsupervised and supervised categorization respectively. In what follows we discuss the validity of some of the assumptions underlying the models we have used and consider some alternative approaches to modeling supervised and unsupervised categorization.

### Stimulus Representation

The Rescorla–Wagner and Rumelhart–Zipser models both assume an *elemental* stimulus representation. For example, in our particular applications of these models we have assumed the presence of an input unit for each of the picture elements that comprise the stimuli. This kind of elemental stimulus representation can be contrasted with *exemplar* stimulus representation. In exemplar stimulus representation, each presented stimulus has its own unique representation. Exemplar models are being increasingly employed in the study of categorization and associative learning because of their proven success in very precisely modeling categorization behavior in certain circumstances (see, e.g., Nosofsky, 1986). There is also some evidence in both humans (e.g., Shanks, Darby, & Charles, 1998) and other animals (e.g., Pearce & Redhead, 1993) that appears to favor exemplar theories over comparable elemental theories. On the other hand, there are phenomena that seem difficult to explain if one assumes a purely exemplar representation but that can be easily explained if elemental representation is assumed (e.g., Gluck, 1991; Kruschke, 1996). There is also some evidence that suggests people can flexibly apply exemplar or elemental stimulus representations in response to differing task demands (e.g., Williams, Sagness, & McPhee, 1994).

It is also likely that, as suggested in General Recognition Theory (Ashby & Townsend, 1986) and stimulus-sampling theory (Estes, 1950), even two physically identical stimuli will have differing input representations due to variations in our perceptual system. The picture is yet further complicated by evidence that suggests the act of categorization can itself affect our stimulus representations (e.g., Schyns & Rodet, 1997).

Overall, it seems likely that the stimulus representations we have employed in this chapter are a simplification of the true nature of stimulus representation.

## Attentional Processes

One way of thinking about the phenomenon of blocking is as a demonstration that learning is driven by surprise. In the Rescorla–Wagner theory, surprise can be thought of as directly affecting learning. This is because the learning rule states that the change in connection strength is proportional to the difference between the predicted status of the outcome ($\Sigma aw$) and its actual status ($\lambda$). Some other associative theories (e.g., Mackintosh, 1975; Pearce & Hall, 1980) suggest that surprise acts indirectly through some kind of attentional process. The phenomenon of blocking does not, in itself, distinguish between these two classes of explanation. Therefore, although our discovery of a blocking-like effect in free classification indicates that unsupervised learning is surprise-driven, it does not uniquely support the Rescorla–Wagner formulation we have employed in our model. An alternative (or additional) approach would have been to add an attentional process to the Rumelhart and Zipser model.

## Plasticity–Stability Dilemma

The plasticity–stability dilemma is that a system must be able to learn in order to adapt to a changing environment (i.e., it must be "plastic") but that constant change can lead to an unstable system that can learn new information only by forgetting everything it has so far learned. The back-propagation algorithm is well known to suffer from stability problems (see, e.g., the discussion of "catastrophic forgetting" in McCloskey & Cohen, 1989). Stability is also a problem for both the Rescorla–Wagner and the Rumelhart and Zipser systems.

Numerous suggestions have been made for solutions to the plasticity–stability dilemma and there is insufficient space to deal with them all here. One solution (the APECS system) is covered in chapter 7. An alternative model that is more directly applicable to unsupervised learning is Grossberg's Adaptive Resonance Theory (see, e.g., Grossberg, 1987). Adaptive Resonance Theory is somewhat related to the Rumelhart and Zipser system, but it adds a top-down process. Like Rumelhart and Zipser, input unit activity leads to one category unit being more active than the others. Unlike Rumelhart and Zipser, this category unit does not necessarily "win." It will do so only if downward connections from the category unit to the input units reproduce the input sufficiently well. If the most active unit does not predict the input very well, the same test is performed for the next most active category unit. If none of the current category units pass the test, a new category unit is created and designated the winner. In this way, the system remains able to learn about new situations while protecting what has already been learned by creating new representations to cater for the new information.

## Decision Processes

In the Rumelhart and Zipser model, and in our model, the category of a presented stimulus is decided by finding the most active output unit. The process by which this happens is not specified, but is assumed to be errorless. In other words, the most active unit will always be the one that is selected. In reality, any process is likely to be imperfect and so sometimes some other unit will be selected, particularly if there are two or more units whose activations are similar. One very common way of representing this decision process is through the ratio rule. Next we consider one particular type of ratio rule, the *exponential ratio rule*.

The ratio rule compares the activity of each output unit to the activity of all other output units. In this way, a highly active output unit is selected with a higher probability if all other output units are quite low in activation than if the other units have a high activation too. In the exponential ratio rule, an additional parameter $k$ adjusts how much influence the relative strengths of the category units have. If $k$ is large, the most activated category is nearly always chosen. If $k$ is small, the relative strengths of activation have very little influence on the category decision.

Formally, the exponential ratio rule is

$$Prob(category\ x) = \frac{e^{ko_x}}{\sum_{j=1}^{v} e^{ko_j}} \tag{6.6}$$

where the activation of output unit $x$ is represented as $o_x$ and $v$ is the number of output units. *Prob(category x)* is the probability that category $x$ is selected.

The ratio rule is widely used in the modeling of categorical decision processes (e.g., Gluck & Bower, 1988; Kruschke, 1993; Nosofsky, 1986). However, there is mounting evidence that the exponential ratio rule is incorrect and that an alternative process based on the mutual inhibition of output units may be more appropriate (see, e.g., Wills et al., 2000) .

## Level of Analysis

In this chapter, we've concentrated on theories that attempt to eluci-
date the specific processes that underlie supervised and unsupervised
category learning. The two models we've looked at in most detail attempt to do this with processes that are neurally plausible. However,
this is not the only approach one can take to understanding categorization. One can, for example, employ a more abstract level of analysis
and consider the general problems that any categorization system
must solve. In this section, we describe one theory that takes this approach—Anderson's rational model.

The core idea of Anderson's rational model (e.g., Anderson, 1991) is
that, as the brain is adapted to its environment, much insight into human information processing can be gained by reflecting on the nature
of information in that environment. If Anderson's model were a *normative* model, it would employ all relevant probability information
about the category structure in the environment. The model is described as rational rather than normative because it also takes into account some considerations about the computational complexities of
processing this information.

The model is expressed through Bayesian mathematics. For example,
the probability that a person is 20 years old, given that they are a student, is quite high. This is called a conditional probability, and is ex-
pressed as P(twenty | student). Imagine you are walking down the
street of a particular town and meet a 20-year-old. How likely is it that
this person is a student? Another way of asking the same question is to
ask for an estimate of P(student | twenty). Your estimate will, of course,
be affected by P(twenty | student), but also by the overall probability
that anyone is a student, P(student).

This is basically the way the rational model calculates the probabilities with which a stimulus comes from a specific category. If a new stimulus has to be categorized, the model determines the probability with
which each stimulus feature would occur, given that the stimulus comes from a particular category. The probabilities for all the features are
multiplied together, giving a single number for each category. The stimulus is considered to belong to the category that produces the largest
number. When no prior knowledge is available, or the calculated
number is below a certain threshold, a new category is created.

## SUMMARY

Categorization—dividing the world into groups of things—has been
studied through two basic types of experiments. The first type consists
of studies where each stimulus is accompanied or followed by accurate
information about category membership. These studies are by far the
most common but the level of feedback given seems unlikely to be

commonly available outside the laboratory. The second type of study—free classification—goes to the opposite extreme and provides no feedback whatsoever.

These two basic types of categorization experiments are reflected in the two basic types of associative categorization models: supervised models and unsupervised models. In this chapter, we concentrated on one comparatively simple associative model of each type. The first was the Rumelhart and Zipser competitive-learning system, which is a model of unsupervised learning. The second was the Rescorla–Wagner theory (aka. simple delta-rule network), which has been widely applied to human and animal data.

We went on to outline the case for integrating models of supervised and unsupervised learning. Our main argument was that only an integrated system could make use of feedback when it was available but not be paralyzed when feedback was unexpectedly absent. We then discussed one way in which competitive learning and the delta rule could be combined to create a comparatively simple integrated model.

The integrated model we proposed predicts that blocking-like effects should also occur in the absence of feedback, whereas the Rumelhart and Zipser model predicts that they will not. The results of our free-classification study suggest that blocking-like effects do indeed occur in the absence of feedback. These results therefore provide another reason for favoring our integrated model over the component models from which it was constructed.

There are a number of respects in which the model we have proposed is likely to be a simplification of a fully adequate model of categorization. These respects include our assumptions about stimulus representation, the absence of an attentional process, the absence of a process that addresses the plasticity–stability dilemma, and the absence of a realistic decision mechanism.

## REFERENCES

Ahn, W.-K., & Medin, D. L. (1992). A two-stage model of category construction. *Cognitive Science, 16,* 81–121.

Anderson, J. R. (1991). A rational analysis of categorization. *Psychological Review, 98,* 409–429.

Ashby, F. G., & Townsend, J. T. (1986). Varieties of perceptual independence. *Psychological Review, 93*(2), 154–179.

Bersted, C. T., Brown, B. R., & Evans, S. H. (1969). Free sorting with stimuli in a multidimensional attribute space. *Perception & Psychophysics, 6B,* 409–413.

Bruner, J. S., Goodnow, J. J., & Austin, G. A. (1956). *A study of thinking.* New York: Wiley.

Dickinson, A. Shanks, D. R., & Evenden, J. (1984). Judgement of act-outcome contingency: The role of selective attention. *Quarterly Journal of Experimental Psychology, 36A,* 29–50.

Estes, W. K. (1950). Toward a statistical theory of learning. *Psychological Review, 57,* 94–107.

Forster, K. I., & Forster, J. C. (2003). DMDX version 3. http://www.u.arizona.edu/~jforster/dmdx.htm

Gluck, M. A. (1991). Stimulus generalization and representation in adaptive network models of category learning. *Psychological Science*, 2, 50–55.

Gluck, M. A., & Bower, G. H. (1988). From conditioning to category learning: An adaptive network model. *Journal of Experimental Psychology: General*, 117(3), 227–247.

Grossberg, S. (1987). Competitive learning: From interactive activation to adaptive resonance. *Cognitive Science*, 11, 23–63.

Hebb, D. O. (1949). *The organization of behavior*. New York: Wiley.

Homa, D., & Cultice, J. C. (1984). Role of feedback, category size, and stimulus distortion on the acquisition and utilization of ill-defined categories. *Journal of Experimental Psychology: Learning, Memory, and Cognition*, 10(1), 83–94.

Hornik, K., Stinchcombe, M., & White, H. (1989). Multilayer feedforward networks are universal approximators. *Neural Networks*, 2, 359–368.

Howell, D. C. (2002). *Statistical methods for psychology*. Belmont, CA: Duxbury Press.

Jones, F. W., Wills, A. J., & McLaren, I. P. L. (1998). Perceptual categorization: Connectionist modelling and decision rules. *The Quarterly Journal of Experimental Psychology*, 51B(3), 33–58.

Kamin, L. J. (1969). "Attention-like" processes in classical conditioning. In M. R. Jones (Ed.), *Miami symposium on the prediction of behavior: aversive stimulation* (pp. 9–31). Miami, FL: University of Miami Press.

Kruschke, J. K. (1993). Human category learning: Implications for backpropagation models. *Connection Science*, 5(1), 3–36.

Kruschke, J. K. (1996). Base rates in category learning. *Journal of Experimental Psychology: Learning, Memory, and Cognition*, 22(1), 3–26.

Mackintosh, N. J. (1975). A theory of attention: Variations in the associability of stimuli with reinforcement. *Psychological Review*, 82, 276–298.

Martin, I., & Levy, A. B. (1991). Blocking observed in human eyelid conditioning. *Quarterly Journal of Experimental Psychology*, 43B, 233–255.

McClelland, J. L., & Rumelhart, D. E. (1985). Distributed memory and the representation of general and specific information. *Journal of Experimental Psychology: General*, 114(2), 159–188.

McCloskey, M., & Cohen, N. J. (1989). Catastrophic interference in connectionist networks: The sequential learning problem. In G. H. Bower (Ed.), *The psychology of learning and motivation* (pp. 109–165). San Diego: Academic Press.

McLaren, I. P. L. (1989). The computational units as an assembly of neurons: An implementation of an error correcting learning algorithm. In R. Durbin, C. Miall, & G. Mitchison (Eds.), *The computing neuron* (pp. 160–178). Amsterdam: Addison-Wesley.

Medin, D. L., & Schaffer, M. M. (1978). Context theory of classification learning. *Psychological Review*, 85(3), 207–238.

Medin, D. L., Wattenmaker, W. D., & Hampson, S. E. (1987). Family resemblance, conceptual cohesiveness, and category construction. *Cognitive Psychology*, 19, 242–279.

Minsky, M. L., & Papert, S. A. (1969). *Perceptrons: An introduction to computational geometry*. Cambridge, MA: MIT Press.

Nosofsky, R. M. (1986). Attention, similarity and the identification-categorisation relationship. *Journal of Experimental Psychology: General*, 115(1), 39–57.

Overall, J. E. (1980). Power of chi-square tests for 2 × 2 contingency tables with small expected frequencies. *Psychological Bulletin*, 87, 132–135.

Page, M. (2000). Connectionist modelling in psychology: A localist manifesto. *Behavioral and Brain Sciences, 23*(4), 443–512.

Pearce, J. M. (1987). A model of stimulus generalization for Pavlovian conditioning. *Psychological Review, 94*, 61–73.

Pearce, J. M., & Hall, G. (1980). A model for Pavlovian learning: Variations in the effectiveness of conditioned but not of unconditioned stimuli. *Psychological Review, 87*, 532–552.

Pearce, J. M., & Redhead, E. S. (1993). The influence of an irrelevant stimulus on two discriminations. *Journal of Experimental Psychology: Animal Behavior Processes, 19*, 180–190.

Rescorla, R. A. (1973). Evidence for a "unique stimulus" account of configural conditioning. *Journal of Comparative and Physiological Psychology, 85*(2), 331–338.

Rescorla, R. A., & Wagner, A. R. (1972). A theory of Pavlovian conditioning: Variations in the effectiveness of reinforcement and nonreinforcement. In A. H. Black & W. F. Prokasy (Eds.), *Classical conditioning II: Current research* (pp. 64–99). New York: Appleton–Century–Crofts.

Rumelhart, D. E., Hinton, G. E., & Williams, R. J. (1986). Learning internal representations by error propagation. In D. E. Rumelhart & J. L. McClelland (Eds.), *Parallel distributed processing: Explorations in the microstructure of cognition* (Vol. 1, pp. 318–362). Cambridge, MA: MIT Press.

Rumelhart, D. E., & Zipser, D. (1986). Feature discovery by competitive learning. In D. E. Rumelhart & J. L. McClelland (Eds.), *Parallel distributed processing: Explorations in the microstructure of cognition* (Vol. 1, pp. 151–193). Cambridge, MA: MIT Press.

Schyns, P. G., & Rodet, L. (1997). Categorization creates functional features. *Journal of Experimental Psychology: Learning, Memory, and Cognition, 23*(3), 681–696.

Shanks, D. R., Darby, R. J., & Charles, D. (1998). Resistance to interference in human associative learning: Evidence of configural processing. *Journal of Experimental Psychology: Animal Behavior Processes, 24*(2), 136–150.

Stone, G. O. (1986). An analysis of the delta rule and the learning of statistical associations. In D. E. Rumelhart, J. L. McClelland, & the PDP Research Group (Eds.), *Parallel distributed processing: Explorations in the microstructure of cognition* (Vol. 1, pp. 444–459). Cambridge, MA: MIT Press.

Werbos, P. J. (1974). *Beyond regression: New tools for prediction and analysis in the behavioral sciences.* Unpublished doctoral dissertation, Harvard University, Cambridge, MA.

Widrow, B., & Hoff, M. E. (1960). Adaptive switching circuits. *Institute of Radio Engineers, Western Electronic Show and Convention, Convention Record,* (Part 4, pp. 96–104).

Williams, D. A., Sagness, K. E., & McPhee, J. E. (1994). Configural and elemental strategies in predictive learning. *Journal of Experimental Psychology: Learning, Memory, and Cognition, 20*, 694–709.

Wills, A. J., & McLaren, I. P. L. (1998). Perceptual learning and free classification. *The Quarterly Journal of Experimental Psychology, 51B*(3), 235–270.

Wills, A. J., Reimers, S., Stewart, N., Suret, M., & McLaren, I. P. L. (2000). Tests of the ratio rule in categorization. *The Quarterly Journal of Experimental Psychology, 53A*(4), 983–1011.

Zwickel, J., & Wills, A. J. (2002). Is competitive learning an adequate account of free classification? In W. Gray & C. Schunn (Eds.), *Proceedings of the 24th Annual Conference of the Cognitive Science Society* (pp. 982–987). Mahwah, NJ: Lawrence Erlbaum Associates.

# Chapter 7

# The Role of Associative History in Human Causal Learning

M. E. Le Pelley and I. P. L. McLaren

Ever since Thorndike (1898) proposed the first theory of associative learning over a century ago, it has been the goal of associative modelers to specify the processes and factors influencing the associative change (i.e., learning) undergone by a given cue on a given learning episode. In this chapter we consider one such factor—the prior training that a cue has received, which might be termed the "associative history" of that cue. We demonstrate that, in a number of studies of human causal learning, the associative history of a cue can be shown to have a profound and selective influence on the learning undergone by that cue.

An ability to learn about causal relationships is vital for our successful functioning in a changing world, as it allows us to "predict the future" based on current events. As such, the field of human causal learning has been the subject of intense debate over the years. In a seminal paper, Dickinson, Shanks, and Evenden (1984) noted a parallel between studies of causal learning in humans and experiments on animal conditioning. The former investigate the development of causal judgments as a result of experience of relationships between causes and effects; the latter the development of conditioned responding as a result of experience of relationships between conditioned stimuli (CSs) and unconditioned stimuli (USs). Beyond this surface similarity, Dickinson et al. noted that similar factors seem to influence both human causal learning and animal conditioning. Both, for instance, show similar sensitivity to the temporal contiguity of events (cause and effect, or CS and US), and the degree of contingency between those events (see Dickinson & Shanks, 1985; Shanks & Dickinson, 1991). Parallels such as these led Shanks and Dickinson (1987) to suggest that models of associative learning developed to account for the results of animal conditioning studies might also be applied to studies of human causal learning, and this approach has met with some success (see De Houwer & Beckers, 2002, for a recent review).

## THE RESCORLA–WAGNER MODEL

Perhaps the most influential of these models of animal conditioning is the theory of Rescorla and Wagner (1972). This theory takes the popular view that the magnitude of associative change (learning) undergone by a given cue on a given trial depends on the discrepancy (or *error*) between the current associative strength of the presented cues and the strength that the outcome following these cues can support. Specifically, the change in associative strength ($\Delta V$) undergone by a cue, A, on a given learning episode is governed by the equation:

$$\Delta V_A = \alpha_A \beta (\lambda - \Sigma V) \tag{7.1}$$

where $V_A$ is the associative strength of cue A, $\alpha_A$ and $\beta$ are learning rate parameters relating to the salience of the CS and the US respectively, $\lambda$ is the asymptote of conditioning supportable by that US, and $\Sigma V$ is the summed associative strength of all presented cues. Hence the Rescorla–Wagner model states that the error governing associative change for any cue presented on a trial is based on the combined associative strength of all cues present on that trial. As such this "summed error term" allows different cues to interact and compete with one another in the determination of associative change. This prediction of cue competition receives considerable empirical support, most notably in the phenomenon of blocking (Kamin, 1969). This refers to the finding that the gain in excitatory strength of a cue, B, following reinforcement of an AB compound is much reduced if cue A has previously been trained as being a good predictor of that US. According to the summed error term view taken by Rescorla–Wagner, when the AB compound is followed by reinforcement the associative change undergone by B will be determined by the discrepancy between $\lambda$ and the combined associative strengths of A and B. As a result of pretraining with A (such that $V_A \approx \lambda$) this discrepancy will be near zero, and hence B will gain little associative strength, yielding the blocking effect. For more on the Rescorla–Wagner model and its account of cue-competition effects such as blocking, overshadowing, and conditioned inhibition, see Rescorla and Wagner (1972).

The reliance of associative change on a summed error term has important ramifications for the role of associative history in the Rescorla–Wagner model. It ensures that the associative change undergone by an element of a compound cue depends only on the current associative strength of the compound and the outcome following that compound, not on the individual associative strength of that element or on how that associative strength was reached. In other words, the associative history of an element of a compound cannot have a selective influence on the associative change undergone by that element relative to other elements of the same compound. Rescorla (2000) noted that, as a result, the Rescorla–Wagner model is constrained to predict that equally salient stimuli presented on the same trial must undergo the same associative change. Imagine the case in which a conditioned excitor, A ($V_A >$ 0) and a conditioned inhibitor, B ($V_B < 0$) are presented in compound, and the AB compound thus formed is paired with the outcome. Applying Equation 7.1 to A and B on these reinforced AB trials gives:

$$\Delta V_A = \alpha_A \beta(\lambda - \{V_A + V_B\}) \qquad (7.2)$$

$$\Delta V_B = \alpha_B \beta(\lambda - \{V_A + V_B\}) \qquad (7.3)$$

The use of $\Sigma V$ ensures that the error term for the two simultaneously presented cues is identical. As such this summed error term can also be referred to as a "common" error term, as it applies to all presented cues. It is easy to see that if the salience ($\alpha$) of A and B is equal (ensured empirically by appropriate counterbalancing of stimuli), Equations 7.2 and 7.3 will be identical. In other words, the Rescorla–Wagner model is constrained to predict that A and B will undergo identical increments in associative strength as a result of AB+ trials, despite the fact that A (an excitor) and B (an inhibitor) begin these trials with very different associative strengths ($V_A > 0$, $V_B < 0$). The use of a summed error term means that the distribution of associative change between the elements of the reinforced compound is independent of the individual associative strengths (and associative histories) of those elements.

It is important to note that this prediction of equal associative change is not peculiar to the Rescorla–Wagner model. Wagner's (1981) SOP model, for example, implements a summed error term mechanism (albeit in less explicit fashion than the Rescorla–Wagner model) and as such is constrained to predict equal change for A and B. Likewise, it does not depend upon the assumption of an elemental scheme of stimulus representation taken by the Rescorla–Wagner and SOP models. Pearce's (1987, 1994) configural model, for instance, proposes that learning about the AB configuration on Stage 2 AB+ trials will generalize equally to the A and B elements, leading to equal associative change for both.

## EXPERIMENT 1: ASSOCIATIVE CHANGE FOR EXCITORS AND INHIBITORS TRAINED IN COMPOUND

This prediction of equal associative change for an excitor and an inhibitor reinforced in compound was tested in a recent study of human causal learning by Le Pelley and McLaren (2001a). The basic design of our experiment (excluding filler trials) is shown in Table 7.1. This study

## TABLE 7.1
### Design of Experiment 1 (Excluding Filler Trials)

| Condition | Stage 1 | | Stage 2 | Test |
|-----------|---------|------|---------|------|
| S2R | A+ | C+ | AB+ | AD |
| | E+ | | CD? | BC |
| | BE– | DE– | | |
| S2NR | F+ | H+ | FG– | FI |
| | J+ | | HI? | GH |
| | GJ– | IJ– | | |

employed an allergy prediction paradigm in which participants played the role of a food allergist investigating the causes of allergic reaction in a fictitious patient, Mr. X. In Table 7.1 the letters A–X represent different foods that Mr. X might eat (cues), "+" indicates the occurrence of allergic reaction (the outcome), "–" indicates that no reaction occurred, and "?" indicates an exposure trial (see later discussion). "AB+", for instance, represents a training trial on which participants were informed that Mr. X ate a meal containing foods A and B, and that he suffered an allergic reaction as a result. The experiment employed a within-subjects design, with participants experiencing all of the different contingencies of each stage concurrently. Following training with the trial types shown in Table 7.1 (eight blocks in each stage), on test participants were presented with various meals and were asked to rate them according to how likely they were to predict allergic reaction in Mr. X. These ratings were given on a scale from +10 to –10, where +10 indicated that a meal was very likely to cause allergic reaction, –10 indicated that a meal was very likely to prevent allergic reactions that other foods were capable of causing, and 0 indicated that a meal had no effect on Mr. X (neither causing nor preventing allergic reactions). Following Dickinson et al. (1984), these causal judgment ratings provided our index of the associative strengths of the meals presented on test.

Let us consider first the "Stage 2 reinforcement" (S2R) condition. During Stage 1, A and C were trained as equivalent excitors, whereas B and D were trained as equivalent inhibitors, able to prevent the occurrence of allergic reactions that would otherwise be expected given the presence of the excitatory E. In Stage 2 the AB compound was reinforced. The question of interest was whether these AB+ trials led to equal increments in the associative strengths of A and B, or whether one element would undergo a greater increment than the other. Rescorla (2000) pioneered a method for assessing relative magnitude of associative change undergone by stimuli differing in their "baseline" associative strength that avoids any strong assumptions regarding the mapping between associative strength and performance. Specifically, he proposed comparing responding to A and B when they were embedded in compounds designed to ensure similar overall levels of responding. Following Stage 1, compounds AD and BC should have had equal strengths—each contained one excitor and one inhibitor. If subsequent AB+ trials resulted in equal changes to the associative strengths of A and B, then the AD and BC compounds would remain equal after Stage 2, as each started at the same level and received the same change. If instead the strength of the excitatory A increased more than that of the inhibitory B, then the rating of AD would be higher than that of BC. Conversely, if $\Delta V_B > \Delta V_A$, then BC would receive a higher rating than AD.

The "Stage 2 nonreinforcement" (S2NR) condition is similar, but in the second stage a combination of an excitor (F) and an inhibitor (G) is nonreinforced. This might be expected to lead to a decrement in $V_F$ and $V_G$, but once again the question of importance is whether this decrement is the same for both cues, or whether one changes more than the other. A theory in which the distribution of associative change among the elements of a compound is independent of the individual associative histories of those elements (such as Rescorla–Wagner) is again constrained to predict equal change for F and G on FG– trials, evidenced by equal ratings for FI and GH on test. If, on the other hand, F underwent a greater decrement than G, we would expect FI to be rated lower than GH; if $V_G$ decreased more than $V_F$ we would expect the opposite.

The Stage 2 "CD?" and "HI?" exposure trials were included to counter a potential confound in this study. For example, AB compound presentation may result not only in development of A–US and B–US associations, but also in development of within-compound A–B associations. Consideration of these A–B associations complicates any inference regarding relative magnitudes of associative change drawn from the results. Suppose $V_A$ and $V_B$ undergo equal changes as a result of AB+ trials. The formation of an A–B association might be expected to enhance responding to the inhibitory B (as it has been paired with an excitor), and reduce responding to the excitatory A (as it has been paired with an inhibitor). Thus even if the change in the A–US and B–US associations were equal, AB+ trials could augment responding to B more than to A. The "CD?" trials allow us to overcome this problem. On these trials subjects saw cues C and D paired, but were not told whether or not the outcome occurred. Specifically, they were told the contents of a meal eaten by Mr. X, but were informed that the data regarding the effects of eating that meal (i.e., whether it caused allergic reaction or not) had been lost. This compound exposure allowed within-compound C–D associations to form while leaving C–US and D–US associations unchanged. The effect of A–B association formation would thus be matched by development of C–D associations, such that any difference between AD and BC following Stage 2 could only be due to unequal changes in A–US and B–US associations on AC+ trials. The same applies for FI and GH in the S2NR condition.

The results of this study are shown in Fig. 7.1a. Recall that Rescorla–Wagner predicts AD = BC and FI = GH. Contrary to these predictions, AD received a significantly higher rating than BC, indicating that on AB+ trials, the excitatory A underwent a greater increment in associative strength than did the inhibitory B. Likewise, FI received a significantly higher rating than GH, indicating that the inhibitory G underwent a greater decrement than the excitatory F on FG– trials. In general, then, the element of the compound that was the better predictor of events (reinforcement or nonreinforcement) on compound trials underwent the greater associative change on these trials. These results clearly demonstrate that the distribution of associative change among the elements of a compound depends on the associative history of those elements, and as such contradict the summed error term view taken by the Rescorla–Wagner model. That is, the associative change undergone by each element of a compound is not determined solely by how well that compound predicts the current outcome; the surprisingness of the outcome given the presence of that cue alone is also an important determinant of associative change.

## APECS AND ADAPTIVE GENERALIZATION

These results are more consistent with the APECS (Adaptively Parameterized Error-Correcting Systems) model of learning and memory that we have developed in recent years (Le Pelley, Cutler, & McLaren, 2000; Le Pelley & McLaren, 2001a, 2001b, 2002; McLaren, 1993, 1994). APECS is based on the backpropagation algorithm (Rumelhart, Hinton, & Williams, 1986), and employs a multilayer architecture. Unlike standard backpropagation, however, the recoding of the input patterns realized by the hidden units is of a more strictly configural nature, in the spirit of Pearce's (1987, 1994) configural theory. Consider a two-layer connectionist network with input units, hidden units, and output units. Suppose now that we have a particular input pattern that we wish to map to a particular output pattern. APECS does this by choosing one hidden unit to carry this particular mapping. That is to say, if two stimuli (X and Y) occur together with an outcome, APECS learns excitatory connections from X and Y to a hidden unit, and an excitatory connection between that unit (representing the co-occurrence of X and Y), and the outcome unit. Thus hidden units come to represent certain configurations of input patterns, and so could equally well be termed "configural units." In common with Pearce's model, each different pattern of stimulation is represented by its own configural unit. If a novel configuration of input patterns is presented to the network, a new configural unit is assigned to represent that configuration. For instance, if the network experienced X+, Y+, and XY+ trials, the situation shown in Fig. 7.2 would develop.

In Pearce's model a new configural unit is recruited each time a novel configuration of inputs (i.e., cues or CSs) is presented. APECS goes one

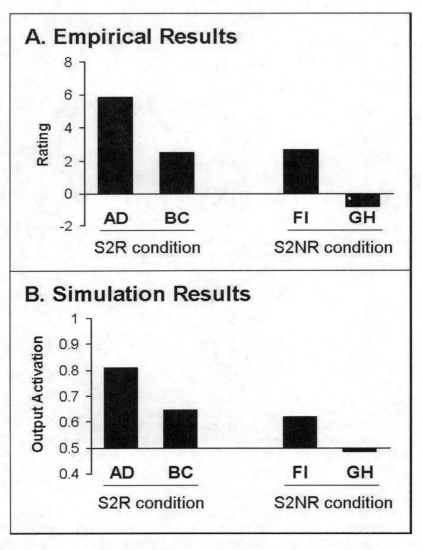

FIG. 7.1. (a) Mean causal judgment ratings received by the test compounds of Experiment 1. A rating of +10 indicates that the meal is perceived as being very likely to cause an allergic reaction, −10 indicates that is perceived as being very likely to prevent allergic reactions that other foods are capable of causing, and 0 indicates that it neither causes nor prevents allergic reactions. (b) Simulation of Experiment 1 using APECS. Results show activation of US output unit as a result of presentation of each test compound to the network following training with the trial types shown in Table 7.1. A perfect predictor of the outcome will produce an activation of 0.9, a neutral cue will produce an activation of 0.5, and an inhibitor will produce an activation between 0 and 0.5.

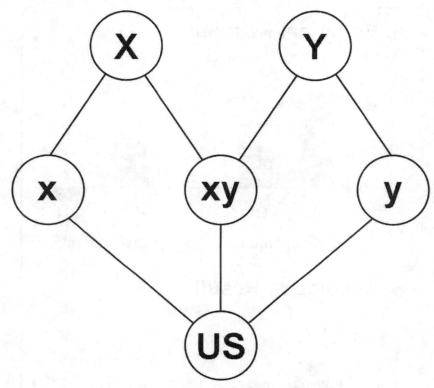

FIG. 7.2. Representations developed by APECS following X+, Y+, and XY+ trials. Letters in uppercase denote the stimulus that each input and output unit represents (where US = unconditioned stimulus outcome unit). Letters in lowercase denote the configurations of stimuli that the hidden units come to represent.

step further than this in its configural nature. In the APECS framework, if a previously experienced pattern of inputs is paired with a novel *outcome*, a new hidden unit will be recruited to carry this new mapping from input to output (input–output mapping). Thus whereas Pearce's theory distinguishes only between configurations of inputs, APECS distinguishes between configurations of inputs and outcomes. If Pearce's model experienced XY+ and XY– trials, it would develop only a single configural unit to represent the configuration "XY." If an APECS network experienced XY+ and XY– trials, on the other hand, it would recruit two hidden units; one carrying an excitatory ("XY+") mapping, the other carrying an inhibitory ("XY–") mapping.

Beyond this configural coding of stimuli, perhaps the most important difference between both the Rescorla–Wagner and Pearce models and the view taken by APECS is that the former employ fixed generalization coefficients, whereas in the latter generalization is able to vary adaptively. That is, according to the Rescorla–Wagner or Pearce models, the generalization between compounds XY and YZ takes a fixed value (on the basis of the shared element, Y) that is unaffected by whether compounds XY and YZ predict the same outcome or different outcomes. APECS, on the other hand, employs adaptive generalization coefficients, such that the amount of generalization between two similar stimuli is modulated according to whether they predict the same or different outcomes. If compounds XY and YZ predict the same outcome, then APECS allows for generalization of responding from one compound to the other on the basis of the shared element, Y. If, on the other hand, XY and YZ predict different outcomes, generalization between them is reduced such that presentation of XY evokes little responding appropriate to YZ. This importance of the outcome in determining the generalization between similar compounds makes the associative history of cues a vital factor in determining the associative change that they undergo on a given trial. As a consequence, even though APECS, like Rescorla–Wagner, relies on summed error terms to determine changes in associative strength, the use of adaptive generalization means that this error term can affect the separable elements of a compound differently, depending on whether these elements have previously been paired with the same outcome as that occurring on compound trials, or different outcomes. As such it is perhaps misleading to refer to APECS as a "common error term" theory in the same sense as the Rescorla–Wagner model.

The predictions made by APECS with regard to Experiment 1 were derived by means of computational simulation. Figure 7.1b shows the averaged results from 20 separate simulations of the experimental design shown in Table 7.1, each simulation representing a different subject. The network and parameters used for this simulation were the same as employed by Le Pelley and McLaren (2001b) and Le Pelley et al. (2000), the only exception being that this simulation also included a unit representing the experimental context, as proposed by Le Pelley (2002), with exactly the same parameters as reported there. In fact the inclusion of this unit makes little overall difference to the pattern of results predicted. Note that the model parameters used in this simulation were not adjusted to provide a best fit to the empirical data of Experiment 1; instead we employed exactly the same parameters as used previously to successfully model a number of other phenomena of human causal learning in order to generate predictions with regard to the current design.

The dependent variable in Fig. 7.1b is the activation of the outcome unit caused by presentation of each of the test compounds (AD, BC, FI, and GH) at the termination of Stage 2. In the APECS model, if the outcome unit receives no stimulation at all, it will have an activation of 0.5. Excitatory input to the outcome unit will tend to increase its activation from this baseline (with a perfect predictor producing an outcome activation of 0.9), and inhibitory input will tend to decrease activation below 0.5. The match between the empirical data of Experiment 1 and the results of the APECS simulation is striking. Unlike the Rescorla–Wagner model, APECS allows the associative history of the separable elements of a reinforced (or nonreinforced) stimulus compound to affect the distribution of associative change among those elements. APECS predicts that AD will cause greater outcome activation than BC, and that GH will cause less outcome activation than FI: This is exactly the pattern observed in the empirical data. Thus APECS seems better-equipped than Rescorla–Wagner to account for the selective effects of associative history on the relative associative change undergone by the two elements of a reinforced (or nonreinforced) compound. But why does the model make these predictions?

We mentioned earlier that APECS allows for modulation of the generalization between similar configurations of stimuli according to whether those configurations are part of input–output mappings predicting the same or different outcomes. Specifically, for cues presented together on trial T, APECS predicts that a cue that was previously part of a mapping predicting the same outcome as that occurring on trial T will (other things being equal) undergo a greater change than a cue that was previously part of a mapping predicting a different outcome. In the former case there will be greater generalization between the mapping in force on trial T and that learned earlier—as both of these mappings predict the same outcome, generalization between the two will remain high. In the latter case, as the previous and current mappings predict different outcomes the generalization between the two will be reduced. Consider how this idea applies to the S2R condition of Experiment 1. Figure 7.3a shows the situation in the APECS network for cues A and B following Stage 1: A is part of an excitatory "A+" mapping, while as a result of the configural coding scheme employed by APECS, B is represented only as part of an inhibitory "BE–" mapping (as B is never experienced in isolation during Stage 1). In Stage 2, the network is presented with AB+ trials. The outcome on these trials (reinforcement) is the same as the outcome that occurred following A during Stage 1. As a result, generalization between the A+ mapping (from Stage 1) and the new AB+ mapping (learnt during Stage 2) remains high—in effect, this means that at the same time as an excitatory mapping between AB and the outcome is learned, the Stage 1 excitatory mapping from A alone to the outcome will also become stronger (Fig. 7.3b). However, the outcome occurring on AB+ trials is different to that which occurred following BE (nonreinforcement) in Stage 1. As a result, generalization between the inhibitory BE– mapping (from Stage 1) and the excitatory AB+ mapping (from Stage 2) will be greatly reduced—in effect, this means that the BE– mapping will be "frozen" on AB+ trials, and so will not suffer any great change in its inhibitory potential. In summary, then, Stage 2 AB+ trials will lead to an increase in the excitatory potential of A+ and AB+ mappings, but will not produce as significant a dec-

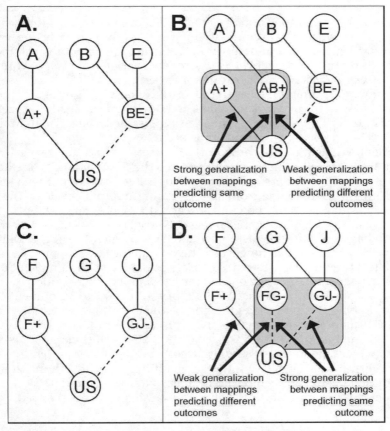

FIG. 7.3. The APECS network as applied to Experiment 1. In all panels input and output units are labeled with the stimuli that they represent (US = unconditioned stimulus outcome unit), whereas hidden units are labeled with the input–output mappings that they come to carry. Solid lines between layers indicate excitatory connections; dashed lines indicate inhibitory connections. (a) Mappings involving A and B developed following Stage 1. (b) Impact of Stage 2 AB+ trials. A novel AB+ mapping is formed; generalization between this novel mapping and the Stage 1 A+ mapping remains high (as both predict the same, correct outcome—reinforcement), whereas generalization between AB+ and BE– is reduced (as these mappings predict different outcomes) such that the BE–mapping is "frozen." The gray box shows the mappings that undergo the greatest increase in excitatory potential as a result of AB+ training. (c) Mappings involving F and G developed during Stage 1. (d) Impact of Stage 2 FG– trials. A novel FG– mapping is formed; generalization between this novel mapping and the Stage 1 GJ– mapping remains high (as both predict the same, correct outcome—nonreinforcement), whereas generalization between FG– and F+ is reduced (as these mappings predict different outcomes) such that the F+ mapping is "frozen." The gray box shows the mappings that undergo the greatest increase in inhibitory potential as a result of FG– training.

135

rement in the inhibitory potential of the BE– mapping. Thus whereas A is subject to two strong excitatory changes, B is subject to only one, with the result being that A undergoes a greater net increment in excitatory strength than does B over the course of these trials—this is, of course, the pattern indicated by the results of Experiment 1.

A similar argument applies to the S2NR condition. Figure 7.3c shows the situation in the network for cues F and G following Stage 1: F is part of an excitatory "F+" mapping, while G is represented as part of an inhibitory "GJ–" mapping. The outcome occurring on Stage 2 FG– trials (nonreinforcement) is the same as that which occurred following GJ in Stage 1. As a result, generalization between the GJ– mapping from Stage 1 and the new FG– mapping learned during Stage 2 will be high—while a novel inhibitory mapping from an "FG" configural unit develops, the inhibitory strength of the previously learned GJ– mapping will also increase (Fig. 7.3d). The outcome on these FG– trials is different, however, to that following F (reinforcement) in Stage 1. Consequently, the generalization between the F+ mapping from Stage 1 and the FG– mapping learned in Stage 2 is reduced, such that FG– trials do not lead to a significant decrement in the excitatory strength of the F+ mapping. Hence during Stage 2, G is subject to two significant inhibitory influences (development of a new FG– mapping and strengthening of the inhibitory potential of the "old" GJ– mapping), whereas F is subject to only one (development of the new FG– mapping). Thus APECS predicts that G will undergo a greater net increment in inhibitory strength than will F, again the pattern seen in the empirical data. Le Pelley and McLaren (2001a) provide a more detailed description of the APECS model with regard to the S2R and S2NR conditions of this experiment, to which the interested reader is referred.

## EXPERIMENT 2: ASSOCIATIVE CHANGE IN RETROSPECTIVE REVALUATION

Our study of the distribution of associative change among the elements of a reinforced compound is not the first time that the ability of the Rescorla–Wagner model to provide a satisfactory account of human causal learning has been called into question. Perhaps the greatest challenge to the Rescorla–Wagner view of causal learning has been provided by demonstrations of retrospective revaluation, indicating that the perceived causal strength of a cue can be altered in the absence of that cue (e.g., Chapman, 1991; Dickinson & Burke, 1996; Le Pelley & McLaren, 2001b; Shanks, 1985). Consider the contingencies shown in the first two lines of Table 7.2. In Stage 1 compounds AB and CD are trained as predictors of the outcome. Then in Stage 2 one of the cues (the competing cue) from each compound is selected for either further training (in the backward blocking condition) or extinction (unovershadowing). The typical result of such studies is that, following Stage 2 training, when the cues that have not received any further training in Stage 2 (the target cues) are tested, D is now rated as a better predictor of the outcome than B. Thus the perceived predictive validity of a cue can be revalued after initial compound training with that cue, either by training the other cue of the compound pair as a valid predictor of the outcome or by extinguishing it. The implication is that the strength of an association between a representation of the target cue (B or D) and the outcome can change on trials on which that cue is not presented (A+ and C–).

The next row of Table 7.2 shows another commonly investigated retrospective revaluation condition: backward-conditioned inhibition (BCI). In this condition, EF– trials precede E+ training. Typically following such training, F is perceived as an inhibitor of the outcome, able to counteract the excitatory effects of other cues (as evidenced by a lower causal efficacy rating for F than for H from the GH–, G– BCI Control contingency). The inhibitory properties of F must have been assumed in retrospect, as E was only established as a good predictor of the US following EF– trials. BCI again indicates that it is possible to change the perceived causal efficacy of a cue in the absence of that cue.

Demonstrations of retrospective revaluation in causal learning are beyond the Rescorla–Wagner model. This model states that a cue's salience, $\alpha$, is positive if that cue is actually presented on a trial, and zero if it is absent. This latter assumption ensures that absent cues cannot engage the learning process, and as there can be no learning about absent cues, there can be no retrospective revaluation.

## The Modified Rescorla–Wagner Model

Van Hamme and Wasserman (1994) proposed a modification to the Rescorla–Wagner model to allow it to account for retrospective effects. They suggested that absent cues, rather than having $\alpha = 0$, should take on a negative value of $\alpha$, allowing them to engage the learning process with a negative sign. Markman (1989) tempered this idea slightly by proposing that only absent-but-expected cues should take on negative $\alpha$, and Dickinson and Burke (1996) suggested that this expectancy arises as a result of the formation of within-compound associations during

TABLE 7.2
Typical Retrospective Revaluation Contingencies

| Contingency | Stage 1 | Stage 2 | Test |
|---|---|---|---|
| Backward blocking | AB+ | A+ | B? |
| Unovershadowing | CD+ | C– | D? |
| BCI | EF– | E+ | F? |
| BCI Control | GH– | G– | H? |

Stage 1 compound training. Thus on the AB+ trials of a backward blocking contingency, subjects learn not only that A and B predict the occurrence of the outcome, but also that A predicts the presence of B and vice versa. On Stage 2 A+ trials, the strength of an association between the presented cue, A, and the outcome will increase. Presentation of A also creates an expectancy of the absent cue B, and this expectancy imbues the cue with negative $\alpha$. Hence as the association between the presented A and the US grows stronger, the association between the absent-but-expected B and the US will grow correspondingly weaker. This logic also applies to the unovershadowing contingency: On Stage 2 C– trials, as the association between the presented cue C and the outcome extinguishes, the association between the absent D (with negative $\alpha$) and the outcome is strengthened. This modified version of the Rescorla–Wagner model is thus able to account for the finding that D is perceived as a better predictor of the outcome than is B on test. Modified Rescorla–Wagner accounts for BCI in a similar fashion. On Stage 2 E+ trials, as E develops an excitatory association to the US, the absent-but-expected F will engage the learning process with the opposite sign and hence will develop an inhibitory association to the US.

We noted earlier that the Rescorla–Wagner model has a summed error term governing the associative change undergone by the separable elements of a compound on a given learning episode, and as such is constrained to predict that equally salient stimuli presented on the same trial will undergo equal associative change. This summed error term view is retained in the modified Rescorla–Wagner model. So while the standard Rescorla–Wagner model is constrained to predict that equally salient stimuli presented on the same trial will undergo equal associative change, this modified Rescorla–Wagner model goes one step further, predicting that equally salient stimuli that are absent-but-expected on the same trial will also undergo equal associative change in retrospect. In other words, just as for cues presented on the same trial, the associative change undergone by cues absent on the same trial is predicted to be independent of the individual associative histories of those cues. And once again, this prediction is not specific to the view of retrospective revaluation in causal learning taken by the modified Rescorla–Wagner theory. For example, another of the most influential associative models of retrospective processing in human causal learning, Dickinson and Burke's (1996) modification of Wagner's (1981) SOP model, would make the same prediction of equal change for cues absent on the same trial. Likewise, in the absence of further assumptions Miller and Matzel's (1988) comparator hypothesis would also seem to predict equal associative change for cues both presented and absent on the same trial.

We investigated this prediction of equal associative change for absent cues in a recent study (Le Pelley & McLaren, 2004), again using an allergy prediction paradigm with human subjects. The basic design of this within-subjects study (excluding filler trials) is shown in Table 7.3. Consider the S2R condition. In the first stage AB is paired with the outcome,

## TABLE 7.3
### Design of Experiment 2 (Excluding Filler Trials)

| Condition | Stage 1 | Stage 2 | Test |
|---|---|---|---|
| S2R | AB+ | AC+ | AG vs. CE |
|  | CD– |  |  |
|  | EF+ | EG? | BH vs. DF |
|  | GH– |  |  |
| S2NR | IJ+ | IK– | IO vs. KM |
|  | KL– |  |  |
|  | MN+ | MO? | JP vs. LN |
|  | OP– |  |  |
| Backward Blocking | QR+ | Q+ | R |
| Unovershadowing | ST+ | S– | T |
| BCI | UV– | U+ | V |
| BCI Control | WX– | W– | X |

CD with no outcome. Then in Stage 2, we combine one element from each compound (A and C), and the novel AC compound thus formed is reinforced. We might expect these AC+ trials to lead to increments in the associative strengths of the presented cues (A and C). Moreover, presentation of A will evoke an expectation of B, and presentation of C will evoke an expectation of D. According to the modified Rescorla–Wagner model, B and D will take on negative $\alpha$, such that $V_B$ and $V_D$ should decrease over these trials (due to processes of backward blocking and BCI respectively). Hence this experimental preparation addresses two questions:

1. Does associative history affect the relative magnitude of associative increment undergone by the presented cues A and C on AC+ trials?
2. Does associative history affect the relative magnitude of associative decrement undergone by the absent-but-expected cues B and D on AC+ trials?

The modified Rescorla–Wagner model, with its summed error term governing associative change, predicts that the associative change undergone by cues that are presented simultaneously, or cues that are absent simultaneously, will be independent of the individual associative histories of those cues. That is, it predicts that, on AC+ trials, A and C will undergo equal increments in associative strength, and B and D will undergo equal decrements in associative strength.

We again assessed relative magnitudes of associative change using Rescorla's (2000) technique of comparing responding to cues when they were embedded in compounds designed to ensure similar overall levels of responding. Thus during Stage 1 compounds EF and GH were trained in identical fashion to AB and CD respectively. This allowed us to compare associative change in presented and absent cues as follows:

1. Presented cues: Following Stage 1 compounds AG and CE should have equal strength—each contains one excitor and one more neutral cue. If Stage 2 AC+ trials lead to a greater increase in $V_A$ than in $V_C$, we would expect a higher rating for AG than for CE; if $\Delta V_C > \Delta V_A$ we would expect a higher rating for CE than for AG.
2. Absent cues: Following Stage 1 compounds BH and DF should have equal strength. If Stage 2 AC+ trials lead to a greater retrospective decrement in $V_B$ than $V_D$, we would expect a lower rating for BH than for DF; if the retrospective decrement is greater for $V_D$ than for $V_B$, we would expect a lower rating for DF than for BH.

In a similar manner to Experiment 1, during Stage 2 participants were also given "EG?" exposure trials on which no information regarding the occurrence or nonoccurrence of the outcome was provided. These trials ensured that any effect of formation of an A–C within-compound association on AC+ trials would be matched by development of E–G associations, such that any difference between AG and CE following Stage 2 could only be due to unequal changes in A–US and C–US associations on AC+ trials. These "exposure" trials also equated any effects of within-compound associations with regard to the absent cues, B, D, F, and H.

The Stage 2 nonreinforcement (S2NR) condition is similar, but the Stage 2 compound IK is nonreinforced. We might expect this treatment to lead to a decrement in the associative strengths of the presented cues I and K, and a retrospective increment in the associative strengths of the related absent cues J and L. Once again the modified Rescorla–Wagner model predicts that each pair of cues (I and K, and J and L) will undergo an equal change in associative strength. Using a similar logic to that employed previously, the actual distribution of associative change between presented cues can be assessed by comparing causal judgment ratings of IO and KM on test, whereas distribution of associative change between absent cues can be assessed by comparing JP and LN.

The final four conditions in Table 7.3 (backward blocking, unovershadowing, BCI, and BCI Control) are the "standard" retrospective revaluation contingencies. These contingencies were included in order to allow us to assess whether our experimental design was indeed able to support learning about absent cues (if not, then we could not expect to see any effects in S2R and S2NR conditions). As discussed earlier, retrospective revaluation would be demonstrated by a lower rating for R (from the backward-blocking contingency) than for T (unovershadowing contingency), and a lower rating for V (BCI contingency) than for X (BCI Control contingency).

## APECS and Retrospective Revaluation

This issue of the effect of associative history on the associative change undergone in retrospective revaluation is of particular interest to us because once again the APECS model, as discussed earlier, predicts a very different pattern of results to the modified Rescorla–Wagner model. Whereas modified Rescorla–Wagner explains retrospective revaluation in terms of novel learning about associatively retrieved representations of absent cues, APECS instead views it as a memory-based effect. In the discussion of Experiment 1 we noted that APECS allows for the generalization between two similar mappings to vary according to whether those mappings predict the same outcome or different outcomes. Specifically, generalization between two mappings remains high if those mappings predict the same outcome, but is dramatically reduced if the two mappings predict different outcomes. The changes occurring in the network to reduce generalization between a novel mapping predicting a certain outcome, and an older, similar mapping predicting a different outcome, lead to a change in the "retrievability" of the older mapping, reducing the extent to which it interferes with the new learning. And according to APECS, it is these changes in retrievability (resulting from changes in generalization) that produce retrospective revaluation. Crucially, these changes in retrievability will be greater when the outcomes following Stage 1 and Stage 2 compounds are different (requiring large changes in the network to reduce generalization between these mappings) than when they are the same (when generalization remains at its "default" high setting). And given that it is changes in retrievability that underlie the revaluation effect, APECS predicts greater revaluation when the outcomes in the two stages are different (as in unovershadowing or backward-conditioned inhibition) than when they are the same (as in backward blocking) (see Le Pelley & McLaren, 2001b, for a more detailed, mechanistic explanation of the effect of associative history on the magnitude of retrospective revaluation in the APECS model).

In the context of the current experiment, then, APECS predicts that on AC+ trials of the S2R condition, B (part of a Stage 1 mapping, AB+, predicting the same outcome as occurs on AC+ trials) will undergo a smaller retrospective decrement in associative strength than will D (part of a Stage 1 mapping, CD–, predicting a different outcome to that occurring on AC+ trials). Similarly it predicts that, on IK– trials of the S2NR condition, J (part of a Stage 1 mapping, IJ+, predicting a different outcome to that occurring on IK– trials) will undergo a greater retrospective increment than will L (part of a Stage 1 mapping, KL–, predicting the same outcome as occurs on IK– trials). In summary, then, for cues that are simultaneously absent on trial T, APECS predicts that a cue that was previously part of a mapping predicting the same outcome as that occurring on trial T will undergo a smaller change than a cue that was previously part of a mapping predicting a different outcome.

Evidence from earlier studies of retrospective revaluation and related phenomena indicates that the view of revaluation as a retrievability process taken by APECS has advantages over the more traditional, learning-based view taken by modified Rescorla–Wagner and modified SOP (Le Pelley et al., 2000; Le Pelley & McLaren, 2001b). Experiment 2 provided a further test of the model of retrospective revaluation offered by APECS, by assessing the influence of associative history on the relative magnitudes of retrospective change undergone by simultaneously absent cues.

Of course APECS also predicts that associative history should influence the relative magnitudes of associative change undergone by the presented cues on Stage 2 trials of the S2R and S2NR conditions of Experiment 2. As explained in the discussion following Experiment 1, APECS predicts that, for cues that are simultaneously presented on trial T, a cue that was previously part of a mapping predicting the same outcome as that occurring on trial T will undergo a greater change than a cue that was previously part of a mapping predicting a different outcome (note this is exactly the opposite of the prediction for absent cues). With regard to Experiment 2, then, we might expect A (part of a reinforced mapping in Stage 1) to undergo a greater increment in associative strength than will C (part of an unreinforced mapping in Stage 1) on Stage 2 AC+ trials of the S2R condition. Likewise, APECS predicts that I (part of a reinforced mapping in Stage 1) will undergo a smaller decrement in associative strength than will K (part of an unreinforced mapping in Stage 1) on Stage 2 IK– trials of the S2R condition.

These predictions were again confirmed by simulation. Figure 7.4a shows the averaged results from 20 separate simulations of the experimental design shown in Table 7.1, each simulation representing a different subject. The network and parameters used were exactly the same as those for the simulation of Experiment 1 (results in Fig. 7.1b). The critical comparisons involve considering the columns of this graph in pairs (AG vs. CE, BH vs. DF, IO vs. KM, JP vs. LN). The simulation results in Fig. 7.4a demonstrate that APECS's use of adaptive generalization coefficients allows the individual associative histories of both presented and absent cues to influence the relative magnitude of associative change that they undergo. These results confirm the predictions of the network laid out earlier, with AG > CE, BH > DF, IO > KM and JP > LN.

The empirical results of Experiment 2 provided clear evidence that our paradigm would support learning about absent cues (validating a comparison between S2R and S2NR conditions). The mean rating of the target cue of the backward blocking contingency, R (rating 2.46), was significantly lower than that of the unovershadowing contingency, T (rating 8.04), and the mean rating of the target cue of the BCI contin-

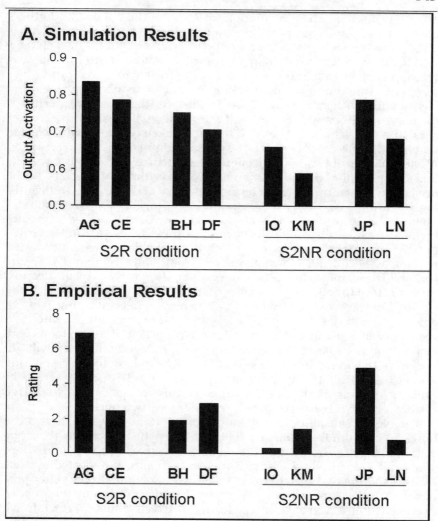

FIG. 7.4. (a) Simulation of Experiment 2 using APECS. (b) Mean causal judgment ratings received by the test compounds of Experiment 2.

gency, V (rating –6.25) was significantly lower than that of the BCI Control contingency (X, rating –2.29).

The empirical data of greatest interest—the mean rating for each test compound—is shown in Fig. 7.4b. Recall that the modified Rescorla–Wagner model specifies a common error term governing associative change for both presented and absent cues and hence specifies no role for associative history in determining the distribution of associative change between the elements of a compound. As such this model (and others taking the same view, e.g., Dickinson & Burke's, 1996, modified SOP) is constrained to predict no difference between the members of each pair, that is, AG = CE, BH = DF, IO = KM, JP = LN. APECS, with its emphasis on adaptive generalization, predicts a profound effect of associative history, with outcome similarity acting in opposite ways on present and absent cues (with similar outcomes in the two stages of the experiment meaning large changes for present cues and small changes for absent cues, and vice versa). In line with the view taken by modified Rescorla–Wagner, the difference between the causal judgment ratings received by BH and DF was not statistically significant; neither was that between IO and KM ($t < 1$ for both comparisons). However, directly contrary to the predictions of summed error term models, AG received a significantly higher rating than CE. This implies that, on Stage 2 AC+ trials, the element of the AC compound that had previously been trained as a predictor of the same outcome as occurred on these trials (A) underwent a greater increment in associative strength than did the element that had previously been trained as a predictor of nonreinforcement (C). This is the prediction made by APECS. Moreover, JP received a significantly higher rating than LN. This implies that, on the IK– trials of Stage 2, the absent-but-expected cue that was part of a mapping predicting a different outcome to that occurring on IK– trials (J) underwent a greater retrospective increase in associative strength than did the cue that was part of a mapping predicting the same outcome (L). Once again this result fits well with the predictions of the APECS model—indeed, to the best of our knowledge APECS is the only existing model of retrospective effects in human learning that is able to predict this influence of associative history on the retrospective change undergone by cues.

The higher causal judgment rating for AG than for CE replicates the observation from Experiment 1 that associative history affects the associative change experienced by presented cues trained in compound. More specifically, this finding fits with the general pattern indicated by that earlier experiment, wherein the cue that was individually the better predictor of following events on compound trials underwent the greater change. The observed difference in ratings between JP and LN extends Experiment 1 by demonstrating that the relative magnitude of retrospective associative change undergone by an absent-but-expected cue can also be selectively affected by the individual associative history of that cue.

These results clearly demonstrate once again the insufficiency of the common error term approach to associative change taken by the modified Rescorla–Wagner model (also taken less explicitly by Dickinson & Burke's, 1996, modified SOP model). Any model that is to encompass these results must specify, either directly or indirectly, a role for associative history in the determination of associative change undergone by different elements that engage the learning process simultaneously, whether those elements represent presented or absent stimuli. APECS is one such model. According to this model, the influence of associative history on the associative change undergone by presented cues is dia-metrically opposed to its effects on the associative change undergone by absent cues. That is, whereas for presented cues it tends to be the case that it is the cue that is the better predictor of the outcome occurring on compound trials that undergoes the greater change, for absent cues it is, if anything, the cue that is the poorer predictor of the outcome occurring on Stage 2 trials that tends to undergo the greater change.

It is important to note, however, that the fit between the predictions of APECS (Fig. 7.4a) and the empirical data of Experiment 2 (Fig. 7.4b) is far from perfect. APECS is successfully able to account for the difference between AG and CE, and that between JP and LN. However, it also predicts greater responding to BH than to DF, and to IO than to KM, whereas in the empirical data neither difference was significant, with both showing a trend in the opposite direction. In other words, though APECS predicts a general pattern wherein, for two cues presented in compound, the cue that has previously been paired with the same outcome as that occurring on compound trials will undergo the greater associative change, in the results of Experiment 2 this effect is seen in one condition (S2R) and not the other (S2NR). Similarly, though APECS makes the general prediction that, for cues that are simultaneously absent but expected, the cue that was previously paired with a different outcome to that occurring on compound trials will undergo the greater associative change, the empirical data again reveal this predicted effect in one condition (S2NR), but not the other (S2R).

The failure to detect greater responding to IO than to KM in the S2NR condition of Experiment 2 (as predicted by APECS) is particularly surprising given the results of Experiment 1, where we found that non-reinforcement of a compound composed of an excitor and an inhibitor led to a greater decrement in the associative strength of the inhibitor than of the excitor. That is, in that case greater change occurred for the element that was part of a Stage 1 mapping predicting the same outcome as occurred on compound trials (nonreinforcement), as compared to an element that was part of a Stage 1 mapping predicting a different outcome (reinforcement). This is the result anticipated by APECS. In Experiment 2, on the other hand, nonreinforcement of a compound composed of an excitor and a neutral cue revealed no difference in the associative change undergone by each, despite the fact that the neutral cue must surely have been a better predictor of nonreinforcement on compound trials than was the excitor.

Why the difference in results between the two experiments? Up to this point, we have discussed effects of associative history in terms of the surprisingness of an outcome given the presence of certain cues, where a more surprising outcome can support more learning than a less surprising one—typically referred to in the animal conditioning literature as "US–processing" effects. Both APECS and Rescorla–Wagner are pure US-processing models. An alternative way in which a cue's associative history might affect the associative change that it undergoes is through learned changes in the processing power devoted to learning about that cue (the "associability" of the cue). Unlike US-processing theories, models of associability changes look at how surprising the presence of a certain cue is, given the occurrence of a certain outcome. That is, these models focus on how well each cue is able to predict the occurrence of the outcome with which it is paired, and adjust the processing power devoted to subsequent learning about that cue appropriately—consequently these are often referred to as "CS-processing" models (for a recent review of the interaction of CS- and US-processing factors in animal conditioning and human causal learning, see Le Pelley, in press). Once again, then, learned changes in associability provide a way in which the individual associative history of a cue can influence the associative change subsequently undergone by that cue, and it is possible that this additional influence of associative history might account for the difference in results between our two similar studies.

One of the most influential models of learned associability in studies of animal conditioning is that of Mackintosh (1975). This states that the associability of a stimulus may vary according to how well that stimulus predicts the occurrence of events of significance. Put simply, this model states that cues that are good predictors of events of significance maintain a higher associability than cues that are poorer predictors of events of significance. Let us suppose that, in the studies of human causal learning outlined earlier, the occurrence of the "Allergic Reaction!" outcome, and the nonoccurrence of an expected reaction (producing inhibitory learning) constitute events of significance, whereas the nonoccurrence of a reaction where none is expected does not. The upshot of this is that cues trained as excitors or inhibitors will develop and maintain a high associability (as they are consistently followed by events of significance), whereas neutral cues will have a lower associability (as they are not). What ramifications does this suggestion have for the S2NR conditions of Experiments 1 and 2? Experiment 1 employed a compound of an excitor and an inhibitor. Both of these cues would begin Stage 2 compound nonreinforced trials with similar, high associabilities, as both were consistently paired with events of significance in Stage 1. This would allow differential effects of associative history in terms of US-processing influences (promoting more rapid learning about the inhibitor than the excitor, as predicted by APECS) to manifest as differences in associative change. Experiment 2 employed a compound of an excitor and a neutral cue in Stage 2. As a result, the excitor might well begin Stage 2 with a higher associability than the neutral cue. Hence CS-processing considerations would tend to promote greater associative change for the excitor than for the neutral cue. US-processing influences, as we have seen, tend to promote greater change in the presented cue that is the better predictor of the outcome on Stage 2 trials. In the S2NR condition of Experiment 2, these two influences oppose one another, with CS processing promoting greater change for I (excitor) than for K (neutral) and US processing promoting greater change for K (better predictor of nonreinforcement) than for I (poorer predictor). The overall effect of these opposing influences, then, could well be no difference in the associative change observed for I and K. In the S2R condition of Experiment 2, on the other hand, these two influences work in concert to ensure that A (an excitor and a better predictor of reinforcement on AC+ trials than C, a neutral cue) undergoes a greater associative change than C, as evidenced by the empirical results of this study.

Associability considerations could also explain the lack of an observed difference between the associative change undergone by the absent cues B (an excitor) and D (a neutral cue) on AC+ trials of Experiment 2. We saw earlier that the US-processing view taken by APECS predicts that the absent cue that is the poorer predictor of the Stage 2 outcome will tend to undergo the greater change. In the S2NR condition, CS-processing influences (promoting greater change in J, an excitor with high associability at the outset of Stage 2, than in L, a neutral cue with lower associability) act in concert with the US-processing mechanisms of APECS (promoting greater change in J, the poorer predictor of non-reinforcement) to ensure greater change for the absent J than for L on IK– trials. In the S2R condition, on the other hand, CS-processing influences (favoring greater change for B than for D) would tend to oppose US-processing influences (favoring greater change for D than for B), resulting in no overall difference in the associative change undergone by the two cues. Thus it would appear that a theoretical framework integrating the US-processing approach to associative history offered by the APECS model with CS-processing mechanisms similar to those suggested by Mackintosh (1975) could potentially provide a full account of the results of Experiments 1 and 2.

## EXPERIMENT 3: LEARNED ASSOCIABILITY IN HUMAN CAUSAL LEARNING

The *post hoc* suggestion that the differences in relative associative change undergone by presented cues in the highly similar S2NR conditions of Experiments 1 and 2 reflect the operation of CS-processing mechanisms is at best extremely tentative. That said, recent evidence has provided good evidence that learned associability processes do indeed operate in human causal learning, and can have a profound influence on the associative change undergone by cues (Le Pelley & McLaren, 2003; Lochmann & Wills, 2003).

The study by Le Pelley and McLaren (2003) employed the within-subjects design shown in Table 7.4 (filler trials are omitted from this table). Once again this experiment used an allergy prediction paradigm with human subjects. In this table, letters A–Y refer to different foods, and the numbers 1–4 represent different types of allergic reaction that patients could suffer as a result of eating these foods (nausea, dizziness, itch, and sweating, with allergies randomly assigned to numbers in the experimental design for each participant).

### TABLE 7.4
### Design of Experiment 3 (Excluding Filler Trials)

| Stage 1 | Stage 2 | Test |
|---|---|---|
| AV → 1 | | |
| BV → 2 | | |
| AW → 1 | AX → 3 | AC |
| BW → 2 | BY → 4 | BD |
| CX → 2 | CV → 3 | VX |
| DX → 1 | DW → 4 | WY |
| CY → 2 | | |
| DY → 1 | | |

In Stage 1, participants were given information about foods and allergies for Mr. X. On each trial they would be told the contents of a meal eaten by Mr. X, and were then asked to predict the type of allergic reaction that he would suffer as a result (given a choice of allergy 1 or allergy 2). During this stage, cues A and D were consistently paired with allergy 1, whereas cues B and C were consistently paired with allergy 2. Cues V–Y, on the other hand, provided no basis for discrimination between the two outcomes, being paired with allergies 1 and 2 an equal number of times. If learned associability processes operate in human causal learning in accordance with the view offered by Mackintosh (1975), wherein good predictors maintain a higher associability than poor predictors, we would expect cues A–D (consistent predictors of Stage 1 outcomes) to maintain higher associability than cues V–Y (inconsistent predictors of Stage 1 outcomes) over the course of Stage 1 training.

In Stage 2, participants were given information regarding foods and allergies for a new patient, Mr. Y. On each of the Stage 2 trial types shown in Table 7.4, a "good predictor" from Stage 1 (A, B, C, or D) is paired with a "poor predictor" (V, W, X, or Y) with which it was not paired in Stage 1, and this novel food compound is paired with a novel outcome: Compounds AX and CV are paired with allergy 3; BY and DW are paired with allergy 4.

Note that, during Stage 2, all cues are objectively equally predictive of their respective outcomes. Cues A and X, for example, are both paired with allergy 3 an equal number of times, and neither is paired with any other outcome. Nevertheless we might expect the differences in predictiveness of cues A–D and V–Y during Stage 1 (in terms of differences in learned associability) to influence the relative rates of causal learning about these cues during Stage 2. Specifically, according to the Mackintosh (1975) view of associability cues A–D will begin Stage 2 training with higher associability than will cues V–Y. As a result, on the first Stage 2 trial of each type, the change in associative strength of the good predictor (from Stage 1) should be greater than that of the poor predictor. Thus, for example, there will be a greater increment in the strength of the association between A and allergy 3 ($V_{A,3}$) than between X and allergy 3 ($V_{A,3}$) on the first AX → 3 trial. Consider now the second AX → 3 trial. Given that $V_{A,3} > V_{X,3}$ as a result of the first trial, A will be a better predictor of allergy 3 than will X on this trial. Therefore the associability of A will remain high, whereas that of X remains low. This idea will apply equally to all subsequent Stage 2 trials, and will ensure that, following Stage 2 training, the associations between the good predictors (from Stage 1) and their respective Stage 2 outcomes will be stronger than the associations between the poor predictors and these same outcomes.

The use of novel outcomes in Stage 2 (allergies 3 and 4, as opposed to allergies 1 and 2 in Stage 1) ensures that Stage 1 training cannot have a direct, "US-processing type" influence on the distribution of associative change between the elements of each Stage 2 compound. That is, whereas in Experiments 1 and 2 the outcome on Stage 2 trials was better-predicted by one element of the stimulus compound than the other, in Experiment 3 the occurrence of the novel outcome on the initial Stage 2 trial is completely unpredicted by either of the two elements of the Stage 2 compound (appropriate randomization and counterbalancing ensured that any generalization between Stage 1 and Stage 2 outcomes could have no selective, systematic effects on learning). Instead, in Experiment 3 the distribution of associative change among the elements of the Stage 2 compound is determined entirely by the difference in associability of the two cues making up this compound, developed during Stage 1.

Following Stage 2, participants were asked to rate the likelihood with which compounds AC, BD, VX, and WY would cause each of allergies 3 and 4.[1] Thus for each meal, subjects would provide two ratings: one of how likely that meal was to cause allergy 3, the other of how likely that meal was to cause allergy 4. As a result of the differences in learned associability discussed earlier, we would expect that $V_{A,3}$ and $V_{C,3}$ would be greater than $V_{X,3}$ and $V_{V,3}$, and $V_{B,4}$ and $V_{D,4}$ would be greater than $V_{Y,4}$ and $V_{W,4}$. As a result we would expect that AC would be judged as strongly predictive of allergy 3 and BD as strongly predictive of allergy 4, whereas VX and WY would be judged as only weakly predictive of allergies 3 and 4 respectively. In other words, the discrimination between compounds AC and BD (made up of good predictors from Stage 1) should be greater than that between VX and WY (made up of poor predictors). In this experiment we were interested in the *differential* predic-

---

[1]Testing compounds, rather than individual cues, prevents alternative interpretations of the results of this study, based on proactive interference or asymmetry of generalization; see Le Pelley and McLaren, 2003 for more details (see also Lochmann & Wills, 2003).

tiveness of each compound for the two allergies—that is, the extent to which it predicted allergy 3 more (or less) than it did allergy 4. Therefore for each compound, the rating on the allergy 4 scale was subtracted from the rating on the allergy 3 scale to yield a difference score. This difference score provides an index of the selective learning of cue–outcome relationships during Stage 2. On this scale, a positive score indicates that a compound is perceived as a stronger cause of allergy 3 than of allergy 4, whereas a negative score indicates that a compound is perceived as a stronger cause of allergy 4 than of allergy 3.

The mean difference score for each of the test compounds of Experiment 3 is shown in Fig. 7.5. These results reveal significant discrimination between compounds made up of good predictors from Stage 1: The mean difference score for AC is significantly higher than that for BD. There is no reliable evidence for discrimination between compounds made up of poor predictors from Stage 1, however: The mean difference scores of VX and WY do not differ significantly. And crucially, in line with the view of learned associability taken by the Mackintosh (1975) model, the discrimination between AC and BD is significantly better than that between VX and WY.

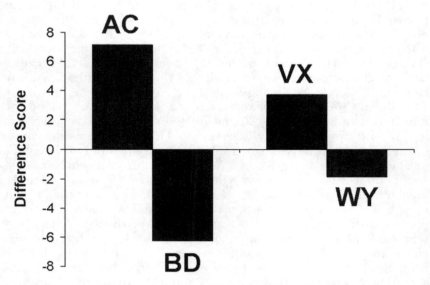

FIG. 7.5. Mean difference scores (allergy 3 rating – allergy 4 rating) for each of the test compounds of Experiment 3. A positive score indicates a greater perceived likelihood of allergy 3 than of allergy 4; a negative score indicates a greater perceived likelihood of allergy 4 than of allergy 3; a score of zero indicates no differential predictiveness.

These results provide clear evidence for an effect of differential predictiveness experienced during Stage 1 training on relative learning rates in Stage 2 (see also Lochmann & Wills, 2003). When, in Stage 2, compounds of good and poor predictors ("good" and "poor," that is, with respect to Stage 1 outcomes) are paired with novel outcomes, learning proceeds more rapidly to the good predictors as a result of this difference in experienced predictiveness. This study thus provides strong evidence for a role of learned associability in determining the distribution of associative change undergone by the elements of a reinforced compound in human causal learning, and this learned associability represents another way in which a cue's associative history can influence the associative change that it undergoes on a given trial.

Earlier we stated that the results of Experiments 1 and 2 contradict any model that specifies the distribution of associative change among simultaneously presented (or simultaneously absent) cues to be wholly governed by a common error term (e.g., the modified Rescorla–Wagner model, or modified SOP). These results were instead proposed to support a model in which the associative change undergone by a cue on a given trial was in some way influenced by the surprisingness of the outcome in the presence of that cue individually. APECS is one such model, in which the differential associative history of simultaneously presented (or simultaneously absent) cues exerts its effects by means of changes in generalization between "old" mappings learned in Stage 1 and "new" mappings learned in Stage 2. We then suggested that a puzzling difference between the results of the S2NR conditions in Experiments 1 and 2 could be accounted for by a further way in which a cue's associative history might influence the associative change undergone by that cue—the operation of learned associability processes ("CS-processing" mechanisms) wherein the processing power devoted to learning about a given cue is able to vary as a function of that cue's history of predictiveness. Experiment 3 provided powerful evidence supporting the operation of these mechanisms in human causal learning. In total, then, we might see the results of Experiments 1–3 as supporting a model in which associative change undergone by a cue is affected by the interaction of two separate influences of associative history—a US-processing influence implementing an effect of the surprisingness of the outcome in the presence of each separate cue, and a CS-processing influence based on the experienced predictiveness of that cue in the past. Given its success in accounting for a range of learning and memory phenomena observed for both presented and absent cues (e.g., Le Pelley et al., 2000; Le Pelley & McLaren, 2001a, 2001b, 2004; McLaren, 1993, 1994) we believe that APECS is a strong candidate for the US-processing component of this integrated model. Experiment 3 indicates that, in human causal learning, cues that are good predictors of events of significance maintain a higher associability than cues that are poorer predictors (see also Lochmann & Wills, 2003), as suggested by the Mackintosh (1975) theory of CS processing. Consequently, it would seem that a model integrating these two distinct approaches to the way in which associative history affects the associative change undergone by a given cue on a given trial might well provide a more satisfying account of the existing empirical data than either component alone.

## REFERENCES

Chapman, G. B. (1991). Trial-order affects cue interaction in contingency judgement. *Journal of Experimental Psychology: Learning, Memory, and Cognition, 17*, 837 –854.

De Houwer, J., & Beckers, T. (2002). A review of recent developments in research and theories on human contingency learning. *Quarterly Journal of Experimental Psychology, 55B*, 289 –310.

Dickinson, A., & Burke, J. (1996). Within-compound associations mediate the retrospective revaluation of causality judgements. *Quarterly Journal of Experimental Psychology, 49B*, 60 –80.

Dickinson, A., & Shanks, D. R. (1985). Animal conditioning and human causality judgment. In L.-G. Nilsson & T. Archer (Eds.), *Perspectives on learning and memory* (pp. 167 –191). Hillsdale, NJ: Lawrence Erlbaum Associates.

Dickinson, A., Shanks, D. R., & Evenden, J. L. (1984). Judgement of act-outcome contingency: The role of selective attribution. *Quarterly Journal of Experimental Psychology, 36A*, 29 –50.

Kamin, L. J. (1969). Predictability, surprise, attention and conditioning. In B. A. Campbell & R. M. Church (Eds.), *Punishment and aversive behavior* (pp. 276 –296). New York: Appleton–Century–Crofts.

Le Pelley, M. E. (2002). *The interaction of learning and memory in human causal behaviour.* Unpublished doctoral dissertation. University of Cambridge, Cambridge, England.

Le Pelley, M. E. (in press). The role of associative history in models of associative learning: A selective review and a hybrid model. *Quarterly Journal of Experimental Psychology B.*

Le Pelley, M. E., Cutler, D. L., & McLaren, I. P. L. (2000). Retrospective effects in human causality judgment. In *Proceedings of the Twenty-Second Annual Conference of the Cognitive Science Society* (pp. 782–787). Mahwah, NJ: Lawrence Erlbaum Associates.

Le Pelley, M. E., & McLaren, I. P. L. (2001a). The mechanics of associative change. In *Proceedings of the Twenty-Second Annual Conference of the Cognitive Science Society* (pp. 534–539). Mahwah, NJ: Lawrence Erlbaum Associates.

Le Pelley, M. E., & McLaren, I. P. L. (2001b). Retrospective revaluation in humans: Learning or memory? *Quarterly Journal of Experimental Psychology, 54B*, 311–352.

Le Pelley, M. E., & McLaren, I. P. L. (2002). The interaction of learning and memory in associative networks. In *Proceedings of the 2002 IEEE World Congress on Computational Intelligence* (pp. 2899–2904). Piscataway, NJ: IEEE.

Le Pelley, M. E., & McLaren, I. P. L. (2003). Learned associability and associative change in human causal learning. *Quarterly Journal of Experimental Psychology, 56B*, 68–79.

Le Pelley, M. E., & McLaren, I. P. L. (2004). Associative history affects the associative change undergone by both presented and absent cues in human causal learning. *Journal of Experimental Psychology: Animal Behavior Processes, 30*, 67–73.

Lochmann, T., & Wills, A. J. (2003). Predictive history in an allergy prediction task. In F. Schmalhofer, R. M. Young, & G. Katz (Eds.), *Proceedings of EuroCogSci 03* (pp. 217–222). Mahwah, NJ: Lawrence Erlbaum Associates.

Mackintosh, N. J. (1975). A theory of attention: Variations in the associability of stimuli with reinforcement. *Psychological Review, 82*, 276–298.

Markman, A. B. (1989). LMS rules and the inverse base-rate effect: Comment on Gluck and Bower (1988). *Journal of Experimental Psychology: General, 118*, 417–421.

McLaren, I. P. L. (1993). APECS: A solution to the sequential learning problem. In *Proceedings of the 15th Annual Conference of the Cognitive Science Society* (pp. 717–722). Hillsdale, NJ: Lawrence Erlbaum Associates.

McLaren, I. P. L. (1994). Representation development in associative systems. In J. A. Hogan & J. J. Bolhuis (Eds.), *Causal mechanisms of behavioural development* (pp. 377–402). Cambridge, England: Cambridge University Press.

Miller, R. R., & Matzel, L. D. (1988). The comparator hypothesis: A response rule for the expression of associations. *Psychology of Learning and Motivation, 22*, 51–92.

Pearce, J. M. (1987). A model for stimulus generalization in Pavlovian conditioning. *Psychological Review, 94*, 61–73.

Pearce, J. M. (1994). Similarity and discrimination: A selective review and a connectionist model. *Psychological Review, 101*, 587–607.

Rescorla, R. A. (2000). Associative changes in excitors and inhibitors differ when they are conditioned in compound. *Journal of Experimental Psychology: Animal Behavior Processes, 26*, 428–438.

Rescorla, R. A., & Wagner, A. R. (1972). A theory of Pavlovian conditioning: Variations in the effectiveness of reinforcement and non-reinforcement. In A. H. Black & W. F. Prokasy (Eds.), *Classical conditioning II: Current research and theory* (pp. 64–99). New York: Appleton–Century–Crofts.

Rumelhart, D. E., Hinton, G. E., & Williams, R. J. (1986). Learning internal representations by error propagation. In D. E. Rumelhart, J. L. McLelland, & the PDP Research Group (Eds.), *Parallel distributed processing* (Vol. 1, pp. 318–362). Cambridge, MA: MIT Press.

Shanks, D. R. (1985). Forward and backward blocking in human contingency judgement. *Quarterly Journal of Experimental Psychology, 37B*, 1–21.

Shanks, D. R., & Dickinson, A. (1987). Associative accounts of causality judgment. *Psychology of Learning and Motivation, 21*, 229–261.

Shanks, D. R., & Dickinson, A. (1991). Instrumental judgment and performance under variations in action–outcome contingency and contiguity. *Memory & Cognition, 19*, 353–360.

Thorndike, E. L. (1898). Animal intelligence: An experimental study of the associative processes in animals. *Psychological Review* (Monograph Supplement, Whole No. 8).

Van Hamme, L. J., & Wasserman, E. A. (1994). Cue competition in causality judgments: The role of nonrepresentation of compound stimulus elements. *Learning and Motivation, 25*, 127–151.

Wagner, A. R. (1981). SOP: A model of automatic memory processing in animal behaviour. In N. E. Spear & R. R. Miller (Eds.), *Information processing in animals: Memory mechanisms* (pp. 5–47). Hillsdale, NJ: Lawrence Erlbaum Associates.

# Chapter 8

# Elemental Representation and Associability: An Integrated Model

Mark Suret and I. P. L. McLaren

How do we learn? What are the processes that drive learning in both animals and humans? Are we simply tracking contingencies between specific events, or does the history and prior knowledge of events have an effect on how we learn about new relationships? Early theories of animal and associative learning (Hebb, 1949; Konorski, 1948; Spence, 1936, 1937) only concerned themselves with simple stimulus–response or input–output connections where both learning and responding were governed principally by the strength of the links between nodes (relative to some asymptote) and the activations of the nodes. More modern versions of this type of approach can account for many of the associative learning phenomena prevalent in the literature, both human and animal, such as blocking, overshadowing, and inhibition (e.g., Rescorla & Wagner, 1972). The types of effect we investigate in this chapter are those that pose problems for these simple yet relatively powerful models of learning.

Phenomena such as the overtraining reversal effect (ORE) (Reid, 1953) and the extradimensional–intradimensional (ED–ID) shift effect (Schwartz, Schwartz, & Teas, 1971; Shepp & Eimas, 1964) both cause particular problems for models that do not take account of the variable salience a stimulus may attain during its previous exposure and training. There are models that recognize the importance of associative history (Mackintosh, 1975; Sutherland & Mackintosh, 1971) and can cope with these types of effects with relative ease. The notion of associability invoked here denotes a parameter controlling learning that is sensitive to previous learning, so that the associative history of a stimulus, that is, how predictive it has been in the past, has an effect on the amount of learning seen on subsequent episodes. The model that we concentrate on

155

in this chapter is that proposed by Mackintosh (1975). His proposal is that a previously good predictor of an outcome will retain a high associability and hence enter into subsequent associations more rapidly than a previously poor predictor.

In the case of the ORE, this can be used to explain the results where a group given overtraining on a discrimination shows faster acquisition of the discrimination when it is reversed than does a group simply trained to criterion before reversal. In experiments such as these, two groups of animals are trained on a particular discrimination, for example the brighter of two stimuli will produce a food reward. One of the groups is trained until they achieve a criterion, commonly 90%, upon which the discrimination task is reversed, and now the darker of the stimuli provides the reward. The other group is trained on the same initial discrimination, but continues with the training for typically 100–200 trials after attaining criterion before the reversal is applied. The finding is that the group overtrained on the initial discrimination requires fewer trials to acquire the reversed discrimination than the group trained to criterion. This result is hard to explain in simple associative terms, as the extended training should have produced stronger associative links between the originally correct stimulus and reward, which would prove more difficult to overcome when the reversal is applied.

In the overtrained case, the associabilities of the predictive stimuli are maintained at a high level during overtraining, which then aids rapid acquisition of the newly reversed discrimination. Conversely, simply training to a criterion will not allow such a high associability to develop; hence, on reversal the new response assignments will be learned at a slower rate.

The idea behind intra- and extradimensional shifts relates to the use of the stimuli in this paradigm, where stimuli typically have two dimensions on which responding could be based, say color and shape, but only one of which is relevant. For example, initially training a group of pigeons on a color discrimination between yellow and blue shapes with form irrelevant, would form the discrimination prior to the dimensional shift. The intradimensional shift (IDS) is where half of the pigeons are then transferred to a new discrimination where color remains the relevant dimension, but now requires discriminating red and green shapes, whereas the extradimensional shift (EDS) requires the subjects to discriminate between the stimuli on the basis of form, star and circle say, with the color dimension (red vs. green) now being irrelevant. The absolute nature of the stimuli is changed between stages to ensure that there can be no direct associative transfer, so that any performance advantage seen for the IDS group must be due to the changes in the associability of the stimuli drawn from the two dimensions. Specifically, the implication is that stimuli drawn from the previously relevant dimension have a higher associability than those drawn from the previously irrelevant dimension.

The evidence for associability processes in humans has been somewhat scarce, and although there have been demonstrations of the ED–ID shift effect (Whitney & White, 1993), it is only recently that human analogues of earlier animal conditioning studies (Rescorla, 2000) have been carried out (Le Pelley & McLaren, 2003; Lochmann & Wills, 2003), demonstrating similar effects to those seen in infra-humans. These experiments have used various allergy prediction paradigms to provide evidence for the presence of associability processes in humans (see also chap. 7). Here we provide further convergent evidence for associability processes in humans using visual discrimination tasks quite unlike the contingency learning experiments just cited. The paradigms we have employed are known to provide good evidence for associability processes when using animal subjects, and the replication of this pattern of results using human participants would adduce compelling convergent evidence for similar processes at work in both humans and animals. Previous experiments have shown that it is possible to obtain an effect known as transfer along a continuum (TAC) with human participants (McLaren & Suret, 2000) and it is this paradigm that we develop further in this chapter. The term TAC was given to a phenomenon first reported by Lawrence (1952) where he demonstrated that a group of rats, trained on a relatively easy brightness discrimination before being transferred to a harder target discrimination on the same dimension, were more accurate at this discrimination than a group of animals trained for an equivalent total length of time solely on the target discrimination.

Our strategy is to look at the role of associability within the TAC paradigm and show that it is possible to obtain results analogous to those found in pigeons by Mackintosh and Little (1970), who included a reversal manipulation in their design. The results they reported are covered in greater detail later in the chapter, but an analysis combining both associability and its generalization to other related stimuli would allow their results to be interpreted along similar lines to the ORE.

As well as presenting empirical results in support of this proposal, this chapter also develops a computational model of associative learning based on the framework given by McLaren and Mackintosh (2000, 2002). Taking the basic components of this model as a starting point, we have added an associability component to the real-time equations governing learning and go on to show that this can be applied to the data reported here. The associability component is based on the algorithm in Mackintosh (1975), although the equations governing its functioning have been modified to fit with a real-time framework.

## EMPIRICAL BACKGROUND

We have shown previously (McLaren & Suret, 2000) that it is possible to obtain a TAC effect in humans using morphed face dimensions; an example of one of the dimensions used in the experiments is shown in Fig. 8.1. The stimuli shown in Fig. 8.1 give some idea of the similarity between both the hard and the easy stimuli, and also the overlap between stimuli that will share the same response during training and

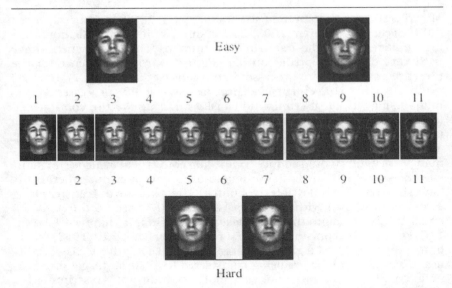

FIG. 8.1. An example of one of the four morphed face dimensions used in the experiments reported here.

pretraining for the easy group. As well as the standard easy-to-hard TAC effect, we demonstrated that it was pretraining on the easy discrimination (whereby feedback is given in order that participants are able to learn the discrimination) rather than simple preexposure to the stimuli (where participants simply looked at the stimuli without making any response) that was crucial in obtaining the TAC effect. Experiment 2 (*ibid*) of that paper shows that preexposure to the easy stimuli affords no advantage for subsequent acquisition of the hard discrimination, whereas preexposure to the hard stimuli gives test performance equivalent to that of pretraining on the hard stimuli. This effect is taken to be the result of perceptual learning as the features common to both hard stimuli are irrelevant to subsequent discrimination, but the unique features are rendered relatively more salient. This allows them to engage in a greater amount of learning when paired with the response during training than the common features and so more accurate discrimination is seen on test. This mechanism for perceptual learning was initially proposed by McLaren, Kaye, and Mackintosh (1989) and further developed in the recent model proposed in McLaren and Mackintosh (2000, 2002).

This set of experiments (and others, see McLaren & Mackintosh, 2002) established that the morphed face stimuli were suitable for use in a procedure designed to demonstrate associative learning, thus validating them for use in subsequent experiments. The studies reported here further develop the TAC paradigm in humans and look for associability effects along the lines of those found by Mackintosh and Little (1970). The design of their experiment is shown in Table 8.1 and it is analogous to the design used in our experiments. Here A, B, C, and D represent stimuli ordered along a dimension, and the + and – indicate reward and nonreward in an animal experiment, or different responses in an experiment with human participants.

The easy reversed condition is identical to the easy condition in terms of the stimuli that are presented, but the responses trained during pretraining are the opposite to those applied in the standard easy group.

Simple associative accounts, such as Rescorla and Wagner (1972), and more complex models such as McLaren and Mackintosh (2000, 2002) will base their predictions of the pattern of results in this experiment on the generalization of the associations formed during the pretraining phase. These generalization-based accounts of TAC, unlike those based on associability, will predict that the easy group should perform the best, followed by hard, with easy reversed performing worst. This latter group will have an initial deficit in performance on starting the training phase, as the responses will be conditioned to inappropriate stimuli on the basis of pretraining. This will eventually be overcome, but the rate at which learning will then proceed should be no greater than that observed for the hard group, as only the hard stimuli are present to drive learning.

Mackintosh and Little's results do not support this type of analysis, as they found that the pigeons in group easy reversed attained the same level of responding as those in group easy at the end of the training phase. Critically, they were significantly better at the hard discrimination at the end of training than the group trained solely on the hard stimuli. This finding fits well with associability accounts as it can easily be accommodated by a theory that takes account of the associative history of the stimuli involved in the discrimination.

## EMPIRICAL EVIDENCE FOR ASSOCIABILITY PROCESSES

Previous attempts to demonstrate the presence of associability processes in humans have met with mixed success (Suret & McLaren, 2003), but

TABLE 8.1

Design of Mackintosh and Little (1970)

|  | Pretraining | Training | Test |
| --- | --- | --- | --- |
| Easy | A+ D– | B+ C– | B vs. C |
| Hard | B+ C– | B+ C– | B vs. C |
| Easy Reversed | A– D+ | B+ C– | B vs. C |

Experiment 3 in our paper showed that it was possible to obtain an analogue of the result reported by Mackintosh and Little (1970), with performance in the easy reversed group being significantly better than that of the hard group. However the experiment presented in that paper was only the beginning of our investigation of this issue, and the empirical portion of this chapter reports additional conditions that shed more light on the processes at work.

Our rationale for the manipulations deployed in our experimental design was as follows: If we are looking to reproduce the results from the animal literature, then it would seem prudent to follow the procedure used within such experiments more faithfully, if not to the letter, then at least in spirit. It would seem unreasonable to expect people to take 2 weeks to acquire a discrimination in the way that pigeons often require, but it would seem sensible to try to match more accurately the relative timings of the stages within the experiment.

The general procedure with most animal experiments is to allow a substantial amount of time between the various stages of the experiment, and this is seldom the case in human experiments. Mackintosh and Little (1970) used daily sessions of training for a 15-day period, so that each training, or pretraining, session was followed by a 24-hour gap. We speculate that it may be that the delay between sessions allows some decay of the associations formed up to that point. This delay may be especially important just before the reversal is applied because, as we see later, it might be that the associabilities ($\alpha$ values) of elements do not decay or that the rate of decay is slower than that for the connections between the stimulus representations and the responses that are required when the stimuli are presented (Holland, 1988). If so, this will allow any changes in associability to persist whereas the associations between stimuli and responses are weakened and hence more readily reversed, as a consequence of the decay that has taken place.

Another crucial component of the Mackintosh and Little effect may be the sheer amount of training given in order to assure successful performance on the reversed problem (Mackintosh, 1969; Reid, 1953). We speculate that the pretraining given must be sufficient to overtrain the subjects on the easy discrimination to such an extent that this will allow generalization of the high associabilities thus obtained to the hard stimuli used in subsequent training, and, if the associability account is to be believed, this will lead to facilitation when learning the hard discrimination.

In line with this analysis, the experiment we report here looks at the effect both of overtraining, and of a delay between pretraining and training within the TAC paradigm, with the focus on determining whether there is any evidence for associability processes in humans. The design looks to test the opposing predictions made by associability and generalization theories on performance with respect to a comparison of the hard and easy reversed conditions in a TAC design. We report the experiment in considerable detail, to give something of the flavor of this type of research, and to clarify the techniques used in transferring an animal paradigm to human subjects.

## EXPERIMENT 1

### Stimulus Construction

The stimuli in Experiment 1 were pictures of faces, all presented as grayscale images. In total there were 44, but these were divided into sets of 11, each of which were generated from two original passport photographs of university undergraduates. These photographs were scanned into a computer and morphed into one another using a standard morphing software package. The photographs were selected so as to be somewhat similar to one another by eye, as this would allow for a smoother morphing process, and more realistic pictures to be generated as a consequence, but picture quality was not paramount, as the primary objective was to have a set of reasonably confusable stimuli. The pictures were size matched using Adobe Photoshop, but no specific attempt was made to explicitly match for brightness or contrast. In total, four pairs of photographs were used, giving four dimensions of stimuli for use in Experiment 1, two female and two male. After morphing one of the photographs into the other, nine intermediate steps between the two endpoints were taken at equal intervals to give a total of 11 pictures for each face dimension. One example of the dimensions used is shown in Fig. 8.1, and due to the original similarity of the photographs and a smooth morphing process, neighboring pictures are very similar to one another. For Experiment 1, pictures 3 and 9 from each dimension were always shown when subjects were dealing with the easy task, and Pictures 5 and 7 were shown as the hard stimuli. On test, all 44 pictures were shown to the subjects to gauge not only discrimination between the critical stimuli at 5 and 7 on each dimension, but also to look at generalization along each dimension.

Although designated as the easy discrimination, Stimuli 3 and 9 on each dimension are still relatively similar to one another, and learning the discrimination is not a trivial matter. This similarity also tends to make learning any sort of rule to differentiate the stimuli difficult, so we assume that the learning proceeds in a more automatic fashion, employing some underlying associative process.

Experiment 1 was written using RealBasic and was run on an Apple Macintosh computer in a quiet, lightly sound-proofed room, away from any external noise. The stimuli measured 3.5 cm by 4.5 cm when presented to the subjects, who were seated approximately 50 cm away from the screen.

### Design

One hundred participants aged between 18 and 35 took part in this study and were divided into eight groups in accordance with the following factors. Experiment 1 used a mixed design, with between–subject factors of Problem (hard/easy reversed), Pretraining Length (long/short) and Gap (present/absent). A within–subjects factor of Dimension Position (11 levels) was also included. The Problem factor is self-explanatory, and the Gap factor relates to the presence or absence of a 20 minute gap between the pretraining and training phases, but Pretraining Length factor indicates how many blocks of training were given during the pretraining phase, either three (long) or one (short). The within–subject factor simply takes account of the participants' responses to the stimuli presented during the test phase.

All subjects experienced pretraining, training, and test phases, but the length of the pretraining and the contiguity of the experiment were changed in accordance with the factors. For all conditions there was no explicit linkage of the pretraining section and the part containing the training and test. No reference was made to previous parts of the experiment, or to the fact that the pretraining would be followed by a phase containing similar stimuli. The training and test phases were linked by asking subjects to respond to the faces on test using the responses that were correct during the training phase.

The pretraining consisted of a concurrent discrimination of four pairs of stimuli, which were determined by the level of Problem assigned to the subject. There were 40 trials in total, with each of the eight stimuli being presented five times in total. The order of the stimuli was constrained so that each of them was presented to the subject before any of the eight pictures were presented again. Within these subblocks of eight stimuli, the pictures were presented in a random order, and the order was different each time the stimuli were presented. There was a time limit of 4.25 seconds for a response to be recorded by pressing either the "x" key on the left-hand side of the keyboard or the ">/." (full-stop) key on the right-hand side. If no response was made within this time, the trial timed out, and the subjects were informed that they had taken too long to respond. The next trial then began. If a response was made, feedback was given on all trials registering whether the response had been correct or not before proceeding to the next trial. At the end of the final block of trials of pretraining, subjects were asked to find the experimenter.

The second stage involved training both groups on the hard problem, again with the same pseudo-random ordering of the stimuli as during pretraining. Subjects were shown 40 pictures in total, with each of the eight pictures being shown five times. This training stage was identical to the pretraining in every sense, apart from the change in stimuli presented to the subjects assigned to the easy reversed condition.

The final stage was a test phase and consisted of five blocks of 44 stimuli, all shown without feedback. All 11 stimuli from each of the four training dimensions were shown during each test block, with each stimulus being presented a total of five times. There was no constraint on the randomization of the stimuli within a block during the test phase, but each block had a different ordering of the stimuli. Despite the absence of feedback, the 4.25-second time limit on responding was retained throughout the test phase.

## Procedure

The participants started the experiment by clicking a button on the screen using a computer mouse, and were told prior to starting that this would initiate a constant stream of stimuli, which would appear on the screen. These stimuli would be in the form of pictures of faces, and the participants' task was to correctly categorize each stimulus as requiring a "left" or "right" response with either the "x" or ">/." key. Feedback would then be given immediately as to the correctness of the response, or if they had taken too long, then this would also be communicated to the subject. Each subject was told that the pictures had been equally and randomly assigned to one of the two response keys and that their task was simply to remember which picture required which response.

The stimuli were presented singly, in the center of the screen. Each trial started with a fixation mark (+) in the center of where the stimulus was to appear, and this was present for 0.7 seconds. A rectangular frame delimiting exactly where the stimulus would appear replaced this mark, and the stimulus itself appeared after another 0.2 seconds. The stimulus was visible for 4.25 seconds and disappeared once a response had been made, or the maximum time allowed had elapsed. Feedback was given for 1 second; either "correct" in the center of the screen, or "error" plus a beep. If the subject had taken too long to make a response, then "timeout" was displayed on the screen, accompanied by beep or if they pressed a key other than one of the two designated keys, then they were prompted with a beep and "invalid key" being shown on the screen. After the 40 pretraining trials, and after a 15-20 min, delay if the subject was in a Gap condition, the subject was given more instructions by the experimenter and then proceeded to the training phase of the experiment. They were told that the second part of the experiment was similar to the first in that they would see some more pictures of faces, and once again they would have to learn, initially by trial and error, which was the correct response to make to each of the pictures. This phase was identical to the pretraining phase except for the change in stimuli for subjects in the easy reversed conditions.

On completion of the training phase, a final set of instructions was given to the subjects detailing the procedure during the test phase. This phase was similar to the two previous phases, except that no feedback was given on any of the responses. Instead, a 1-second pause replaced the previous presentation of the feedback text. There were 44 trials in each of five blocks during the test phase, with each picture from each dimension being presented in every block. Subjects were told that they would see the same pictures that they had been responding to in the training phase, and that they should retain the responses that were correct in that phase. They were also told that they would be seeing some new pictures of faces, and that they should respond to those with the key they felt was most appropriate based on their experience in the training phase. There was a short break allowed between test blocks, and subjects continued once they were ready.

## Results

Average response scores for the easy reversed groups in the four conditions collapsed across the four dimensions are shown in Fig. 8.2a, and those for the hard groups are summarized in Fig. 8.2b. These scores are obtained by assigning one of the response keys a score of +0.5, and the other −0.5. Hence the results on test give an index of which response has been made to each stimulus. In all the graphs of results presented here, the response appropriate for Stimulus 7 is assigned a value of +0.5. The results displayed in Figs. 8.2a and 8.2b show that the extended pretraining and the presence of a gap seems to have had the greatest effect in the easy reversed group, with similar performance shown by all conditions where the pretraining was on the hard stimuli.

The data in Fig. 8.3 show a shift in ordering from hard being better than easy reversed in three of the four conditions, with the only condition where the easy reversed group outperforms the hard group being the long + gap condition. A three-way analysis of variance (ANOVA), using the discrimination score as the dependent measure, gave a main effect of pretraining length, $F(1,92) = 6.10$, $p = 0.015$, with long pretraining giving significantly better performance than short pretraining. Although this may seem unsurprising at first, as increased pretraining on the hard stimuli will doubtless lead to better performance, the application of the extended training to the easy reversed condition has a less certain outcome, especially if the processes in operation are solely driven by generalization. As it turns out, there is an advantage for extended training on the easy reversed, at least under some circumstances (Fig. 8.3). The dependent measure in this figure is mean discrimination score, which is calculated by subtracting the response score for Stimulus 5 from that for Stimulus 7, that is to say the hard stimuli. This means that perfect discrimination has a score of 1, a chance score is 0, whereas negative scores indicate that the responses being made are inappropriate based on the assignments that were taught during the training phase.

An alternative way to analyze this data is to perform a regression analysis on the mean response scores for each condition, and compare the gradients of the discrimination slopes along the dimension. These data are shown in Table 8.2 and report the gradient of the slope for each condition and the associated standard error estimate. Looking at the easy reversed data in Fig. 8.2a, it appears as though the long + gap

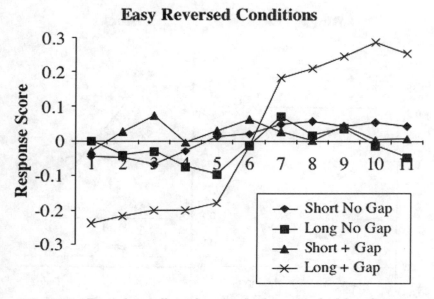

FIG. 8.2a. All test data collapsed across the four morphed face dimensions for the easy reversed conditions.

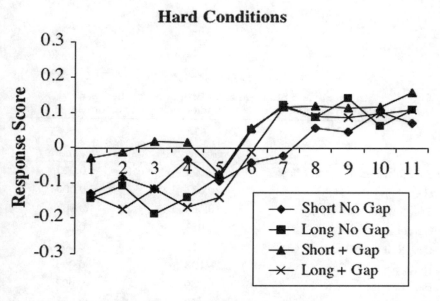

FIG. 8.2b. All test data collapsed across the four morphed face dimensions for the hard conditions.

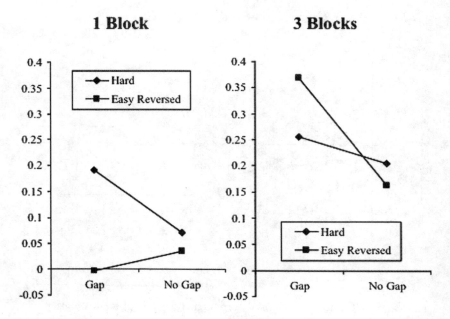

FIG. 8.3. Mean discrimination scores for all groups in the experiment.

TABLE 8.2
Gradients and Standard Error Estimates for the Mean
Response Scores From All Conditions in the Experiment

|  | Gradient | Standard Error Estimate |
|---|---|---|
| Easy Reversed, Long, No Gap | 0.004 | 0.005 |
| Hard, Long, No Gap | 0.033 | 0.003 |
| Easy Reversed, Long, Gap | 0.064 | 0.007 |
| Hard, Long, Gap | 0.033 | 0.006 |
| Easy Reversed, Short, No Gap | 0.013 | 0.004 |
| Hard, Short, No Gap | 0.023 | 0.006 |
| Easy Reversed, Short, Gap | 0.000 | 0.002 |
| Hard, Short, Gap | 0.019 | 0.003 |

group is different to not only the other easy reversed groups, but also all the hard groups in Fig. 8.2b. The gradient of the response slope for this condition is significantly greater than any of the other conditions, smallest $t(20) = 3.36, p < 0.005$. Taking the comparisons of theoretical interest and a significance level of 0.01 to guard against Type 1 error, comparing easy reversed and hard groups in the long + gap conditions reveals a significant difference between the slopes for these conditions, with the easy reversed group having the larger gradient, $t(20) = 3.36, p < 0.005$, and the corresponding comparison for the long no–gap condition shows that in this case the hard group's slope is significantly greater than that for the easy reversed group, $t(20) = 3.71, p < 0.005$. Combining these two analyses to look at the interaction in the linear trends reveals a significant difference between the differences in these two comparisons, $t(40) = 4.96, p < 0.001$. It seems that long pretraining with a gap as opposed to without a gap differentially affects the groups trained on the easy reversed and hard stimuli. That is, long pretraining on the easy reversed stimuli followed by a gap leads to better learning of the subsequent hard discrimination than if pretraining were on the hard discrimination, whereas long pretraining on the easy reversed stimuli without a gap leads to poorer learning of the subsequent hard discrimination than if pretraining were on the hard discrimination

A similar analysis can be applied to all the easy reversed conditions. Here there is a significant advantage for long + gap over long no gap, $t(20) = 6.97, p < 0.001$ and the converse applies to the conditions with short pretraining, where there is an advantage for short no gap over short + gap, $t(20) = 3.61, p < 0.005$. Putting these two analyses together gives another significant difference of differences for the generalization gradients, with the presence of a gap benefiting long pretraining significantly more than short pretraining, where the effect is in the opposite direction, $t(40) = 7.83, p < 0.001$.

## Discussion

The most important result from Experiment 1 is that we have been able to demonstrate better performance on the target discrimination during test for a group of subjects pretrained on the easy reversed condition compared to a group pretrained on the target hard discrimination. This has provided a conceptual replication of the results obtained by Mackintosh and Little (1970), and lends weight to the involvement of associability processes in human associative learning (Le Pelley & McLaren, 2003; Lochmann & Wills, 2003; Whitney & White, 1993). As noted previously, the subjects in Mackintosh and Little's easy reversed group started out at a lower performance level than those in the hard group at the start of training, but surpassed the hard group with a greater amount of training. Humans appear to be able to perform this reversal extremely rapidly, as they have only experienced one block of training with these hard stimuli. Despite this apparently sparse amount of training, with each picture being shown only five times during the block of training, those subjects in the easy reversed condition are more able to form appropriate associations between the target stimuli and the responses taught during the training stage than subjects that have been presented with this target discrimination throughout the experiment.

One parameter influencing these results is revealed by the factorial ANOVA, where the main effect of extended pretraining was significant. As discussed before, this can only have strengthened any connections between the representations for the pretraining stimuli and the responses. This would have had a detrimental effect on the performance of the easy reversed group if performance were being mediated solely by a generalization mechanism. There is also no indication of an interaction in this analysis and as such no evidence that the extended pretraining is benefiting one condition more than the other.

The analysis based on the generalization gradients provides an easy and relatively transparent way to perform further comparisons, which allows a more complete characterization of the data. This analysis gave significant interactions, or more correctly differences between the differences in gradient, for the easy reversed groups with the inclusion of a gap between pretraining and training and long pretraining having differential effects. The difference of differences in the easy reversed groups comes from an increase in gradient, indicating better performance, with the addition of a gap after long pretraining, but a decrease in the short pretraining conditions when the gap is included. There was also a differential effect for the groups with a gap when dealing with the easy reversed versus hard pretraining and the length of pretraining. Pretraining on the easy reversed stimuli showed a benefit over hard pretraining for long pretraining, but the converse was true for short pretraining.

The first of these two analyses points to the importance of including a gap and long pretraining when seeking the maximum performance benefit, whereas the second shows that as well as long pretraining being important it is also necessary to experience the easy reversed stimuli during pretraining. On an associability account the long pretraining on the easy reversed stimuli should give the best performance, and this is what is seen here. The pretraining on the easily discriminable easy reversed will allow these stimuli to be established as good predictors of an outcome, even though the features of these stimuli are associated with different responses during pretraining and training. We take it that the long pretraining allows the associability of these stimuli to increase to a high enough level that they are able to effectively transfer a high value to the hard stimuli and this associability remains high during the initial trials of the reversal. Pretraining either for a smaller number of trials or on the hard stimuli will reduce these benefits and manifest itself in a shallower generalization gradient.

An associability account can explain relatively easily why the easy reversed condition in conjunction with long pretraining confers an advantage, but why should including a gap between pretraining and training have such a strong effect on the results?

There may be a number of reasons for the effect of the gap within the paradigm we have used. The least interesting of these is that subjects become confused in the easy reversed/long no-gap condition when they are transferred to the hard stimuli during the training phase. During the pretraining phase, subjects will have formed strong associations between the easy stimuli and the response appropriate for the initial phase. When immediately changed to the hard stimuli with the reversed response assignments, the new stimuli may be perceived as being very similar to the pictures encountered previously, but the swap in response assignments may have led to confusion. As the easy stimuli are themselves very similar to the respective hard stimuli, subjects may have been attempting to apply whatever strategy had been working during pretraining to the training stage, as they were able to accurately remember their response assignments, and perhaps became frustrated when these appeared to be inconsistent between the two stages. A gap might alleviate this confusion. The weakness of this class of account is that it does not easily explain why better acquisition of the trained discrimination is observed, merely why it should not be inferior to the other groups in Experiment 1. Something more is required.

A different, perhaps more interesting possibility is that the effect of the gap may be due to the relative rates of decay of the alpha values and the weights between stimuli and responses. The associability, $\alpha$, of a stimulus or element may remain relatively constant over time, with no real reduction in its value, whereas the weights that are built up between elements and various outcomes decline over time. This would seem a plausible way to set things up, as it may well be important to retain the information that a certain event is a good predictor of an outcome.

If we propose that the $\alpha$s decay much less rapidly than the weights, then adding an intervening period between pretraining and training will have reduced the strength of the connections between the stimulus elements and the previously associated responses more than it will the $\alpha$s that have built up previously. This combination of decay in weight strength and maintenance of the $\alpha$ values will make it easier to reverse the response assignments, as there will be less inappropriate generalization from the pretraining, while still allowing rapid formation of the correct element–response association. This will mean that the inclusion of a gap in the experimental procedure will have a beneficial effect, whereas transferring straight from the pretraining to the training will not allow time for the weights to decay. This lack of decay will leave greater inappropriate connection strengths from the initial pretraining that will need to be unlearned.

Although we have thus far given an account of the data reported in this chapter couched solely in terms of associability, there are other possible explanations for the easy reversed group performing better than the hard group under certain conditions. The first alternative we consider is the idea of "transferred acquired distinctiveness." Let us suppose that during the first stage, subjects learn to associate Stimulus 3 with the left key (3-left), and Stimulus 9 with the right (9-right), and that they learn this well due to the relatively low overlap between the stimuli. We can also assume that these associations will generalize to similar stimuli, so there will be somewhat weaker representations of 5-left and 7-right at the end of the pretraining phase. After the reversal, it is these learned responses that transfer to the hard stimuli, with the proviso that the representation of 5-left now corresponds to the right key and 7-right to the left during the training phase. Although this account seems rather strange, the idea of acquired equivalence/distinctiveness dates back to Lawrence (1949) and it is just the application of the idea that is novel in this case.

However, this account would predict that introducing a gap can only degrade performance as we would not expect these stimulus–response associations to became stronger in the absence of stimulus presentation. Although this drop in performance could be said to occur for the easy reversed short pretraining conditions, where we find a significant decrement in generalization gradient, exactly the opposite is true for the easy reversed long pretraining conditions where the inclusion of a gap significantly improves performance.

A different explanation that might be able to deal with the inclusion of a gap can be considered as a more cognitive approach to the problem. The proposal could be that when a gap is present within Experiment 1, subjects take this as a cue that the task may have changed in some respect. After again learning the discrimination between the easy stimuli during pretraining, the reversed transfer to the hard problem will cause mistakes to be made if subjects are continuing to respond, quite reasonably, in line with the mappings learned during the pretraining phase. These errors may cause the subject to realize that the responses from the pretraining phase are no longer correct but, instead of being randomly reassigned, have simply been reversed. Our argument is that this realization is the more likely if the subjects believe that the task has changed in some respect. After the gap in the hard pretraining condition, subjects continue as they have been during pretraining once they establish that there has been no change in the response assignments.

There are, however, a number of challenges that this explanation might encounter when attempting to explain all the data from this chapter. Although this cognitive account can explain the difference between the easy reversed and hard groups when experiencing long pretraining with the presence of a gap, it would also predict similar results for the short pretraining conditions, but this is not what we observe in the data. There is no advantage when including the gap for the short pretraining; in fact the trend is reversed, with the hard group being significantly better than the easy reversed group. This argument could be countered by proposing that the discrimination has not been learned well enough during the initial stage, although this seems unlikely for the easy discrimination. There are further difficulties with the notion of the gap as a separator between experimental stages given the following analysis. Under the procedures used here, there is an explicit break in proceedings between the pretraining and training phases, as further instructions are given to the subjects. Hence we could propose that this explanation should apply to all the conditions where the pretraining has been on the easy reversed stimuli. This line of argument would have to consider the gap and no-gap conditions as essentially equivalent, in that both signaled a change in experimental stage at the same point in the experiment, and so should give the same results for both conditions. This is not what is seen for the long pretraining no-gap condition, where the performance on the hard condition is significantly better than that on the easy reversed condition, $t(20) = 3.71, p < 0.005$.

In summary, the results reported here indicate that overtraining improves performance on the TAC task in general, and more specifically, even when the response assignments are reversed between pretraining on the easy stimuli and then training on the hard stimuli. This result reproduces the finding from Mackintosh and Little (1970), who showed an identical effect using pigeons trained on a wavelength discrimination. It would seem that the results reported in this chapter can be explained most effectively by an associability-based account rather than the other possibilities we have discussed and adds to the evidence that there may be associability processes present in humans as well as animals.

The version of the McLaren and Mackintosh (2000, 2002) model used to simulate our previous work is unable to cope with this set of results as it has no associability component built into it. However, this model, and its predecessor (McLaren et al., 1989), has shown itself to be adept at dealing with a wide range of associative learning phenomena and so we would like to retain these mechanisms while incorporating the idea of associability into the model. Our task now becomes one of integration of these results into the computational framework established by McLaren and Mackintosh (2000, 2002). Having established that, as predicted by Mackintosh (1975), extended pretraining will make the success of transfer after a reversal more likely, we now have to incorporate the idea of associability into a revised model.

## MODELING ASSOCIABILITY IN REAL TIME

The results just presented provide good evidence for associability processes being present in humans, as we have managed to reproduce the results from Mackintosh and Little's (1970) first experiment using a TAC paradigm with human subjects. This adds further weight to the argument that we need a theory that takes account of the associative history of a cue when attempting to model TAC, or indeed the results of any experiment where a reversal in response assignment is imposed yet yields an advantage in performance (Mackintosh, 1969; Reid, 1953).

We have shown previously (Suret & McLaren, 2002, 2003) that a model based on generalization (McLaren & Mackintosh, 2000, 2002) has been able to account for all of the empirical data to date using this relatively complex paradigm. The results from McLaren and Suret (2000) appealed to the notion of salience modulation, but there was no need to employ the idea of associative history with reference to stimulus–outcome associations, as the results here were due to stimulus preexposure in the absence of any outcome. Later use of the reversal manipulation within the TAC paradigm gave no advantage for groups experiencing the reversal, despite easy pretraining, with the results always favoring a generalization explanation.

What follows is an exposition of how the Mackintosh (1975) model can account for the data from Experiment 1, not just using unitary stimulus representations, but at a more elemental level as well, where the associability of the stimuli can generalize across the elements of the stimulus dimension. The final part of this section details how the equations governing behavior in the original Mackintosh model have been developed to fit in with the real-time distributed representation that the McLaren and Mackintosh (2000, 2002) model employs.

## AN ELEMENTAL ANALYSIS OF REVERSAL AND TRANSFER ALONG A CONTINUUM

This section gives an overview of how an associability-driven theory, such as Mackintosh (1975), is able to deal relatively easily with the problem of reversal within TAC. Equation 8.1 shows how the weight change, $\Delta V$, is calculated, where $\alpha$ is the salience of the conditioned stimulus (CS), $\theta$ is the salience of the US, and $\lambda$ is the asymptotic value for learning about the unconditioned stimulus (US). The initial modification made to the basic theory is in that same paper, where Mackintosh proposes that if the weight change for some stimulus $A_1$ is:

$$\Delta V_{A_1} = \alpha_{A_1} \theta \left( \lambda - V_{A_1} \right) \tag{8.1}$$

then the weight change for a similar stimulus, $A_2$, will be defined by the similarity of the two stimuli, here $S_{A1,A2}$, where $0 < S_{A1,A2} < 1$.

$$\Delta V_{A_2} = S_{A_1 A_2} \alpha_{A_1} \theta \left( \lambda - V_{A_1} \right) \tag{8.2}$$

If we consider one of our stimulus continua of 11 faces, Fig. 8.1, then what will be established during the pretraining phase for the hard and easy reversed conditions? Taking an elemental approach to the problem will provide a more coherent analysis of what may actually be happening during a TAC procedure and how learning transfers between the pretraining and training stages. Let us propose that the stimuli are composed of elements, and that the closer the stimuli are on the dimension, the more elements they share with one another. For the purposes of this discussion we use the definition of representation on a dimension as detailed in McLaren and Mackintosh (2002), where:

1. Stimuli are represented as patterns of activity over sets of elements making up these stimuli, and all things being equal, this pattern will be Gaussian in nature.
2. A dimension is represented by an ordered set of elements.
3. One can move along a stimulus dimension by replacing elements of the stimulus with the provisos that a replaced element is not resampled, and nor are the replacing elements themselves replaced.

These assumptions allow a fairly natural representation of a dimension to be constructed, with a set of elements that are assumed to be present in all the stimuli along the dimension and are available for activation whenever a stimulus is presented. The Gaussian pattern of activation over these elements when a stimulus is presented leads naturally to some form of generalization, where neighboring elements are activated to a greater or lesser extent depending on their proximity to the presented elements. Each element will form its own associations to the two possible responses in the experiments under consideration, becoming more strongly associated, after sufficient training, with one than the other.

Combining the idea of associability generalization with this elemental dimensional framework, we can now look at how the various conditions under test might be predicted to behave on the basis of such a model.

## A NEW MODEL: FROM TRIAL-BASED TO A REAL-TIME FRAMEWORK

The description we provided previously of an elemental version of the Mackintosh (1975) model is only a first step on the path of integrating it into a real-time system. There are many assumptions inherent in the original model, and in the explanation given earlier, which must be explained more clearly to show how the system might function in a more realistic setting. The following section details the modifications that have been made in transition from the original model to the one developed here to explain the data, not only from the current experiment, but also from other reversal experiments. The core of the model is identical to that reported in McLaren and Mackintosh (2000, 2002), and has already been used to model TAC with the simulations reported in Suret and McLaren (2002) demonstrating that the model can cope with this type of associative phenomenon (McLaren & Suret, 2000), but the necessary addition is some way of changing the associability that each representational element is assumed to possess. Here we briefly introduce the algorithms used in McLaren and Mackintosh

(2000, 2002) as a preliminary step in their later modification to incorporate variable associability.

One major difference between the original Mackintosh (1975) model, or indeed any classic associative learning theory (Pearce, 1987, 1994; Pearce & Hall, 1980; Rescorla & Wagner, 1972), and the model developed here, is that these previous theories have assumed that the learning is artificially segmented into trials, and that weight and associability changes occur only on a trial-by-trial basis. Such a model tends to focus on the "learning" episodes, rather than any change in weights or associability that may occur during any intertrial interval (ITI) unless these are specifically factored in, and again considered as discrete trials.

However, a real-time system at least treats the presence or absence of stimuli with some consistency. There is no limitation on when learning is allowed to occur and all values within the system are continually updated in accordance with the appropriate algorithms, and it is just the input to the system that varies as a function of time. This change in external input as stimuli, both CSs and USs, are turned on and off, drives the formation of appropriate connections within the system in a continuous fashion without the need to break a simulation into a series of discrete episodes.

Another major difference concerns the use of elemental representation within the model. In the original Mackintosh (1975) model, stimuli were treated as unitary objects, with their representations being simply attributed to a single node within the computational framework. These stimulus input nodes were totally isolated, with no mechanism for generalization between nodes. The nodes were also limited in the values that their activations could take. Activations were set either to 1 when the stimulus represented by the node was present, or to zero when it was absent. Both the representation and activation of stimuli within the system considered here take on different properties to the unitary, binary node used previously.

As in McLaren and Mackintosh (2002), representations are taken to be a distributed pattern of activation across an ordered series of units rather than a unitary representation. This pattern of activation is governed by the presence, or absence, of an input at a specific node, and the value of the activation at a given node is dependent on the distance from this node to the one that has been given maximal activation by having the appropriate stimulus presented. In all the simulations reported, only one stimulus is ever presented at a time, leading to a single pseudo-Gaussian pattern of activation over the units.

Hence, the representational differences between the model provided in this chapter and the Mackintosh (1975) model are essentially twofold:

1. The activation of a node within the network can vary from 0 to some maximal value, defined by the model parameters rather than the binary values of 1 and 0 allowed previously.

2. Stimuli are represented by a set of nodes rather than a single node, and these nodes may have different activations, depending on their distance from the currently presented stimulus and the amount of time elapsed since they were last active.

An important consequence of these differences is that a distributed representation will allow generalization between similar stimuli to occur. Activation of a novel stimulus, but one similar to that previously presented, will tend to activate a similar representation, to a similar degree, and hence performance on this new stimulus will be governed by the connections formed previously.

The differences just outlined take us no further than McLaren and Mackintosh's (2000, 2002) model of generalization. What is needed now is a novel integration of the concept of associability into the real-time model developed in this chapter. There are a number of differences between the algorithm used in our model and that proposed by Mackintosh (1975) for the changes in associability that come about as a consequence of the differences between the models highlighted earlier, but, as far as possible, the spirit of the original has been preserved despite the necessary modifications.

To start, let us consider the two equations used for the modification of the associability parameter, $\alpha$. Equations 8.3 and 8.4 give the original formulation for changing the $\alpha$ value of a stimulus, whereas Equations 8.5, 8.6, and 8.7 describe the algorithm used in the model being developed for simulating the results of Experiment 1.

$$\Delta\alpha_A > 0 \text{ if } |\lambda - V_A| < |\lambda - V_X| \tag{8.3}$$

$$\Delta\alpha_A < 0 \text{ if } |\lambda - V_A| \geq |\lambda - V_X| \tag{8.4}$$

The original Mackintosh (1975) model has at its core, the idea that the value of $\alpha$ that a stimulus has is dependent on how predictive that stimulus has been previously. Good predictors maintain high values of $\alpha$, which allows them to engage in further learning rapidly, whereas poor, that is, inconsistent, predictors have lower values of $\alpha$, which, relatively speaking, retards learning about these stimuli. Equations 8.3 and 8.4 show how this change in $\alpha$ should be driven, where $V_A$ is the associative strength between A and the US and $V_X$ is the sum of the associative strengths between all other stimuli present and the US. The equations dictate that if stimulus A is better at predicting the outcome than all other stimuli present on that trial, that is, its error is lowest, then its value of $\alpha$ will increase, but if it is predicting the occurrence of the outcome less accurately than all other stimuli, then its $\alpha$ will decline.

Equation 8.5 gives the form of the equation used for changing the value of a in the real-time simulations, which takes the idea of a stimulus element being a good predictor of the outcome and modifies it for use in a real-time model.

$$\partial \alpha_i = \varepsilon \sum_j a_i \left( U - \alpha_i \right) \left( \alpha_i - L \right) \gamma_j \left( w_{ij} - \overline{w}_{ij} \right) \tag{8.5}$$

$$\text{if } \Delta_j \geq 0 \text{ then } \gamma_j = 10 \times (1 - \Delta_j) \tag{8.6}$$

$$\text{if } \Delta_j < 0 \text{ then } \gamma_j = \Delta_j \tag{8.7}$$

where $\Delta_j$ is the discrepancy between the external input applied to unit $j$, by virtue of the presence or absence of a US, and the internal input applied to the unit from all other units activated at the same time. A large positive $\Delta$ indicates that the US is not well predicted, whereas a small positive or zero value of $\Delta$ shows that the US is being well predicted, although a negative value of $\Delta$ means that the outcome is being overpredicted. A positive $\Delta$ will increase the strength of the associative links between unit $j$ and the US as well as the associability of unit $j$, whereas negative values of $\Delta$ will decrease both these attributes.

As with the original Mackintosh model, each node is assigned its own value of $\alpha$, but now nodes represent elements of the stimulus rather than the entire stimulus. The change in $\alpha$ is more difficult to control in a real time system, as the strict co-occurrence of element and response is often limited; hence there is only a small window of opportunity for the system to learn whether a particular element is a good or bad predictor of an outcome. There is also the problem of determining whether an element is actually a consistent predictor of an outcome, as with a large number of elements it is unlikely, especially at the outset, that any one element will have greater predictiveness for the outcome than all other elements put together. The original Mackintosh (1975) model normally assumed the presence of just two stimuli, only one of which was predictive, and thus this problem never tended to arise. The absence of a singularly predictive element presents a problem, as if no single element is more predictive than the rest, then the $\alpha$ values of all stimulus elements must decline. This problem has been avoided by comparing the associative strength between each element ($i$) and a given outcome ($j$), with the average for all associative strengths between all other elements and that outcome, denoted by ($w_{ij} - \overline{w}_{ij}$). This will mean that elements that have a higher associative strength than average, and hence are better predictors of the outcome will have a positive value for this term, and hence the change in the magnitude of $\alpha$ will be positive. The converse will apply to elements whose associative strength to a particular outcome is less than average, where their $\alpha$ value will tend to decline.

The $(U - \alpha_i)(\alpha_i - L)$ term in Equation 8.5 implements the idea of "sticky" alpha, borrowed from Sutherland and Mackintosh (1971), where $U$ and $L$ are the upper and lower bounds on the value of $\alpha$. This term limits the rate of change of $a$ when it approaches one of these extremes, and then large values of $(w_{ij} - \overline{w}_{ij})$ will tend to have less of an effect on $\alpha$ than otherwise. The change in $\alpha$ for a given element is also modulated by the activation, $a_i$, of that element, as it is necessary to ensure that only active elements engage in $\alpha$ change, be this positive or negative, as it would be inconsistent to change the $\alpha$ of an element when it was not active at a given time. The modification to the algorithm for $\alpha$ change detailed in Equations 8.6 and 8.7 relates to the predictiveness of a given element, but in this case is based on the $\Delta$ for a given outcome $(j)$. Equation 8.6 describes what happens when $\Delta_j \geq 0$, and in this case the multiplier $1 - \Delta$ is used. If the $\Delta$ for an outcome is small and positive, then it is well predicted by the elements present at that time, and the change in $\alpha$ should therefore be relatively large; however if $\Delta$ is large and positive, then the outcome is poorly predicted, and $\alpha$ should change rather less. If the $\Delta$ for the outcome is negative, however, then this will tend to indicate that the outcome is overpredicted, and hence the value of $\alpha$ should decline accordingly, which is achieved by setting the multiplier to $\gamma_j = \Delta_j$. This state will occur only when the system continues to predict the presence of a particular outcome despite its absence. The factor of 10 applied to the $\gamma$ parameter when $\Delta$ is positive is simply to boost the magnitude of a change for a good predictor allowing more rapid change in the value of $\alpha$ when the correct outcome is being predicted. As mentioned previously, the time frame for significant $\alpha$ change is limited due to the fact that the elements and outcomes are never maximally activated simultaneously. The activations of the elements are decaying while the representations are present, so this extra boost will allow reasonable learning during this relatively short period.

Finally, the algorithm includes the sum over all outcomes, which takes account of how predictive an element is in general, rather than being solely tied to a single outcome and $\varepsilon$ is a general learning rate parameter.

Despite the extensive modifications outlined here, the aim of the $\alpha$ change algorithm in this model is to preserve the functioning of the rules for changing the associability presented in the original description of the Mackintosh (1975) model. The simulations that follow use this modified version of the McLaren and Mackintosh (2000, 2002) model and are intended to reproduce the pattern of results seen empirically. Despite the modifications applied to the McLaren and Mackintosh model, the previous predictions of the model when dealing with preexposure effects are unchanged. The inclusion of a variable CS associability parameter works alongside the mechanism for the change in salience and determines how quickly previously encountered elements can change their associations as a function of their previous predictiveness as well as their previous exposure.

## SIMULATIONS OF EXPERIMENT 1

### Simulation Design

The focus of these simulations was to demonstrate an advantage for extended training preceding a reversal as found in Experiment 1. All simulations used 20 virtual subjects per condition. The conditions run were identical to those in the experiment, with the critical phase being the pretraining session where the amount and type of pretraining was manipulated. Training consisted of presenting the stimulus representations for the hard stimuli to the network, and the test phase presented all 11 stimulus representations in the absence of any teaching signal. The activations of the response units were then calculated and this gave the response activation measure.

### Simulation Procedure

The simulations reported in this chapter used a single dimension, rather than the four used in the experiment, to reduce the complexity of the system. Using four separate dimensions made no difference to the results because, although the responses are the same for each dimension, all representations of the dimensions are essentially kept separate as there are no connections from the output units back to the input layer, which would allow interference between dimensions to occur. Though acknowledging that there is undoubtedly interference between the morphed face dimensions, as all the stimuli used are pictures of faces, it was judged to be too difficult to assess how much interference there was between dimensions, and for simplicity it was ignored in what follows.

The aim of the simulations was to reproduce the experimental procedure as accurately as possible. Despite there only being one dimension used in the simulation, the procedure used for the experiment was mapped as closely as possible onto the code used for running the simulation. Each stimulus was still presented five times during the pretraining and training phases, and once during each of five blocks during test, although the total number of stimuli presented to the network was necessarily reduced by a factor of four. The relative timings were also kept the same as those in the experiment. The stimuli were presented for the equivalent of 4.25 seconds within the simulation, with the gap between stimulus offset and feedback onset, the length of time feedback was present, and the intertrial interval all being the same relative length of simulation time.

When each stimulus was presented to the network, the external input to all the elements on the input layer were set to the values generated by the exponential input function (McLaren & Mackintosh, 2002), giving maximal activation at the presented stimulus, which decreased with distance along the dimension away from the presented stimulus. As stated earlier, this alteration in external inputs was the only change applied to the model while the simulation was running and these changes occurred on a predictable timescale, congruent with the empirical experimental procedure. On completion of the pretraining and training phases of the simulation, all test data were recorded in a fashion analogous to that used for the experiments.

As there is no decision mechanism within the model, the equivalent of the empirical response score was obtained by subtracting the asymptotic activation of one output unit from the other when a stimulus was presented on test. This gives some measure of how likely one response is to be chosen compared to the other when presented with a stimulus in the absence of feedback based on the relative activations of the two responses, and is intended to parallel the experimental test stage, as the response scores generated give some indication of how well associated a stimulus was with the two responses, and to which it is most strongly associated. On test, no learning was allowed, and the activations were reset to their levels at the end of training after the presentation of each stimulus. Once these response activations have been obtained, then it is trivial to calculate the corresponding discrimination activation by simply subtracting the activation for Stimulus 5 from that for Stimulus 7 to produce dependent measures that are analogous to those used in the empirical work.

## SIMULATION RESULTS

It should be noted that the model makes no attempt to differentiate between- and within-subject designs as we made no provision for any interference that doubtless occurs between the dimensions used in the empirical studies. We also made no attempt to model the influence of the gap on learning as we feel this is still not fully understood, preferring instead to concentrate on the easy/hard problem and long/short pretraining factors. All simulations reported here include a delay between pretraining and training equivalent in length, relative to the timings used for stimulus presentation, to that used in the empirical studies. That is to say that the mapping between simulation "time" and the time for actual presentations or any delay within the experiment was one-to-one.

Figure 8.4 shows the results for the simulation of the experiment, with the data sets showing the switch in ordering as the amount of pretraining increases, with easy reversed showing better performance than the hard after extended pretraining. The Pearson's correlation coefficient is 0.971, which gives an $r^2$ value of 0.942. Using a Spearman's

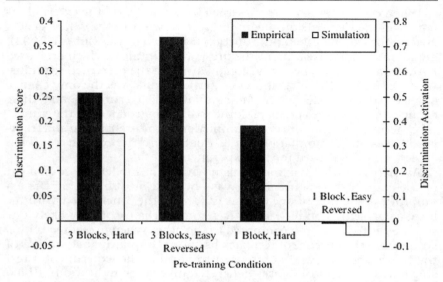

FIG. 8.4. Empirical and simulation data following the designs from the experiment.

Rank correlation, due to the small number of data points, the value of r obtained is 1, $p = 0.042$. The ordering of the results was identical in both simulation and empirical data, where 3 blocks, easy reversed showed best performance, followed by 3 blocks, hard, then 1 block, hard, with 1 block, easy reversed showing poor performance in both sets of data.

Figure 8.5 shows the simulation of Experiment 2 from Suret and McLaren (2003) where a within-subject version of the TAC paradigm was used. Although this has already been modeled in that paper, that was using the original McLaren and Mackintosh (2000, 2002) model, and needs to be redone with the modified version to show that the inclusion of associability has not changed the ordering of the results. The Pearson's correlation coefficient is 0.958, which gives an $r^2$ value of 0.917. Using a Spearman's Rank correlation, due to the small number of data points, the value of $\rho$ obtained is 1, $p = 0.042$. The ordering of the results was identical in both simulation and empirical data, where easy showed best performance, followed by hard, then hard reversed, with easy reversed being the worst-performing condition in both sets of data.

The new version of the model appears to be able to cope well with the previously reported results, with the pattern of results being the same in both the new simulation and the empirical data. The standard TAC effect is present in the new simulation work, as is the apparent reliance on generalization when there is a limited amount of pretraining, with easy reversed being numerically worse than hard reversed.

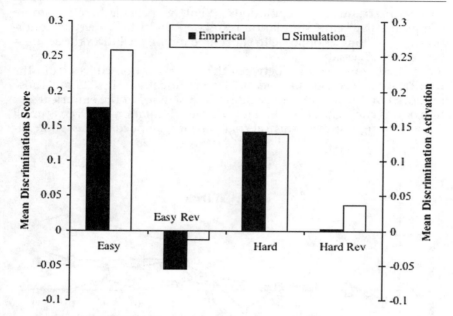

FIG. 8.5. Empirical and simulation results reported in Suret and Mc-Laren (2003), Experiment 2.

## DISCUSSION

The modified version of McLaren and Mackintosh (2000, 2002) developed in this chapter has been able to accurately model the results from the experiment reported in the first half of this chapter as well as the data from Experiment 2 in Suret and McLaren (2003), both of which contain a reversal manipulation between the pretraining and training stages of the experiment. Even though a reversal was contained within these empirical studies, it was only with the addition of extended pretraining on the easy stimuli that this facilitated later learning of the hard discrimination during training (Fig. 8.5).

This model can be equally well applied to animal learning studies, where training prior to a reversal facilitates later acquisition of a discrimination (Mackintosh, 1969; Mackintosh & Little, 1970). All that is required is to again propose that the stimuli used in these experiments possess the same properties as the face dimensions used in the human studies and can be represented in a distributed fashion, an idea that is widespread (McClelland & Rumelhart, 1985).

A greater understanding of the model developed in this chapter can be gained from a more detailed analysis of the results produced by the model and a closer inspection of what happens to the values of $\alpha$ after various pretraining manipulations. What we provide here is a more comprehensive set of simulation results on the critical reversal conditions, where long as opposed to short pretraining facilitates the acquisition of the reversal.

The first comparison is between the generalization curves from the empirical data set (Fig. 8.6a, adapted from the data in Fig. 8.2) and those produced by the model (Figure 8.6b). As discussed in the empirical section of this chapter, rather than just the discrimination between Stimuli 5 and 7 being reversed, this reversal has been applied to the whole di-

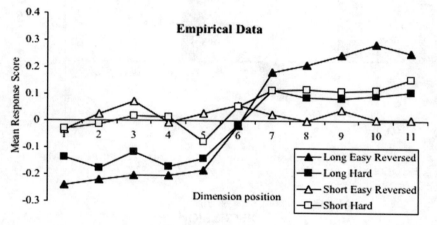

FIG. 8.6a. Comparison of the generalization curves obtained empirically.

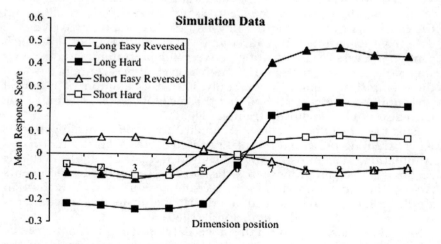

FIG. 8.6b. Comparison of the generalization curves obtained using the computational model developed in this chapter.

mension, with, at least, numerically better performance being shown on discrimination between the easy stimuli, which had originally been trained with the reverse response assignments. Figure 8.6b shows the same pattern of results for the simulation data, with better responding to Stimuli 3 and 9 being seen for the long pretraining group. The other groups show very similar patterns of generalization in the simulation and empirical data, with the only slight discrepancy being in the short easy reversed group. Whilst the empirical data shows a fairly flat function, with some evidence for the acquisition of the hard discrimination during training, the simulated data shows responding is still being governed by the reversed pretraining.

This pattern of results in the simulation must mean that the associability of the stimuli is having a very large effect on the acquisition of the hard discrimination during the training stage. The interaction of the associability with the generalization mechanism already present within the McLaren and Mackintosh (2000, 2002) model would allow this pattern of results to occur, as the high associability associated with the units will allow rapid links to form between the active units and the appropriate outcomes, and on test this will generalize across the dimension. Figure 8.7 shows the values of $\alpha$ after the 10 trials of training for the four simulated conditions shown in Fig. 8.6b, and this provides some surprising insights.

Looking at the $\alpha$ values for the long, hard group, there is a counter-intuitive result for the $\alpha$ value for Element 6, the one that is shared be-

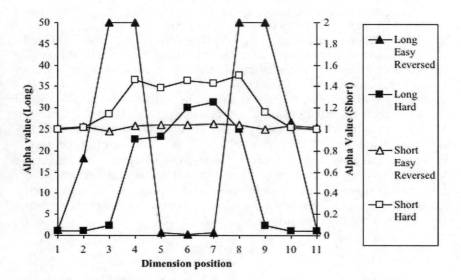

FIG. 8.7.  A comparison of the $\alpha$ values for stimuli along the dimension after different types of pretraining.

tween the two hard stimuli. Earlier analyses had supposed that this element would have a low associability as it is a relatively poor predictor of the outcomes, given it is activated equally by the two stimuli to which different responses are required. What we see from the simulation is that the $\alpha$ value for that element is comparable to the values for Elements 5 and 7, which are more predictive of the appropriate outcome. Although this may appear surprising, it is actually this high value of $\alpha$ that is making the hard discrimination so difficult. Because Element 6 has a high $\alpha$, it engages in learning to the response, in conjunction with the element appropriate to the stimulus presented; but the activation of Element 6 will tend to activate, not only the correct response, but also the incorrect one, leading to slower acquisition of the discrimination. If the $\alpha$ value for Element 6 had been driven low immediately, this would have in fact aided the discrimination, as there would have been much lower activation of the incorrect response from this element. We would expect the associability of this element to decline eventually, as expected for a poor predictor, with a larger amount of training.

Analysis of the other conditions is less surprising, with the two short conditions having had relatively little time to change their values of $\alpha$, although in the hard condition, we can observe the start of the increase of all the $\alpha$ values in the center of the dimension. The long, easy reversed group has very high values of $\alpha$ for Elements 3, 4, 8, and 9, which are the pretrained elements (3 and 9) and the elements that are, presumably, the most predictive elements during training, taking into account the overlap and activation from the opposing stimulus.

The amalgamation of the Mackintosh (1975) theory with the model outlined in McLaren and Mackintosh (2000, 2002) has provided a good framework for simulating experimental results that appear to need an associability explanation. Despite the difficulties that were inherent in combining the ideas from a theory based on unitary stimuli employing binary activation nodes with those of a distributed, elemental, real-time network, the spirit of the Mackintosh (1975) model has been retained. Elements that are predictive of a given outcome will tend to see their associabilities rise, whereas those that are unpredictive will attain a low value of $\alpha$. When a small amount of training is given the $\alpha$ value will not have developed sufficiently to dominate learning, so the pattern seen is that predicted by generalization; but after extended pretraining, some elements' $\alpha$ values have risen to such a level that they can drive learning rapidly enough to reverse the predictions of a strict generalization account.

## CONCLUSIONS

The empirical and simulation work within this chapter has focused on the TAC paradigm, where the basic result is that pretraining an easy discrimination on a dimension before training on a hard discrimination on the same dimension facilitates learning compared to an equivalent total amount of pretraining and training solely on the hard discrimination (Lawrence, 1952). Although this result can easily be explained via generalization, the findings in Mackintosh and Little (1970) challenge the completeness of this explanation. They showed that pretraining on the easy discrimination followed by a reversal in response assignment before transferring to the hard problem also ultimately results in better performance than the same total amount of training on the hard discrimination. It is this result that prompted the extension of our research to the role of associability processes in humans. The experiment reported in this chapter looks at reversal within the TAC paradigm using human subjects, but this time with the additional proposal that overtraining (Reid, 1953) could be the key element missing from previous experiments. This experiment has managed to reproduce the critical result from Mackintosh and Little where pretraining on the easy discrimination followed by a reversal before training on the hard stimuli showed significantly better performance than training on the hard stimuli alone without a reversal in response assignment. This success was due to extended pretraining with a significant benefit being found for three times as much pretraining as had originally been given.

This result falls in line with the majority of the work from the animal literature, where the phenomenon is known as the ORE (Reid, 1953), and lends weight to the argument that associative history is as important in human learning and memory as it is in animals (Le Pelley & McLaren, 2003; Lochmann & Wills, 2003). Associative learning theories, such as that of Mackintosh (1975), can easily account for this pattern of performance by attributing high associabilities (and hence high learning rates) to previously good predictors of an outcome, however, integrating this into a more elemental, real-time model was something of a challenge. We have demonstrated how a real-time model, McLaren and Mackintosh (2000, 2002), that has previously been shown to provide a good fit to other experimental data (McLaren & Suret, 2000; Suret & McLaren, 2003), and a theory of associability, Mackintosh (1975), can be successfully amalgamated (after some adaptation). As noted in the discussion of the model, although the rules for a change within the modified version of McLaren and Mackintosh are somewhat altered from those proposed in the original Mackintosh theory, the spirit of their applications is the same. Previously good predictors of an outcome possess high associabilities and are able to learn new element–outcome mappings rapidly, whereas poor predictors possess low $\alpha$ values and are relatively slow to form new associations, all other things being equal.

This combination of the two models, one concerned with representation development and one with stimulus–outcome learning, is the first of its kind, and the demonstration that associability can be integrated into a real-time model, which has considerable success in describing the data reported here, is important. Perhaps the result of greatest significance is the successful modeling of the difference in the pattern of responding after a reversal with different amounts of training. There should be relatively little difficulty in applying the model to the majority of the reversal data present in the animal literature, as the processes at work are assumed to be the same, and the paradigms used are generally less complicated than the TAC paradigm used here, constituting just a simple reversal of response assignment after a training period of variable length. It is the successful development of this novel, computational model that encourages us to believe that, at a basic level, there are a set of associative processes that drive learning in humans and infra-humans.

## REFERENCES

Hebb, D. O. (1949). *The organization of behavior*. New York: Wiley.

Holland, P. C. (1988). Excitation and inhibition in unblocking. *Journal of Experimental Psychology: Animal Behavior Processes, 14,* 261–279.

Konorski, J. (1948). *Conditioned reflexes and neuron organization.* Cambridge, England: Cambridge University Press.

Lawrence, D. H. (1949). Acquired distinctiveness of cues. I. Transfer between discriminations on the basis of familiarity with the stimulus. *Quarterly Journal of Experimental Psychology, 39,* 770–784.

Lawrence, D. H. (1952). The transfer of a discrimination along a continuum. *Journal of Comparative and Physiological Psychology, 45,* 511–516.

Le Pelley, M. E., & McLaren, I. P. L. (2003). Learned associability and associative change in human causal learning. *Quarterly Journal of Experimental Psychology, 56B,* 68–79.

Lochmann, T., & Wills, A. J. (2003). Associative history in an allergy prediction task. In F. Schmalhofer, R. M. Young, & G. Katz (Eds.), *Proceedings of the EuroCogSci 03* (pp. 217–222). Mahwah, NJ: Lawrence Erlbaum Associates.

Mackintosh, N. J. (1969). Further analysis of the overtraining reversal effect. *Journal of Comparative and Physiological Psychology, Monograph, 67(2,* Pt. 2).

Mackintosh, N. J. (1975). A theory of attention: Variations in the associability of stimuli with reinforcement. *Psychological Review, 82,* 276–228.

Mackintosh, N. J., & Little, L. (1970). An analysis of transfer along a continuum. *Canadian Journal of Psychology, 24,* 362–369.

McClelland, J. L., & Rumelhart, D. E. (1985). Distributed memory and the representation of general and specific information. *Journal of Experimental Psychology: General, 114,* 159–188.

McLaren, I. P. L., Kaye, H., & Mackintosh, N. J. (1989). An associative theory of the representation of stimuli: applications to perceptual learning and latent inhibition. In R. G. M. Morris (Ed.), *Parallel distributed processing: Implications for psychology and neurobiology* (pp. 102–130). Oxford, England. Oxford University Press.

McLaren, I. P. L., & Mackintosh, N. J. (2000). An elemental model of associative learning: I. Latent inhibition and perceptual learning. *Animal Learning and Behavior 28,* 211–246.

McLaren, I. P. L., & Mackintosh, N. J. (2002). An elemental model of associative learning: II. Generalization and discrimination. *Animal Learning and Behavior, 30,* 177–200.

McLaren, I. P. L., & Suret, M. B. (2000). Transfer along a continuum: differentiation or association? In *Proceedings of the Twenty-Second Annual Conference of the Cognitive Science Society* (pp. 340–345). Mahwah, NJ: Lawrence Erlbaum Associates.

Pearce, J. M. (1987). A model for stimulus generalization in Pavlovian conditioning. *Psychological Review, 94*, 61–73.

Pearce, J. M. (1994). Similarity and discrimination: A selective review and a connectionist model. *Psychological Review, 101*, 587–607.

Pearce, J. M., & Hall, G. (1980). A model for Pavlovian conditioning: Variations in the effectiveness of conditioned but not of unconditioned stimuli. *Psychological Review, 87*, 532–552.

Reid, L. S. (1953). The development of noncontinuity behavior through continuity learning. *Journal of Experimental Psychology, 46*, 107–112.

Rescorla, R. A. (2000). Associative changes in excitors and inhibitors differ when they are conditioned in compound. *Journal of Experimental Psychology: Animal Behavior Processes, 26*, 428–438.

Rescorla, R. A. and Wagner, A. R. (1972). A theory of Pavlovian conditioning: Variations on the effectiveness of reinforcement and non-reinforcement. In A. H. Black & W. F. Prokasy (Eds.), *Classical conditioning: II. Current research and theory* (pp. 64–99). New York: Appleton–Century–Crofts.

Saksida, L. M. (1999). Effects of similarity and experience on discrimination learning: A non-associative connectionist model of perceptual learning. *Journal of Experimental Psychology: Animal Behavior Processes, 25*, 308–323.

Schwartz, R. M., Schwartz, M., & Tees, R. C. (1971). Optional intradimensional and extradimensional shifts in the rat. *Journal of Comparative and Physiological Psychology, 77*, 470–475.

Shepp, B. E., & Eimas, P. D. (1964). Intradimensional and extradimensional shifts in the rat. *Journal of Comparative and Physiological Psychology, 57*, 357–361.

Spence, K. W. (1936). The nature of discrimination learning in animals. *Psychological Review, 43*, 427–449.

Spence, K. W. (1937). The differential response in animals to stimuli varying within a single dimension. *Psychological Review, 44*, 430–444.

Suret, M. B., & McLaren, I. P. L. (2002). An associative model of human learning on an artificial dimension. In *Proceedings of the 2002 International Joint Conference on Neural Networks* (pp. 806–811). Piscataway, NJ: IEEE.

Suret, M. B., & McLaren, I. P. L. (2003). Representation and discrimination on an artificial dimension. *Quarterly Journal of Experimental Psychology, 56B*, 30–42.

Sutherland, N. S., & Mackintosh, N. J. (1971). *Mechanisms of animal discrimination learning.* New York: Academic Press.

Whitney, L., & White, K. G. (1993). Dimensional shift and the transfer of attention. *Quarterly Journal of Experimental Psychology, 46B*, 225–252.

# Chapter 9

# Applications and Extensions

A. J. Wills

In the final two chapters of this book, we turn to phenomena whose practical implications are more direct than some of the phenomena previously discussed. In Chapter 10, Robin Murphy and colleagues discuss the "depressive realism" effect. This effect, first reported by Alloy and Ambramson (1979), concerns the difference between depressed and nondepressed individuals in their ability to rate zero contingencies. Zero contingencies ($\Delta P = 0$) are where, for example, an individual's action does not change the probability with which an event occurs. When subsequently asked to rate the level of contingency, depressed individuals are generally *more* accurate than nondepressed individuals. Depressed and nondepressed individuals' ratings do not appear to differ when the contingency is nonzero. Taken at face value, these results seem to pose certain questions for the position that depression is related to faulty thought processes (e.g., Beck, 1976).

Robin Murphy and colleagues dissect the original Alloy and Ambramson (1979) result from the perspective of known phenomena in human associative learning. First, they note that in nondepressed individuals the magnitude of overestimation of zero contingencies is modulated by the base rate of the outcome. The most common result is that as the outcome becomes more likely to occur overall, the zero contingency becomes progressively more overestimated (Vallée-Tourangeau, Holingsworth, & Murphy, 1998). However, this result is not always found (e.g., Wasserman, Chatlosh, & Neunaber, 1983) and Robin and colleagues suggest that, where it is not found, this may be due to the action–stimulus interval employed. In this context, action–stimulus interval (ASI) is the time between an action and the occurrence of the event that it caused. In some experiments ASI is virtually zero, whereas in others it is about 500 ms. Robin and colleagues go on to demonstrate systematically that ASI modulates the extent to which zero contingencies are overestimated. This result is in line with previous demonstrations that ASI modulates ratings of nonzero contingencies (Shanks, Pearson, & Dickinson, 1989).

A central conclusion from this sort of study is that aspects of experimental design that may appear incidental to a particular experimenter, such as the inclusion of a short ASI, can importantly affect the conclusions one draws. The connection to "depressive realism" is that previous studies of the effect have generally used very long intertrial intervals (ITIs), and studies that have failed to replicate the depressive realism effect (e.g., Dobson & Pusch, 1995) have used relatively short ITIs. From these results, Robin and colleagues suggest that depressed individuals are particularly prone to include the ITI in their assessments of contingency. In other words, depressed individuals are more likely to count the unfilled gap between trials as an example of a situation where they did not act and the outcome did not occur ("cell D" on a standard contingency table), whereas nondepressed people are more likely to ignore the ITI. Robin and colleagues then go on to provide evidence for this position by manipulating ITI systematically with both depressed and nondepressed individuals. One may therefore conclude that although depressed and nondepressed individuals approach the judgment of zero contingencies differently, it is not straightforwardly the case that the depressed individuals are more accurate.

In chapter 11, we move on to a research area with commercial implications as Andy Field introduces the concept of evaluative conditioning (EC). The basic idea of EC is to set up a situation where a neutral stimulus repeatedly predicts the occurrence of a stimulus that is already well-liked. EC has occurred if the neutral stimulus becomes more liked as a result of this treatment. The idea behind EC can be seen in many forms of product promotion. For example, one might follow a product launch with an excellent free lunch, hoping thereby to increase liking of the product. Similarly, the use of pleasant music (or pleasant individuals) in television commercials can be seen as an attempt to increase liking for a product by EC.

Does EC really work? Andy Field reviews the evidence, starting with a broad range of studies that appear to show successful EC for visual, taste, and odor stimuli. However, things do not remain optimistic for long, as Andy reveals a whole host of methodological problems with these initial demonstrations. After one has worked through the claims and counterclaims, it seems likely that EC of tastes reliably occurs and that EC of visual stimuli can occur but is perhaps less reliable.

Andy Field then addresses the question of whether EC is qualitatively different from other types of conditioning. For example, considerable evidence suggests that, in humans, awareness is required for classical conditioning to occur (see chap. 3, this volume). In contrast, some researchers (and presumably some advertisers) seem to assume that EC can occur in the absence of awareness. The evidence for this position seems equivocal at best. Additionally, some researchers assume that EC is highly resistant to extinction, and EC's usefulness as an efficient marketing technique seems dependent on this being true. Some resistance to extinction can be seen in a design where acquisition trials are followed by an equal number of extinction trials. In this situation the extinction trials can fail to reliably change the size of the EC effect. However, such a finding is not unique to EC.

## REFERENCES

Alloy, L. B., & Ambramson, L. Y. (1979). Judgement of contingency in depressed and non-depressed students: Sadder but wiser? *Journal of Experimental Psychology: General, 108*(4), 441–485.

Beck, A. T. (1976). *Cognitive therapy and the emotional disorders.* New York: International University Press.

Dobson, K. S., & Pusch, D. (1995). A test of the depressive realism hypothesis in clinically depressed subjects. *Cognitive Therapy and Research, 19*(2), 179–194.

Shanks, D. R., Pearson, S. M., & Dickinson, A. (1989). Temporal contiguity and the judgement of causality by human subjects. *The Quarterly Journal of Experimental Psychology, 41B*(2), 139–159.

Vallée-Tourangeau, F., Holingsworth, L., & Murphy, R. A. (1998). "Attention bias" in correlation judgments: Semdslund (1963) revisited. *Scandinavian Journal of Psychology, 39*, 221–233.

Wasserman, E. A., Chatlosh, D. L., & Neunaber, D. J. (1983). Perception of causal relations in humans: Factors affecting judgements of response–outcome contingencies under free-operant procedures. *Learning & Motivation, 14*, 406–432.

# Chapter 10

# Signal–Outcome Contingency, Contiguity, and the Depressive Realism Effect

Robin A. Murphy, Frédéric Vallée-Tourangeau, Rachel Msetfi,
and Andy G. Baker

Learning about predictive contingent relationships allows a window into the underlying causal structure of the environment. The alternative might be to work out the true physical mechanism of any caused event. For example, that flowers on fruit trees precede the arrival of fruit can be understood on the basis of a complete understanding of the ontogenesis of fruit, but even this knowledge is based on a chain of predictive contingencies. The epistemological nature of causal knowledge has been questioned for centuries (see also chap. 2, this volume). The idea that causal knowledge might be founded on an understanding of correlation is attributed to Hume (1739/1960). He suggested that detecting a positive contingency between flowers and fruit is enough information to infer a causal connection or, minimally, to allow us to act as if there was an understanding of the causal relation. Unlike working out the complete physical model, learning a contingency simply requires remembering the likelihood of fruit following flowers and comparing this memory with one of the likelihood of fruit in the absence of flowers.

A great deal of research first with laboratory animals (Rescorla, 1968) and then with humans (for reviews, see Allan, 1993; Baker, Murphy, & Vallée-Tourangeau, 1996; Shanks, 1993) has been devoted to showing sensitivity to contingent relationships. Psychological theories have been applied to the data to try and explain the processes that allow this learning to take place. We would argue that the most successful to date have been those based on the formation of associations (Baker, Murphy, Vallée-Tourangeau, & Mehta, 2001).

Doubts have been raised as to the adequacy of these accounts (e.g., Buhener & May, 2003; Cheng, 1997; De Houwer, chap. 3, this volume;

Melz, Cheng, Holyoak, & Waldmann, 1993). Not surprisingly, some of the evidence that has been recruited to undermine the associative account is from experiments showing that judgments sometimes deviate from the predictions of associative models. We discuss how this problem may be a general issue related to the fact that the associative models that have been recruited are sometimes used in a manner that omits important temporal parameters that may influence judgments. This problem is also relevant for theories that use normative statistical measures of contingency. In both cases the models assume that causes and events are binary and that some of the temporal variables that can be used to relate events are irrelevant.

We first discuss experimental evidence examining how people respond to contingent relationships and illustrate how associative models were crucial in distinguishing between contingency learning and learning based on simpler heuristics. We then discuss some experimental evidence that illustrates how varying some of the temporal variables in contingency tasks can influence learning. These results suggest that we need to modify our models. But generally they also suggest that both contingency-based and associative accounts still have much to offer (e.g., Allan, 2003).

## ASSOCIATIVE THEORY AND CONTINGENCY

Associative theories generally have a single common mechanism to account for learning. They rely on the close pairing of two events in space and time. This experience leads to an internal connection between events. The strength of the connection is determined in part by how often the events are paired, how often either one occurs alone, and how often both are absent. Research into human learning of event–outcome contingency relationships has attempted to relate the underlying learning processes to associative models originally developed to account for animal learning phenomenon (c.f. Baker, Berbrier, & Vallée-Tourangeau, 1989; Dickinson, Shanks, & Evenden, 1984; Shanks, 1987). For example, Pavlovian learning has been carefully analyzed from an associative framework. Learning that a particular conditioned stimulus (CS) occurs immediately prior to an unconditioned stimulus (US) is helped if the CS and US occur together with greater regularity than they occur apart. One interpretation of these events is that an association between the CS and US is formed. The strength of this association provides an accurate representation of the predictive relatedness of the two events. Some human learning involves conditioning with the same sorts of biologically significant events and neutral sensory stimuli that have been shown with animals, but human learning also involves linguistically based stimuli such as words. With the full range of sensory input, associative models have been quite successful. In the causal learning literature, where differences have been found between judgments of relatedness and the experimenter's programmed relationship, some researchers have proposed that, in addition to associative learning, causal schemas influence how judgments are made (e.g., Cheng, 1997) or that inherent biases or predispositions influence stimulus processing (Alloy & Abramson, 1979; Wasserman, Elek, Chatlosh, & Baker, 1993).

## SIGNAL–OUTCOME PAIRINGS VERSUS CONTINGENCY

Early theories of learning relied on the pairing between two events to determine the strength of the association between them. For instance, Hull's (1943) theory for Pavlovian conditioning assumed that conditioned behavior resulted from pairing an outcome with a signal. A neutral CS (e.g., a 10-second light presentation) could be paired with a US (e.g., food). Conditioning was successful if experimental animals acquired a conditioned response (e.g., food searching) when the CS was presented. Associative accounts of this learning relied on the number of spatially and temporally contiguous pairings between the two events to explain the strength of the association and thus the level of responding. If the CS was presented without the US, behavior would diminish, presumably reflecting the weakened association between the two events. In terms of heuristics conditioning was thought to be determined by the likelihood of the US in the presence of the CS, $P(US|CS)$. This was shown to be inadequate by experiments demonstrating that it was the CS's overall contingency that mattered.

Experiments by Rescorla (e.g., 1968) were the first to unambiguously demonstrate that the likelihood of the outcome in the absence of the CS $[P(US|{\sim}CS)]$ also contributed to the strength of conditioned responding. In turn this result led to the development of an explanation of contingency sensitivity using associative principles. To accommodate this result, Rescorla and Wagner (1972) suggested that learning about a single CS actually involves forming two associations: (a) an association between the CS and the US (as before), but also, (b) an association involving the context, in which the CS occurred, and the US. Moreover, these two associations are involved in a competition with one another for association with the US. This idea allows associative models to be sensitive to the overall contingency between the CS and the US. If the likelihood of the US is greater in the presence of the CS [i.e., $P(US|CS) > P(US|{\sim}CS)$], then the CS–US association will be stronger than the context–US association. Whereas, if the likelihood of the US in the absence of the CS is greater, then the context–US association will be stronger (for a more detailed review of associative accounts of contingency learning, see Baker et al., 2001).

However, it is important to remember throughout this somewhat superficial discussion that some of the temporal characteristics related to the CS and US are lost in this analysis. For example, CSs, contexts, and USs are temporally extended and importantly the temporal characteristics of these events and their contiguity influence the course of learning. For example, whether the CS and the US are presented simultaneously or sequentially influences the strength of learning. Even if, as is usual, the CS and the US are presented sequentially, the degree to which they overlap also influences the extent of learning. As a general rule, the closer the two events are presented in time the stronger the learning. But there are important qualifications to be made as a function of the organism and the type of conditioning. For example, rabbit eyeblink conditioning is most effective with a relatively brief 500-millisecond CS–US onset interval (the time between the onset of the CS and the onset of the US). For pigeon key-pecking, the optimal period is of the order of seconds. For rats learning a fear response, the optimal CS–US interval is longer still. Finally, food aversions with rats can develop even with CS–US intervals several hours in length (Mackintosh, 1983). This simply demonstrates that both between species and even within species these temporal parameters influence learning beyond the basic notion of temporal contiguity. One could argue that the animals have different causal models that guide their learning. In some sense this might be true. We still find it productive to argue that contingency remains the primary driver of learning, but there are differences between CSs and USs that influence how they will be learned. One of the reasons for this confidence is that in spite of the differences in optimal period, in all cases learning is dramatically interfered with if another stimulus occurs in the period between CS onset and US onset.

Research into animal conditioning has proceeded to develop real-time models of association formation (e.g., Schmajuk, 1997; Wagner & Brandon, 2001), precisely to deal with some of these issues. However, no such development has occurred in the field of human contingency learning (although see chaps. 7 and 8, this volume). It is possible of course that these variables are irrelevant for human learning. However, we already know that contingency learning in humans is sensitive to the delay between signal and outcome (Dickinson & Shanks, 1995). One of the goals of this chapter is to look at the influence of other temporal variables.

Because of the conceptual similarity between an animal acquiring a conditioned response on the basis of CS–US contingency and a human reasoner gauging the relationship between a cue and an outcome, the Rescorla–Wagner (1972) model of associative learning has been applied to human contingency learning. Similar to early animal associationists, researchers studying human contingency learning suggested that participants were simply sensitive to either the number of times that the signal and the outcome co-occurred or the rate at which the outcome occurred in the presence of the signal (Smedslund, 1963; Ward & Jenkins, 1965). We discuss one such study and illustrate using data from our lab how this original theoretical bias led to experiments that failed to test whether humans were sensitive to contingencies.

## MEASURING SIGNAL–OUTCOME CONTINGENCY

Researchers have devised a number of procedures for assessing human contingency learning. They can be categorized as involving either actively learning a response–outcome relationship or passively learning a signal–outcome relationship. In the prototypical case of the latter type, participants are required to learn a relationship between one signal and an outcome. The task for the participant is to report whether the signal is a reliable predictor of the outcome. Because the signal and outcome in these tasks are binary, there are four types of events that can occur: The signal and outcome occur together, either the signal or the outcome occur in the absence of the other, or neither event occurs. The four trial types can be represented in a contingency table (see Fig. 10.1). The underlying logic has been to present a sequence of trials and then ask participants to rate the strength of the relationship between the signal and the outcome. You might then be able to learn how accurate people were and the cognitive strategy they use by comparing judgments with various methods of combining the four cells of the table (e.g., Arkes & Harkness, 1983; Shaklee & Tucker, 1980). Judgment accuracy is defined by how the participants are able to integrate information consistent with a positive relationship, a negative relationship, or no relationship between the two events.

|  | OUTCOME | |
| --- | --- | --- |
|  | Present | Absent |
| **SIGNAL** Present | A | B |
| **SIGNAL** Absent | C | D |

$$\text{Delta } P = (A/(A+B)) - (C/(C+D))$$
$$= P(O|S) - P(O|\text{-}S)$$

FIG. 10.1.  2 × 2 contingency table.

The accepted normative measure of the contingency between events in such a table is called Delta P ($\Delta P$). $\Delta P$ is the difference between the conditional probability of an outcome (O) in the presence of the predictor signal (S), or $P(O|S)$ and the probability of the outcome in the absence of the signal, $P(O|\sim S)$ (Allan, 1980). A positive value of this difference indicates that the outcome occurs more frequently following the signal than in its absence, whereas a negative value indicates the converse. Positive values suggest a facilitatory causal relationship and negative ones a preventive or inhibitory cause. When the two probabilities are equal, no contingency exists between the two events.

To calculate the contingency, and the conditional probabilities, the frequencies of four different types of evidence or event conjunctions must be known. The probability of the outcome in the presence of the signal, $P(O|S)$, requires knowing how often the two events have occurred together (Cell A) and how often the signal has occurred in the absence of the outcome (Cell B). The proportion of A cells relative to the sum of A and B cells provides the likelihood of the outcome in the presence of the signal. The second conditional probability, $P(O|\sim S)$, requires knowing how often the outcome has occurred during the absence of the signal (Cell C) and how often the absence of the outcome has occurred in the absence of the signal (Cell D).

However, notice that this analysis ignores the temporal duration of the predictive signal, the duration of the outcome, the actual signal–outcome onset interval. It can code the length of time between signals by increasing the number of Cell D occurrences, but even this has its problems.

Logically each of these conjunctions of events is equally informative about the overall relationship, but Cell D poses problems for both the experimenter and the participant. The absence of both events provides positive information about a contingency but is difficult to define experimentally and indeed epistemologically (Nisbett & Ross, 1980). Given a finite period in which nothing has happened how can one determine how many conjunctions of no-signal and no-outcome have occurred? For example, because increasing frequencies of Cell D increase $\Delta P$, if participants overestimate the number of times that neither event has occurred then their estimates should exhibit a positive bias.

The following sections illustrate how the notion of contingency has been useful for our understanding of human learning in these contingency paradigms. We then show how two aspects of the temporal relationship, which are difficult to define, can influence learning. This in itself is not novel (see also Shanks & Dickinson, 1987); however, we discuss how a failure to recognize this issue has contributed to two possibly erroneous conclusions in the contingency learning literature. The first is that judgment of instrumental contingencies is more influenced by the presence of the outcome than by its absence. The second is that people who exhibit mild symptoms of depression might be better judges of contingency than those without these symptoms.

## ASSESSING CONTINGENCY LEARNING

Initial studies of human contingency learning implied that the pairing between signal and outcome exerted an inordinate influence on judgments relative to the other events of the contingency table. A number of studies in different areas of psychology showed that in the absence of an overall positive signal–outcome contingency [i.e., $P(O|S) = P(O|\sim S)$], participants often judged there to be a positive relationship when there was a high frequency of event pairings. This "illusory correlation" phenomenon has been observed in simulated medical diagnosis tasks (e.g., Smedslund, 1963), in the interpretation of psychodiagnostic tests (e.g., Chapman & Chapman, 1969), and in stereotype formation (Hamilton & Gifford, 1976). A similar finding has been reported in animal conditioning (Quinsey, 1971).

In each of these cases there are two potential problems with interpretation of participants' positive judgments of a putative zero contingency. The first involves assumptions about how participants use the measurement scale. The second involves assumptions about the perceived frequency of events. Participants' judgments might not transparently map onto the measurement scale imposed on them by researchers. If participants are trained with a noncontingent relationship and asked to make a judgment of the relationship on a scale of –100 to +100, a rating of 0 is generally the expected outcome. However, this assumes that participants align their subjective experience of a noncontingent relationship with the value 0 on the rating scale. Most studies have implicitly assumed that a positive judgment implies that the subjects are above psychological zero. A fairer test requires comparing these judgments with judgments from a range of other contingencies. The minimal evidence for sensitivity to the noncontingent relationship should be that participants judge all noncontingent relationships similarly, but different from positive and negative contingencies. Therefore, there should be a direct relationship between changes in contingency and changes in judgments, but not necessarily a direct mapping between the experimenter's programmed contingency and the dependent variable.

The second, somewhat related, problem is whether the contingency presented is really noncontingent. The assumption is that the experimenter is in the privileged position of being able to objectively measure and present the appropriate events that define a zero contingency. However, the experimenter must be able to assume that the four cells of the contingency table are equally under their control. Certainly a case can be made for the number of times two things are paired together (Cell A), or either event occurs alone (Cell C and Cell B), but even these events are crucially determined by the level of contiguity between the signal and the outcome. For instance, do the two events need to occur simultaneously or, as is usual, does the signal occur before the outcome and, if so, how long before? Is it possible that people will mistakenly consider some conjunctions to be individual pairings and hence overestimate

Cells B and C at the expense of Cell A? Or might they think some disjoint presentations to be conjunctions with the opposite effect? In addition Cell D, the absence of both events, is even more difficult to control (Shanks & Dickinson, 1987).

A participant's perception of the contingency between events can depart significantly from the experimenter's intended contingency if participants estimate the frequency of the nonoccurrence of both events in a manner different than programmed by the experimenter. For example, if they overestimate the frequency of Cell D this will reduce $(P(O|\sim S)$ and thus generate a positive bias. Thus, from the perspective of the experimenter two events may occur independently of each other. The experimenter has defined a task as noncontingent, but this *experimenter contingency* is based on assumptions about how the participant should partition time, and also assumes that the subject should use only a certain type of evidence for their decision.

For example, if participants overestimate the frequency of Cell D observations, then they may form the impression of a positive contingency. The *participants' perceived contingency* may be positive whereas the *experimenter's* is zero. Neither estimate is more "correct" than the other in any true sense, and therefore experimenters must be careful how they interpret differences between expected judgments and actual judgments. Evidence that judgments were positive following zero contingency training might say very little about learning noncontingent relationships. Importantly, this could indicate a failure of the experimenter to control the contingency rather than a failure of the participant to respond appropriately.

The first problem described relates to whether it is reasonable to expect that participants' judgments should map transparently onto the experimenter's scale. Therefore, does the possibility that participants judge a zero contingency positively on the experimenter's scale indicate that they have misinterpreted the evidence? Early work studying contingency learning concluded that they had. Smedslund (1963) claimed to show that participants were excessively reliant on Cell A events to inform their judgments, suggesting that they were not able to use all four types of events, and therefore were not naturally sensitive to contingencies. He suggested that his findings reflected a tendency to rate relationships as positively contingent based on the frequency of signal–outcome co-occurrences alone. We work through how contingency theory usefully helped develop our understanding of human learning before illustrating how its misinterpretation may have misled researchers.

In Smedslund's (1963) study, student nurses were presented with a deck of 100 cards; each card represented a patient (and one instance of a cell in the contingency matrix) and indicated the presence or absence of a symptom and the presence or absence of a disease. Smedslund designed the deck such that (a) 70% of the cards (the patients) showed the disease and (b) that the symptom was a poor predictor of the disease because the probability of the disease in the presence and in the absence of the symptom was 0.69 and 0.72, respectively (see Table 10.1). Thus the disease was approximately as likely to occur in the presence as in the absence of the symptom. Smedslund reported that half of the student nurses "said there was a relationship [between the symptom and the disease] because the number of symptom–disease cards was the largest or was large" (p. 171). This was indeed the most frequent patient type (see the second column of Table 10.1).

On the basis of this finding, Smedslund concluded that humans were very poor reasoners about correlations, and that what little sense could be made of such information was driven entirely by consideration of the symptom–disease frequencies, a conclusion granted textbook legitimacy even now (e.g., Baron, 2000; Sutherland, 1992). However, Smedslund did not attempt to dissociate the impact of the disease base rate from the actual symptom–disease correlation. The idea that participants might judge the presented relationship as less predictive than one actually containing a positive contingency was not tested, and therefore requires that the participants' perceptions map directly onto the measurement scale. Subsequent work in a number of laboratories using different procedures was able to show that participants could discriminate positive, zero contingencies, and negative contingencies, irrespective of the number of signal–outcome pairings (e.g., Dickinson et al., 1984; Wasserman et al., 1993).

Using Smedslund's symptom–disease scenario, Vallée-Tourangeau, Hollingsworth, and Murphy (1998) presented participants with five different symptom–disease relationships (see Table 10.1). In two of

TABLE 10.1

Frequency of the Four Trial Types in Smedslund (1963, Experiment 2) and in the Five Conditions of Vallée-Tourangeau, Hollingsworth, and Murphy (1998, Experiment 1)

| | Smedslund | Vallée-Tourangeau, Hollingsworth, & Murphy | | | | |
|---|---|---|---|---|---|---|
| | Zero | Neg | .30 Zero | .50 Neg | .70 Zero | Pos |
| Symptom-Disease | 37 | 9 | 9 | 15 | 21 | 21 |
| Symptom-No Disease | 17 | 21 | 21 | 15 | 9 | 9 |
| No Symptom-Disease | 33 | 21 | 9 | 15 | 21 | 9 |
| No Symptom-No Disease | 13 | 9 | 21 | 15 | 9 | 21 |
| P(Disease) | 0.70 | 0.50 | 0.30 | 0.50 | 0.70 | 0.50 |
| P(Disease\|Symptom) | 0.69 | 0.30 | 0.30 | 0.50 | 0.70 | 0.70 |
| P(Disease\|No Symptom) | 0.72 | 0.70 | 0.30 | 0.50 | 0.70 | 0.30 |
| $\Delta P$ | −0.03 | −0.40 | 0.00 | 0.00 | 0.00 | 0.40 |

these, the symptom–disease contingency was nonzero, either negative 0.4 or positive 0.4, whereas in the remaining three it was zero; that is, the disease was as likely to be observed in patients with the symptom as in those without. These three zero-contingency conditions differed in the disease base rate, either 30%, 50%, or 70%. Therefore, the disease occurred relatively more frequently for patients with and without the symptoms as the percentage increased.

The mean judgments in all five conditions are plotted in Fig. 10.2. Participants did indeed rate zero-contingency relationships as slightly positive and, as the disease base rate increased, they were more likely to rate the symptom–disease relationship positively. This is consistent with Smedslund's early work. However, high or low disease base rates did not irremediably blunt the participants' judgment accuracy. Despite the fact that the high-density zero contingency contained a higher disease base rate than the positive correlation condition (0.7 vs. 0.5), the mean judgment was significantly higher in the positive condition than in the high–base rate zero condition. Similarly, although the disease base rate was lower in the low base rate zero correlation condition than in the negative correlation condition (0.3 vs. 0.5), the mean judgment in the negative condition was significantly lower than in the low-density zero condition.

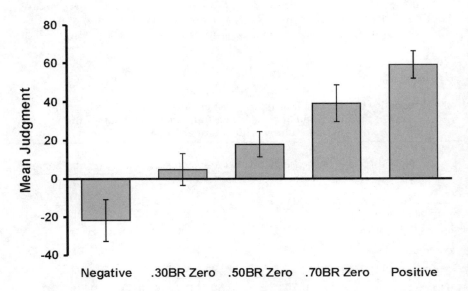

FIG. 10.2. Symptom–disease correlation judgments in the five conditions of Vallée-Tourangeau, Hollingsworth, and Murphy (1998, Experiment 1). The disease base rate was 0.5 in both the negative- and positive-correlation conditions. The disease base rate in the three zero-correlation conditions was 0.30, 0.50, and 0.70, respectively.

Thus, unlike Smedslund's original experiment, our experiment enabled us to clearly document people's ability to discriminate zero from nonzero symptom–disease contingencies. The disease base rate did have a significant impact on judgments as revealed by the order of the mean judgments across the three zero-correlation conditions. It is this finding that lends credence to our thesis that Smedslund's results were driven by the very high disease base rate used in the zero symptom–disease correlation presented to his group of student nurses. The fact that in our study the three zero contingencies were judged differently suggests that contingency is not all that is being judged.

In summary, people are able to discriminate different levels of contingency, but judgments of zero contingencies sometimes seem to be different from the objective contingency programmed by the experimenter. There are a number of possible explanations for this departure. It may reflect a bias in processing the four different types of trial that provide evidence for the contingency (e.g., Baron, 2000). Alternatively, it is also possible that causal inferences are influenced by more than $\Delta p$. The outcome base rate is an integral part of this inferential process (see, Cheng's power probabilistic contrast theory, 1997). We now examine some of the data on base rate effects and attempt to show that some of these effects might be better explained with reference to a more precise mapping of experience onto the events of the contingency table.

## BASE RATE DEPARTURES FROM CONTINGENCY

The base rate effect in contingency learning is the finding that judgments of similar contingencies seem to show influences beyond the contingency. To make matters even more confusing, there are two base rate effects reported in the literature that seem to relate to the type of task used by the experimenter. Passive tasks, like those used in Smedslund (1963) in which participants simply view a series of events, seem to result in judgments that increase with increasing outcome density, whereas tasks, in which a participant's instrumental behavior or response is the signal for the possible outcome, seem to result in weaker discrimination of different contingencies with increasing outcome frequency (Wasserman et al., 1993).

In one study we demonstrated the impact of the effect base rate within different correlation conditions (Vallée-Tourangeau, Murphy, Drew, & Baker, 1998). Using a virus–disease scenario, different contingencies were instantiated over a series of discrete trials (or "patients") much like Smedslund's task. We recorded judgments in two contingency conditions: zero and positive. At each level of contingency, the disease (outcome) base rate could be low at 0.25 (i.e., the overall probability of the disease was 25%), medium at 0.50, or high at 0.75. Terminal mean judgments in these six treatments are shown in the left panel of Fig. 10.3. The influence of the actual virus–disease contingency and the

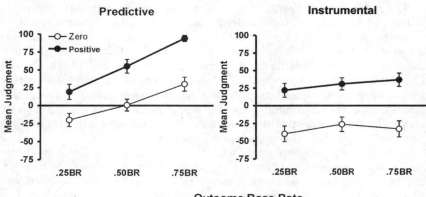

FIG. 10.3. Mean virus–disease contingency judgments as a function of the base rate of the effect (.25BR, .50BR, and .75BR) and the actual cause–effect correlation (zero, and positive) in a predictive task are shown in the left panel. Mean response–outcome contingency judgments as a function of the base rate of the outcome (.25, .50, .75) and the actual response–outcome contingency (zero, and positive) in an instrumental learning are shown in the task right panel.

disease base rates are clearly apparent. Thus, participants' judgments in the positive conditions were significantly more positive than judgments in the zero conditions. But, within each of the three levels of virus–disease contingency, the disease base rate significantly influenced judgments: Thus, the more frequent the overall likelihood of the disease the more positive the attribution of causal importance to the virus.

The influence of the effect base rate on judgments is a robust phenomenon. Earlier descriptions are found in the work of Alloy and Abramson (1979, with nondepressed participants), Allan and Jenkins (1980), Dickinson et al. (1983), Shanks (1985, 1987), and Baker et al. (1989). Commentators from opposite ends of the theoretical spectrum have attempted to explain the finding that the same contingency defined with different base rates often elicits different ratings. Some have suggested that it is a reflection of incomplete learning; that, is the different judgments reflect the different experience with the outcome but that with more experience judgments would eventually become more similar. Alternatively, Shanks has suggested that it may reflect a within-participants training artefact (Shanks, Lopez, Darby, & Dickinson, 1996). However, we have looked for this difference in our data and found no consistent evidence for this effect. Similarly, Shanks (1985) elegantly demonstrated that the effect base rate significantly influenced judgments in a between-subjects design, hence the cross-condition interference hypothesis offers little explanatory value.

Cheng (1997) has argued that the base-rate effect in zero-contingency conditions reflects either incomplete learning (the judgments are preasymptotic) or interference from nonzero correlation conditions in within-subjects design. However, in positive contingencies Cheng's power PC theory describes an extra causal learning process that attributes increased causal efficacy to signals that are related to higher outcome densities (see chap. 2, this volume, for a fuller discussion). A further feature of these density effects is that they are seemingly dependent on some unspecified aspect of the task. For instance, the outcome effect described by Vallée-Tourangeau, Murphy, Drew, and Baker (1998) is typical of other findings; however, using a quite different preparation without discrete trials, Wasserman and his colleagues (1993) have shown a completely opposite density effect.

## THE INSTRUMENTAL LEARNING DENSITY EFFECTS

In an instrumental learning preparation, participants are asked to judge the contingency between an action they perform and a subsequent outcome. In the laboratory, that action might be pressing a key on a computer keyboard, and the outcome a brief presentation of a geometric figure on the monitor. Though many researchers had studied this type of learning using discrete trials in which the opportunity to respond was signaled, Wasserman used a free-operant procedure in which participants responded as often as they liked during a specified training session (Wasserman, Chatlosh, & Neunaber, 1983; Wasserman et al., 1993). This procedure was adapted from a standard contingency learning procedure used in instrumental conditioning with animals described by Hammond (1980). Hammond noticed the problem involved in programming a contingency for experimental subjects. He chose one method although it is not the only solution. By systematically mapping contingency judgments as a function of a wide range of experimenter programmed action–outcome contingencies, Wasserman et al. (1993) have reported an impressive degree of accuracy. Not only were the contingency judgments closely aligned with the actual degree of action–outcome contingency but they were also largely unaffected by the base rate of the outcome (Benassi & Mahler, 1985; Wasserman et al., 1983). The latter finding contrasts rather sharply with the robust impact of the effect base rate in noninstrumental contingency judgment tasks such as ours.

Wasserman et al. (1993) used the Rescorla–Wagner model to explain their results. They showed an impressive correspondence between judgments and predictions of the Rescorla–Wagner model by assuming that the parameter that codes learning on outcome trials was higher than the parameter coding learning on no-outcome trials. However, this is not the only set of parametric assumptions that produces this pattern. In particular, if one assumes that there is a bias in the interpretation of the four cells of the contingency table in Wasserman's procedures, then this pattern of results can also be reproduced. There is good reason for positing that this might happen.

A particular feature of the Hammond schedule used by Wasserman is that, although the participant is unaware of the segmentation of time, the experimental period is segmented into 1-second bins. The conditional probabilities for the occurrence of the outcome in the presence and the absence of a response are mapped onto the bins. If the participant performs at least one response during any 1-second bin, then it is deemed a response and an outcome occurs at the end of the bin according to the probability of an outcome given a response, $P(O|R)$. If no response is made during the 1-second bin, then the outcome occurs with the probability $P(O|{\sim}R)$. One consequence of this procedure is that on average there is a .5-second delay between a response and an outcome. If the participant happens to respond at the start of a bin, then the outcome is delayed by 1 second; similarly, if the participant happens to respond near the end of the bin, then the delay is close to 0 seconds. This has three possible effects on the perception of contingency. The first is that responses that actually generate an outcome might be categorized as having not been paired with the outcome, especially if there is a 1-second delay. This is akin to reducing the impact of Cell A events. There is good evidence that even a relatively short delay between a signal and an outcome can seriously attenuate the perception of contingency (Dickinson & Shanks, 1995). In addition, outcomes that are nominally produced by responding might be categorized as not being contingent on responding. This is like increasing the number of Cell C events. Finally, because participants can respond as often as they like, they may respond more than once during a given 1-second bin, but still receive only one outcome presentation. This has the effect of increasing the number of Cell B events, in which a response is presented and no outcome occurs (Shanks & Dickinson, 1987). The overall effect of these factors is that the actual perceived contingency might be very difficult to establish. To the extent that judgments map onto estimates of contingency, the experimenter can be hopeful that this mapping is meaningful. However, any attempt to interpret departures from the estimates of contingency by resorting to auxiliary assumptions may be mistaken because the perceived contingencies might be different than the programmed one. We sought to explore whether the differences in density effects may reflect the attenuated contiguity in the Hammond schedule.

## TEST OF THE CONTIGUITY HYPOTHESIS OF DENSITY EFFECTS

To test whether the attenuated contiguity present in Wasserman et al. (1993) might be responsible for the pattern of density effects observed in that study, we report here some unpublished work in which we examined contingency judgments with an instrumental learning methodology in six conditions analogous to the ones run in Vallée-Tourangeau, Murphy, Drew, and Baker (1998). These conditions reflected the factorial combination of two levels of action–outcome contingency (zero, $\Delta P = 0$; and positive, $\Delta P = .5$) with three levels of outcome density (low at .25, medium at .5, high at .75). In the task, participants were asked to assess the causal importance of pressing the spacebar in producing the appearance of a geometrical figure on the computer screen. They could press the bar as many or as few times as they wished. As in any instrumental learning preparation, the experimenter did not control precisely the frequency and timing of delivery of the reinforcer (the outcome); rather, these were determined by the participants' behavior. The outcome would appear on the computer screen with probability $P(O|R)$ given an action and with a probability $P(O|\sim R)$ given the absence of an action after a certain amount of time elapsed. The difference between these two conditional probabilities determined the level of action–outcome contingency. The programmed conditional probabilities in the six conditions are shown in Table 10.2 along with the mean actual conditional probabilities experienced by the participants. In the three zero-contingency conditions, the outcome was as likely to occur following an action as following no action; that is, $P(O|R)$ equaled $P(O|\sim R)$. However, the overall probability of the outcome occurring varied from 0.25 to 0.75. In the three positive-contingency conditions, the outcome was programmed to occur more often following an action than following no action; that is, $P(O|R)$ was larger than $P(O|\sim R)$, and as in the zero-contingency conditions, the base rate of the outcome varied from 0.25 to 0.75. This experimental design enabled us to determine the degree of discrimination between two levels of action–outcome contingency and the impact of the outcome base rate on judgments.

## TABLE 10.2
### Programmed and Actual Contingencies in the Six Conditions of the First Instrumental Learning Experiment

|  | Programmed | | | Actual | | |
|---|---|---|---|---|---|---|
|  | $P(O|A)$ | $P(O|\sim A)$ | Delta P | $P(O|A)$ | $P(O|\sim A)$ | Delta P |
| Zero .25 | 0.25 | 0.25 | 0.00 | 0.27 | 0.24 | 0.03 |
| Zero .50 | 0.50 | 0.50 | 0.00 | 0.49 | 0.49 | 0.00 |
| Zero .75 | 0.75 | 0.75 | 0.00 | 0.73 | 0.77 | −0.04 |
| Pos .25 | 0.50 | 0.00 | 0.50 | 0.49 | 0.00 | 0.49 |
| Pos .50 | 0.75 | 0.25 | 0.50 | 0.73 | 0.25 | 0.48 |
| Pos .75 | 1.00 | 0.50 | 0.50 | 1.00 | 0.50 | 0.50 |

Each of the six action–outcome contingencies was instantiated over a sequence of 40 sampling intervals whose maximum duration was 1 second. During that 1-second segment, the computer program monitored whether the spacebar had been pressed. If so, then the outcome would be shown on the screen immediately after the bar press with probability $P(O|R)$ for a quarter of a second, and then a new 1-second sampling interval would be initiated. The stronger contiguity of response and outcome pairings was a departure from the Hammond schedule used by Wasserman et al. If, at the end of the 1-second segment, no bar presses had been detected, then the outcome would be presented on the computer monitor with probability $P(O|{\sim}R)$ and a new 1-second segment was initiated. Participants were not informed of this segmentation, nor was it marked in any manner during the task. Rather, they pressed the spacebar and stared at a blank computer screen on which a geometrical shape sometimes appeared. In contrast to the 45-minute testing sessions with the procedure of Vallée-Tourangeau, Murphy, Drew, and Baker (1998), participants were exposed to each of the six conditions for at most 40 seconds. Hence the experiment took between 5 and 10 minutes to complete, including reading the task instructions and making judgments at the end of each condition.

Participants were exposed to all six treatments. To minimize cross-treatment interference, unique geometrical figures were assigned to different treatments. The treatment orders as well as the assignment of figures to treatments were partially counterbalanced across participants. Twenty-six psychology undergraduates received course credits for their participation.

The mean contingency judgments for the six conditions are plotted in the right-hand panel of Fig. 10.3. Contingency discrimination appeared very good. Judgments in the three positive conditions were much more positive than judgments in the three zero conditions. Unexpectedly, judgments in the three positive conditions were not as positive as those recorded in the positive conditions of Vallée-Tourangeau, Murphy, Drew, and Baker (1998). The average judgment in the three positive conditions was 29.9 in this study whereas it was 56.1 in Vallée-Tourangeau et al. In turn, judgments across the three zero conditions were more negative (overall mean of −32.9) than the judgments in the analogous zero-contingency conditions of Vallée-Tourangeau et al. (mean of 9.1). Of primary interest is the fact that participants discriminated between the two levels of contingency.

But what of the impact of the outcome base rate on judgments? In both levels of contingency, mean judgments in the low–base rate treatments were lower than in the high–base rate treatment, which suggests that the outcome base rate did influence judgments. But importantly this pattern of results was opposite to that shown by Wasserman et al. (1993). A two-way repeated measures analysis of variance (ANOVA) on these data supported these observations (all tests for this and subsequent experiments assume a .05 alpha level). The main effect of contingency was reliable, $[F(1, 50) = 65.1]$, but neither the main effect of base rate, $[F < 1]$, nor the interaction, $[F < 1]$, were reliable.

The potentially important difference between our findings, and Wasserman et al.'s finding that increased outcome density dampened judgments, was our improved contiguity between response and outcomes. In our procedure an outcome programmed to occur after a response did so immediately following the response and the 1-second sampling interval was reset to 0. Thus the contiguity between response and outcome was consistently perfect. As described earlier, with Wasserman et al.'s (1993) the high outcome base rates, that is, when $P(O|R)$ is greater than .5, this degraded *contiguity* may contribute to a degraded perception of *contingency*. That is, any delay between a response and an outcome may sometimes lead reasoners to attribute the occurrence of the outcome not to their behavior, but rather to the absence of a response, thereby inflating the perception of $P(O|{\sim}R)$. The higher the outcome base rate the larger the subjective perception of $P(O|{\sim}R)$, and the more degraded the perception of contingency (see Shanks & Dickinson, 1987).

To test this hypothesis, we conducted a second study but this time directly compared the two experimental procedures. We tested participants with both the Hammond schedule and our revised version with stronger contiguity on the two positive $\Delta P = .75$ contingencies from Wasserman et al. (1993) that showed the biggest effect on the Hammond schedule. The two contingencies involved either low outcome density with the following two conditional probabilities for the likelihood of the outcome $[P(O|R) = .75$ and $P(O|{\sim}R) = 0; \Delta P = .75 - 0 = .75]$ or high outcome density $[P(O|R) = 1.0$ and $P(O|{\sim}R) = .25; \Delta P = 1.0 - .25 = .75]$. In Wasserman et al. (1993) these two contingencies elicited judgments corresponding to .65 and .51 respectively. Both judgements are lower than the actual $\Delta P$, but these judgments are both higher than any judgment of a lower contingency, and therefore are perfectly in line with the notion of sensitivity to contingency. However, the crucial concern here is the fact that the higher outcome density elicited lower judgments (.51) than did the lower outcome density (.65).

In a within-subjects design, participants rated the effectiveness of their response in producing an outcome in the two positive-contingency conditions using our perfect contiguity procedure, and using Wasserman's original procedure. The order of the two contingencies within each contiguity procedure was counterbalanced, as was the degree of contiguity. The results are displayed in Fig. 10.4 and clearly show both outcome effects. With the original variable contiguity schedule, judgments were higher with the lower density contingency and with the modified, higher contiguity schedule, judgments of the higher density were higher. The statistical analysis supports this observation. The interaction between type of schedule and contingency was reliable, $[F(1,31) = 14.60]$. These results confirm the quite fine sensitivity of hu-

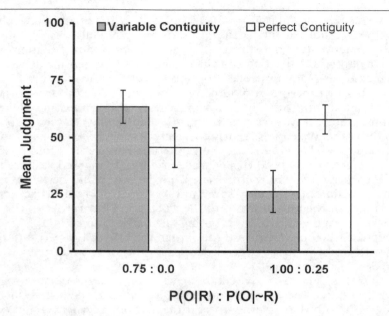

FIG. 10.4. Mean action–outcome contingency judgments in positive contingency conditions ($\Delta P = .75$) as a function of level of contiguity (perfect or variable) and two levels of the outcome base rate (.375 in condition .75:0.0, .625 in 1.0/0.25).

man judgments to variations in contiguity (see also Shanks et al., 1989). They also suggest that the interpretation posited by Wasserman et al. (1993), involving the differential effectiveness of outcome and no-outcome trials as an explanation of the density effect, is incomplete or incorrect.

In summary, previous work had shown that people are quite accurate at judging contingencies. These judgments were relatively consistent with predictions from $\Delta P$, and an associative analysis based on the Rescorla–Wagner model. However, if one assumes that the experimenter has correctly manipulated the contingent relationship, then both models fail to predict the influence of outcome density. However, we have argued that the departures from this profile might most easily be accounted for by issues related to the contingency presentation rather than contingency learning per se. We have shown how modification of the temporal contiguity between responding and the outcome seems to elicit the positive base rate effect; judgments increase with increasing base rate.

Some researchers might conclude that this analysis is appropriate only for instrumental tasks in which there is an ill-defined intertrial interval (ITI), but this is incorrect. The same analysis can be applied to predictive tasks in which discrete trials are presented to the participant. Consider a standard signal–outcome scenario used to teach a positive contingency. The participant might be presented with trials representing patients either with or without some fictitious disease and virus labels. The presence or absence of the disease and virus might be fairly easy to parse, although the signal–outcome onset period is ignored. But, how is the participant meant to estimate the number of no-virus/no-symptom instances, Cell D from the contingency table? The experimenter might hope that the participant is using only the experience of patients described in the experimental protocol, but it is not too much of a stretch to assume that people have prior experience of the absence of viruses and the absence of diseases. Any causal scenario one might imagine might be similarly influenced.

Although we have discussed how manipulating the contiguity between signal and outcome can have important influences on judgments, we now show how varying the amount of context exposure can also influence judgments. We have already suggested that problems related to the presentation of the D cell in contingency tables (the absence of the signal and the absence of the outcome) may also contribute to affect judgments. In particular, increases in Cell D should produce a consequent increase in judgments because these events confirm that neither event or outcome occur by themselves. We now discuss one experiment that investigated the influence of Cell D exposure with respect to the depressive realism effect.

## TESTING THE ROLE OF THE CELL D IN DEPRESSIVE REALISM

In addition to the general interest for human cognition that contingency learning has attracted, it has also been implicated in the study of individual differences. In particular, there is a long history of applying contingency analyses to the study of psychopathology. While studying conditioned reflexes in dogs, Pavlov (1927) noted the relation between learning conditional or contingent relationships and the development of emotional disturbances. However, Alloy and Abramson (1979) were the first researchers to imply that the contingency judgment paradigm with humans could be used as a tool to study individual differences including the symptoms of depression. Their experiments were designed to test predictions derived from theories that proposed that depressed people were characterized by a sense of a lack of control. They fail to properly evaluate the contingency between their behavior and its outcomes. This research was inspired in part by the learned helplessness theory of depression (Seligman, 1975), which argues that depressed people should be less able to learn response–outcome contingencies.

The experimental procedure employed by Alloy and Abramson involved an instrumental contingency learning task similar to the one described by Wasserman et al. (1993) except that participants were not free to respond at any time during the training session, but had to restrict their response to particular signaled intervals. Participants were asked to learn the relationship between pressing a key and the illumination of a light. Strong differences were observed between normals and dysphorics in their judgments of zero contingencies that varied in terms of outcome density. In the low–base rate condition, the outcome occurred 25% of the time [P(O) = .25] regardless of participants' pressing, whereas with the high base rate the outcome was presented 75% of the time [P(O) = .75]. These contingencies are the same as the .25BR zero and .75BR zero contingencies described in previous experiments. During trials, which were signaled by the occurrence of a yellow light lasting 3 seconds, participants were instructed to either press the key once or leave the key alone and the outcome (a green light) would or would not occur. Trials were separated by a variable 14-second interval (10–25 seconds). It was assumed that if subjects "realistically" assessed these contingencies there would be no differences in their judgments because, in spite of the density differences, both were zero contingencies. Moreover, it was implicitly assumed that the judgments if "realistic" should equal zero. Alloy and Abramson (1979) found that nondysphoric students' judgments increased with higher levels of outcome density. In contrast, students categorized as dysphoric, based on their score on a depression inventory, showed unchanged judgments in these two conditions. It is this increase in nondysphorics' judgments, which occurs as a function of higher levels of outcome density, that has been interpreted as an "optimistic" bias or a departure from "realism." The lack of a density effect on the part of the dysphoric students was purported to be reflective of their tendency to be more realistic or accurate in their perceptions. Thus, the density effect, that we have argued may be a consequence of distorted perceptions of cell frequencies, is argued by Alloy and Abramson to be a consequence of unrealistic, but adaptive, optimism in nondysphorics.

Since Alloy and Abramson's study, a number of replications of the depressive realism effect have been attempted. Much of the evidence suggests dysphoria influences judgments in situations in which the response does *not* control the outcome (zero contingencies) but the outcome occurs frequently; in these cases judgements are closer to zero—and therefore more accurate—than the judgments of nondysphorics (Alloy, Abramson, & Kossman, 1985; Benassi & Mahler, 1985; Martin, Abramson, & Alloy, 1984; Vasquez, 1987). This research has also shown that there is little difference between these two groups of participants when the contingencies to be judged are positive, suggesting that there is something special about the noncontingent conditions.

A number of explanations have been generated for the depressive realism effect. Alloy and Abramson (1979) suggested that conditions of zero contingency may be consistent with dysphoria and the expectations that it engenders concerning control over events in one's environment. This match between their expectations and the task allows them to accurately judge the two zero contingencies as being the same. In contrast, nondysphorics may have an optimistic bias that suggests they are much more in control than they actually are. As a consequence, some noncontingent situations are judged to be positive. Other proposals by Ackerman and DeRubeis (1991) are that motivation and perceptions of self, rather than expectations, drive the difference between the two groups. Self-esteem is somehow related to the person's perceived instrumentality in controlling environmental events. Depression weakens this motivation to maintain self-esteem. Either or both motivation and expectation could contribute to the observed depressive realism effect.

However, returning to the associative perspective on human contingency learning, it is quite easy to predict more positive judgments with higher outcome density for zero contingencies if one simply assumes that, whereas the programmed contingency is intended to reflect a zero contingency, the participants perceive a positive contingency. This can happen simply if they overestimate the number of Cell D occurrences, that is the frequency of absences of the signal and the outcome. Even if every care is used by the experimenter to explicitly guide the participants, ITIs may also be construed as possible Cell D events. Controlling the perception of the absence of events and outcomes has been a particular problem in other contingency learning domains.

In animal conditioning, for example, in spite of evidence that rats learn a conditioned response on the basis of CS–US contingency, subsequent work has argued against this (c.f. Papini & Bitterman, 1990). For example, strong conditioning is sometimes found following zero-contingency training, or animals may be found to be insensitive to changes in contingency caused by introducing USs in the absence of the CS (Hallam, Grahame, & Miller, 1992; Jenkins & Shattuck, 1981; Quinsey, 1971). However, if the rats' perception of the frequency of events in the contingency table differed from the experimenter's programmed contingency, as we have suggested, then it might not be surprising that responding did not mirror the "objective" contingency. We have recently reported an experiment that showed strong discrimination between positive- and zero-contingency training with rats using a procedure in which the Cell D events were explicitly marked with a stimulus (Murphy & Baker, 2004). We showed, using an explicit contextual cue, how competition between contextual cues and the target signal predicted sensitivity to CS–US contingency. Therefore, it is important in any contingency learning task that the experimenter have adequate control over the likelihood of the outcome in the absence of the signal. The following experiment attempted to show the influence of the absence of the signal on contingency learning in dysphoric and nondysphoric students.

It is also worth noting that associative theories can model the effect. The Rescorla–Wagner model treats adding extra trials, in which the absence of the signal occurs without the outcome (Cell D), as increasing the amount of context extinction. This decreases the context's associative strength, thereby allowing the signal to retain a stronger association with the outcome. Thus, adding either real or perceived Cell D events would be predicted to elicit stronger judgments of a contingency.

The two contingencies described by Alloy and Abramson were a low-density and a high-density zero contingency. The low-density zero contingency was constructed by presenting the outcome on 25% of the trials when the response occurred, and 25% of the trials when the response did not occur. If participants include some of the intertrial time in their processing of the information, in associative terms this will involve extra context extinction that will indirectly generate more associative strength to the response and, hence, a slight positive bias in judgments. From the perspective of $\Delta p$ this would be represented by extra Cell D experience, which would reduce the conditional probability of an outcome in the absence of the response, $P(O|{\sim}R)$. This would increase the perceived $\Delta P$ and thus would also generate a bias. The limit of this bias would be .25 for the low-density contingency as large numbers of Cell D event would cause $P(O|{\sim}R)$ to approach zero whereas as $P(O|R)$ would remain at .25. With the high-density zero contingency in which both unconditional probabilities are .75, the limit of this process would be a $\Delta p$ of .75 because $P(O|R)$ would be maintained at .75. A similar increased bias would also be predicted by the associative analysis. Therefore, by incorporating the ITI both the $\Delta P$ contingency and the Rescorla–Wagner predictions suggest that judgments should exhibit a bias that increases with outcome density.

In fact, most of the successful depressive realism studies that we have found have involved training with somewhat longer ITI time periods than is traditionally used in the field of learning (Shanks, 1985; Wasserman et al., 1993). Furthermore, at least one study that has been published that failed to replicate the depressive realism effect used relatively shorter ITIs of less than 5 seconds (e.g., Dobson & Pusch, 1995). The following experiment sought to replicate both the presence and absence of the depressive realism effect by assuming that the crucial variable underlying the two findings was the difference in ITI.

Ninety-six participants were assigned to dysphoric (n = 48) and nondysphoric (n = 48) groups on the basis of their scores on the Beck Depression Inventory (BDI; Beck, Ward, Mendelson, Mock, & Erbaugh, 1961). Scores of 8 or below were taken to indicate no depression. BDI scores were higher in the depressed groups than in the nondepressed groups [$F(1,81) = 133.6$]. Groups were successfully matched on gender, digit span and age, but differed on the National Adult Reading Test [$F(1,89) = 4.74$] and years of education [$F(1,89) = 5.68$].Therefore, subsequent data analysis included these factors as covariates to ensure that any variance in judgements attributable to these factors was removed from the analysis.

The experiment involved a 2 (mood) × 2 (ITI length) × 2 (outcome density) fully factorial between-subjects design. Each participant made judgments of only one contingency problem—a high-density zero-contingency $[P(O|R) = P(O|{\sim}R) = .75]$ or a low-density zero-contingency $[P(O|R) = P(O|{\sim}R) = .25]$. The experimental conditions differed as to whether the ITI was short (3 seconds) or long (15 seconds) and the participants' mood—dysphoric or nondysphoric. Experimental events were presented via computer monitor.

Participants were asked to judge how much pressing of a button controlled a light switching on. They were further instructed that it was necessary to press the button on some occasions and not press it on an approximately equal number of occasions. Each trial was constructed such that there was a 3-second opportunity for the participants to make their response. This period was signaled by an on-screen message saying, "You may press the button now!" This was followed by a 2-second period, in which the light either switched on or remained off. During the ITI period, the unlit light bulb remained on the screen. After the contingency judgment task was completed, participants were debriefed.

The results confirmed the findings of Alloy and Abramson (1979): Using the long, 15-second ITI conditions, dysphoric participants showed little evidence of a density effect whereas the non-dysphoric group did; however, neither mood group exhibited an outcome density effect when the ITIs were short. The mean judgments of the contingency between button pressing and occurrence of the outcome are presented in Fig. 10.5.

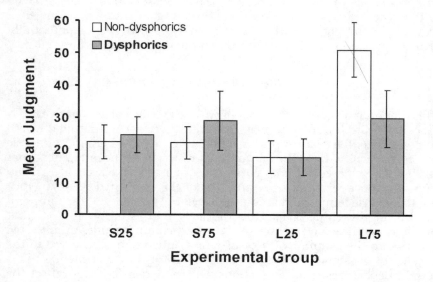

FIG. 10.5. Mean judgment of control in dysphoric and nondysphoric participants as a function of short (S) and long (L) ITI and low (25%) and high (75%) outcome base rate.

A 2(ITI) × 2 (density) × 2 (mood) × 2 (gender) fully factorial between subjects ANOVA confirmed these observations. The three-way interaction between length of ITI, outcome density (low, high) and mood (dysphoric, nondysphoric) was reliable [$F(1,78) = 4.27$]. Further analysis of the three-way interaction showed that when ITIs were short, there was no reliable density by mood interaction [$F < 1$], but there was when ITIs were long, [$F(1,78) = 4.46$]. Furthermore, there was no difference between mood groups in the low-density/long-ITI condition [$F < 1$], but as expected, nondepressed people's judgments were higher than depressed people's judgements in the high-density/long-ITI condition [$F(1,78) = 11.6$]. Taken together these results support the hypothesis that the increase in contingency estimates found with the increase in outcome density is a function of the relative amounts of context extinction. The higher outcome density groups receive less context extinction and thereby perceive the contingency as more positive.

Unlike the interpretation offered by Alloy and Abramson (1979) our interpretation of the difference between dysphorics and nondysphorics suggests that judgments of zero contingencies may not easily inform us about perceptions of realism. Instead, programmed contingencies may elicit judgments that differ from experimenter expectations for a number of reasons including the segmentation of $\sim$O|$\sim$R experience. Although this work does not explain why there is a difference with dysphoric participants, it raises the possibility that some of it relates to contextual learning, and this requires further investigation. Our interpretation is also a new direction for the use of associative models, in particular the idea that contextual conditioning in human contingency learning is influenced by the ITI. This analysis also offers a potentially fruitful direction to advance our understanding of depression.

## SUMMARY AND CONCLUSIONS

This work has attempted to show how the flexibility of associative models can account for outcome density effects thereby eliminating the need to invoke auxiliary assumptions concerning causal schemas, optimistic biases, or sensitivity to the reinforcing properties of the outcome. What the associative account does require in order to make accurate predictions is a more accurate representation of the associated events including the precise temporal relations between the variables. If the temporal resolution governing the segmentation of time is different from that predicted by the experimenter, or if the participant includes unpredicted events into the estimate of how often no outcome has occurred in the absence of the signal, then it will be difficult for the experimenter to interpret departures from predictions. Outcome density may reflect the additional processes that have been developed to account for judgments, but they may also reflect poor experimental control or understanding of which events participants deem useful for judging a contingent relationship. Our research has shown that associative theory is well able to account for seeming departures from predictions based on normative reasoning models by ensuring that both contiguity and contextual exposure are controlled.

## REFERENCES

Ackermann, R., & DeRubeis, R. J. (1991). Is depressive realism real? *Clinical Psychology Review*, *11*(5), 565–584.

Allan, L. G. (1980). A note on measurement of contingency between two binary variables in judgment tasks. *Bulletin of the Psychonomic Society*, *15*(3), 147–149.

Allan, L. G. (1993). Human contingency judgments: Rule based or associative? *Psychological Bulletin*, *114*, 435–448.

Allan, L. G. (2003). Assessing PowerPC. *Learning and Behavior*, *31*, 192–204.

Allan, L. G., & Jenkins, H. M. (1980). The judgment of contingency and the nature of the response alternatives. *Canadian Journal of Psychology*, *34*(1), 1–11.

Alloy, L. B., & Abramson, L. Y. (1979). Judgement of contingency in depressed and non-depressed students: Sadder but wiser? *Journal of Experimental Psychology: General*, *108*(4), 441–485.

Alloy, L. B., Abramson, L. Y., & Kossman, D. A. (1985). The judgement of predictability in depressed and nondepressed college students. In F. R. Brush & J. B. Overmier (Eds.), *Affect, conditioning, and cognition: Essays on the determinants of behavior* (pp. 229–246). Hillsdale, NJ: Lawrence Erlbaum Associates.

Arkes, H. R., & Harkness, A. R. (1983). Estimates of contingency between two dichotomous variables. *Journal of Experimental Psychology: General*, *112*, 117–135.

Baker, A. G., Berbrier, M. W., & Vallée-Tourangeau, F. (1989). Judgements of a 2 × 2 contingency table: Sequential processing and the learning curve. *Quarterly Journal of Experimental Psychology*, *41B*(1), 65–97.

Baker, A. G., Murphy, R. A., & Vallée-Tourangeau, F. (1996). Associative and normative models of causal induction: Reacting to versus understanding cause. In D. R. Shanks, K. J. Holyoak, & D. L. Medin (Eds.), *The psychology of learning and motivation* (Vol. 34, pp. 1–45) . San Diego: Academic Press.

Baker, A. G., Murphy, R. A., Vallée-Tourangeau, F., & Mehta, R. (2001). Contingency learning and causal reasoning. In R. R. Mowrer & S. B. Klein (Eds.) *Handbook of contemporary learning theories* (pp. 255–306). Mahwah, NJ: Lawrence Erlbaum Associates.

Baron, J. (2000). Thinking and deciding (3rd ed.). Cambridge, England: Cambridge University Press.

Beck, A. T., Ward, C. H., Mendelson, M., Mock, J., & Erbaugh, J. (1961). An inventory for measuring depression. *Archives of General Psychiatry*, *4*, 561–571.

Benassi, V. A., & Mahler, H. I. M. (1985). Contingency judgements by depressed college students: Sadder but not always wiser. *Journal of Personality and Social Psychology*, *49*(5), 1323–1329.

Buehner, M. J., & May, J. (2003). Rethinking temporal contiguity and the judgement of causality: Effects of prior knowledge, experience and reinforcement procedure. *Quarterly Journal of Experimental Psychology*, *56A*, 865–890.

Chapman, L. J., & Chapman, J. P. (1969). Illusory correlation as an obstacle to the use of valid psychodiagnostic signs. *Journal of Abnormal Psychology*, *74*, 271–280.

Cheng, P. W. (1997). From covariation to causation: A causal power theory. *Psychological Review*, *104*(2), 367–405.

Dickinson, A., & Shanks, D. R. (1995). Instrumental action and causal representation. In D. Sperber, D. Premack, & A. J. Premack (Eds.), *Causal cognition* (pp.
5–36). Oxford, England: Clarendon Press.

Dickinson, A., Shanks, D., & Evenden, J. (1984). Judgment of act–outcome contingency: The role of selective attribution. *Quarterly Journal of Experimental
Psychology, 36A*(1), 29–50.

Dobson, K. S., & Pusch, D. (1995). A test of the depressive realism hypothesis in
clinically depressed subjects. *Cognitive Therapy and Research, 19*(2), 179–194.

Hallam, S. C., Grahame, N. J., & Miller, R. R. (1992). Exploring the edges of Pavlovian contingency space: An assessment of contingency theory and its various metrics. *Learning and Motivation, 23*, 225–249.

Hamilton, D. L., & Gifford, R. K. (1976). Illusory correlation in interpersonal
perception: A cognitive basis of stereotypic judgments. *Journal of Experimental Social Psychology, 12*, 392–407.

Hammond, L. J. (1980). The effects of contingencies upon appetitive conditioning in
free-operant behavior. *Journal of Experimental Analysis of Behavior, 34*, 297–304.

Hull, C. L. (1943). *Principles of behavior.* New York: Appleton–Century–Crofts.

Hume, D. (1960). *A treatise of human nature.* Oxford, England: Clarendon Press.
(Original work published 1739)

Jenkins, H. M., & Shattuck, D. (1981). Contingency in fear conditioning a reex-
amination. *Bulletin of the Psychonomic Society, 17*, 159–162.

Mackintosh, N. J. (1983). *Conditioning and associative learning.* Oxford, England: Clarendon Press.

Martin, D. J., Abramson, L. Y., & Alloy, L. B. (1984). Illusion of control for self
and others in depressed and non-depressed college students. *Journal of Personality and Social Psychology, 46*(1), 125–136.

Melz, E. R., Cheng, P. W., Holyoak, K. J., & Waldmann, M. R. (1993). Cue competition in human categorisation: Contingency or the Rescorla–Wagner learning rule? Comments on Shanks (1991). *Journal of Experimental Psychology:
Learning, Memory, and Cognition, 19*, 1398–1410.

Murphy, R. A., & Baker, A. G. (2004). A role for CS–US contingency in Pavlovian
conditioning. *Journal of Experimental Psychology: Animal Behavior Processes,
30*, 229–239.

Nelson, H. (1982). *National adult reading test (NART): Test manual.* Windsor,
England: NFER-Nelson.

Nisbett, R. E., & Ross, L. (1980). *Human Inference: Strategies and Shortcoming.*
Englewood Cliffs, NJ: Prentice-Hall.

Papini, M. R. & Bitterman, M. E. (1990). The role of contingency in classical conditioning. *Psychological Review, 97*, 396–403.

Pavlov, I. (1927). *Conditioned reflexes.* Oxford, England: Oxford University Press.

Quinsey, V. L. (1971). Conditioned suppression with no CS–US contingency in
the rat. *Canadian Journal of Psychology, 25*, 69–82.

Rescorla, R. A. (1968). Probability of shock in the presence and absence of CS in
fear conditioning. *Journal of Comparative and Physiological Psychology, 66*, 1–5.

Rescorla, R., & Wagner, A. (1972). A theory of Pavlovian conditioning: Variations in the effectiveness of reinforcement and non-reinforcement. In A.
Black & W. Prokasy (Eds.), *Classical conditioning II: Theory and research* (pp.
64–99). New York: Appleton–Century–Crofts.

Schmajuk, N. A. (1997). *Animal learning and cognition: A neural network approach.* Cambridge, England: Cambridge University Press.

Seligman, M. E. P. (1975). *Helplessness: On development, depression and death.*
New York: Freeman.

Shaklee, H., & Tucker, D. (1980). A rule analysis of judgments of covariation between events. *Memory and Cognition, 8,* 459–467.

Shanks, D. R. (1985). Continuous monitoring of human contingency judgment across trials. *Memory & Cognition, 13*(2), 158–167.

Shanks, D. R. (1987). Acquisition function in contingency judgment. *Learning and Motivation, 18,* 147–166.

Shanks, D. R. (1993). Human instrumental learning: A critical review of data and theory. *British Journal of Psychology, 84,* 319–354.

Shanks, D. R., & Dickinson, A. (1987). Associative accounts of causality judgment. In G. H. Bower (Ed.), *The psychology of learning and motivation* (Vol. 21, pp. 229–261). San Diego: Academic Press.

Shanks, D. R., Lopez, F. J., Darby, R. J., & Dickinson, A. (1996). Distinguishing associative and probabilistic contrast theories of human contingency judgment. *The psychology of causal learning and motivation* (Vol. 34, pp. 265–311). San Diego: Academic Press.

Shanks, D., Pearson, S. M., & Dickinson, A. (1989). Temporal contiguity and the judgement of causality by human subjects. *The Quarterly Journal of Experimental Psychology, 41B*(2), 139–159.

Smedslund, J. (1963). The concept of correlation in adults. *Scandinavian Journal of Psychology, 4*(3), 165–173.

Spellman, B. A. (1996). Conditionalizing causality. In D. R. Shanks, K. J. Holyoak, & D. L. Medin (Eds.), *The psychology of learning and motivation* (Vol. 34, pp. 167–206). San Diego: Academic Press.

Sutherland, S. (1992). *Irrationality, the enemy within.* London: Penguin.

Vallée-Tourangeau, F., Hollingsworth, L., & Murphy, R. A. (1998). "Attentional bias" in correlation judgments: Smedslund (1963) revisited. *Scandinavian Journal of Psychology, 39,* 221–233.

Vallée-Tourangeau, F., Murphy, R. A., Drew, S., & Baker, A. G. (1998). Judging the importance of constant and variable candidate causes: A test of the Power PC theory. *Quarterly Journal of Experimental Psychology, 51A*(1), 65–84.

Vasquez, C. (1987). Judgement of contingency: Cognitive biases in depressed and nondepressed subjects. *Journal of Personality and Social Psychology, 52*(2), 419–431.

Wagner, A. R., & Brandon, S. E. (2001). A componential theory of Pavlovian Conditioning. In R. R. Mowrer and S. B. Klein (Eds.), *Handbook of contemporary learning theories.* Mahwah, NJ: Lawrence Erlbaum Associates.

Ward, W. C., & Jenkins, H. M. (1965). The display of information and the judgment of contingency. *Canadian Journal of Psychology, 19*(3), 231–241.

Wasserman, A. R., & Brandon, S. E. (2001). A componential theory of Pavlovian conditioning. In R. R. Mowrer and S. B. Klein (Eds.), *Handbook of contemporary learning theories.* Mahwah, NJ: Lawrence Erlbaum Associates.

Wasserman, E. A., Chatlosh, D. L., & Neunaber, D. J. (1983). Perception of causal relations in humans: Factors affecting judgments of response–outcome contingencies under free-operant procedures. *Learning and Motivation, 14*(4), 406–432.

Wasserman, E. A., Elek, S. M., Chatlosh, D. L., & Baker, A. G. (1993). Rating causal relations: Role of probability in judgments of response–outcome contingency. *Journal of Experimental Psychology: Learning, Memory, and Cognition, 19*(1), 174–188.

# Chapter 11

# Learning to Like (or Dislike): Associative Learning of Preferences

Andy P. Field

Preferences influence virtually all aspects of human behavior; they impact upon the foods we eat, the products we buy, the stimuli we approach or avoid, and the people with whom we spend time. Despite their huge influence, relatively little is understood about how we develop these preferences. One candidate to explain preference learning is associative learning: For example, associative learning has a long history as an explanation for why extreme emotional responses, such as fear, develop (e.g., Watson & Rayner, 1920; and for reviews, see Davey, 1997; Field & Davey, 2001). The interest in explaining preferences as conditioned responses dates back to the 1930s when Razran did several studies (all reported only as abstracts) in which various stimulus materials (musical selections, photographs, verbal statements, and paintings) were presented during a luncheon (two sandwiches, two desserts, and a beverage no less!). Evaluations of the stimuli became more positive because of the association between the stimulus and pleasant experience of the luncheon. Conversely, when paired with a noxious odor ratings decreased (see Razran, 1938a, 1938b, 1940a, 1940b).

Hot on Razran's trail were C. K. Staats and A. W. Staats (1957; see also A. W. Staats & C. W. Staats, 1958) who investigated the conditioning of attitudes through a verbal paradigm by presenting participants with either national names (e.g., German, Swedish, French) or male names (e.g., Harry, Tom, Jim) as a conditioned stimulus (CS). These CSs were then paired with orally presented positively or negatively valenced words (A. W. Staats & C. K. Staats, 1958). The paradigm is like a CS+/CS− discrimination paradigm in that one target word was always paired with positive words (CS+), whereas a second target word was always paired with negative words (CS−) and the CSs were coun-

terbalanced across groups. This procedure formed the basis of a neutral-like, neutral-disliked, CS–US (unconditioned stimulus) paradigm.
Each US word was used only once and so Staats and Staats reasoned
that the evaluation, rather than the specific US, would be associated
with the CS. The remaining CSs were paired with neutral words such
as *chair*. After conditioning, participants rated each of the CS words
along a 7-point scale ranging from pleasant to unpleasant. Seventeen
people who indicated an awareness of some of the CSs and USs were
excluded from the analysis (awareness was measured in terms of ver-
balizing the specific contingency that the participant experienced). The
results showed differential responding to names paired with positive
and negative words and, *prima facie*, provided evidence of some kind of
affective transfer through conditioning. What's more, because conditioning had occurred in participants who were classified as unaware of
the contingencies, Staats and Staats concluded that this conditioning
was an unconscious process.

Two subsequent studies challenged Staats and Staats' conclusions.
Cohen (1964) and Insko and Oakes (1966) both replicated Staats and
Staats' experiment but using different measures or criteria for assessing
contingency awareness: Both found a strong relationship between contingency awareness and the alleged conditioned attitudes. More convincingly, Page (1969, 1971, 1973, 1974) in, what turned out to be, a
debate of some magnitude took Staats and Staats to task using very detailed measures of contingency awareness and demand awareness and
concluded that "the so-called conditioned attitudes are entirely artefacts
of demand characteristics" (Page, 1969, p. 185).

A. W. Staats was not happy. In a reply (A. W. Staats, 1969), he de-
fended his work by suggesting that these other studies created the apparent demand characteristics by prompting participants to report that
they saw through the purpose of the experiment. Page countered this
argument empirically with a set of studies that manipulated aspects of
awareness (1974) and the assessment of awareness (1971, 1973); his
conclusions remained unchanged.

In the last 30 years, the strands of this work have been taken up by
researchers from many different disciplines, and a broad database now
exists that goes a long way to informing us about the role that associative learning has in preference learning. However, as we shall see, the
specter of cynicism still floats around the ether, causing trouble at every
available opportunity. This chapter asks whether preferences really can
be conditioned, and if so, is the mechanism the same as for other forms
of associative learning?

## A BRIEF(ISH) HISTORY OF EVALUATIVE CONDITIONING

Evaluative conditioning (EC) is a process by which neutral stimuli acquire affect through contiguous pairing with a stimulus that already
evokes an emotional response. In conditioning terms, the affectively

neutral stimulus is the CS and is paired with either a liked or disliked US, resulting in the CS evoking a response congruent with the US with which it was paired.

## A Typical Experiment Using Visual Stimuli

The EC literature really began in 1975 when Levey and Martin introduced a paradigm that forms the basis of many of the studies that have subsequently been done. A generic visual EC experiment would begin with participants evaluating a set of novel stimuli, usually by ranking them, or rating them on some form of scale [e.g., disliked (–100) through 0 (neutral) to +100 (liked)]. A selection of the most positive and negatively rated pictures would then be removed to be used as USs, and a selection of stimuli rated around zero (neutral) would be removed to be used as CSs. CSs would then be allocated to a given US either using some criterion (such as perceptual similarity) or on a random basis.

During conditioning the CS–US pairs would be presented several times in semirandomized order. Typically the CS appears for a short time (1 second might be typical), there would be a trace interval of a few seconds, and then the US would appear (again 1 second might be typical). There would then be a longer gap (8 seconds perhaps) before the next trial began. The exact timings and the number of times each CS–US pair is presented has, not surprisingly, differed across studies over the years; these are merely representative values.

Following the conditioning stage, participants would again rate the stimuli using whatever rating scale was used to establish the original evaluative responses. This forms the core framework of a typical experiment. Over the years different measurement techniques have been used such as ranking pictures (Field, 2003; Johnsrude, Owen, Zhao, & White, 1999; Levey & Martin, 1975), rating scales (Baeyens, Crombez, Van den Bergh, & Eelen, 1988; Baeyens, Eelen, & Van den Bergh, 1990; Baeyens, Eelen, Van den Bergh, & Crombez, 1989a, 1989b, 1990, 1992; Baeyens, Hermans, & Eelen, 1993; Baeyens, Kaes, Eelen, & Silvermans, 1996; Baeyens, Wrzesniewski, De Houwer, & Eelen, 1996; Field & Davey, 1999; Field & Moore, in press; Fulcher & Cocks, 1997; Hammerl & Grabitz, 1993, 2000; Stevenson, Boakes, & Prescott, 1998, to name but a few), physiological measures (Hermans, Vansteenwegen, Crombez, Baeyens, & Eelen, 2002; Purkis & Lipp, 2001), and implicit attitude measures (Field, 2003; Hermans et al., 2002; Olson & Fazio, 2001), but other aspects of the paradigm remain relatively similar across studies.

Figure 11.1 shows an idealized set of results from such a study. CSs begin life as fairly neutral stimuli, but become viewed as more positive or negative depending on whether they are paired with a liked or disliked US respectively during conditioning. Sometimes control pairings are included in which neutral CSs are paired with other neutral stimuli. The ratings of these stimuli should not change.

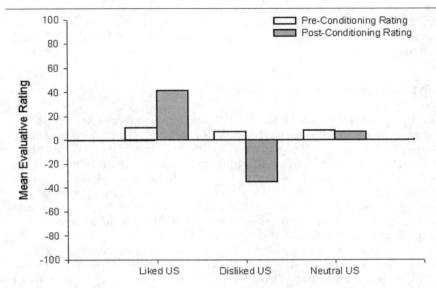

FIG. 11.1. An idealized (but completely fabricated) set of results from an EC study. All CS ratings start off being relatively neutral. However, when paired repeatedly with a liked US they increase, but when the US is disliked they decrease. When the US is also neutral ratings should not change across the conditioning procedure.

## A Typical Experiment Using Taste Stimuli

The typical paradigm for looking at taste preferences is not dissimilar to the visual paradigm. In essence, a CS+/CS– differential conditioning paradigm is used. Before conditioning, participants rate a series of novel flavored drinks. During conditioning, participants receive presentations of a CS+ compound (a fruit-flavored drink mixed with either a positive or negative US: sugar or Tween20[1] respectively) and a CS– (a different fruit flavor mixed with water). A typical conditioning trial might consist of looking at the drink for 5 seconds, then smelling it for 5 seconds, then taking the fluid into their mouths and tasting it for 5 seconds before swallowing. After 5 seconds of waiting they might then consume some bread to clear the palette and then 20 seconds later the next trial would begin. They might typically taste around 6 or 12 randomly ordered trials each of the CS+ and CS–, so 12 or 24 trials in all (Baeyens, Crombez, Hendrickx, & Eelen, 1995). Following this, they would rerate the CS flavors. The typical finding is much the same as for visual stimuli (see Fig. 11.1): Neutral tastes paired with noxious USs become less liked compared to those not paired with another taste (e.g., Baeyens, Eelen, Van den

[1]Tween 20 is a chemical that has a bitter aftertaste—rather like eating soap!

Bergh, & Crombez, 1990, Baeyens et al., 1995a, 1996; Baeyens, Hendrickx, Crombez, & Hermans, 1998; Baeyens, Vanhouche, Crombez, & Eelen, 1998), whereas tastes paired with pleasant USs are viewed more favorably after conditioning (in Zellner, Rozin, Aron, & Kulish, 1983; but not in Baeyens, Eelen, Van den Bergh, & Crombez, 1990).

This paradigm differs from the visual paradigm in one important respect: One flavor is always reinforced (either negatively or positively), whereas the other is never reinforced. As such, this paradigm can be considered a well-controlled discriminative paradigm, because all CSs are paired with all USs across participants. In the visual paradigm, CSs and USs are often chosen based on an individual's initial ratings and so CSs and USs cannot be counterbalanced across different groups. This, as we shall see, is important.

### Preferences for Visual Stimuli: Basic Findings

Over the past 30 years, numerous studies have been done using variants on the typical paradigm already described. The basic finding was demonstrated by Levey and Martin (1975) using works of art as stimuli, and they replicated these effects in a series of experiments (Martin & Levey, 1978), which led them to conclude that EC is highly dependent on the similarity between CS and US (which enhances the conditioning effect): Dissimilarity between CS and US abolishes the EC effect and too much similarity between the stimuli impedes conditioning. They also found that participants with an appreciation for the visual arts were less likely to condition (perhaps because they already have fairly fixed tastes in art), as were participants making aesthetic judgements rather than going with their feelings. Levey and Martin's (1987) final empirical contributions showed that the strength of the US might also moderate learning: One-trial learning could be established for CSs paired with intense USs, and conditioning in five trials was achievable with moderate USs. Around the same time Eifert, Craill, Carey, and O'Connor (1988) used a very similar paradigm to demonstrate that preferences for Greek letters could be increased or decreased by using positive or negative music (respectively) as a US. In addition, using positive music while exposing animal phobics to their feared stimulus appeared to facilitate the positive effects of this treatment (at the group level).

Frank Baeyens and his colleagues followed up Martin and Levey's ideas with a quite remarkable body of work, all of which made attempts to improve the methodology. His work undoubtedly was responsible for garnering a wider interest in conditioned preferences—especially among learning theorists. Baeyens replicated the basic EC effect but using pictures of human faces (Baeyens et al., 1988, 1989a, 1989b, 1993; Baeyens, Eelen, & Van den Bergh, 1990; Baeyens, Eelen, Van den Bergh, & Crombez, 1990, 1992) and unearthed many of the functional characteristics of EC (as we see in due course). The same research group also demonstrated that evaluations of affectively neutral words, and nonwords, could be changed through pairing with affectively positive and negative words (De Houwer, Baeyens, & Eelen, 1994; De Houwer, Hendrickx & Baeyens, 1997)—although the results were somewhat inconsistent (see De Houwer et al., 1997; Field, 2000b).

Around the same time, a parallel strand of research was being undertaken by consumer researchers. Gorn (1982) carried out a simple study in which participants watched a slide that featured either a blue or beige pen while listening to a piece of music that was either pleasant (the theme music from *Grease*, which apparently some people find pleasant) or unpleasant (classical Indian music, which apparently some people find unpleasant, although personally I'm convinced that the USs were the wrong way around!). At the end of the study, participants chose a blue or beige pen as their reward. Participants chose a pen congruent with the "pleasant" music—even preferences for pens appear to be conditionable!

However, as Allen and Madden (1985) noted, the demands of the task were somewhat obvious in Gorn's study. They replicated the study using humor as a US (Bill Cosby as a positive US and an offensive comedian called Redd Fox as an unpleasant US), not music, and took thorough postexperimental assessments. They found virtually no demand awareness using these measures, but also found no evidence of conditioning. They concluded that any apparent conditioning observed in the positive US group could be explained by several participants believing that the experiment was about consistency theory, and deliberately choosing a pen consistent in color with the slide they had been shown! Kellaris and Cox (1989) also replicated the Gorn study and failed to find any significant effects. However, they did find a significant effect when they ran a role-playing nonexperiment where participants imagined themselves in the experimental situation and predicted the response they would give. They concluded that Gorn's results were due to demand awareness. So, perhaps preferences for pens can't be conditioned after all.

Shimp, Hyatt, and Snyder (1991) challenged these replications, accusing the authors of accepting a demand–awareness account in favor of looking at the procedural differences in the replications. Shimp et al. attempted to estimate the degree of demand awareness that might have contributed to Gorn's results. When they reanalyzed Gorn's data, controlling for this demand awareness, the test results were still significant. So, preferences for pens can be conditioned then? Actually, no: Darley and Lim (1993) noted several errors in the assumptions made by Shimp et al. in their estimations of demand awareness. When these errors were rectified, and Gorn's data reanalyzed, the results lost their significance.

Leaving pens aside, Bierley, McSweeney, and Vannieuwkerk (1985) conducted a more methodologically rigorous exploration of the classical conditioning of preferences. They used red, blue, and yellow geometric shapes as CSs and the music from the movie *Star Wars* as a positive US. Participants were screened to ensure that they were not color-blind and that they liked the music from *Star Wars*. CSs were counterbalanced across groups, and two control groups were used: a CS-only group, where the geometric shapes were presented but the *Star Wars* music was never played, and a random control group, where the *Star Wars* music was played randomly after the CSs (so, no color reliably predicted the onset of the music). At face value they found significant conditioning effects: Shapes paired with the music were preferred. However, they failed to make the necessary statistical comparisons between the experimental and control groups to demonstrate that the learning was associative (see Field, 1997).

Stuart, Shimp, and Engle (1987) carried out four experiments using an analogous paradigm to Bierley et al. except that a neutrally valenced product (Brand L toothpaste) acted as a CS and positively valenced pictures acted as USs (a mountain waterfall, a sunset over an island, blue sky and clouds seen through the mast of a boat, and a sunset over an ocean). Alongside these, several filler items were used, which included three other products (brand R cola, brand M laundry detergent, and brand J soap) and 12 neutrally valenced scenes (dirt, radar dish, license plate). One key difference between this study and that of Bierley et al., was that Stuart et al. did not incorporate a second CS that was always paired with the absence of a US. They found that conditioned preferences (compared to the control group) could be found but did not depend on how many times the CS–US pairs were presented (they tried 1, 3, 10, or 20 conditioning trials) and that preexposure to CSs (latent inhibition) and backward presentations (i.e., the US appears before the CS in a given trial) inhibited conditioning.

In a later study, Shimp, Stuart, and Engle (1991) reported 21 experiments using an identical paradigm to their earlier study, but with actual brands of cola that were classed as either well known (Pepsi and Coca-Cola), moderately known (Royal Crown and Shasta—two local brands well known to the campus population but seldom advertised), and unknown (Cragmont, Elf, My-te-fine, and Target colas—all nonlocal brands unheard of by the participants used). The brand of cola was used as a CS and was paired with the same picture USs as used by Stuart et al. (1987). The remaining cola brands were used as filler items and were paired with neutral USs that were the same as in their earlier study.

Throughout the 21 studies, Shimp et al. (1991) varied the brand of cola used as the CS and the context within which it was placed (i.e., whether known or unknown brands were used as the filler stimuli). All other aspects of the studies were the same as those used by Stuart et al. (1987). Out of the 21 experiments, only 11 revealed significant differences in the preferences toward CSs between the paired and control conditions. It is possible that some of these effects were due to the role of context (i.e., the filler items that were used); however, in five of the failures this explanation can be ruled out (see Field, 1997). Another interesting moderating variable appeared to be contingency awareness (see the section later in this chapter). The last nine studies in the set were analyzed with respect to whether participants were contingency aware or unaware, and seven of these showed significant conditioning effects in participants classified as contingency aware compared to both those classified as unaware and control participants. The participants classified as unaware of the contingencies did not respond significantly differently to the random control participants, indicating that conditioning was dependent on awareness (we return to this point later).

### Preferences for Tastes: Basic Findings

Zellner, Rozin, Aron, and Kulish (1983) discovered over three experiments that preferences for flavored teas could be conditioned by using sugar as a US: When presented after conditioning in unsweetened form, ratings for the flavored tea (CS+) previously presented in compound with sugar were higher than ratings of the tea (CS–) previously presented in compound with only water. Baeyens, Eelen, Van den Bergh, and Crombez (1990) followed up this work to see the effects of flavor-flavor and color-flavor conditioning using a CS+/CS– differential conditioning paradigm (described earlier). They found evidence that flavor preferences depended on the US paired with the flavor: Flavors paired with positive USs became more liked, whereas those paired with disliked USs became more disliked. There was also some evidence that these conditioned preferences were present (albeit attenuated somewhat) a week later. Baeyens et al. looked also at the effect of color in the CS+ (again presented in compound with either a liked or disliked US) with the same result: Color preference depended on the US with which it was paired. However, Field and Davey (1997) noted one curious feature of the data: Color and taste preferences for CS+ compounds did not change according to whether the US was positive or negative; instead, they all just became more disliked (even when a positive US was used). The CS– ratings (the control CSs), however, did shift according to whether a positive or negative US had been used (even though this US was never paired with the CS–). This shift in the CS– created a differential response pattern in the CS+ stimuli, but this was due, not to changes in the CS+ ratings, but to differential changes in the CS– ratings (see also Field & Davey, 1998). As Baeyens, De Houwer et al. (1998) acknowledge this kind of "anchoring" problem is inevitable in a discriminative paradigm; but because the CS– acts as a baseline for change, it is the relative difference in ratings to the CS+ and CS– that is important.

Baeyens, Crombez, Hendrickx, and Eelen (1995) conducted a similar study, based again on the typical paradigm described earlier, in which the number of acquisition trials, the color of the liquid, and the flavor used as CS+ were counterbalanced across groups. The results showed a significant differentiation between ratings of fruit flavors paired with

the CS+ and fruit flavors (CS–) paired with a sugar US. No such differentiation was found when the CS– had no US (i.e., just water was used).
So, fruit flavors paired with a negative US were rated significantly
lower than fruit flavors paired with a positive US but not significantly
lower than a CS paired with a control US. These effects were not influenced by the number of acquisition trials, but there was a rather complicated interaction between the number of acquisition trials and whether
the color of the liquid at acquisition and test was the same or different.

These basic results have been replicated in several more recent studies
(Baeyens, Crombez, De Houwer, & Eelen, 1996; Baeyens, Hendrickx et
al., 1998; Baeyens, Vanhouche et al., 1998) and, in general, it would be
fair to conclude that whereas conditioned dislikes (i.e., when the US is a
nasty taste) have been robustly and regularly observed, conditioned
preferences (i.e., when the US is a positive taste such as sugar) have been
found only erratically (see De Houwer, Thomas, & Baeyens, 2001). For
example, Baeyens et al. (1990) failed to replicate Zellner et al.'s results.
This could be due to the relative salience of the negative USs: Indeed,
when positive USs of (presumably) greater salience than water or sugar
are used, such as caffeine, flavor preferences to novel drinks can be conditioned (e.g., Yeomans, Jackson, Lee, Nesic, & Durlach, 2000; Yeomans,
Jackson, Lee, Steer et al., 2000; Yeomans, Ripley, Lee, & Durlach, 2001;
Yeomans, Spetch, & Rogers, 1998).

## Preferences for Odors: Basic Findings

Stevenson and colleagues (Stevenson et al., 1998; Stevenson, Boakes, &
Wilson, 2000a, 2000b; Stevenson, Prescott & Boakes, 1995) have developed a paradigm that mirrors the standard taste paradigm already described, but uses odors as CSs. In this paradigm, novel odors are paired
with either a pleasant taste (sucrose) or an unpleasant one (citric acid). In
these studies, the expectation would be that liking for odors increases when
they're paired with pleasant tastes, but decreases when they are paired
with unpleasant tastes. However, they have found inconsistent evidence
that this is true: Stevenson et al. (1995—two experiments), Stevenson et al.
(2000b—Experiment 2), and Stevenson et al. (1998) found no evidence for
changes in liking of the CSs paired with different USs, yet Stevenson et al.
(2000b—Experiments 3 and 4) did find some evidence for preference
change. Interestingly, although there is only inconsistent evidence that
preferences for odors can be conditioned, other stimulus properties that
could arguably contribute to preferences, such as sweetness and sourness,
were reliably conditioned in all of these studies.

## Preferences Conditioned Cross-Modally

Stevenson's paradigm uses CSs and USs from different modalities (taste
and smell) and found very little evidence that preferences (at least in

terms of explicit evaluative ratings of liking) could be conditioned. Does this simply mean that cross-modal EC doesn't work?

We have already seen several examples of cross-modal EC: geometric shape CSs paired with music USs (Bierley et al., 1985), pen CSs paired with music (Gorn, 1982) or humor USs (Allen & Madden, 1985), and Greek letters paired with music (Eifert et al., 1988). However, Todrank, Byrnes, Wrzesniewski, and Rozin (1995) also carried out four experiments using olfactory USs and visual CSs. They used 36 of the pictures of human faces that Baeyens has used throughout his research (e.g., Baeyens et al. 1988, 1990a) as CSs and 11 odorants judged as people-related as USs (i.e. lotions, sweat, soap). In the first three experiments, photos with slightly positive ratings were selected to be paired with the liked US, and photos with slightly negative ratings were chosen to be paired with the negative US, but in a fourth CS–US allocation was entirely random. The odors were presented several times, followed by a CS, in a backward presentation schedule.

The results in all four experiments showed a significant difference between the changes in ratings of pictures paired with liked and disliked odors. However, the change in the ratings of CSs from N-L (Neutral-Like) pairs was not significantly different from the ratings of neutral-odor control pairs (N-N) or neutral pictures presented without an odor (a CS-only control, N–). However, the changes in ratings of the CS pictures from N-D pairs were significantly different to the N-N and N– control pictures. Van Reekum, Van den Bergh and Frijda (1999) likewise found that preferences for novel paintings could be conditioned using pleasant or unpleasant odors as USs, but also when liked or disliked sounds were used as USs. Johnsrude et al. (1999) also found that preferences for novel patterns could be conditioned using desirable foods (Willy Wonka's Dweeb candies or raisins) as a US. This particular form of preference learning appeared to be impaired in patients with unilateral lesions that included the amygdaloid nuclear complex, but not in those with unilateral damage confined to the frontal cortex (Johnsrude, Owen, White, Zhao, & Bohbot, 2000). This study is one of few that attempts to localize conditioned preference learning in the brain.

However, Baeyens et al. (1996) found less clear-cut evidence of cross-modal conditioning in two "naturalistic" experiments. They investigated how evaluations of different odors were influenced by experiencing the odor concurrently with a positive or negative event: In a first quasi-experiment the event was visiting a toilet room (participants rated this experience positively or negatively prior to the experiment), and in a second experiment the event was a positive or negative massage (the negative massage was judged to be unpleasant by a trained practitioner). In both the toilet room and the massage experiments, participants rated both the odor used during conditioning and a control odor, which was not paired with the US (the two odors were counterbalanced). In the toilet room study, only a marginal conditioning effect was found, and in the massage study, conditioning was observed in participants who experienced the positive massage but not in those who received the negative massage. Also, although conditioning was observed when comparing the experimental odor with the control odor, there was no significant differential responding between the positive US and negative US groups.

## Interim Summary

So far we've seen that many studies have attempted to show that preferences for neutral stimuli can be conditioned using emotionally valenced USs. These studies have involved visual stimuli, tastes, and odors as CSs and USs, and have been both intramodal and cross-modal. Across this body of work many studies seem to have shown the basic effect that preferences for visual stimuli and tastes can be successfully changed, but cannot always be changed for odors. However, we've also seen throughout this review that there are some inconsistencies in the data. It is to these that we now turn.

## ENTER THE HARBINGER OF DOOM

Although at first glance, the body of work so far reviewed appears to support the idea that associative learning can create preferences for novel stimuli, EC has been an elusive and controversial phenomenon. Stevenson et al. (2000b) and Lovibond and Shanks (2002) recently noted that EC experiments using visual stimuli had come under considerable criticism. The controversy surrounding EC stems from both failures to obtain the basic effect (e.g., Field, 1997; Field & Davey, 1999; Field, Lascelles, & Davey, 2003; Rozin, Wrzesniewski, & Byrnes, 1998) and demonstrations that EC effects can be elicited through nonassociative processes (Field & Davey, 1997, 1999).

### The Squid of Despair

The seeds of doubt were initially sewn by Davey (1994), who pointed out that because the typical EC paradigm did not include nonpaired control conditions against which to compare conditioning effects, there was little evidence that the effects observed were associative learning. This criticism applies considerably more to the typical visual paradigm in which CSs and USs are not counterbalanced than to taste experiments in which typically CSs and USs are counterbalanced with one CS acting as a CS-only control. Shanks and Dickinson (1990) have eloquently highlighted the problem: In early visual EC paradigms CSs and USs were selected by participants (and often paired on the basis of perceptual similarity) and this CS–US assignment procedure may have interacted with the effects of stimulus exposure to create the illusion of conditioning. Furthermore, Shanks and Dickinson argue that true conditioning effects can be isolated only if the pairing of a particular CS with a particular US is counterbalanced across participants (as is usually done in when taste stimuli are used).

When CSs and USs are counterbalanced across stimuli it is possible to rule out any effects of the particular stimulus materials chosen. What is more, if one CS is never paired with a US (a true CS–) then the paradigm incorporates a comparison between CSs that enter into associations (CS+s), and CSs that do not. Therefore, any effect in the CS+ can be attributed to the association it entered into. To infer a causal role of "associations" in the change of preferences, a Popperian view of science dictates that conditions in which the cause is present (in this case associations are present) must be compared with situations in which the cause is absent (in this case associations are absent)—see Field and Hole (2003) and Field and Davey (1998). The problem is that in the typical visual paradigm the only controls are pairings in which neutral CSs are paired with other neutral stimuli: Therefore the proposed cause (the association between stimuli) is still present. Therefore, we cannot infer that changes in the evaluative response to CSs paired with valenced USs compared to those paired with neutral USs are due to associations: because associations (the proposed causal variable) are present in both types of pairings.

Understandably, Baeyens and his colleagues maintain that the typical paradigm that has been employed incorporates sufficient within-participant controls to infer associative learning (Baeyens & De Houwer, 1995; Baeyens, De Houwer, Vansteenwegen, & Eelen, 1998; De Houwer et al., 2001). However, Field and Davey (1998) have argued, based on the preceding logic, that to infer a causal connection between CS–US associations and conditioned responding a nonpaired control condition is necessary (or CS-only pairings). They recommend a control condition in which all CS–US associations are eliminated: the block/subblock, or BSB, control (Field 1996, 1997). In this control condition CSs and USs are paired with themselves (rather than with each other) such that they are presented the same number of times, and for the same duration as in the associated experimental condition. This set of self-presentations forms a subblock. All subblocks of CSs are presented together in random order to form a block of CS presentations. Likewise subblocks of USs are randomly presented to form a block of US presentations. The order of presentation of the CS and US blocks is counterbalanced. As such, this control procedure will be identical to the associated experimental group in all aspects (number of stimulus presentations, temporal aspects of presentation) *except* that CSs cannot enter into associations with USs.

The debate surrounding the EC paradigm has a novel twist in that when nonpaired controls have been used, conditioning-type effects were observed when no CS–US associations could have been made (Field & Davey, 1997, 1999; Shanks & Dickinson, 1990) and even when participants saw no CSs or USs at all during conditioning (Field & Davey

1997, 1999). Field and Davey (1999) also showed that conditioning–like effects could be produced when participants used similarity-based category-learning strategies in the visual EC paradigm. In short, participants based their responses on how perceptually similar a particular CS was to salient exemplars of the categories of "liked" and "disliked" rather than responses being influenced by the US with which the CS was paired. However, because of the way in which CSs were assigned to USs (USs were chosen to be highly salient exemplars and CSs were assigned to the USs on the basis of perceptual similarity), the illusion of an effect caused by the pairing of CSs and USs was created. Crucially, this study highlighted that this artefact was likely to have been present in an important subset of the early evaluative conditioning studies (but see De Houwer, Baeyens, Vansteenwegen, & Eelen, 2000).

Although the artifact unearthed by Field and Davey (1999) does not apply to all research (just an important subset) the methodological debate has cast doubt over whether preferences can really be acquired through associative learning. However, this is not the end of the story: There are published reports of numerous failures to obtain EC in both the laboratory (Field & Davey, 1999; Rozin et al., 1998) and real-world settings (Rozin et al., 1998). Based on personal communications, Field (1997) reports a further 19 unpublished failures to obtain EC from a variety of laboratories (Field & Davey, Baeyens and colleagues, and Rozin and colleagues) 10 of which utilize the visual paradigm. Field et al. (2003) also report 11 other laboratory studies including the taste and visual paradigms that have not shown significant differential conditioning or shown only fairly weak effects. These findings cannot simply be ruled out on the basis of experimenter incompetence, or analysis errors, because the vast majority of them come from laboratories in which EC has been found on other occasions with ease (Baeyens and colleagues) and with less ease (Field and Davey).

Rozin et al. (1998) reports two failures to find EC when odors were used as CSs and positive experiences were used as USs (Experiments 3 and 4), and a further two failures when odors were used as CSs and pictures were used as USs. It was also mentioned earlier that Baeyens, Eelen, Van den Bergh, and Crombez (1990; Baeyens et al., 1996a) failed to find evidence that preferences for colors could be conditioned using taste USs. These findings cast doubt, in particular, over the robustness of cross-modal conditioning; however, it is worth remembering that some of these studies used odors as CSs and, as we have seen, odors appear to be relatively insensitive to evaluative change (see Stevenson et al., 1995, 1998, 2000a, 2000b).

A final point worth making is that in many EC studies the demands of the task will be fairly self-evident to participants. Often (especially when small numbers of CSs and USs are used) it will be obvious that some stimuli are paired with nice stimuli during conditioning and others are paired with nasty stimuli. It may not take a genius to then surmise that the evaluations are expected to change. This is known as *demand awareness*, and if participants respond according to this demand awareness then any apparent learning is merely a reflection of their desire to comply with the demands of the task.

Allen and Janiszewski (1989) specifically addressed this issue in two experiments. Participants played a computer "game" in which they were presented with a letter string and then one of five Norwegian words; they had to decide whether the Norwegian word could be spelled from the preceding letter string. In fact, this task was virtually impossible because the initial letter string appeared for only a short time. Some of the Norwegian words, which were CSs, were followed by positive information (participants were told that their decision was correct and were congratulated) whereas others were followed by nothing. This positive information acted as a positive US, and it always followed a specific word and never a different word (these two words were counterbalanced to make a true CS+/CS− discriminative paradigm). There were other filler words, which were sometimes paired with positive information and sometimes not. After the game, participants completed a semantic differential scale indicating whether they liked or disliked each word.

In both experiments a postexperimental interview assessed whether participants were unaware, contingency aware (i.e., aware that a certain word always predicted a successful response from the participant), or demand aware (i.e., aware that the game should influence their positiveness toward the word that was followed by positive information). The results showed that preferences for the CS+ were significantly greater than for the CS−. When the groups were split according to awareness there was no conditioning effect in participants unaware of the contingencies, but there was in participants who were contingency aware or demand aware.

## THE HAMSTER OF HOPE

Although the methodological debates and the studies that fail to replicate past findings demonstrate the fragility of the EC phenomenon, some considerable progress has been made in recent years to clear the foreboding air. Of course, the sense of foreboding differs somewhat: Field and Davey (1998, 1999) and Field (1997) question the very existence of EC, whereas Rozin et al. (1998) and De Houwer et al. (2000, 2001), rather more cheerily, allude to the possibility of boundary conditions that moderate conditioned responding.

The first issue to address is whether EC can be established in conditions that even the cynics would agree are rigorous. One problem is when CSs and USs are not counterbalanced across participants. Clearly this counterbalancing has been done in some of the studies (especially those using tastes that rely on a CS+/CS− discriminative paradigm), but less often in others (such as in the visual domain—e.g., Baeyens,

Crombez, Van den Bergh, & Eelen, 1988; Baeyens, Eelen, & Van den Bergh, 1990; Bayens et al., 1989a, 1989b, 1992, 1993; Levey & Martin, 1975; Martin & Levey, 1978, 1987). However, some studies have used random CS–US assignments which goes some way to preventing the problem (e.g., Baeyens et al., 1989b, 1992, 1993). De Houwer et al. (2000) report a "typical" visual paradigm in which CSs were randomly allocated to USs and evaluative responding was found. Likewise, Hammerl and Grabitz (2000) report significant EC effects when using haptic stimuli and random CS–US assignments. However, in a study using picture CSs randomly assigned to disgusting (and affectively neutral) USs, no evaluative learning was found (Schienle, Stark, & Vaitl, 2001). Although random assignment does much to reduce systematic biases from the pairing of CSs and USs (and does rule out Field & Davey's, 1999, artifact, which was based on CSs and USs being matched based on perceptual similarity), it does not completely eliminate them. If Shanks and Dickinson's (1990) advice is to be heeded then CSs must be counterbalanced across USs. Some studies have done this (Bierley et al., 1985; De Houwer et al., 1994, 1997) but in these cases the evidence for affective learning is not always robust (see earlier). Three very recent studies have used counterbalanced CS–US allocations for pictorial stimuli. Olson and Fazio (2001) conducted a study in which Pokemon characters (pretested to be neutral in adults) were paired with either positive or negative words and images. No single US was used and instead a series of different words and pictures of the same valence was used as USs for a particular CS. Which CS was paired with the array of positive stimuli and negative stimuli was counterbalanced. The results showed significant preferences for the CS paired with positive stimuli compared to the one paired with negative stimuli. Field (2003) did a similar study but with 7- to 13-year-old children. He showed them pictures of novel cartoon characters ("andimon" and "helemon," who were created especially for this experiment) paired with either liked (ice cream) or disliked (Brussels sprouts) pictures of foods. Evaluative responses toward the cartoon characters changed accordingly. Field and Moore (in press) used pictures from the International Affective Picture System (IAPS; Lang, Bradley, & Cuthbert, 1997) to enable them to pair "universally" neutral CSs with "universally" liked or disliked USs and counterbalanced CSs and USs accordingly. Again, they found evidence of evaluative learning. However, these positive results should be contrasted with the failures reported by Field et al. (2003) using a similar paradigm.

The next issue that critics have raised is whether the effects shown in EC studies represent associative learning. Again, in the taste domain, CS-only trials are routinely employed, which allow firm conclusions about the associative nature of effects. However, in the visual domain, these pairings are infrequently used and instead neutral CSs are paired with neutral USs (which still involves an association). Again, we can turn to more recent evidence. Hammerl and Grabitz (2000) incorporated Field's BSB control into their experiment using haptic stimuli and showed conditioned responding relative to this control. Likewise, Field and Moore (in press) and Lascelles, Field, and Davey (2003) both demonstrated conditioned responding using visual stimuli relative to a BSB control (and when CS–US allocations were counterbalanced). Finally, Diaz, Ruiz, and Baeyens (in press) have shown that evaluations of Japanese letters (CSs) can be changed by pairing with affective words (USs) relative to a BSB control group.

Finally, there is the issue of demand awareness, which could certainly go some way to explaining results in paradigms in which relatively few CSs are used. As Field and Moore (in press) point out, for demand awareness to explain conditioned responding participants need to be aware of the contingencies *and* to have an expectation that the experimenter wants CS ratings to change in the direction of the US with which it was paired. Without contingency awareness, any expectation that CS ratings should change in the direction of the US cannot translate into behavior because the participant does not know on which US to base the change. Also, the participant has to be able to control their responses: They have to be able to behave in the way that is expected of them. As such two possibilities for ruling out demand awareness explanations immediately suggest themselves: Eliminate contingency awareness so that any demand awareness cannot be translated into behavioral responses, or change the evaluation task so that participants have little or no ability to consciously influence it.

Again, some recent studies have done just that. In terms of reducing contingency awareness, several studies have used rapidly presented stimuli to reduce contingency awareness (see later section) and have still found evidence for evaluative learning (e.g., De Houwer et al., 1994, 1997; Field & Moore, in press; Krosnick, Betz, Jussim, & Lynn, 1992). Other studies have looked at alternative measures of evaluative responses that would be difficult to consciously influence. For example, Olson and Fazio (2001) used an implicit association task (Greenwald, McGhee, & Schwartz, 1998) as an indirect measure of affective responses and found significant differences between CSs paired with liked and disliked USs. Field (2003) and Hermans et al., (2002) both employed affective priming as an index of evaluative learning and both found positive evidence. In all of these studies it is hard to think how demand awareness could explain the results because participants either were unaware of the contingencies of conditioning (and so could not act upon them even if they were aware of the demands of the task), or would find it extremely difficult to deliberately respond in certain ways because indirect measures of evaluative responses were used.

Although these recent findings have advanced things considerably (at least in terms of ruling out alternative explanations), there is still the alarming occurrence of failures to replicate previously "well-established" findings. De Houwer et al. (2000, 2001) and Rozin et al. (1998) have alluded to boundary conditions that moderate evaluative learning. What might these conditions be? Unfortunately, no one seems to know and there is little systematic research to draw upon. De Houwer et al. (2001) suggested that "belongingness" between the CS and US might be important (based largely on Todrank et al.'s, 1995, findings). Field (2000a, 2001) has made a similar point by suggesting that the ecological relevance of the learning episode is important: Learning will occur only when the CS and US "make sense" ecologically. This is partially supported by the fact that the evidence for cross-modal conditioning appears to be somewhat weaker than for intramodal conditioning. Also Martin and Levey (1978) believed that the similarity between CS and US enhances the conditioning effect. Furthermore, Lascelles et al. (2003) recently found evidence for selective associations in EC: Ratings of pictures of foodstuffs (CSs) changed negatively only after pairing with pictures of obese body shapes (USs)—thin and normal body shapes had no effect. Lascelles et al. also showed that these results could be explained in part by an a priori expectancy bias: that is, expectancies that are brought into the experimental situation influence what is learned. However, Field et al. (2003) report several experiments that aim to manipulate the conceptual similarity between the CS and US, all of which fail to provide evidence that the conceptual relationship between the CS and US is important.

Other plausible candidates for boundary conditions relate to procedural aspects such as the number of trials, the timing parameters, the number of CS–US pairs, the intensity of the US, or the way in which responses are measured. The number or trials used has varied across different studies, but Baeyens et al.'s (1992) systematic manipulation of this variable (see also Baeyens, Crombez, et al., 1996) revealed no effect of the number of trials. Also Levey and Martin (1987) and Stuart et al. (1987) both showed learning in only one trial. In terms of timing parameters, these have varied considerably in different studies, from trials lasting 10 or more seconds (Baeyens, Eelen, & Van den Bergh, 1990; Baeyens et al., 1988, 1990, to name just a few) to others in which trials last only 1.5 seconds (Olsen & Fazio, 2001). In terms of whether the gap between the CS and US makes a difference, effects have been shown using trace-conditioning procedures with gaps of several seconds (e.g., Baeyens, Eelen, & Van den Bergh, 1990) or only 200 milliseconds (Field & Moore, in press) as well as delay conditioning in which presentations of the CS and US overlap (Field, 2003; Fulcher & Cocks, 1997). Yet again, no consistent evidence emerges for the importance of the timing parameters. The number of CS–US pairs could make a difference because the more pairs there are, the greater the cognitive load placed upon a participant. However, effects have been found with as many as nine CS–US pairs (e.g., Baeyens et al., 1988; Baeyens, Eelen, & Van den Bergh, 1990) and as few as two (e.g. Field, 2003). Although Field et al. (2003) suggest that in general they have greater success with fewer CS–US pairs; this does not explain why others have succeeded with as many as nine pairs. With regard to US intensity, arguably the greater consistency in experiments using taste stimuli could be due to the relatively more intense USs employed in those studies (especially the negative US). Indeed, Levey and Martin (1987) showed that the strength of the US moderated learning, and some recent successes in methodologically stringent paradigms have used very extreme USs (e.g., Field & Moore, in press). However, this doesn't explain why learning effects have also been established with mild USs such as human faces (e.g., Baeyens et al., 1988; Baeyens, Eelen, & Van den Bergh, 1990), affective words (e.g., De Houwer et al., 1994, 1997), and even pictures of Brussels sprouts (Field, 2003)! We are also left none the wiser about measures of the evaluative response because a variety of measurement techniques have been used such as ranking pictures (Field, 2003; Johnsrude et al., 1999; Levey & Martin, 1975), rating scales (Baeyens, Crombez et al., 1995; Baeyens, Eelen, & Van den Bergh, 1990; Baeyens, Eelen, Van den Bergh, & Crombez, 1989a, 1989b, 1990, 1992; Baeyens, Hermans, & Eelen, 1993; Baeyens, Crombez, Hendrickx, & Eelen, 1995; Baeyens, Kaes, Eelen, & Silvermans, 1996; Baeyens, Wrzesniewski, De Houwer, & Eelen, 1996; Field & Davey, 1999; Field & Moore, 2003; Fulcher & Cocks, 1997; Hammerl & Grabitz, 1993, 2000; Stevenson et al., 1998, to name but a few), physiological measures (Hermans et al., 2002; Purkis & Lipp, 2001), and implicit attitude measures (Field, 2003; Hermans et al., 2002; Olsen & Fazio, 2001). It is not consistently obvious whether one measurement technique produces stronger effects than another.

One boundary condition that has been investigated is attention. Field and Moore (in press) manipulated aspects of attention in a visual evaluative conditioning experiment. The results of these experiments indicated that although associative EC effects were not disrupted by a lack of contingency awareness, dividing attention did eliminate conditioning. However, even this is not a clear-cut result because Hammerl and Grabitz (2000) also distracted participants, albeit when using haptic stimuli, and found conditioning only when attention was divided! Field and Moore (in press) found that contingency awareness remained relatively unaffected by distraction; therefore, it is not simply the case that participants ignored all of the CSs and USs because their attention was focused on the distraction task. Katkin, Weins, and Öhman (2001) found that when an aversive US was used, learning was best predicted by an ability to sense internal cues. Field and Moore reason that because evaluative responses are based on such gut feelings (at least in terms of how they are operationalized in experiments), they may be moderated by individuals' abilities to sense internal responses to the experimental stimuli. So, although a lack of attention does not distract participants from the stimuli per se, it may distract them from processing the emotional content of these stimuli by preventing attention to visceral cues. However, future research is needed to verify this explanation and this explanation doe not account for Hammerl and Grabitz's findings.

## Interim Summary

Research into the associative learning of preferences has been dogged by methodological problems and failures to replicate basic findings. Perhaps the most consistent evidence comes from studies using tastes, which have been well designed and controlled and are, it seems, more widely replicable. The evidence using visual stimuli is less clear-cut, partly because of methodological weaknesses in some of the earlier studies, but also because of ubiquitous accounts of failed attempts to get effects. However, some recent work has done much to quash the methodological criticisms and to demonstrate convincingly that preferences for visual material can result from associative learning, even if it may not always be replicable. This had led to speculation of boundary conditions, but without clear candidates emerging that explain the variability between studies. If we accept that there is now convincing evidence that preference can be learned, the remaining issue becomes whether this learning is qualitatively distinct from other forms of associative learning.

## IS EVALUATIVE CONDITIONING A QUALITATIVELY DISTINCT FORM OF ASSOCIATIVE LEARNING?

### Learning Without Contingency Awareness

Many early studies reported anecdotally, or through measures, that participants were unaware of the contingencies of learning (just a few examples are Baeyens et al., 1988, 1989, 1992; Baeyens, Eelen, & Van den Bergh, 1990; Levey & Martin, 1975; Martin & Levey, 1978). Conditioning without contingency awareness is particularly important theoretically because, as Lovibond and Shanks (2002) point out, it rarely—if ever—occurs in autonomic conditioning. Lovibond and Shanks distinguish single-process models, in which propositional learning causes contingency awareness which in turn causes the conditioned response, from dual-process models, in which propositional learning causes contingency awareness, but conditioned responding is caused by some nonpropositional system (so contingency awareness and learning need not correlate). If EC can occur without awareness then a dual-process model is implied—EC would be a nonpropositional learning process. One further inference might, therefore, be that EC is a qualitatively distinct form of Pavlovian learning.

However, Field (2000b) did an extensive review of the literature on EC without contingency awareness and concluded that although there was good evidence that contingency awareness was not necessary for learning about tastes; the evidence that learning using visual stimuli could occur without awareness was controvertible. This view was endorsed by Lovibond and Shanks (2002) in a detailed review of the role of contingency awareness in conditioning in general. The crux of Field's argument was that (a) early studies showing conditioning in the absence of contingency awareness using visual stimuli utilized a paradigm that was sub-sequently shown to be flawed (Field & Davey, 1999); (b) later studies that did not use this paradigm (such as Baeyens, Crombez, Van den Bergh, & Eelen, 1988; Baeyens, Eelen, Van den Bergh, & Crombez, 1989b; Baeyens, Eelen, Crombez, & Van den Bergh, 1992; Baeyens, Hermans, & Eelen, 1993; Hammerl & Grabitz, 1993) looked at contingency awareness only as a tangential theme; (c) there is an important distinction to be made be-tween demand awareness (a lack of which should not influence condi-tioning) and contingency awareness (a lack of which could influence conditioning) and some studies cited as evidence for conditioning without awareness probably actually measure demand awareness (e.g., Hammerl & Grabitz, 1993; Stuart et al., 1987); (d) the majority of studies investi-gating contingency awareness in EC did not use between-group controls to demonstrate that learning is associative (see Davey, 1994; Field & Davey, 1998) and if the learning in these studies was nonassociative then there is no reason why contingency awareness should affect it; and (e) the validity of post hoc measures of contingency awareness will always be controversial (for reasons detailed by Lovibond & Shanks, 2002; Shanks & St. John, 1994) and so systematic attempts to manipulate contingency awareness should be attempted.

The evidence for the role of awareness in EC is complex, not least of all because many of the studies use noncomparable measures of aware-ness. Shanks and St. John (1994) have identified two criteria for assess-ing awareness in implicit learning tasks. The first is the *information criterion*, which is the need to establish that the information obtained by the awareness measure is the same information responsible for the per-formance changes observed in the experiment. This criterion addresses the problem that participants might form conscious hypotheses that af-fect responding, but that are not detected by the awareness measure be-cause the measure is directed at a different, but correlated, set of hypotheses. This argument is particularly pertinent to the learning of complex systems and artificial grammars, where it is possible for partic-ipants to extract correlated rules that could result in above-chance responding at test (for reviews, see Berry, 1994; Berry & Dienes, 1993).

The second criterion identified by Shanks and St. John (1994), the *sensitivity criterion*, addresses the need to construct a measure that is sensitive enough to detect awareness: If an insensitive measure is used then it is possible to conclude erroneously that awareness is not present. Of course, the converse problem is that a measure can be oversensitive, leading to participants being classified as aware when they believe that they are guessing (cf. Berry, 1994). The resolution of these two prob-lems depends on whether it is important to detect conscious knowledge, or tap unconscious knowledge. This choice, in turn, will depend on how consciousness is defined. Baeyens, De Houwer, and Eelen (1994) believe that awareness in EC should be linked to participative, phenomenological experience and so their verbal measures of awareness are sufficiently sensitive. Nevertheless, Field (2000b) suggested that recognition measures of contingency awareness should be used in EC research to increase sensitivity.

Some of the problems identified by Field (2000b) have, as we've seen, been overcome: Control groups and counterbalanced CS–US allocations have been used (e.g., Field & Moore, in press). Two recent studies (Field & Moore, in press; Fulcher & Hammerl, 2001) in particular have attempted to reduce awareness systematically (through distraction tasks and subliminal presentations of stimuli). Field and Moore also employed a recognition measure of awareness and a BSB control group. Both studies found some evidence for conditioning without contingency awareness. Krosnick et al. (1992) and De Houwer et al. (1994, 1997) have also had some success demonstrating EC with subliminally presented stimuli.

However, as Field (2001) points out, there is still much confusion about the role that contingency awareness plays: There is evidence that contingency awareness facilitates conditioning (see Field, 2000b; Field & Davey, 1998, for reviews) *does not* influence learning one way or another (e.g., Baeyens, Eelen, & Van den Bergh, 1990; Field & Moore, in press; Fulcher & Cocks, 1997; Hammerl, Black, & Silverthorne, 1997; Levey & Martin, 1987, 1975; Martin & Levey, 1987; Todrank et al., 1995), and that it actually *impedes* learning (Fulcher & Hammerl, 2001; Hammerl & Grabitz, 2000). There is also evidence that EC can occur without awareness (e.g., Baeyens, Eelen, & Van den Bergh, 1990; Field & Moore, in press; Fulcher & Hammerl, 2001) and that EC *cannot* occur without awareness (for reviews, see Field, 2000b, Field & Davey, 1998).

The more important issue is whether conditioning without contingency awareness makes EC distinct from other forms of associative learning. Lovibond and Shanks (2002) would presumably argue that it does; however, there is evidence of associative learning without contingency awareness in different paradigms. The notion of conditioning without contingency awareness is certainly compatible with recent expectancy models of conditioning (Davey, 1992; see also Davey, 1997), which assume that the CS–US association "can be influenced by factors other than the experienced contingency … [and that] the strength of the CR is determined by nonassociative factors which influence the evaluation of the US" (Davey, 1992, p. 41). This expectancy model does not assume that expectancies are formed verbally (although they can be) and it, therefore, incorporates a notion that learning could take place without awareness. In addition, Öhman, Dimburg, and Esteves (1989) argue that autonomic conditioned responses can be learned through preattentive analysis, which activates an automatic processing of the CS–US relationship.

Furthermore, many researchers have demonstrated that learning of a repeating sequence (as measured by the serial reaction time task), which Nissen and Bullemer (1987) characterize as associative learning, was not affected by a lack of awareness of what was being learned in "normals" (e.g., Destrebecqz & Cleeremans, 2001, 2003; Nissen & Bullemer, 1987; Willingham, Greeley, & Bardone, 1993) and amnesiacs (Reber & Squire, 1994, 1998). Although debate exists regarding whether this evidence shows true learning without awareness (see, e.g., Shanks & Channon, 2002; Shanks, Wilkinson, & Channon, 2003; Wilkinson & Shanks, 2004), at face value, these findings do make it unclear whether learning without awareness would qualify EC as a distinct form of learning.

Razran (1955) proposed a levels-of-learning approach, which at the lowest level consists of nonassociative learning. Lower-level reflexive stimulus–response (S–R) associations may be formed when the response is relatively salient and overshadows other internal or external stimulation that is contiguous with the CS (Davey, 1983). Responses to noxious tastes (e.g., Baeyens, Crombez, Hendrickx, & Eelen, 1995; Baeyens, Crombez, De Houwer, & Eelen, 1996; Baeyens, Hendrickx et al., 1998b), odors (Stevenson et al., 2000a, 2000b; Todrank et al., 1995), touch (Fulcher & Hammerl, 2001; Hammerl & Grabitz, 2000), and extreme visual material (Field & Moore, in press) may well be salient, and if so, would not require contingency awareness because S–R associations rather than CS–US associations are the driving force behind learned responses. However, given that S–R learning in both animals and humans is also normally associated with a stage of goal-directed action that becomes progressively automated, future research clearly needs to be done to see whether this explanation is plausible.

## Resistance to Extinction

The second important characteristic of EC is that it appears to be highly resistant to extinction. This finding was first intimated by Levey and Martin (1975), who noted that after 18 months participant's ratings of the CSs had not changed. The first systematic study exploring whether evaluative responses could be extinguished was conducted by Baeyens et al. (1988). In this study, participants underwent the same basic visual EC procedure (described earlier), but after the postconditioning evaluative ratings had been taken, participants experienced an extinction phase in which the CSs were randomly presented 5 or 10 times without contingent presentations of the USs. Participants then rerated the CSs for a third time. Baeyens et al. found that EC was resistant to extinction: Even when the CSs were presented several times without reinforcement, the acquired valence of the CS remained. In a follow-up study 2 months later, the ratings of the CSs had still not changed. Baeyens et al. (1989a) replicated this finding.

However, these findings have been criticized: Davey (1994) argued that the experimental subterfuge surrounding these studies encouraged participants to respond congruently to their earlier evaluations. In addition, these studies assigned CSs and USs on the basis of perceptual similarity and so could be prone to the artifact described by Field and Davey (1999). Finally, no between-group controls were used to demonstrate that learning was associative.

More recent studies have tried to overcome these problems. De Houwer et al. (2000) reported resistance to extinction in a visual paradigm using random CS–US assignments. Although they used relatively few extinction trials (5), this basic effect has been replicated by Diaz et al. (in press) using more extinction trials (14) and compared to a BSB control group. Furthermore, Field (2003) reports resistance to extinction in conditioned preferences to novel cartoon characters using 10 extinction trials. This again was compared to a BSB control, and when CSs were counterbalanced across USs. In addition, when the taste paradigm has been used, Baeyens et al. (1995a, 1996a, 1998b) have all found good evidence that CS-only presentations do not attenuate learned responses. In these paradigms, the number of extinction trials are typically the same as, or similar to, the number of acquisition trials (e.g., six in Baeyens et al., 1995a, 1996a) and CS and USs have been counterbalanced.

Resistance to extinction is an intriguing characteristic because associative learning theory (e.g., Pavlov, 1927; Rescorla & Wagner, 1972) predicts that successive, unreinforced presentations of the CS should result in successive reductions in the strength of the CR—which in this case is the acquired valence. If EC is resistant to extinction, then this characteristic may make it functionally different from other forms of Pavlovian conditioning (and some have argued this to be the case, e.g., Baeyens et al., 1995). However, Sclafani (1991), in a review, has shown resistance to extinction in Pavlovian conditioning paradigms using food stimuli with rats. Stevenson et al. (2000b) report resistance to extinction of CS properties of odors (such as sweetness and sourness). Also, Eysenck and Kelly (1987) suggested that the conditioning of ecologically important responses such as illness, fear, and anxiety are unlikely to extinguish and that it is even possible that the strength of the conditioned response will increase over extinction trials (incubation). So, EC may not be as unique as it first appears.

Interestingly, Hermans, Crombez, Vansteenwegen, Baeyens, and Eelen, (2000) found that although behavioral indicators of affect were unaffected by extinction, indices of expectancy learning were affected by extinction. They conclude that this supports the idea the two forms of learning are distinct. However, as De Houwer et al. (2000) note, stimulus associations do actually survive extinction (Rescorla, 1996; see also Bouton, 1993, 1994,) in normal Pavlovian learning. This opens up the possibility that any apparent distinctions between EC and other forms of associative learning in terms of extinction are simply due to differences in the expression of responses rather than differences at the mechanistic level. Put another way: The underlying process may be the same, but the expression of responses may vary according to how learning is measured (at what level even?). Hermans et al.'s results are equally consistent with this position.

## Contingency

Baeyens et al. (1993) exposed different groups of participants to different levels of contingency between the CS and US. One group was exposed to 10 trials where the CS and US were perfectly contingent, a second group received 20 such trials, a third group saw 10 presentations of the CS and US alongside 10 CS-only presentations (making a 50% contingency), and a final group was exposed to 10 CS–US presentations along with 10 CS-only and 10 US-only presentations. So, in all but one condition, participants were exposed to the same number of contiguous CS–US presentations, but with differing contingency between the stimuli. Baeyens et al. found no significant differences between any of the groups and concluded that contingency was not an important feature of evaluative learning.

Again, these findings seem to suggest differences between EC and other forms of associative learning in which the degree of statistical contingency between the CS and US is an important fact in the strength of conditioned responses (e.g., Rescorla, 1968, and characterized in the Rescorla–Wagner model, 1972). However, these findings may also be explained not by differences at the mechanistic level, but by differences at the level of expression. Rescorla (2000) has shown that although CS–US contingency is important for eliciting conditioned responses, it does not appear to affect the underlying association between a CS and US, which can form quickly and is not broken by the weakening of the contingency. This is completely consistent with findings from EC: CS–US associations are unaffected by contingency; it is merely the expression of conditioned responses that is affected.

## Feature Modulation

Rescorla (1991) has also demonstrated that if a CS is reinforced if, and only if, it is accompanied by another stimulus (called a "feature"), the conditioned responses likewise occur only if that feature is present. This is sometimes called occasion setting. Baeyens et al. (1996, 1998) failed to find such effects using a taste EC paradigm. Again, at face value this suggests differences between EC and other forms of associative learning. However, Hardwick and Lipp (2000) have demonstrated occasion setting using visual stimuli. In particular, affective learning to the CS is modulated by the feature, which itself acquires an evaluative response.

## Other Characteristics

So far I hope to have shown that although at first glance there are important differences between EC and conventional associative learning, these differences are not inconsistent with associative learning in a broader context. There are also situations in which EC behaves consistently with classical associative learning.

*US Revaluation.* According to models of associative learning, revaluation of the US should cause responses to the CSs to change accordingly. Baeyens et al. (1992) conducted a study in which USs were revalued using positive or negative verbal descriptions of the stimuli. Participants underwent a standard EC paradigm using pictures of human faces as the stimuli followed by the revaluation procedure. The results showed significant differential responding to CSs when participants had received US information of the same affective value as the US (e.g., positive information about a US already regarded as positive), but no shifts when the information given had the opposite affective valence to the US (e.g., negative information about a US regarded as positive). So, when the US was revalued to become a neutral stimulus, CSs were also rated neutrally. Although not explicitly a revaluation procedure, Hammerl, Bloch, and Silverthorne (1997) also found that habituation to USs reduced evaluative responses to CSs paired with these stimuli.

*Sensory Preconditioning.* Sensory preconditioning is a form of behaviorally silent learning (see Dickinson, 1980). Procedurally, it consists of three stages: (a) a CS1 is paired with a different CS2 resulting in no, obvious, behavioral change; (b) the CS2 is paired with a US on a number of occasions; and (c) the CS1 is presented alone and is found to elicit a conditional response appropriate to the US. So, although the CS1 is never directly paired with the US, it elicits the same conditioned response as if it had been. In the first stage, some learning about the two CSs has gone on, but with no obvious behavioral indication. Hammerl and Grabitz (1996) found evidence for this in a visual EC paradigm.

*Latent Inhibition.* Latent inhibition is found when preexposure to the CS retards the acquisition of a conditioned response to the CS when subsequently the CS is paired with a US. Latent inhibition is found in all animal models of classical conditioning (see Mackintosh, 1983), and in human autonomic conditioning (Siddle & Remington, 1987). Stuart et al. (1987) did report latent inhibition effects in an advertising paradigm, and De Houwer et al. (2000) found broadly consistent effects. However, research is a little thin on the ground to make firm conclusions.

## SUMMARY

This chapter has explored the evidence that preferences for stimuli can be acquired through associative learning. I hope to have shown that although researchers have traveled a turbulent road, there is evidence from a variety of sources that affective responses to stimuli can be acquired through associative processes. I also hope to have demonstrated that the view that EC appears to be distinct from other forms of associative learning in many important respects, and may, therefore, stem from different learning mechanisms, is overly simplistic. The little evidence around suggests that EC behaves like Pavlovian learning in many respects, and where it does differ it is not alone: There is evidence of associative learning with awareness and resistance to extinction in other domains. Perhaps more important, there is evidence that the CS–US associations that drive traditional associative learning are not moderated by extinction, statistical contingency, or contingency awareness. As such, EC may likewise be driven by the same underlying associative mechanisms as Pavlovian learning, but may differ (if at all) only in how responses are moderated. Researchers now need to address the issues of what is learned in an EC paradigm: Are the associative substructures the same as in associative learning, and, if so, why does the expression of conditioned responses behave differently?

## REFERENCES

Allen, C. T. & Janiszewski, C. A. (1989). Assessing the role of contingency awareness in attitudinal conditioning with implications for advertising research. *Journal of Marketing Research, 26,* 30–43.

Allen, C. T. & Madden, T. J. (1985). A closer look at classical conditioning. *Journal of Consumer Research, 12,* 301–315.

Baeyens, F., Crombez, G., De Houwer, J., & Eelen, P. (1996). No evidence for modulation of evaluative flavor-flavor associations in humans. *Learning and Motivation, 27,* 200–241.

Baeyens, F., Crombez, G., Hendrickx, H., & Eelen, P. (1995). Parameters of human evaluative flavor-flavor conditioning. *Learning and Motivation, 26,* 141–160.

Baeyens, F., Crombez, G., Van den Bergh, O., & Eelen, P. (1988). Once in contact always in contact: Evaluative conditioning is resistant to extinction. *Advances in Behaviour Research and Therapy, 10,* 179–199.

Baeyens, F., & De Houwer, J. (1995). Evaluative conditioning is a qualitatively distinct form of classical conditioning: a reply to Davey (1994). *Behaviour Research and Therapy, 33,* 825–831.

Baeyens, F., De Houwer, J., & Eelen, P. (1994).Awareness inflated, evaluative conditioning underestimated (Peer Commentary to D. C. Shanks and M. F. St. John, 1994). *Behavioural and Brain Sciences, 17,* 396–397.

Baeyens, F., De Houwer, J., Vansteenwegen, D., & Eelen, P. (1998). Evaluative conditioning is a form of associative learning: On the artificial nature of Field and Davey's (1997) artifactual account of evaluative learning. *Learning and Motivation, 29,* 461–474.

Baeyens, F., Eelen, P., & Van den Bergh, O. (1990). Contingency awareness in evaluative conditioning: A case for unaware affective-evaluative learning. *Cognition and Emotion, 4,* 3–18.

Baeyens, F., Eelen, P., Van den Bergh, O., & Crombez, G. (1989a). Acquired affective evaluative value: Conservative but not unchangeable. *Behaviour Research and Therapy, 27,* 279–287.

Baeyens, F., Eelen, P., Van den Bergh, O., & Crombez, G. (1989b). The influence of CS–US perceptual similarity/dissimilarity on human evaluative learning and signal learning. *Learning and Motivation, 20,* 322–333.

Baeyens, F., Eelen, P., Van den Bergh, O., & Crombez, G. (1990). Flavour-flavour and colour-flavour conditioning in humans. *Learning and Motivation, 21,* 434–455.

Baeyens, F., Eelen, P., Van den Bergh, O., & Crombez, G. (1992). The content of learning in human evaluative conditioning: Acquired valence is sensitive to US-revaluation. *Learning and Motivation, 23,* 200–224.

Baeyens, F., Hendrickx, H., Crombez, G., & Hermans, D. (1998). Neither extended sequential nor simultaneous feature positive training result in modulation of evaluative flavor conditioning in humans. *Appetite, 31,* 185–204.

Baeyens, F., Hermans, D., & Eelen, P. (1993). The role of CS–US contingency in human evaluative conditioning. *Behaviour Research and Therapy, 31,* 731–737.

Baeyens, F., Kaes, B., Eelen, P., & Silvermans, P. (1996). Observational evaluative conditioning of an embedded stimulus element. *European Journal of Social Psychology, 26,* 15–28.

Baeyens, F., Vanhouche, W., Crombez, G., & Eelen, P. (1998). Human evaluative flavor-flavor conditioning is not sensitive to post-acquisition US-inflation. *Psychologica Belgica, 38,* 83–108.

Baeyens, F., Wrzesniewski, A., De Houwer, J., & Eelen, P. (1996). Toilet rooms, body massages, and smells: Two field studies on human evaluative odour conditioning. *Current Psychology, 15*(1), 77–96.

Berry, D. C. (1994). Implicit learning: Twenty-five years on. A tutorial. In C. Umilta & M. Moscovitch (Eds.), *Attention and performance XV: Conscious and nonconscious information processing* (pp. 755–781). Cambridge, MA: MT Press.

Berry, D. C., & Dienes, Z. (1993). *Implicit learning: Theoretical and empirical issues.* London: Lawrence Erlbaum Associates.

Bierley, C., McSweeney, F. K., & Vannieuwkerk, R. (1985). Classical conditioning of preferences for stimuli. *Journal of Consumer Research, 12,* 316–323.

Bouton, M. E. (1993). Context, time, and memory retrieval in the inference paradigms of Pavlovian learning. *Psychological Bulletin, 114,* 80–99.

Bouton, M. E. (1994). Context, ambiguity and classical conditioning. *Current Directions in Psychological Science, 3,* 49–53.

Cohen, B. H. (1964). Role of awareness in meaning established by classical conditioning. *Journal of Experimental Psychology, 67,* 373–378.

Darley, W. K., & Lim, J.-S. (1993). Assessing demand artefacts in consumer research: An alternative perspective. *Journal of Consumer Research, 20,* 489–495.

Davey, G. C. L. (1983). An associative view of human classical conditioning. In G. C. L. Davey (Ed.), *Animal models of human behaviour: Conceptual, evolutionary, and neurobiological perspectives* (pp. 95–114). Chichester, England: Wiley.

Davey, G. C. L. (1994). Is evaluative conditioning a qualitatively distinct from of classical conditioning? *Behaviour Research and Therapy, 32,* 291–299.

Davey, G. C. L. (1992). Classical conditioning and the acquisition of human fears and phobias: a review and synthesis of the literature. *Advances in Behaviour Research and Therapy, 14,* 29–66.

Davey, G. C. L. (1997). A conditioning model of phobias. In G. C. L. Davey (Ed.) *Phobias: A handbook of theory, research and treatment* (pp. 301–322). Chichester, England: Wiley.

De Houwer, J., Baeyens, F., & Eelen, P. (1994). Verbal evaluative conditioning with undetected US presentations. *Behaviour Research and Therapy, 32,* 629–633.

De Houwer, J., Baeyens, F., Vansteenwegen, D., & Eelen, P. (2000). Evaluative conditioning in the picture-picture paradigm with random assignment of conditioned stimuli to unconditioned stimuli. *Journal of Experimental psychology: Animal Behavior Processes, 26*(2), 237–242.

De Houwer, J., Hendrickx, H., & Baeyens, F. (1997). Evaluative learning with "subliminally" presented stimuli. *Consciousness and Cognition, 6,* 87–107.

De Houwer, J., Thomas, S., & Baeyens, F. (2001). Associative learning of likes and dislikes: A review of 25 years of research on human evaluative conditioning. *Psychological Bulletin, 126,* 853–869.

Destrebecqz, A., & Cleeremans, A. (2001). Can sequence learning be implicit? New evidence with the process dissociation procedure. *Psychonomic Bulletin & Review, 8,* 343–350.

Destrebecqz, A., & Cleeremans, A. (2003). Temporal effects in sequence learning. In L. Jiminez (Ed.), *Attention and implicit learning* (pp. 181–213): Amsterdam: John Benjamins.

Diaz, E., Ruiz, G., & Baeyens, F. (in press). Resistance to extinction of human evaluative conditioning using a between-participants design. *Cognition and Emotion.*

Dickinson, A. (1980). *Contemporary animal learning theory.* Cambridge, England: Cambridge University Press.

Eifert, G. H., Craill, L., Carey, E., & O'Connor, C. (1988). Affect modification through evaluative conditioning with music. *Behaviour Research and Therapy, 26,* 321–330.

Eysenck, H. J., & Kelly, M. J. (1987). The interaction of neurohormones with Pavlovian A and Pavlovian B conditioning in the causation of neurosis, extinction, and incubation of anxiety. In G. C. L. Davey (Ed.), *Cognitive processes and Pavlovian conditioning in humans* (pp. 251–286). Chichester, England: Wiley.

Field, A. P. (1996). *An appropriate control condition for evaluative conditioning.* (Cognitive Science Research Paper No. 431). Brighton, England: University of Sussex, School of Cognitive and Computing Science.

Field, A. P. (1997). *Re-evaluating evaluative conditioning.* Unpublished doctoral dissertation, University of Sussex, Brighton, England.

Field, A. P. (2000a). Evaluative conditioning is Pavlovian conditioning: Issues of definition, measurement and the theoretical importance of contingency awareness. *Consciousness and Cognition, 9,* 41–49.

Field, A. P. (2000b). I like it, but I'm not sure why: Can evaluative conditioning occur without conscious awareness? *Consciousness and Cognition, 9,* 13–36.

Field, A. P. (2001). When all is still concealed: Are we closer to understanding the mechanisms underlying evaluative conditioning? *Consciousness and Cognition, 10,* 559–566.

Field, A. P. (2003, March). *I don't like it because it eats Brussels sprouts: Evaluative conditioning in children.* Paper presented at the British Psychological Society Annual Conference, Bournemouth, England.

Field, A. P., & Davey, G. C. L. (1997). Conceptual conditioning: Evidence for an artifactual account of evaluative learning. *Learning and Motivation, 28,* 446–464.

Field, A. P., & Davey, G. C. L. (1998). Evaluative conditioning: Arte-fact or -fiction?¡a reply to Baeyens, De Houwer, Vansteenwegen & Eelen (1998). *Learning and Motivation, 29,* 475–491.

Field, A. P., & Davey, G. C. L. (1999). Reevaluating evaluative conditioning: A nonassociative explanation of conditioning effects in the visual evaluative conditioning paradigm. *Journal of Experimental Psychology: Animal Behavior Processes, 25,* 211–224.

Field, A. P., & Davey, G. C. L. (2001). Conditioning models of childhood anxiety. In W. K. Silverman & P. A. Treffers (Eds.), *Anxiety disorders in children and adolescents: Research, assessment and intervention* (pp. 187–211). Cambridge, England: Cambridge University Press.

Field, A. P., & Hole, G. (2003). *How to design and report experiments*. London: Sage.

Field, A. P., Lascelles, K. R. R., & Davey, G. C. L. (2003). *Evaluative conditioning: Missing presumed dead*. Manuscript under review.

Field, A. P., & Moore, A. C. (in press). Dissociating the effects of attention and contingency awareness on evaluative conditioning effects in the visual paradigm. *Cognition & Emotion*.

Fulcher, E. P., & Cocks, R. P. (1997). Dissociative storage systems in human evaluative conditioning. *Behaviour Research and Therapy, 35*(1), 1–10.

Fulcher, E. P., & Hammerl, M. (2001). When all is revealed: A dissociation between evaluative learning and contingency awareness. *Consciousness and Cognition, 10*, 524–549.

Gorn, G. J. (1982). The effects of music in advertising on choice behaviour: A classical conditioning approach. *Journal of Marketing, 46*, 94–101.

Greenwald, A. G., McGhee, D. E., & Schwartz, J. L. K. (1998). Measuring individual differences in implicit cognition: The implicit association test. *Journal of Personality and Social Psychology, 74*, 1464–1480.

Hammerl, M., Bloch, M., & Silverthorne, C. P. (1997). Effects of US-alone presentations on human evaluative conditioning. *Learning and Motivation, 28*, 491–509.

Hammerl, M., & Grabitz, H.-J. (1993). Human evaluative conditioning: Order of stimulus presentation. *Integrative Physiological and Behavioural Science, 28*, 191–194.

Hammerl, M., & Grabitz, H.-J. (1996). Human evaluative conditioning without experiencing a valued event. *Learning and Motivation, 27*, 278–293.

Hammerl, M., & Grabitz, H.-J. (2000). Affective-evaluative learning in humans: A form of associative learning or only an artifact? *Learning and Motivation, 31*, 345–363.

Hardwick, S. A. & Lipp, O. V. (2000). Modulation of affective learning: An occasion for evaluative conditioning? *Learning and Motivation, 31*, 251–271.

Hermans, D., Crombez, G., Vansteenwegen, D., Baeyens, F., & Eelen, P. (2000). *Expectancy-learning and evaluative learning in human classical conditioning: Differential effects of extinction*. Unpublished manuscript.

Hermans, D., Vansteenwegen, D., Crombez, G., Baeyens, F., & Eelen, P. (2002). Expectancy–learning and evaluative learning in human classical conditioning: Affective priming as an indirect and unobtrusive measure of conditioned stimulus valence. *Behaviour Research and Therapy, 40*, 217–234.

Insko, C. A., & Oakes, W. F. (1966). Awareness and "conditioning" of attitudes. *Journal of Personality and Social Psychology, 67*, 1–11.

Johnsrude, I. S., Owen, A. M., White, N. M., Zhao, W. V., & Bohbot, V. (2000). Impaired preference conditioning after anterior temporal lobe resection in humans. *The Journal of Neuroscience, 20*, 2649–2656.

Johnsrude, I. S., Owen, A. M., Zhao, W. V., & White, N. M. (1999). Conditioned preference in humans: A novel experimental approach. *Learning and Motivation, 30*, 250–264.

Katkin, E. S., Wiens, S.,& Öhman, A. (2001). Nonconscious fear conditioning, visceral perception, and the development of gut feelings. *Psychological Science, 12*, 366–370.

Kellaris, J. J., & Cox, A. D. (1989). The effects of background music in advertising: A reassessment. *Journal of Consumer Research, 16*, 113–118.

Krosnick, J. A., Betz, A. L., Jussim, L. J., & Lynn, A. R. (1992). Subliminal conditioning of attitudes. *Personality and Social Psychology Bulletin, 18*, 152–162.

Lang, P. J., Bradley, M. M. & Cuthbert, B. N. (1997). *International Affective Picture System (IAPS)* [CD-ROM]. Gainesville, FL: NIMH Center for Emotion and Attention (CSEA).

Lascelles, K. R. R., Field, A. P., & Davey, G. C. L. (2003). Using food CSs and body shapes as UCSs: A putative role for associative learning in the development of eating disorders. *Behavior Therapy, 34*, 213–235.

Levey, A. B., & Martin, I. (1975). Classical conditioning of human "evaluative" responses. *Behaviour Research and Therapy, 13*, 221–226.

Levey, A. B., & Martin, I. (1987). Evaluative conditioning: A case for hedonic transfer. In H. J. Eysenck and I. Martin (Eds.), *Theoretical foundations of behaviour therapy*. New York: Plenum.

Lovibond, P. F., & Shanks, D. R. (2002). The role of awareness in Pavlovian conditioning: Empirical evidence and theoretical implications. *Journal of Experimental Psychology: Animal Behaviour Processes, 28*, 3–26.

Mackintosh, N. J. (1983). *Conditioning and associative learning*. Oxford, England: Oxford University Press.

Martin, I., & Levey, A. B. (1978). Evaluative conditioning. *Advances in Behaviour Research and Therapy, 1*, 57–101.

Martin, I., & Levey, A. B. (1987). Learning what will happen next: Conditioining, evaluation and cognitive processes. In G. C. L. Davey (Ed.), *Cognitive processes and Pavlovian conditioning in humans*. Chichester, England: Wiley.

Nissen, M. J., & Bullemer, P. (1987). Attentional requirements of learning: evidence from performance measures. *Cognitive Psychology, 19*, 1 < @1500 > 32.

Öhman, A., Dimberg, U., & Esteves, F. (1989). Preattentive activation of aversive emotions. In T. Archer & L.-G. Nilsson (Eds.), *Aversion, avoidance and anxiety* (pp. 169–193). Hillsdale, NJ: Lawrence Erlbaum Associates.

Olson, M. A., & Fazio, R. H. (2001). Implicit attitude formation through classical conditioning. *Psychological Science, 12*, 413–417.

Page, M. M. (1969). Social psychology of a classical conditioning of attitudes experiment. *Journal of Personality and Social Psychology, 11*(2), 177–186.

Page, M. M. (1971). Postexperimental assessment of awareness in attitude conditioning. *Educational and Psychological Measurement, 31*, 891–906.

Page, M. M. (1973). On detecting demand awareness by postexperimental questionnaire. *Journal of Social Psychology, 91*, 305–323.

Page, M. M. (1974). Demand characteristics and the classical conditioning of attitudes experiment. *Journal of Personality and Social Psychology, 30*, 468–476.

Pavlov, I. P. (1927). *Conditioned reflexes*. Oxford, England: Oxford University Press.

Purkis, H. M., & Lipp, O. V. (2001). Does affective learning exists in the absence of contingency awareness? *Learning and Motivation, 32*, 84–99.

Razran, G. (1938a). Conditioning away social bias by the luncheon technique [Abstract]. *Psychological Bulletin, 35*, 693.

Razran, G. (1938b). Music, art and the conditioned response [Abstract]. *Psychological Bulletin, 35*, 532.

Razran, G. (1940a). Conditioned response changes in rating and appraising sociopolitical slogans [Abstract]. *Psychological Bulletin, 37*, 481.

Razran, G. (1940b). Music Determinants of the consolidation or *Praegnanz* of conditioned preferences [Abstract]. *Psychological Bulletin, 37*, 562.

Reber, P. J., & Squire, L. R. (1994). Parallel brain systems for learning with and without awareness. *Learning and Memory, 1*, 217–229.

Reber, P. J., & Squire, L. R. (1998). Encapsulation of implicit and explicit memory in sequence learning. *Journal of Cognitive Neuroscience, 10*, 248–263.

Rescorla, R. A. (1968). Probability of shocks in the presence and absence of CS in fear conditioning. *Journal of Comparative Physiological Psychology, 66,* 1–5.

Rescorla, R. A. (1991). Combinations of modulators trained with the same and different target stimuli. *Animal Learning and Behavior, 19,* 355–360.

Rescorla, R. A. (1996). Preservation of Pavlovian associations through extinction. *Quarterly Journal of Experimental Psychology, 49B,* 245–258.

Rescorla, R. A. (2000). Associative changes with a random CS–US relationship. *Quarterly Journal of Experimental Psychology, 53B,* 325–340.

Rescorla, R. A., & Wagner, A. R. (1972). A theory of Pavlovian conditioning: Variations in the effectiveness of reinforcement and non-reinforcement. In A. H. Blake & W. F. Prokasy (Eds.), *Classical conditioning II: Current research and theory* (pp. 64–199). New York: Appleton–Century–Crofts.

Rozin, P., Wrzesniewski, A., & Byrnes, D. (1998). The elusiveness of evaluative conditioning. *Learning and Motivation, 29,* 397–415.

Schienle, A., Stark, R. & Vaitl, D. (2001). Evaluative conditioning: a possible explanation for the acquisition of disgust responses? *Learning and Motivation, 32,* 65–83.

Sclafani, A. (1991). Conditioned food preferences. *Bulletin of the Psychonomic Society, 29,* 256–260.

Shanks, D. R., & Channon, S. (2002). Effects of a secondary task on "implicit" sequence learning: Learning or performance? *Psychological Research, 66,* 99–109.

Shanks, D. R., & Dickinson, A. (1990). Contingency awareness in evaluative conditioning: A comment on Baeyens, Eelen and van den Bergh. *Cognition & Emotion, 4,* 19–30.

Shanks, D. R., & St. John, M. F. (1994). Characteristics of dissociable human learning systems. *Behavioural and Brain Sciences, 17,* 367–447.

Shanks, D. R., Wilkinson, L., & Channon, S. (2003). Relationship between priming and recognition in deterministic and probabilistic sequence learning. *Journal of Experimental Psychology: Learning Memory and Cognition, 29,* 248–261.

Shimp. T. A., Hyatt, E. M., & Snyder, D. J. (1991). A critical appraisal of demand artefacts in consumer research. *Journal of Consumer Research, 18,* 273–283.

Shimp, T. A., Stuart, E. W., & Engle, R. W. (1991). A program of classical conditioning experiments testing variations in the conditioned stimulus and context. *Journal of Consumer Research, 18,* 1–12.

Siddle, D. A. T., & Remington, R. (1987). Latent inhibition and human Pavlovian conditioning: Research and relevance. In G. C. L. Davey (Ed.), *Cognitive processes and Pavlovian conditioning in humans* (pp. 115–146). Chichester, England: Wiley.

Staats, A. W. (1969). Experimental demand characteristics and the classical conditioning of attitudes. *Journal of Personality and Social Psychology, 11*(2), 187–192.

Staats, A. W., & Staats, C. K. (1958). Attitudes established by classical conditioning. *Journal of Abnormal and Social Psychology, 57,* 37–40.

Staats, C. K., & Staats, A. W. (1957). Meaning established by classical conditioning. *Journal of Experimental Psychology, 54,* 74–80.

Stevenson, R. J., Boakes, R. A., & Prescott, J. (1998). Changes in odor sweetness resulting from implicit learning of a simultaneous odor-sweetness association: An example of learned synesthesia. *Learning and Motivation, 29,* 113–132.

Stevenson, R. J., Boakes, R. A., & Wilson, J. P. (2000a). Counter-conditioning following human odor-taste and color-taste learning. *Learning and Motivation, 31,* 114–127.

Stevenson, R. J., Boakes, R. A., & Wilson, J. P. (2000b). Resistance to extinction of conditioned odor perceptions: evaluative conditioning is not unique. *Journal of Experimental Psychology: Learning Memory and Cognition, 26,* 423–440.

Stevenson, R. J., Prescott, J., & Boakes, R. A. (1995). The acquisition of taste properties by odours. *Learning and Motivation, 26,* 433–455.

Stuart, E. W., Shimp, T. A., & Engle, R. W. (1987). Classical conditioning of consumer attitudes: Four experiments in an advertising context. *Journal of Consumer Research, 14,* 334–349.

Todrank, J., Byrnes, D., Wrzesniewski, A., & Rozin, P. (1995). Odours can change preferences for people in photographs: A cross-modal evaluative conditioning study with olfactory USs and visual CSs. *Learning and Motivation, 26,* 116–140.

Van Reekum, C. M., Van den Berg, H., & Frijda, N. H. (1999). Cross-modal preference acquisition: Evaluative conditioning of pictures by affective olfactory and auditory cues. *Cognition and Emotion, 13,* 831–836.

Watson, J. B. & Rayner, R. (1920). Conditioned emotional reactions. *Journal of Experimental Psychology, 3,* 1–14.

Wilkinson, L., & Shanks, D. R. (2004). Sequence knowledge and intentional control. *Journal of Experimental Psychology: Learning, Memory and Cognition, 30,* 354–369.

Willingham, D. B., Greeley, T., & Bardone, A. M. (1993). Dissociation in a serial response time task using a recognition measure: Comment on Perruchet and Amorim (1992). *Journal of Experimental Psychology: Learning, Memory, and Cognition, 19,* 1424–1430.

Yeomans, M. R., Jackson, A., Lee, M. D., Nesic, J. S., & Durlach, P. J. (2000). Expression of flavour preferences conditioned by caffeine is dependent on caffeine deprivation state. *Psychopharmacology, 150,* 208–215.

Yeomans, M. R., Jackson, A., Lee, M. D., Steer, B., Tinley, E. M., Durlach, P. J. et al. (2000). Acquisition and extinction of flavour preferences conditioned by caffeine in humans. *Appetite, 35,* 131–141.

Yeomans, M. R., Ripley, T., Lee, M. D., & Durlach, P. J. (2001). No evidence for latent learning of liking for flavours conditioned by caffeine. *Psychopharmacology, 157,* 172–179.

Yeomans, M. R., Spetch, H., & Rogers, P. J. (1998). Conditioned flavour preference negatively reinforced by caffeine in human volunteers. *Psychopharmacology, 137,* 401–409.

Zellner, D. A., Rozin, P., Aron, M., & Kulish, C. (1983). Conditioned enhancement of human's liking for flavor by pairing with sweetness. *Learning and Motivation, 14,* 338–350.

# Author Index

## A

Abramson, L. Y., 189, 195, 204, 211–212, 215–216
Ackerman, R., 213
Ahn, W. –K., 101
Aitken, M. R. F., 56
Allan, L. J., 16, 25, 33, 35, 41, 66–67, 70, 72–73, 75–82, 84, 86–89, 193–194, 198, 204
Allen, C. T., 226, 230, 234
Alloy, L. B., 189, 195, 204, 211–212, 215–216
Almaraz, J., 53, 70, 73, 75
Anderson, J. R., 120
Arcediano, F., 69
Arkes, H. R., 197
Aron, M., 225, 228–229
Ashby, F. G., 97, 117
Austin, G. A., 101

## B

Baddeley, A., 97
Barnet, R. C., 66
Baeyens, F., 54, 56, 223–226, 228–230, 232–245
Baker, A. G., 17, 21, 23–26, 28–32, 52–53, 67, 70, 193–195, 201, 203–210, 212–214
Bardone, A. M., 241
Baron, J., 201, 203
Beck, A. T., 189
Beckers, T., 42, 45–48, 55, 57, 126
Been, S., –L.49
Beers, J. R., 44, 57
Benassi, V. A., 205, 212

Berbrier, M. W., 194, 204
Berry, D. C., 240
Bersted, C. T., 101
Betz, A. L., 236, 241
Bierley, C., 226, 230, 235
Bitterman, M. E., 213
Bjork, R. A., 55
Bloch, M., 241, 245
Boakes, R. A., 56, 223, 229, 231, 233, 238, 242–243
Bohbot, V., 230
Bouton, M. E., 49, 243
Bower, G. H., 101, 106, 119
Bradley, M. M., 235
Brewer, W. F., 41–43, 57–58
Brown, B. R., 101
Bruner, J. S., 101
Buehner, M. J., 25, 193
Bullemer, P., 241
Burke, J., 3, 136–138, 144
Byrnes, D., 230–231, 233–234, 236–237, 241–232

## C

Caño, A., 70, 73
Carey, E., 225, 230
Chapman, G., 24, 68, 136
Channon, S., 242
Chapman, L. J., 199
Chapman, J. P., 199
Charles, D., 117
Chatlosh, D. L., 17, 24–25, 28, 52, 189, 195, 201, 203, 205–206, 208–210, 212, 214
Cheng, P., 3, 15, 17, 19, 25, 27, 38, 41, 51–52, 193–195, 203–204
Clayton, N. S., 57

Cleeremans, A., 241
Cobos, P. L., 70, 73
Cocks, R. P., 223, 237–238, 241
Cohen, B. H., 222
Cohen, N. J., 118
Colgan, D. M., 45
Collins, D. J., 53, 84
Cook, S. W., 3, 45
Cox, A. D., 226
Craill, L., 225, 230
Crombez, G., 223–225, 228–230,
       233, 235–240, 242–244
Cultice, J. C., 122
Cuthbert, B. N., 235
Cutler, D. L., 130, 133

**D**

Darby, R. J., 46, 117, 204
Darley, W. K., 226
Davey, G. C. L., 42, 221, 223, 228,
       231–238, 240–242
Dawson, M. E., 42–44, 54, 56–57
De Houwer, J., 42, 45–48, 54–57,
       126, 193, 225–226,
       228–230, 232–238,
       240–243, 245
De Marez, P., –J.53
DeNike, L. D., 44
DeRubeis, R. J., 213
Destrebecqz, A., 241
Diaz, E., 236
Dickinson, A., 3, 30, 42, 56–57, 67,
       111, 125, 128, 136–138,
       144, 190, 194, 196, 198,
       200, 204, 206, 209–210,
       231–232, 235, 245
Dienes, Z., 240
Dimberg, U., 241
Dobson, K. S., 190, 214
Dougherty, M. R., 58
Drew, S., 26, 203, 205, 207–208
Durlach, P. J., 229

**E**

Ebbinghaus, H., 96
Eelen, P., 223–226, 228–230,
       232–245
Eifert, G. H., 225, 230
Eimas, P. D., 155

Elek, S. M., 17, 24–25, 28, 52, 195,
       201, 203, 205–206,
       208–210, 212, 214
Engle, R. W., 227, 237, 240, 245
Epstein, S., 44
Estes, W. K., 117
Esteves, F., 241
Evans, S. H., 101
Evenden, J. L., 30, 67, 111, 125,
       128, 194, 200, 204
Eysenck, H. J., 243

**F**

Fazio, R. H., 223, 235–238
Fernandez, P., 53, 75
Field, A. P., 221, 223, 226–228,
       231–243
Fodor, J. A., 51, 54
Forster, K. I., 112
Forster, J. C., 112
Fouquet, N., 23
Frank, R., 27, 30, 32, 67, 70
Fratianne, A., 70
Frijda, N. H., 230
Frohart, R., 49
Fulcher, E. P., 223, 237–238,
       241–242

**G**

Gantt, W. H., 5
Garcia, J., 15
Gettys, C. F., 58
Gifford, R. K., 3, 199
Glautier, S., 47–48
Gluck, M. A., 101, 106, 117, 119
Glymour, C., 59
Goodnow, J. J., 101
Gopnik, A., 59
Gorn, G. J., 226, 230
Grabitz, H. –J., 223, 235, 238,
       240–242, 245
Grahame, N. J., 66, 213
Greeley, T., 241
Green, R. E. A., 41–42
Greenwald, A. G., 236
Grossberg, S., 4, 118

**H**

Haberlandt, K., 23, 65, 67

Hagmayer, Y., 70
Hall, G., 4, 21–22, 118, 174
Hallam, S. C., 213
Hamilton, D. L., 3, 199
Hammond, L. J., 205
Hammerl, M., 223, 235, 238,
        240–242, 245
Hampson, S. E., 102
Hardwick, S. A., 244
Harkness, A. R., 197
Harris, R. E., 3, 45
Hebb, D. O., 55, 97, 102, 155
Hendrickx, H., 56, 224–226,
        228–229, 235, 238,
        241–243
Hermans, D., 223, 225, 228,
        235–236, 238, 240,
        242–243
Hinton, G. E., 4, 97, 107, 130
Hoff, M. E., 105
Hole, G., 232
Holland, P. C., 160
Hollingsworth, L., 189, 201
Holyoak, K. J., 15, 32–34, 37,
        51–52, 68–70, 73, 76,
        80–81, 83, 88, 194
Homa, D., 111
Hornik, K., 107
Howell, D. C., 122
Hull, C. L., 4, 195
Hume, D., 13, 96, 193
Hyatt, E. M., 226

I

Insko, C. A., 222

J

Jackson, A., 229
Jacoby, L. L., 55
James, W., 46
Janiszewski, C. A., 234
Jenkins, H. M., 196, 204, 213
Johnsrude, I. S., 223, 230, 238
Jones, F. W., 113
Jourban, R., 55
Jussim, L. J., 236, 241

K

Kaes, B., 223, 233, 238, 243–244

Kahneman, D., 53
Kamin, L. J., 65–66, 110, 126
Kant, I., 13
Kao, S. F., 69, 73
Katkin, E. S., 239
Kaye, H., 158, 171
Kellaris, J. J., 226
Kelly, A., 44, 57
Kelly, M. J., 243
Koelling, R. A., 15
Konorski, J., 4, 155
Kossman, D. A., 212
Krosnick, J. A., 236, 241
Kruschke, J. K., 4, 106, 117, 119
Kulish, C., 225, 228–229

L

Langley, P. J., 235
Larkin, M. J. W., 56
Lascelles, K. R. R., 231, 233,
        235–237
Lawrence, D. H., 99, 157, 170, 185
Lee, M. D., 229
Lee, M. G., 55
Le Pelley, M. E., 56, 127, 130, 133,
        136, 138, 141–142,
        146–147, 149, 151, 157,
        167, 185
Levey, A. B., 111, 223, 225, 235,
        237–239, 241–242
Lim, J. S., 226
Lipp, O. V., 223, 238, 244
Little, L., 99, 157, 159–160, 167,
        171, 181, 185
Lober, K., 26
Lochmann, T., 98, 147, 149, 151,
        157, 167, 185
Logan, F. A., 23, 65, 67
López, F. G., 33, 53, 69–70, 73,
        75–76, 204
Lovibond, P. F., 42–43, 45–46,
        49–50, 54–55, 57, 59, 231,
        239–241
Lynn, A. R., 236, 241

M

Mackintosh, N. J., 4, 41–42, 98–99,
        118, 146–151, 156–159,

167, 171–177, 179–181,
183–185, 196, 245
Madden, T. J., 226, 230
Mahler, H. I. M., 205, 212
Maltzman, I., 58
Markman, A. B., 137
Marr, D., 27
Martin, D. J., 212, 241
Martin, I., 122, 223, 225, 235,
237–239, 242
Matute, H., 53, 69
Matzel, L. D., 21, 36, 138
May, J., 193
McClelland, J. L., 3, 96, 106, 181
McCloskey, M., 118
McGhee, D. E., 236
McLaren, I. P. L., 41–42, 56, 99,
102, 108–109, 111, 113,
119, 127, 130, 133, 136,
138, 141–142, 147, 149,
151, 157–160, 167,
171–175, 177, 179–181,
183–185
McPhee, J. E., 117
McSweeney, F. K., 226, 230, 235
Medin, D. L., 101–102
Mehta, R., 28, 30, 35, 52–53, 67,
193, 195
Melz, E. R., 33, 194
Mercier, P., 29, 30, 32, 67, 70
Miller, R. R., 21, 36, 66, 69, 138,
213
Minsky, M. L., 4, 106
Mitchell, C. J., 46, 49
Moore, A. C., 223, 235–238,
241–242
Murphy, R. A., 21, 23, 26, 31,
52–53, 189, 193, 195, 201,
203, 205, 207–208, 213

N

Nesic, J. S., 229
Neunaber, D. J., 189, 205
Nisbett, R. E., 198
Nissen, M. J., 241
Nosofsky, R. M., 117, 119
Novick, L. R., 15, 17, 41, 52

O

Oakes, W. F., 222

O'Connor, C., 225, 230
Ogden, E. E., 58
Öhman, A., 54, 57, 238, 241
Olson, M. A., 223, 235–238
Overall, J. E., 115
Owen, A. M., 223, 230, 238

P

Page, M., 103
Page, M. M., 222
Pan, M., 27, 30, 32, 67, 70
Papini, M. R., 213
Papert, S. A., 4, 106
Park, J., 15
Parton, D. A., 44
Pavlov, I. P., 1–4, 41, 96, 211, 243
Pearce, J. M., 4, 21–22, 116–118,
127, 130, 174
Pearson, S. M., 190, 210
PDP research group, The, 3, 96
Prescott, J., 56, 223, 229, 233, 238
Price, P. C., 69, 73, 89
Price, T., 23, 65, 67
Purkis, H. M., 223, 238
Pusch, D., 190, 214
Pylyshyn, Z. W., 51, 54

Q

Quinsey, V. L., 199, 213

R

Rayner, R., 3, 221
Razran, G., 3, 41–42, 221, 242
Reber, A. S., 95
Reber, P. J., 242
Redhead, E. S., 117
Reid, L. S., 160, 172, 185
Reimers, S., 109, 119
Remington, R., 245
Rescorla, R. A., 4, 21–23, 25, 55, 59,
66–67, 98, 105–106,
126–128, 140, 155, 157,
159, 174, 193, 195–196,
243–244
Richardson-Klavehn, A., 55
Ripley, T., 229
Robbins, S. G., 24, 68
Rodet, L., 118

Rogers, P. J., 229
Roupenian, A., 44
Ross, L., 198
Rozin, P., 225, 228–231, 233–234, 236–237, 241–242
Ruiz, G., 236
Rumelhart, D. E., 3–4, 96–97, 104, 106–107, 109, 116, 130, 181

**S**

Sadeghi, H., 35
Sagness, K. E., 117
Schaffer, M. M., 101
Schell, A. M., 42–44, 54, 56–57
Schienle, A., 235
Schmajuk, N. A., 196
Schneider, W., 57
Schulz, L. E., 59
Schwartz, J. L. K., 236
Schwartz, M., 155
Schwartz, R. M., 155
Schyns, P. G., 118
Sclafani, A., 243
Seligman, M. E. P., 211
Shaklee, H., 197
Shanks, D. R., 26, 30, 33, 42–43, 46, 50, 52–55, 67, 69–70, 73, 75–76, 84, 111, 117, 125, 128, 136, 190, 193–194, 196, 198, 200, 204, 206, 209–210, 214, 231–232, 235, 239–242
Shattuck, D., 213
Shepp, B. E., 155
Shiffrin, R. M., 57
Shimp, T. A., 226–227, 237, 240, 245
Shultz, T. R., 14, 27
Siddle, D. A. T., 245
Siegel, S., 67
Silvermans, P., 223, 233, 238, 243–244
Silverthorne, C., 241, 245
Sloman, S. A., 41
Smedslund, J., 3, 196, 199–200, 203
Snyder, D. J., 226
Soares, J. J., 54
Sobel, D. M., 59
Spellman, B. A., 31–32

Spence, K. W., 4, 155
Spetch, H., 229
Squire, L. R., 242
Staats, A. W., 221–222
Staats, C. K., 221
Stark, R., 235
Steer, B., 229
Stevenson, R. J., 56, 223, 229, 231, 233, 238, 242–243
Stewart, N., 109, 119
Stinchcombe, M., 107
St. John, M. F., 43, 55, 240
Stuart, E. W., 227, 237, 240, 245
Stone, G. O., 106
Suret, M., 109, 119, 157, 159, 172–173, 180–181, 185
Sutherland, N. S., 155, 177
Sutherland, S., 201

**T**

Tangen, J. M., 33, 35, 70, 72–73, 75–82, 84, 86–89
Tees, R. C., 155
Thomas, S., 54, 56, 229, 232, 234, 236–237
Thorndike, E. L., 4, 96, 125
Tinley, E. M., 229
Todrank, J., 230, 237, 241–242
Townsend, J. T., 117
Tucker, D., 197
Tversky, A., 53

**V**

Vaitl, D., 235
Vallée-Tourangeau, F., 21, 26, 29, 30–32, 52–53, 67, 70, 189, 193–195, 201, 203–205, 207–208
Van den Bergh, O., 223–225, 228–230, 233, 235, 237–242, 244
Vandorpe, S., 42, 47, 55
Van Hamme, L. J., 21, 69, 73, 137
Vanhouche, W., 225, 228, 243–244
Vannieuwkerk, R., 226, 230, 235
Van Reekum, C. M., 230
Vansteenwegen, D., 223, 228, 232–238, 243, 245
Vasquez, C., 212
Vegas, S., 53

## W

Wagner, A. R., 4, 21–23, 25, 42, 55,
    59, 65–67, 98, 105,
    126–127, 138, 155, 159,
    174, 195–196, 243–244
Waldmann, M. R., 32–34, 37,
    46–47, 57, 68–70, 73, 76,
    80–81, 83, 88–89, 194
Ward, W. C., 196
Wasserman, E. A., 17, 21, 24–25,
    28, 51–52, 67, 69, 73, 137,
    189, 195, 201, 203,
    205–206, 208–210, 212,
    214
Watson, J. B., 3, 221
Wattenmaker, W. D., 102
Werbos, P. J., 4, 107
White, H., 107
White, K. G., 156, 167
White, N. M., 223, 230, 238
Whitney, L., 156, 167
Widrow, B., 105
Wiens, S., 238
Wilkinson, L., 242
Williams, D. A., 117

Williams, R. J., 4, 97, 107, 130
Willingham, D. B., 241
Wills, A. J., 98, 102, 109, 111, 113,
    115, 119, 147, 149, 151,
    157,167, 185
Wilson, J. P., 229, 231, 233,
    242–243
Wrzesniewski, A., 223, 230–231,
    233–234, 236–237–238,
    241–242

## Y

Yarlas, A. S., 15
Yates, F., 69, 73, 89
Yeomans, M. R., 229
Yu, K. S., 57

## Z

Zellner, D. A., 225, 228–229
Zhao, W. V., 223, 230, 238
Zipser, D., 104, 109, 116
Zwickel, J., 111, 115

# Subject Index

## A

Allergy prediction, 128, 148
Anderson's rational model, 120
APECS model, 130–136, 141–147, 151
Associability, 146–147, 155–157, 159–160, 167–169
Associative history, 125–127, 130, 139–140, 142–147, 151, 185
Awareness, 43–44, 50–51, 55–56, 57–58, 222, 226, 234, 236, 239–242

## B

Back-propagation, 107, 118, 130
Backward blocking, 136–140
Blocking, 44–45, 46–49, 55, 65, 66–68, 110–111, 126

## C

Catastrophic forgetting, 118
Categorization, 101–102
Causal
    asymmetry, 70, 88–89
    direction, 28, 32–33, 73, 80, 88
    model theory, 68–70, 73, 88
Common error term, 133, 144, 151
Comparator hypothesis, 138
Competitive learning, 103–105
Conditioning
    autonomic, 43, 49–50
Configural theories, 117, 127, 130–133

## C

Contiguity, 14–15, 55–56, 65, 195, 199, 206–211
Contingency table, 16, 197
Cue interaction, 69–70, 72

## D

Delta P, 16–17, 70–72, 89, 197–198
Delta rule, 105–108
Depressive realism, 211–216
Dual–process theories, 41, 54–57, 88

## E

Elemental models, 117, 174
Evaluative conditioning, 221–246
    block / sub–block control, 232
    boundary conditions, 236–239
    contingency, 243–244
    crossmodal, 229–231
    latent inhibition, 245
    nonassociative explanations, 231–233
    odors, 229
    resistance to extinction, 242–243
    sensory preconditioning, 245
    taste, 224–225, 228–229
    US revaluation, 244–245
    visual223, 225–228
Exemplar models, 117

## F

Feature emergence, 118
Free classification, 101–2

**G**

General recognition theory, 117–118
Generalization, 12, 130–136,
    141–144, 159, 168
Generative transmission, 14

**H**

Hebbian learning, 102–103
Hidden layer, 107, 130

**I**

Illusory correlation, 199

**M**

Mackintosh (1975) theory, 118,
    146, 155, 157, 172–177,
    185
McLaren & Mackintosh theory,
    172–175, 183

**O**

Occam's razor, 108
Outcome density, 24, 203–204,
    207–210, 216
Overtraining reversal effect,
    155–156, 185

**P**

Pearce–Hall theory, 118
Plasticity–stability dilemma,
    118–119
PowerPC theory, 17–21

**R**

Ratio rule, 119
Reasoning, 11–12, 13–15, 46–50,
    58–59, 68–70
Relative validity, 23, 65–67
Rescorla–Wagner theory, 21–23, 25,
    30, 32–33, 66–67,
    105–108, 126–127, 145,
    196
Retrospective revaluation, 136–139,
    141–142

**S**

Salience, 23, 66, 126, 137, 172
SOP model, 235
Summed error term, 126–127,
    138–139
Supervised learning, 102, 105

**T**

Transfer along a continuum,
    157–158, 160
Trial order effects, 53

**U**

Unovershadowing, 136–137, 140
Unsupervised learning, 102,
    103–105

**W**

Within–compound associations,
    129, 137–138, 140